SELF, IDENTITY

SOCIAL MOVEMENTS

Sheldon Stryker, Timothy J. Owens,
and Robert W. White, Editors

Social Movements, Protest, and Contention
Volume 13

University of Minnesota Press
Minneapolis • London

Published by the University of Minnesota Press
111 Third Avenue South, Suite 290
Minneapolis, MN 55401-2520
http://www.upress.umn.edu

Library of Congress Cataloging-in-Publication Data

Self, identity, and social movements / Sheldon Stryker, Timothy J. Owens, and Robert W. White, editors.
p. cm.—(Social movements, protest, and contention ; v. 13)
Includes bibliographical references and index.
ISBN 0-8166-3407-6 (HC : alk. paper)—ISBN 0-8166-3408-4 (PB : alk. paper)
1. Social movements—Psychological aspects—Congresses. 2. Identity (Psychology)—Congresses. I. Stryker, Sheldon. II. Owens, Timothy J. (Timothy Joseph) III. White, Robert W. IV. Title. V. Series.
HM881 .S45 2000
303.48′4—dc21 00-008265

Printed in the United States of America on acid-free paper

11 10 09 08 07 06 05 04 03 02 01 00 10 9 8 7 6 5 4 3 2 1

For our children and our wives—Alyce, Susan, and Terry—
and to Bob's sister Barbara

Contents

Acknowledgments

During the 1995 academic year, Shel Stryker and Tim Owens had a series of conversations about the present state and future of social psychology in general and self and identity research in particular. It wasn't long before we were talking about how ideas of self and identity could benefit work on social movements and vice versa. Those conversations took root in a series of grant proposals that grew into an international miniconference and blossomed into this volume. After our grants were secured, we recruited Bob White as a coeditor and began inviting seventeen sociologists and psychologists (including ourselves) to a two-and-one-half-day conference in April 1996 at Indiana University–Purdue University at Indianapolis. The participants represented new and senior scholars interested in linkages between or among the self, social identities, personal identities, and social movement participation. In order to foster discussion and cross-fertilization, each participant prepared a conference working paper that was distributed to all the other participants a few weeks before the conference. The ensuing debate and discussion resulted in a very challenging and constructive conference. Since our purpose for the whole enterprise was to bridge specialties and disciplines, each participant was directed to treat the relations of *at least two* of the conference's central concepts: self/identity, social identity, and social movements. The fruit of that conference is this book, a truly collaborative effort between an extraordinarily energetic and dedicated group of scholars. The papers were initially divided among the editors into the topics of self (Owens), identity (Stryker), and social movements (White). We then worked within these areas, and together across the areas, to produce a cohesive and fully collaborative volume.

We owe thanks to many people and begin with a special thank you to Ligaya Lindio-McGovern for helping Owens and Stryker organize the conference. Diane Lihota, Jacqui Cook Chester, and Bruce Beal served as our diligent, fastidious, and always cheerful assistants. Georganna Priest also helped with many clerical tasks with her usual accuracy and efficiency. In keeping with the international, catholic flavor of the conference, our caterer, Sara Reed-Purvis, created a cake of the world that identified each participant by state or country. It was so beautiful that everyone was afraid to cut into it. We bet it was delicious. Support for the conference was provided by several external and internal sources. We gratefully acknowledge financial assistance from the American Sociological Association/National Science Foundation Fund for the Advancement of the Discipline as well as the Indiana University President's Council on the Arts and Sciences, the IU Center on Philanthropy, the IU Graduate School, the IUPUI Office of Faculty Development, the IU Department of Sociology, and the IUPUI School of Liberal Arts.

Introduction

Social Psychology and Social Movements: Cloudy Past and Bright Future

Sheldon Stryker, Timothy J. Owens, and Robert W. White

This volume seeks to develop the potential of social psychological work on self and identity for the theory of and research on social movements. The preparation and presentation of such a volume are timely: today, a strong current of interest in social psychological concepts and ideas exists among social movement scholars, and a good deal of that interest reflects the concepts of self and identity. Yet there is also considerable confusion about the meaning and implications of diverse conceptions of self and identity in the social psychological literature as well as the diverse disciplinary and theoretical traditions from which these conceptions stem; and there is considerable confusion in the social movement literature about such matters and their relevance for social movement analyses. This circumstance means that the concepts of self and identity are less useful to students of social movements than they might otherwise be. The present volume reflects an effort to improve that situation.

A brief review of the history of social movement theorizing and research, particularly among sociologists in the United States, sets the stage for the remaining chapters in the volume. Those who know this history will be aware that there is considerable irony in the assertion, made above, that social movement scholars currently find something of interest in social psychological concepts and ideas. Much early work on social movements was strongly rooted in a social psychology that concerned itself with "collective behavior," a subtopic of which was "social movements." Nevertheless, not too long ago and in some respects even today, the suggestion that social psychological concepts and theory relating to self and identity might be useful to social scientists, particularly sociologists, interested in social movements would generally have been rejected out of hand. Today, as noted, the suggestion is respectfully, albeit perhaps also more than a bit skeptically, attended. Why this is so requires examining the fall from grace of earlier attempts to understand social movement phenomena in social psychological terms, the more recent rediscovery of social psychological concepts and theories by social movement theorists and researchers, and the reasons for the earlier fall and the more recent rediscovery.

The 1960s were watershed years in the theoretical treatment of social movements. Earlier, the social movement literature took many of its cues from one (or more) of three sources. The first is the writings of Le Bon (1895) and Tarde (1890), who, reacting to the French Revolution, offered their respective emphases on the irrationality of crowd behavior and imitation as the foundation of social life. The second was provided by Blumer's (1939) model of collective behavior, in which movements were seen as born of efforts to redress the impact of social disorganization and consequent personal disorganization and crowd behavior. And the third can be found in the pervasive treatment of pre– and post–World War II political movements of Right and Left as "the politics of unreason" (Lipset and Raab 1970).

A result of these lines of literature was a marked tendency to view protest movements of the 1960s and earlier as products of alienation (Kornhauser 1959), relative deprivation (Gurr 1970), frustrations derived from status inconsistency (Lenski 1954), the actions of misfits (Hoffer 1951), and even unresolved oedipal conflicts (Feuer 1969).[1] In brief, social movements were viewed largely as the products of unbridled affect, of nonrational and irrational wellsprings of action. Social movements were taken to be anything but well-considered responses to legitimate concerns about real but oppositional interests.

Not surprisingly, a reaction set in, fueled in part by the fact that the very social scientists who studied social movements often were themselves active movement participants who could hardly be expected to accept quietly a characterization of their behavior as nonrational or, especially, irrational. A dramatic expression of this reaction is Gamson's (1975,130–36) use of the words "straightjacket" and "stultifying" in describing the impact of the earlier application of social psychological theories and concepts to social movements.

A major reaction came via resource mobilization theory (McCarthy and Zald 1973, 1977; Zald and Ash 1966; see also Oberschall 1973), overwhelmingly emphasizing organizational variables in deliberate efforts to mobilize resources in accounting for the growth, development, success, and decline of social movements. Another reaction, akin in spirit and tone to resource mobilization—indeed, the two shade into each other—but stressing political structures, processes, and opportunities, came in the form of political process theory (McAdam 1982; Tarrow 1988, 1994; Tilly 1978). Emphasizing organizational and political variables, these theories deemphasized social psychological variables (Zurcher and Snow 1981). Two observations are pertinent. First, the antagonism of these theories to a nonrational model of the human being, rather than a rejection of a *particular* (limited and in that sense peculiar) social psychology, was generalized to social psychology of whatever kind; the implicit—and sometimes explicit (see, e.g., Gamson 1975; McCarthy and Zald 1973, 1977)—demand was that social psychological theorizing be eschewed in the study of social movements. Second, rejecting social psychology in the study of movements, theorists nevertheless incorporated a social psychology by adopting a "rational man" model (Snow and Oliver 1995; Stryker 1980; Zurcher and Snow 1981). That is, social psychology, by definition, is the study of the relations of the social and the personal. A theory or model attributing qualities relevant to their interaction to human beings is perforce a social psychological theory or model. There is, of course, a contradiction entailed in rejecting social psychology on the one hand and adopting a particular social psychology on the other. Of considerable importance and relevance in the present context, however, is what that theoretical move gains (and why) and what it loses (and why).

The why in both cases is the same. By adopting a rational man social psychology, movement theorists can assume the essential equivalence of all persons entering movements. Since every person is the equivalent of every other, the theorists can remain largely indifferent to the entering humans and concentrate on structural constraints and opportunities affecting movements and on the mobilization of resources to achieve social movement objectives.[2]

However, assuming the equivalence of human beings also imposes serious limits on questions raised in social movement research and the possibility of understanding important features of movements. As Snow and Oliver (1995) observe, movements typically recruit only a small fraction of the persons whose apparently identical social structural niches and ideological orientations make them equally likely to join. Minimally, this implies the need to go beyond social structural and ideological variables in accounting for movements' recruitment experiences. Along the same lines, it becomes difficult to raise and pursue effectively any number of questions, for example: How are we to understand variations in persons' being nominal members as opposed to becoming heavily involved? How are we to understand the differential willingness of movement members to provide resources to further movement ends? How are we to understand the fissions and conflicts that occur within many social movements and the consequences of these? How are we to understand differences in who stays in and who drops out of movements? Dealing with such questions requires introducing concepts and theories that allow seeing the human material of movements in variegated terms. It requires a social psychology that recognizes and accommodates variation in human beings.

That requirement has not gone unremarked by social movement theorists and researchers, including some who were vociferous earlier in insisting that students of movements downplay social psychology and approach their work from a more or less purely social organizational standpoint. Gamson (1992, 56), even though his call to bring social psychology back into social movements work is apparently not ready to admit darker possibilities in the interplay of social psychological variables and social movement phenomena, writes about social psychological theory: "Cleansed of its assumptions about a spoiled or ersatz identity, there is a central insight that remains. Participation in social movements frequently involves enlargement of personal identity for participants and offers fulfillment and realization of self." The volume in which Gamson's (1992) paper appeared (Morris and Mueller 1992; see, in particular, chapters by Mueller and by Taylor) called for a revived interest of social movement theory in social psychology; and that call is now sounded—and responded to—regularly (e.g., Johnston 1995 and other papers in Johnston and Klandermans 1995; Klandermans 1984, 1997; McAdam and Paulson 1993; Snow and Oliver 1995; Zurcher and Snow 1981).

Although they were marginalized with the growing dominance of the resource mobilization and political process perspectives through the 1970s and 1980s, there continued to be sociologists and social psychologists who pursued their interests in social movements from the standpoint of social psychology (e.g., Snow, Zurcher, and Ekland-Olson 1980; Turner 1969; Turner and Killian 1957; see also the reviews of the social psychology of social movement literature contained in (Snow and Oliver 1995) and Zurcher and Snow 1981). Notable in this respect is a psychologist, Bert Klandermans (1984, 1997). Klandermans (1984) explicitly sought to bridge resource mobilization theory and social psychology by introducing into the former a theory of differential motivation for movement participation based on the concept of expectations. Later, he (Klandermans 1997; chapter 3, this volume; Klandermans and Oegema 1987) extended his bridging efforts by incorporating political process variables as well as an expanded set of social psychological concepts, including identity concepts, into work on social movements. Obviously, this continuity also bespeaks a recognition of the need for a social psychology in work on social movements.

Given agreement on that need, the question becomes: What kind of social psychology? This volume argues that it is a social psychology giving central place to concepts of self and identity that will prove especially useful to students of social movements.

This argument is not entirely novel; it has been anticipated in the literature of past decades (see, e.g., Isaacs 1975; Klapp 1969; Zurcher and Snow 1981), and today we can find in the social movement literature a wide range of discussions invoking one or another conception of self and identity. Indeed, such discussions have become ubiquitous, as the following range of works illustrates: Gamson 1995; Gould 1995; Grant and Brown 1995; Hunt, Benford, and Snow 1994; Klandermans 1997; Laraña, Johnston, and Gusfield 1994; McAdam and Paulson 1993; Melucci 1988; Snow and Oliver 1995; Sparks and Shepard 1992; Tajfel and Turner 1986; Taylor and Whittier 1992.

Why, then, a volume (re)making the argument? What justifies a volume devoted to exploring the relevance of concepts of self and identity to social movement behavior? The answers to this question are basically twofold and in some measure contradictory. First, a considerable price is being paid for the current popularity—the ubiquity previously remarked—of discussions of self and identity (particularly the latter) in work addressing social movement issues; second, despite this popularity of usage, social movement theorists and researchers have yet to take advantage of the full range of intellectual resources present in various conceptions of self and identity.

To expand these answers briefly, since they are treated at greater length in the next chapter ("Identity Competition: Key to Differential Social Movement Participation?" by Sheldon Stryker): the very ubiquity of usage implies the strong possibility that the usage has been imprecise and indiscriminate—and it has been both. Often, the terms *self* and *identity* are used in work without any attempt to specify their complex meanings. At an extreme, the language of self and identity represents simply the use of alternative words for well-established social science concepts such as culture or ethnicity. More important, perhaps, is a failure to recognize that there is a difference among various self and identity concepts with respect to levels of application—to an individual; to a social category; to a social collectivity; to a society as a whole—and a related tendency to use conceptions of self and identity appropriate to analyses on one level as though they were equally appropriate to analyses on another level. This state of affairs in its turn reflects the unclear relation between personal identities and identities defined in categorical or collective terms, as well as between identities of whatever kind and self. It reflects as well confusion resulting from the use of different self and identity terminology to mean the same thing and the use of the same term to mean quite different things, not to speak of unrecognized or "fuzzy" overlap among a variety of self and identity conceptualizations.

One consequence of indiscriminate and imprecise use of various self and identity concepts in social movement analyses is the failure to ask questions about the relations among collective, categorical, group, and individual identities, the ways in which these may (or may not) fit together and the consequences of fit or lack of fit, questions that could supply a much more refined sense than currently exists of the whys of multifarious social movement processes and outcomes. This failure relates not only to the noted indiscriminate and imprecise usage but also to the fact that various usages of the terms *self* and *identity* are linked to differing disciplinary and theoretical traditions. Thus, for example, the concept of identity carries the connotation of sameness or continuity of individual self-concepts through time in the psychoanalytic tradition represented by Erik Erikson (1968). In the theoretical tradition of symbolic interactionism in sociology (see, e.g., Stryker 1980), the concept of identity refers to an internalized set of meanings attached to a role played in a network of social relationships, with a person's self viewed as, in important part, an organization of the various identities held by the person. As it derives from the theoretical tradition of cognitive social psychology dominant among psychologists taking self as their object of study, social identity refers to a person's view of self as a member of a social category, to—in Turner's (1987) terms—grouping cognitively oneself and some class of stimuli as the same. Collective identity refers to emergent shared beliefs about membership, boundaries, and activities of a social movement held by movement members; this concept of identity tends to be "localized" among students of social movements, often but not necessarily sociologists, and it often takes on a strong cultural connotation. Too often, those representing different disciplinary and theoretical traditions incorporating concepts of identity have little contact with those representing other traditions. Again, the useful application of identity concepts to social movement issues is more limited than it might be.

Disciplinary and terminological challenges have also hampered meaningful and fruitful linkages between students of self per se, particularly self-esteem, and social movements. Unlike the problems discussed in relation to various forms of identity, and the debate over social psychology's relevance to social movements notwithstanding, concepts of self and self-esteem have had very little impact on the social movement literature. (An exception is the "irrational actor" view that sees people gravitating to social movements to shore up their sense of self and self-esteem or immersing themselves in a movement that effectively subordinates self to a larger cause; see chapter 10, this volume.) Even though self-concept and self-esteem have appeared in the social science literature for more than a century, these concepts have rarely been linked to macro social phenomena such as collective behavior and social movements; given the intellectual traditions and histories involved, this is hardly surprising. Students of self and self-esteem, then, face the same generic challenges of other social psychologists in affecting work on social movements. There is, however, one major difference: these students have experienced an even more delayed (re)entry into the social movement literature. This volume is also devoted to reestablishing the linkage and exploring how the rich literature on the self and self-esteem can expand our knowledge of social movements.

As noted in the preface, this effort to bridge more usefully work on the social psychology of self and identity and work on social movements began by bringing together in a conference four kinds of social scientists: social psychologists whose disciplinary background is sociology, for whom the concept of personal identity is central in their thinking and work; social psychologists whose disciplinary background is psychology, for whom the concept of social identity is central; social psychologists of whatever disciplinary background whose work focuses on the larger concept of self rather than the more particular concept of identity; and sociologists who are primarily students of social movements. The hope in bringing together this diverse set of persons was that the mutual stimulation that then occurred would result in a clearer sense of how the variety of conceptualizations of self and identity relate to one another. The further aspiration was to show that the incorporation of one or another (or more) of the conceptualizations of self and identity into work on social movements could enrich the theory of and research on movements.

The chapters that follow in this volume collectively demonstrate the validity of both hope and aspiration. The volume is organized in three parts, aside from this introductory chapter. Part I moves toward meeting our objectives by offering three chapters dealing with the relationships among various forms of identity and their impact on social movement participation.

In his chapter, Sheldon Stryker ("Identity Competition: Key to Differential Social Movement Participation?") is concerned not so much with relating personal identity and social identity, or personal identity and collective identity, as with clarifying the distinctions among these conceptualizations and with suggesting the implications of the distinctions for social movement analyses. In particular, he asserts that, as compared with alternative conceptualizations, the conceptions of self and of personal identity as these are developed in identity theory offer important advantages for the analysis of differences in levels and kinds of participation of persons in social movements, from none to considerable and from trivial to consequential. Specifically, he argues that a conception of self as composed of multiple identities varying in salience, their salience linked to but not totally dependent on embeddedness in networks of role relationships supportive of the identities, enables a theoretically grounded analysis of identity competition (or mutual reinforcement) useful in explaining variable participation of persons in social movements.

David A. Snow and Doug McAdam ("Identity Work Processes in the Context of Social Movements: Clarifying the Identity/Movement Nexus") distinguish personal and collective identities and point to various processes through which the personal and collective identities of social movement activists are aligned. To clarify the "identity/movement nexus," they elaborate ways in which personal and collective identities may be linked and examine the implications of these linkages for movement dynamics and processes. Noting the insufficiencies of dispositional and structural accounts of social movements, they build on the constructionist approach to movement collective identities to differentiate two forms of identity work, identity convergence and identity construction. The former refers to the coalescence of movement and individuals who already agree with it, the latter to the process through which personal and collective identities are aligned and become consistent with individuals' self-conceptions and interests. Snow and McAdam then examine the mechanisms that mediate forms of identity work and the dynamics of identity work over the life course of movements, suggesting that different forms of identity work tend to dominate movement recruitment over time and that movement dynamics are influenced by these identity work processes.

Whereas Snow and McAdam focus on links between individual and collective identities and the impact of these links for social movement processes, Bert Klandermans and Marga de Weerd ("Group Identification and Political Protest") concentrate their efforts on the relationships of collective identity and social identity. They argue that the two forms of identity are distinct but related, tied together through processes of group identification. In turn, they assert that group identification processes are essential to the construction of the collective identities many claim as essential to effective movement actions. Klandermans and de Weerd illustrate their argument with data from a longitudinal survey of Dutch farmers' protests against government agricultural policies. Finding strong and stable ingroup identification among Dutch farmers, they demonstrate that group identification influences action preparedness, the intention to participate in protest activity of Dutch farmers.

The chapters constituting Part II continue to contribute to the objectives of the volume in part by developing distinctions between as well as relationships among various conceptions of self and identity. Yet their concerns are not so much with such distinctions and relationships as with some particular aspect of, or issue implicating, self or identity and with relating this aspect or issue to movement participation.

Part II is organized into three subsections, the first of which comprises two chapters focusing on personal identity. Criticizing current work on collective identity as not going far enough in incorporating culture in the form of value systems and ideology, nor far enough in incorporating individual self-concepts or self-motives, Viktor Gecas ("Value Identities, Self-Motives, and Social Movements") proposes as a corrective focusing on value-based identities. He observes that current social psychological discourse approaches identity largely in terms of social location (i.e., social relationships and memberships) and argues that a consideration of identities based on values has been neglected. Drawing in part on work on values by Milton Rokeach, Gecas describes such identities as more diffuse and more transcendent than identities based on social roles and memberships, consequently having special relevance for understanding social movements. Since the value systems and ideologies associated with movements have identity implications affecting members' commitment and sense of authenticity, considering value-based identities will enable social movement researchers to understand members' motivations better.

Jill Kiecolt ("Self-Change in Social Movements") notes, along with many contemporary social movement analysts, that a central task of a social movement is to ensure that its members incorporate the movement's collective identity into their own self-definitions. She asks: How is this accomplished? More specifically, how does social movement participation affect self-concept change? She begins her development of an answer to these questions by distinguishing two general features of self-concepts that are open to change: (1) the hierarchy of traits/identities included in the self-concept and (2) the meaning of the identities that are part of the self-concept (an idea also touched on by Owens and Aronson, chapter 9, this volume).

Hierarchies of identities can change by adding or discarding identities, modifying the salience of identities, or shifting the rankings of identities; meanings can change though altering definitions of what can be accomplished by acting out an identity, by shifting the image projected in an identity, or by transforming the linkages among identities. Having illuminated these various kinds of changes in identities that are possible, Kiecolt is able to offer a set of propositions or hypotheses relating the possibilities for change to Gamson's delineation of movement identities (organizational activist, movement activist, solidary group activist), illustrating the processes involved by reference to particular social movements.

The second section of Part II shifts attention to social identities and collective identities. Elizabeth C. Pinel and William B. Swann Jr. ("Finding the Self through Others: Self-Verification and Social Movement Participation") begin this shift by first reviewing the evidence for a strong self-verification motive in persons' behavior with respect to their individual self-views and then pursuing the question of whether that motive is equivalently operative with respect to social identities. Finding that self-verification strivings do occur when social identities are involved, Pinel and Swann relate these strivings to social movement participation. They argue that people will not join movements frustrating self-verification needs and that successful movement recruitment techniques appeal to those needs; that people will more likely join movements when movement collective identities align with their highly salient identities, thus relating self-verification to Stryker's argument in chapter 1. Drawing on the social movements discussed by Roth in chapter 14 and by White and Fraser in chapter 15, they suggest that *withdrawal* of participation in movements relates to conflicts between collective identities and self-views, a theme consistent with, though coming from a different direction than, chapter 9. Furthermore, they extend Kiecolt's analysis by suggesting that changes in self-concepts, often a motivation in social movement participation, are made possible in the context of self-verification.

Marilynn B. Brewer and Michael D. Silver ("Group Distinctiveness, Social Identification, and Collective Mobilization") are concerned with the determinants of the strength and importance of social identities. Assuming that such identities are a critical group resource for mobilizing collective action, they assert that understanding how, when, and why large numbers of persons belonging to a given social category adopt category membership as an important social identity is critical to predicting and explaining collective movements. To that end, they offer Brewer's theory of optimal distinctiveness, postulating that social identification derives from two universal human motives: a need for inclusion and assimilation and a need for differentiation from others. The theory predicts that social identification will be highest in those groups making members feel they are valued and representative members of an exclusive category, providing a general model for understanding the formation, maintenance, and fission of social movements. Bolstering their argument by reference to the empirical work of Brewer and her colleagues, and echoing the work of Taylor, chapter 13, as well as others, they assert that the close tie between cognitive representations of self and representations of the collective that group identification reflects could well be the sine qua non of collective action.

The remaining chapter in the second section of Part II deals with an emergent theme in work by social psychologists trained in psychology, namely, the potential significance of turning away from individualism to collectivism as a foundational premise for social psychological theorizing and research. Kay Deaux and Anne Reid ("Contemplating Collectivism"), discerning such a turn in social psychology, propose a group-specific conception of collectivism as more amenable—as compared with either an individualistic or a cultural conception—to social psychological theorizing and more useful in exploring relationships between social identity and social movement behavior. Introducing a new measure of collectivism, a multifactor scale assessing theoretically relevant aspects of group-focused collective values, Deaux and Reid go on to consider the implications of this conceptual approach for investigating social movement participation. One particular aspect of their analysis echoes Klandermans and de Weerd in chapter 3. Drawing a distinction between collectivism and the strength of social (group) identification, and noting that social identity is a necessary component of collectivism whereas the reverse is not, they theorize that strength of collectivism as associated with a particular group identification will predict whether collective action is or is not taken.

The chapters in the third section of Part II focus attention on the relevance of the self-esteem component of self, as well as on the links of individual and social or collective identities to social movement behaviors.

Timothy J. Owens and Pamela J. Aronson ("Self-Concept as a Force in Social Movement Involvement") link aspects of self and identity to the impetus to become involved in social movements. To achieve that goal, they connect social and collective identity to what they term individual and social self-esteem and then bring the literatures on these topics to bear on social movement participation. They also seek to anchor self-esteem and social movement participation in perceptions of fairness and justice. Developing these aspirations, Owens and Aronson offer three hypotheses (or models). The first hypothesis, that individual self-esteem is itself sufficient to move persons to movement activism, is recognized as an oversimplification, reflecting a sympathetic reaction to Snow and McAdam's criticism, in chapter 2, of dispositional accounts of movement activism. The second and third hypotheses are proposed to remedy this oversimplification. The second argues, in a manner recalling status inconsistency arguments, that a disparity between positive individual self-esteem and social self-esteem expands the motivation to engage in appropriate social movement activity. The third theorizes that high self-esteem people will be active movement participants when their social justice concerns are coupled with a perception of chronic injustice accorded a group to which they are attached via salient social identities.

Detecting a new appreciation in the literature for the "marginal man" thesis of social movement participation that antedated resource mobilization theory, Howard B. Kaplan and Xiaoru Liu ("Social Movements as Collective Coping with Spoiled Personal Identities: Intimations from a Panel Study of Changes in the Life Course between Adolescence and Adulthood") boldly and provocatively seek to recast and reinvigorate the classical (McAdam 1982) or dispositional perspective on social movement participation. They make their case though an empirical examination of a "spoiled identity thesis" drawing on data from Kaplan's four-wave longitudinal study whose subjects were initially seventh-graders in the Houston, Texas, school system in 1971 were restudied as ninth-graders, when they were in their twenties, and most recently when they were from thirty-five to thirty-nine years old. The hypothesis tested is that persons with "spoiled identities" in general and those who have experienced rejection by others in particular are motivated to rehabilitate their negative sense of self by joining social movements, especially when the movements challenge mainstream society, the assumed source of their misfortune. Since social movements are seen as vehicles for redefining societal or group norms, which self-rejecters presumably have failed to meet, Kaplan and Liu believe that social movements serve as a way to combat or correct the source of earlier negative experience by redefining the normative standards of behavior and evaluation by which they were previously found wanting.

Roy F. Baumeister, Karen L. Dale, and Mark Muraven ("Volition and Belongingness: Social Movements, Volition, Self-Esteem, and the Need to Belong") observe that psychologists studying self have emphasized cognitive processes and the self as executive initiating actions and making choices and that they have (relatively) neglected the interpersonal self defined by personal relationships and social roles. Asserting that self is a tool for building and sustaining interpersonal relationships and recognizing the fundamentally social nature of human beings, they assume (recalling Brewer and Silver) that people have a basic motivation to form and maintain social bonds and that self-esteem is an internal measure of how well they are doing on this score. Thus self-esteem mediates the link between belongingness needs and social movements. In contrast to Owens and Aronson's focus on high self-esteem people, Baumeister, Dale, and Muraven suggest that persons with low self-esteem may find social connectedness especially problematic and that social movement recruitment appeals with the implied message of banding with a group may be especially attractive to such persons. With regard to the executive function of self, the authors point to research implying not only severe limitations on the exercise of volition that must be carefully tapped but also a finite volitional reserve. They note that joining a movement may require an act of volition. However, once a person is in a movement, the need for individual volition may be removed by group influences, making it easier to remain than *deciding* to leave. The authors show how distinguishing between choosing to join and choosing specific participatory acts is useful for understanding apparently paradoxical aspects of social movement participation.

Lory Britt and David Heise ("From Shame to Pride in Identity Politics") draw in part on Kaplan's earlier work to deal with spoiled, here stigmatized, identity—specifically that attached to being gay—to explicate how a social movement, gay rights, converts shame and loneliness into pride and solidarity and a fight for justice. (The chapter thus hearkens back to Kiecolt's concern, in chapter 5, with how self-change occurs and Owens and Aronson's look, in in chapter 9, at injustice and feelings of indignation.) More generally, Britt and Heise seek to integrate emotion into the study of social movements, doing so by developing a model describing how social movements engage in identity politics based on their analysis of the gay rights movements. Assuming that persons with a stigma are favorably disposed toward a social movement ameliorating their stigma, creating a latent willingness to participate in the movement, the model asserts that increasing levels of participation in social movement–related activities begins a process by which initial shame converts to fear, fear to anger, anger to pride. It also asserts that pride in the context of shared attributes among those participating in a movement increases the solidarity of the participants. The role of social movements, claim Britt and Heise, is to incite emotion; social movements, that is, do emotion work that raises emotional capital for mobilization efforts.

The Britt and Heise chapter, given its empirical grounding in a specific social movement, bridges to Part III of the volume, whose three chapters each deal with a particular social movement. It links especially to the chapter by Verta Taylor ("Emotions and Identity in Women's Self-Help Movements"), who also is a strong advocate of integrating emotion into work on social movements. Taylor draws heavily on the sociology of emotions literature as well as the individual and collective identity literatures in her analysis of participation in the postpartum depression self-help movement. Using both individual and organizational data collected over ten years of fieldwork, she demonstrates, echoing themes in Kiecolt and Brewer and Silver, that involvement in this movement helps activists reconstruct their individual identities around a collective identity that transforms negative emotions into positive emotions. More specifically, she traces the transformation in movement members of the negative and stigmatized emotions (guilt, anxiety, depression, anger) associated with failure to demonstrate the self-sacrificial love normatively expected of mothers into pride at having survived an ordeal. Stressing that to suggest emotions play a part in social movements does not negate the evidence arguing the instrumental and strategic nature of social movements, Taylor ends with the summary judgment that "a full understanding of social movements requires that we attend both to the cognitive and the emotional aspects of social protest."

Silke Roth ("Developing Working-Class Feminism: A Biographical Approach to Social Movement Participation") presents a case study of members of the Coalition of Labor Union Women (CLUW), an organization that was formed as a strategy to bridge the gap between the women's movement and the labor movement. Her study demonstrates the validity of Stryker's contention concerning the import of variations in personal identities for issues of variable participation and maintenance of membership in social movements. Roth combines survey data, life history, and in-depth interview methods with a biographical perspective on social movement participation emphasizing how the lives of participants shape social movement organization and identities while at the same time shaping those participants. She identifies four ideal types of women who joined CLUW: founding mothers, rebellious daughters, political animals, and fighting victims. She shows that the personal identities of members of CLUW are distinct from the collective identity of the organization; that the indicated four types of women are different in their motives for involvement in CLUW, in their expectations for activism, and in their careers within the movement; that these types of women had differential impact in the construction of the movement's collective identity; and that these types of women experience differently the movement's collective identity, with different consequences for their movement-related behaviors.

Robert W. White and Michael R. Fraser ("Personal and Collective Identities and Long-Term Social Movement Activism: Republican Sinn Féin") capitalize on intensive interview data from White's long-term study of Irish Republicans to examine a movement's collective identity and the individual identities of movement members. In so doing, they demonstrate not only that individual identities influence collective identity but also that collective identity affects activists' personal lives and identities and their movement careers as well. Examining a new political party, Republican Sinn Féin, created in a split from an existing political party, Provisional Sinn Féin, White and Fraser argue that a movement's collective identity is constructed out of shared aspects of individual identities of subgroups of activists. They suggest that the collective identity of Republican Sinn Féin is more complex than the sense of "we-ness" and solidarity in terms of which collective identity is often defined; rather, it has two major dimensions, one based on social solidarity, the other on ideology or what it means for activists to be a "Republican." They show that collective identity is not necessarily agreed on by activists and that what a movement means to activists may vary across subgroups, sometimes leading to factionalism and splits.Having offered the reader "appetizers" in the form of brief synopses of the chapters that follow, we are now ready for the "entrees" themselves.

Notes

1. The picture being presented is overdrawn. Not all social movement theorists and researchers up to and into the 1960s are appropriately characterized in these terms; see, among others, Turner and Killian (1957). Nevertheless, the description given is valid as a portrayal of a generalized tendency.

2. See Zurcher and Snow (1981) for a critique of rational man social psychology in the specific context of social movement work.

References

Blumer, Herbert. 1939. "Collective Behavior." In *Principles of Sociology,* edited by Robert E. Park, 219–88. New York: Barnes and Noble.

Erikson, Erik H. 1968. *Identity: Youth and Crisis.* New York: Norton.

Feuer, Lewis S. 1969. *The Conflict of Generations.* New York: Basic Books.

Gamson, William A. 1975. *The Strategy of Social Protest.* Homewood, Ill.: Dorsey.

———. 1992. "The Social Psychology of Collective Action." In *Frontiers of Social Movement Theory,* edited by Aldon D. Morris and Carol Mueller, 53–76. New Haven: Yale University Press.

———. 1995. "Constructing Social Protest." In *Social Movements and Culture,* edited by Hank Johnston and Bert Klandermans, 85–106. Minneapolis: University of Minnesota Press.

Gould, Roger V. 1995. *Insurgent Identities: Class, Community, and Protest in Paris from 1848 to the Commune.* Chicago: University of Chicago Press.

Grant, Peter R., and Rupert Brown. 1995. "From Ethnocentrism to Collective Protest: Responses to Relative Deprivation and Threat to Social Identity." *Social Psychology Quarterly* 58:195–212.

Gurr, Ted. 1970. *Why Men Rebel.* Princeton: Princeton University Press.

Hoffer, Eric. 1951. *The True Believer.* New York: Harper and Row.

Isaacs, Harold R. 1975. *Idols of the Tribe: Group Identity and Political Change.* Cambridge: Harvard University Press.

Johnston, Hank. 1991. *Tales of Nationalism: Catalonia, 1939–1979.* New Brunswick, N.J.: Rutgers University Press.

Johnston, Hank, and Bert Klandermans, eds. 1995. *Social Movements and Culture.* Minneapolis: University of Minnesota Press.

Johnston, Hank, Enrique Laraña, and Joseph R. Gusfield. 1994. "Identities, Grievances, and New Social Movements." In *New Social Movements: From Ideology to Identity,* edited by Enrique Laraña, Hank Johnston, and Joseph R. Gusfield, 3–35. Philadelphia: Temple University Press.

Klandermans, Bert. 1984. "Mobilization and Participation: Social-Psychological Expansion of Resource Mobilization Theory." *American Sociological Review* 49:583–600.

———. 1997. *The Social Psychology of Protest.* Oxford: Blackwell.

Klandermans, Bert, and Dirk Oegema. 1987. "Potentials, Networks, Motivations, and Barriers: Steps toward Participation in Social Movements." *American Sociological Review* 52:519–32.

Klapp, Orrin. 1969. *Collective Search for Identity.* New York: Holt, Rinehart and Winston.

Kornhauser, William. 1959. *The Politics of Mass Society.* New York: Free Press.

Laraña, Enrique, Hank Johnston, and Joseph R. Gusfield, eds. 1994. *New Social Movements: From Ideology to Identity.* Philadelphia: Temple University Press.

Le Bon, Gustave. 1895. *The Crowd: A Study of the Popular Mind.* London: Ernest Benn.

Lenski, Gerhard. 1954. "Status Crystallization: A Non-Vertical Dimension of Social Status." *American Sociological Review* 9:405–13.

Lipset, Seymour Martin, and Earl Raab. 1970. *The Politics of Unreason.* New York: Harper and Row.

McAdam, Doug. 1982. *Political Process and the Development of Black Insurgency, 1930–1970.* Chicago: University of Chicago Press.

McAdam, Doug, and Ronnelle Paulson. 1993. "Specifying the Relationship between Social Ties and Activism." *American Journal of Sociology* 99:640–67.

McCarthy, John D., and Mayer N. Zald. 1973. *The Trend of Social Movements in America.* Morristown, N.J.: General Learning Press.

———. 1977. "Resource Mobilization and Social Movements." *American Journal of Sociology* 82: 1212–42.

Melucci, Alberto. 1988. "Getting Involved: Identity and Mobilization in Social Movements." *International Social Movement Research* 1:329–48.

Morris, Aldon D., and Carol Mueller, eds. 1992. *Frontiers of Social Movement Theory.* New Haven: Yale University Press.

Oberschall, Anthony. 1973. *Social Conflicts and Social Movements.* Englewood Cliffs, N.J.: Prentice-Hall.

Snow, David A., and Pamela E. Oliver. 1995. "Social Movements and Collective Behavior: Social Psychological Dimensions and Considerations." In *Sociological Perspectives on Social Psychology,* edited by Karen S. Cook, Gary Alan Fine, and James S. House, 571–99. Boston: Allyn and Bacon.

Snow, David A., Louis A. Zurcher Jr., and Sheldon Ekland-Olson. 1980. "Social Networks and Social Movements: A Microsociological Approach to Differential Recruitment." *American Sociological Review* 45:787–801.

Sparks, Paul, and Richard Shepherd. 1992. "Self-Identity and the Theory of Planned Behavior: Assessing the Role of Identification with Green Consumerism." *Social Psychology Quarterly* 55:388–99.

Stryker, Sheldon. 1980. *Symbolic Interactionism: A Social Structural Version.* Menlo Park, Calif.: Benjamin/Cummings.

Tajfel, Henri. 1981. *Human Groups and Social Categories.* London: Academic Press.

Tarde, Gabriel. 1890. *The Laws of Imitation.* New York: Holt.

Tarrow, Sidney. 1988. "National Politics and Collective Action: Recent Theory and Research in Western Europe and the United States." *Annual Review of Sociology* 14:421–40.

———. 1994. *Power in Movements: Social Movements, Collective Action, and Politics.* New York: Cambridge University Press.

Taylor, Verta, and Nancy E. Whittier. 1992. "Collective Identity in Social Movement Communities: Lesbian Feminist Mobilization." In *Frontiers of Social Movement Theory,* edited by Aldon D. Morris and Carol Mueller, 104–30. New Haven: Yale University Press.

Tilly, Charles. 1978. *From Mobilization to Revolution.* Reading, Mass.: Addison-Wesley.

Turner, John C. 1987. *Rediscovering the Social Group: A Self-Categorization Theory.* New York: Blackwell.

Turner, Ralph. 1969. "The Theme of Contemporary Movements." *British Journal of Sociology* 20:390–405.

Turner, Ralph H., and Lewis Killian. 1957. *Collective Behavior.* Englewood Cliffs, N.J.: Prentice-Hall.

Zald, Mayer N., and Roberta Ash. 1966. "Social Movement Organization: Growth, Decline, and Change." *Social Forces* 44:327–41.

Zurcher, Louis A., and David A. Snow. 1981. "Collective Behavior: Social Movements." In *Social Psychology: Sociological Perspectives,* edited by Morris Rosenberg and Ralph H. Turner, 447–82. New York: Basic Books.

Part I
The Theoretical and Conceptual Frame

1

Identity Competition: Key to Differential Social Movement Participation?

Sheldon Stryker

How can we best understand variation in forms and levels of social movement participation? Why do some join, whereas others with the same ideology and interests do not? Why is there variation in quitting, responsiveness to leaders' appeals, devoting resources to movement activities? Why does variation occur over time? Can we account for participation and nonparticipation parsimoniously, in the same conceptual and theoretical terms?

This chapter argues for a need to turn to social psychological theory and concepts of a particular sort for answers to such questions. It further argues that identity theory and its concepts fill the bill.[1] This theory invokes concepts pointing to differences among persons while rooting those differences in social structure, social location, and social interaction. It invokes a concept of self composed in part of multiple identities linked to interaction in networks of social relations. These identities are potential competitors in producing behavioral choices. The theory also invokes concepts of commitment and identity salience, both variable among persons, and proposes processes linking commitment to identity salience and identity salience to role-related choices. The framework underlying the theory suggests that identities reciprocally affect commitment and can become functionally autonomous; they can affect persons' choice behavior independent of the commitment underwriting their salience.

Identity theory is not the only social psychological theory using *identity*. The term is basic to social identity theory (Tajfel 1981), which deals with conflicts stemming from in-group/out-group categorizations. Further, the term appears in literatures of political science, social history, and historical sociology, doing so without explicit ties to social psychology. *Conceptualizations* of identity—when offered—in these literatures are diverse, confusing discussions of its applicability to social movements. Appreciating the possibilities of identity theory for analyses of variable participation in movements requires distinguishing usages in the social movement and social psychological literatures.

I turn first to this task. Given my focus on its potential for social movement analysis, identity theory and its concepts are more fully described than alternatives. The heart of the chapter discusses why and how this theory is useful in explaining variable movement participation. A brief coda concludes the chapter.

Clearing the Ground

Cultural and Collective Conceptions of Identity

The concept of "identity" often remains unproblematized and untheorized in the social science literature. When identity is explicitly addressed, its conceptualization is frequently cultural: identity is made equivalent to the ideas, beliefs, and practices of a society, its features implicitly ascribed to all members of that society. Although network theorists invoke identity from a structural rather than a cultural perspective, their conception also ascribes its features to those sharing a common social location and, implicitly, a culture, without differentiating further among persons to whom the term applies.

Nowhere is the practice of leaving identity undefined or equivalent to culture clearer than in work by political scientists and historical sociologists on contemporary resurgences of ethnicity and nationalism and "the politics of identity." Nagel (1995), discussing the revival of American Indian ethnic identity, does not define identity, obscuring what is gained in using the term rather than referencing American Indian ethnicity. Scheff's (1994) "Emotions and Identity: A Theory of Ethnic Nationalism" contains no mention of identity apart from the title, suggesting that identity and ethnicity are equivalents, that identity has no independent analytic significance in the theory developed.

Taking identity for granted is demonstrated in essays by Somers and Gibson (1994), Wiley (1994), and Zaretsky (1994). The last approaches issues of action, agency, and identity by linking identity and narrativity. Using "identity" ubiquitously, they offer no definition or conceptual analysis of it. Nonetheless, these authors, and the others cited, clearly hold a cultural conception of identity—they are concerned with ideas, beliefs, practices, characterizing entire peoples.

Isaacs (1975, 38), writing on identity and political change, offers a definition of basic group identity: "the ready-made set of endowments and identifications that every individual shares with others from the moment of birth by the chance of the family into which he is born at that given time in a given place." He elaborates by noting that basic group identity is formed of primordial attachments or affinities, pointing to individuals' values deriving from unique histories of their people and to "a deep commonality known only to those who shared in it, and only expressible in words more mythical than conceptual." He locates identity in the core of the individual *and* the core of communal culture, indeed in the identity of the two identities. His attributes of group identity—body, name, history, religion, nationality—testify to its status as a cultural concept with minimal (in a sociological sense only trivial) variation in the individuals incorporating the identity.

The New Social Movement perspective sees a collective search for identity as a fundamental movement activity. For Melucci (1985), collective identity refers to shared beliefs making collective action possible. "The concept of collective identity refers to the (often implicitly) agreed upon definition of membership, boundaries, and activities for the group" (Johnston, Laraña, and Gusfield 1994, 15). Taylor (1989) defines collective identity as a shared definition of a group deriving from common interests, experiences, and solidarity, involving a we-feeling, constructed, activated, and sustained through interaction in movement communities (Taylor and Whittier 1992). Collective identities are shaped by commonalities bringing persons into movements and by interaction and common experiences in them. They represent emergent cultures; as such, they are supra-individual, indifferently describing movement participants.[2]

Theorists of social movements drawing on network perspectives recently have introduced identity into their work. Although moving toward usages that enable an understanding of differential involvement of persons in movement activities, they fall short of fully doing so, because they retain a focus on collective identity (Gould 1995) or treat movement identities as existing in isolation from other identities (Kim and Bearman 1997).

Social Identity Theory and Category-Based Identities

Social identity theory developed to explain large-scale religious, ethnic, and national conflicts. Assuming that self-definition is affected by specific membership groups, this theory defines *social identity* as "that part of the individual's self-concept which derives from his knowledge of his membership in a social group (or groups) together with the value and emotional significance attached to that membership" (Tajfel 1981, 225). The theory assumes strong needs to identify as a member of a group (or groups) and to regard one's own group(s) positively, needs satisfied through social comparisons derogating out-groups.

Self-categorization theory (Turner et al. 1987), embedded in social identity theory, defines self-categorizations as cognitive groupings of oneself and some class of stimuli as the same and in contrast to another class of stimuli. Incorporating this concept of self-categorization, social identity theory collapses "group" and "social category."

Other Social Psychological Sources and Uses of Identity

Noting other uses of identity in social psychology helps clarify identity theory's potential for social movement theory. Arguing that various theories of identity fill explanatory gaps left by alternatives, Thoits and Virshup (1995) distinguish individual ("me") or role-based identities from collective ("we") group or category-based identities. The former are "identifications of the self *as* a certain kind of person, claimed and enacted for the self alone." The latter are identifications of the self *with* a group or category as a whole, claimed and enacted with or for other members. Roles are situationally specific; sociodemographic categories are transsituational, carrying across particular situations. Role-based identity conceptions are oriented to stability, social order, and the reproduction of social structure.[3] Collectivity-based conceptions of identity are oriented to group competition and conflict, and thus to social change. Problematic here are separating "role" from "group"; collapsing the "group"/"category" distinction; asserting that role-based identities are claimed and enacted for self alone; and implicitly arguing that since roles are situationally specific, role-based identities are situationally specific. Consequences of these conceptual "moves" for theorizing the relation of identity to variable social movement participation are considered below.

Some New Social Movement theorists invoke an individual identity concept, appropriating a symbolic interactionist approach, and offer claims about identities: movement collective identities become bases for members' definitions of self; the relation of individual and collective is blurred; movement action is a mix of individual and collective identity confirmations (Johnston, Laraña, and Gusfield 1994, 7); claimed by persons in movements is the right to be whatever they wish, and embedded in this right is pervasive everyday acting out of identities that are the objectives of movement action (Melucci 1980, 1994). For New Social Movement analysts in general, blurring individual and collective identities is automatic (echoing Isaacs's merging of individual and culture); and relationships and identities anchored outside movements deliver commitment and solidarity of members to movements (Gamson 1992; Melluci 1994). As this suggests, New Social Movement theorists tend to restrict identity considerations to persons already in social movements, with attention focused on those whose ties to persons not directly involved in a movement reinforce movement participation (see, e.g., Johnston, Laraña, and Gusfield 1994). Thus, implicit in much movement literature is an ideology; neglected is the possibility that relationships outside movements and identities rooted in outside relationships can subvert collective identities tied to movements. In short, little attention is paid to external identities inhibiting the joining of movements or minimizing participation in movements joined. Insofar as they merge individual and collective identity, conceptions of identity in the New Social Movement literature obviate the utility of the concept to account for differential involvement in movement activities.

Others move toward individualizing social and collective identities. Klandermans (1997; Klandermans and de Weerd, chapter 3, this volume) argues that persons adopt idiosyncratic subsets of beliefs from a body of collective beliefs, and he recognizes movement members' variable attachment to a collective identity. Yet Klandermans fails to realize the potential of an individualized sense of identity for movement analyses by not placing collective identities in the context of other significant identities persons hold.

Deaux (1996) notes that identities based on relationships are viewed as more central and desirable than those not so based, and she distinguishes between fate interdependence (believing one shares a destiny with similar others) and task interdependence (involvement with others in pursuit of a goal). Both observations imply the utility of distinguishing "group" and "category," for groups are relationship-based social units, whereas categories are not; and categories link to a sense of common fate, groups to task interdependence. Thus, Deaux, whose starting point is social identity theory, moves toward a sense of identity compatible with that of identity theory. McAdam and Paulson (1993) suggest that identity salience, a concept central to identity theory, can specify links between social ties and movement activism. However, they infer the salience of an identity from commitments supporting that identity. Doing so, they neglect the independent impact of identity salience on movement-related choices. Further, they focus on single, movement-related identities, losing the analytic power of conceptualizing self as a structure of interdependent identities. These observations hold for others (e.g., Gould 1995) working from a network perspective.

A summary of major problems with alternative treatments of identity can help make clear the potential of identity theory for social movement theory and research. These are:

1. Treating "group" and "social category" as conceptual equivalents and separating the role conception from its bases in groups disable the asking and answering of important questions about the relations of movements and their members.
2. Cultural, categorical, or collective concepts of identity, sufficient for analyses of movements as "wholes" or comparative analyses crossing movements, are problematic for analyses of variable behavior of members within movements.
3. Merging individual and collective identities by definition or theoretical fiat obviates important theoretical and empirical issues in relations between individual and collective identities.
4. Assuming the reinforcing character of individual and collective identities also obviates important issues.
5. Analyzing movement behavior as if only a movement-embedded identity were operative is insufficient to understand variable relations of identity and movement participation.
6. Inferring salience of an identity from commitments supporting that identity fails to recognize that identities affect behavior independent of supportive relationships.

Identity Theory

Identity theory is a theory of role-related choice behavior deriving from a structural symbolic interactionism (Stryker 1980) whose prototypical question is: Why, on a free afternoon, do some persons play golf with friends and others take their children to the zoo?[4] A scope condition is contained in the question: it applies when alternative courses of action are reasonably open.

A symbolic interactionist frame assumes that humans are actors, recognizing the possibility of choice in human life. It further assumes that action and interaction are shaped by definitions of situations; definitions are based on shared meanings developed in interaction; meanings persons attribute to themselves—self-conceptions—are critical to interaction and action; and self-conceptions, like other meanings, are shaped in interaction and are outcomes of others' responses to persons. These assumptions lead to the basic proposition of symbolic interactionism: society shapes self shapes social behavior. The proposition includes the possibility of reciprocity among parts.

Differentiating traditional and structural symbolic interactionism is the assumption that social structure constrains—facilitates or inhibits—though it does not determine human action. Identity theory builds on this additional assumption, as well as refinements of the traditional frame and on specifications of its basic proposition.

The refinements concern conceptualizations of society and self and the relative weight given social structure as compared with interpretive processes in accounts of social behavior. The traditional interactionist frame views societies as ephemeral reflections of individual lines of action and transient, shifting patterns of interaction (Blumer 1969). In this view, structure has little place in accounts of humans' behavior, and there is little sense of constraints on behavior. Further, the traditional frame tends to dissolve structure in a solvent of subjective definitions, to view definitions as unanchored, open to any possibility, failing to recognize that some *possibilities* are more *probable* than others.[5] On the premise that self reflects society, this view leads to seeing self as undifferentiated, unorganized, unstable, and ephemeral.

Current sociology's image of society recognizes durability in patterned interactions and relationships, emphasizing resistance to change and a tendency of structure to reproduce itself. In this image, society is a complex mosaic of relations, groups, organizations, institutions, and communities, crosscut by demarcations based on categorical distinctions (race, ethnicity, and so on). This diversity is seen as organized in multiple, overlapping ways—interactionally, functionally, hierarchically—its parts sometimes highly interdependent and sometimes not, sometimes cooperating and sometimes conflicting.

The interactionist premise that self reflects society requires conceiving self in the image of society. Self must be seen as multifaceted, composed of parts sometimes highly interdependent and sometimes not, some conflicting and some reinforcing, a self organized variously. Viewing both society and self as complex, multifaceted, and variously organized permits theorizing the relations among characteristics of the two going beyond the generality of "society shapes self shapes social behavior."

Identity theory developed by specifying this interactionist formula. Social behavior is specified by focusing on role-related choices. Identity salience, specifying self, is taken to affect role choice; and commitment, specifying society, is taken to affect identity salience. The theory's basic proposition becomes: commitment affects identity salience affects role choice. Reflecting its sociological heritage, the theory emphasizes the asserted directionality but recognizes reciprocity among its elements. The choice of the word *affect* implies that the proposition eschews strict determination.

The identity salience concept builds on a multifaceted self composed of identities or internalized role designations. Persons potentially have as many identities as sets of role relations in which they participate. Identities are self-cognitions tied to roles and thus to positions in organized social relations.[6] Self is taken to be organized; one mode of organization is hierarchy. The theory assumes that identities vary in salience and are organized in a salience hierarchy. Identity salience is defined as the likelihood an identity will come into play in a variety of situations as a function of its properties as a cognitive schema (Stryker and Serpe 1994). The theory proposes that choice among behaviors expressive of particular roles reflects relative location in a salience hierarchy of identities associated with those roles.

Four implications of identity and identity salience so conceived warrant stress: persons "carry" cognitive schemata across situations, predisposing them to perceive and act in situations in line with extant identities; identities (and identity salience) can be self-reinforcing, given the noted process and the reciprocal impact of behavior on self-concepts; identities are motivational, moving people to actions expressing their meaning behaviorally; as a consequence of being transsituational, self-reinforcing, and motivational, identities can influence action independent of relationships supporting the identities—they can be functionally independent of the commitments affecting them.

Commitment's referent is in social groups or in networks of relationships. In complex, differentiated societies, persons live not in society as a whole but in small, relatively specialized units composed of others to whom they relate through occupancy of social positions and playing associated roles. Saying persons are committed to a group or social network is saying their relations to others depend on playing particular roles and having particular identities.[7] Two analytically and empirically independent types of commitment exist: interactional, the number and frequency of relationships entered by playing a role; and affective, the depth of emotional attachment to particular sets of others (Serpe 1987).

Applying Identity Theory to Social Movement Participation

Preliminary Considerations

Analysts have addressed social movement participation largely in terms of recruitment, focusing on persons already recruited. Evidently, most persons sharing social characteristics of the already recruited and equivalently ideologically ready for recruitment do not in fact participate in movement action of any kind (Klandermans and Oegema 1987). Why not? Analysts note that recruitment of new members is facilitated by preexisting network ties. But linkages to friends or other social networks, such as family or workplace contacts, *and* the identities related to these linkages may keep others *out* of movement membership.

Entering or declining to enter a movement is not the only choice important to social movements' growth, effectiveness, transformations, and longevity. Union members must decide whether to join strikes, cross picket lines, and honor boycotts. Members of ethnic or national movements must decide whether to give time, money, and, in extreme circumstances, lives. Members of movements must choose to seek or accept leadership roles, to stay in or leave their movements. Variation in movement involvement over time and life course deserve theoretical explanation. Just as a theory accounting in the same conceptual terms for both recruitment and failure to recruit is preferable for reasons of parsimony, so too is a single theory accounting for movement choices with opposing consequences. New Social Movement theorists distinguish between life in a movement and "everyday life" outside. Despite its utility, the distinction obscures the important fact that life both in and outside a movement is social and can be expected to reflect principles operative in the social more generally. One principle is that segments of persons' lives and activities affect one another; relationships are mutually implicative, as are identities. A segment can be expected to affect other segments—family problems are introduced into work settings; work demands affect family life. New Social Movement theorists assert that movement collective identity is expressed in everyday activities of movement members and that relationships to networks external to movements reinforce network commitments and ideology. But if a movement's collective identity can be expressed *outside* movement settings, so identities external to movements can be expressed *inside* them, in ways not necessarily benign or reinforcing with respect to movement identities and ideology. Variation in movement participation should be explicable in the same theoretical terms as variation in nonmovement participation.

Within movements, participation is variable. It is axiomatic that explanations of variability must be built on variables. Thus a theory built on a cultural conception of identity will not suffice. Nor will a theory invoking collective identities, even one sensitive to identities built around local, spatially bounded arenas of relations and interaction (as in Gould 1995).

Such theories suffice for many movement problems: this is not a claim of hegemony for identity theory, only that for the problem at hand, identity theory is in principle able to explain variation in movement participation because it incorporates concepts of identity that translate into variables.

When persons categorized equivalently are attributed the same identity, that desideratum is lost. Differences in conceiving identity, however, go beyond the variable-constant distinction. Identity in identity theory is rooted in social groups: membership is a matter of playing a role in a network of reciprocal roles. Identity in social identity theory is a concept rooted in social categories; membership in a category is assigned on the basis of a shared characteristic. Relatedly, social identity theory treats "group" and "category" as synonyms, understandable in a theory whose objective is explaining conflict between categories of persons. Such theory perhaps need not concern itself with variation among persons within categories. Identity theory differentiates groups and categories. While a category is inclusive of persons sharing some characteristic (Catholics, Serbs, Catalonians, gays), a group is a functioning unit of interacting persons typically occupying differentiated positions within the unit and playing complementary roles that organize members to deal with a task.

This distinction permits marking properties of groups vis-à-vis categories relevant for analyses of variation in social movement participation. As noted, identities based on relationships in groups are generally more central and desirable to persons than identities not based on relationships (Deaux 1996). More graphically, people do not live in categories; they live in groups. That fact gives groups power and influence over members that categories do not have and cannot be expected to have except when categories approach *being* groups. Involved is the distinction between interdependence of fate based on a shared characteristic and task interdependence that marks social groups' activities. Often, and under most circumstances, the latter take precedence, implying that group- rather than category-based identities will more effectively shape behavior.

Although, for emphasis, the category/group distinction has been drawn without subtlety, the distinction is not absolute. Groups perhaps typically form of subsets of persons having common categorical characteristics; categories reflect social boundaries, making it more likely that persons with common characteristic will form the role-based relationships underlying commitments. Importantly for social movement analyses, category-based movements (e.g., most ethnic-based movements) will typically incorporate multiple groups, with consequent potential for intramovement rivalry and conflict. Further, since within-movement group formations are not equally likely to develop, groups that do form may reap advantages not available to others. Finally, social movements may exhibit varying degrees of groupness, or degrees of groupness may vary across a movement's life cycle. All these possibilities hold implications for movement organization, cohesion, discipline, potential for unified activity, and success.

Commitment and Variation in Social Movement Participation

Although identity theory argues that the impact of commitment on role choice is through identity salience, I focus here on possible direct effects of variations in commitment on participation.

Commitment, again, refers to persons' relationships to others in groups and networks: persons are said to be committed to a group or network of others when their relations to these others depend on their playing particular roles and having particular identities. This conceptualization was stimulated by social movement research by Kornhauser (1962). He asks: Why do some leaders of a radical organization, committed to overthrowing the U.S. government but faced with strong evidence that this would not happen in their lifetime, remain in leadership positions despite the objective hopelessness of their cause? And why do some leaders abandon their leadership positions? His answer: Leaders remain as leaders when their social relations are circumscribed by the party—when their spouses are also party members involved in party activities; when their party position is also the source of their income; when their friends are drawn from party ranks; when, in short, they are isolated from relationships external to the party. When this is true, they are inured to objective evidence of failure from outside the movement, they are committed to the party, and they continue to play their roles as leaders. The process of abandoning party positions and roles begins when commitments erode—when, for example, they have financial needs not met by the party and they take jobs unrelated to party role, or when they establish relations to persons not party members. When that happens, their role-related performances erode.

At minimum, commitments absorb time and energy. Thus, every commitment to networks or groups not directly tied to a movement itself threatens the hegemony of the movement in securing persons' allegiance and participation.

However, matters are more complicated than the foregoing suggests. Persons have multiple commitments: they are typically involved in multiple sets of relations. Some of the sets overlap in degree, from partial to total, which is to say that (some of) the same others are in more than one set of relations. With regard to persons' commitment to movements and the consequences of that commitment for movement-related choices, key questions become: To what degree do movement relationships overlap with nonmovement relationships—for example, are others in persons' families also movement members? Are all, most, few, or no friends movement members? When nonmovement relationship networks are independent of movement relationships, do various nonmovement sets of relationships reinforce or compete with commitment to movement relationships? In the event that nonmovement and movement relationships compete, what is the level of commitment to social movement relationships relative to commitments to nonmovement relationships?

If movement and nonmovement relationships overlap greatly, it is likely that persons' multiple commitments will reinforce one another; if these are independent, they may still reinforce one another but are more likely to compete for the loyalty of movement members. The implications for variation in social movement activity of various kinds are apparent. If one has few or weak commitments to family, friends, or other groups outside the social movement—if major commitments are to relationships within the movement—there are few limits on what a movement can ask and is likely to receive. If commitments to family, friends, or other groups outside the movement are relatively weak, there will be little competition when movement leaders call for participation even of a demanding, all-encompassing sort. Conversely, however, if commitments to family, friends, or other social units are strong, the potential competitive edge of these units may well be high, in part because these units (more so than movements) are likely to be groups, and group-based expectations are likely to be more insistent, more powerful, than non-group-based expectations. Then, responsiveness to movement demands for participation will likely reflect the degree to which external commitments nevertheless support movement demands. If this support is weak or absent, responsiveness to those demands will be weak or absent. If, however, external support for a movement is great—when, for example, there are family traditions of movement support, as seems to be the case of Irish Republicanism (see chapter 15)—movement demands will be more insistent and members' responsiveness to those demands more assured.

Commitments, it should be noted, are dynamic; they change in response to whatever may interrupt extant relationships or create new relationships—changes in personal circumstance such as shifting jobs, receiving a promotion, changing living quarters, developing a new recreational activity. Geographic mobility can decisively break prior commitments and force the development of new commitments; social mobility may weaken or attenuate extant relationships. Persons' commitments will be affected by changes occurring in the lives of others to whom they relate as well as by changes occurring in their own lives. An important source of commitment dynamics are life-course changes: for instance, getting married establishes a new commitment; having children expands commitments to family; the death of a spouse or of a friend changes prior commitments in which spouse or friend were central. Changes in commitment from these sources or from others can be expected to alter the kinds and levels of members' movement participation, the precise changes depending on just what changes in commitment occur. Finally, and to repeat, high commitments to groups outside a movement may reinforce the power of the movement to ask for and get participation from its members *if* the groups share movement expectations, norms, values, and goals. If, however, outside groups to which persons are highly committed do not share movement expectations, norms, values, and goals, movement recruitment and participation will be dampened.

Identity Salience and Variation in Movement Participation

According to identity theory, the proximate source of role-choice behavior is identity salience; but the theory asserts that variation in commitment is the source of variation in identity salience. This poses an issue: if role choice reflects identity salience but identity salience reflects commitment, are the two concepts redundant with respect to their impact on role choice? If the argument of this chapter is accepted, considerable data demands are imposed on those seeking explanations of variable membership participation in movement activities. At minimum, they must gather individual-level data either on a range of commitments of movement members or on the salience of the identities implicated in those commitments. If the answer to the question posed is yes, data on one or the other will suffice. If the answer is no, gathering data on both commitment and identity salience becomes necessary. Thus, there is much at stake in the answer.

Unfortunately, the answer must be no. This is partly because of the "principled indeterminacy" of social life, partly because no single variable (commitment) of a social psychological theory will totally explain an expected outcome (identity salience), partly because no single intervening variable (identity salience, with respect to role-related choices) will mediate all the impact of an antecedent variable (commitment). In important part, however, it is because of the way identity theory conceptualizes identity and identity salience and the way identity theory links identity salience to role-related choices.

Identity has been conceptualized as a cognitive schema whose meaning lies in expectations for behavior reflecting the role on the basis of which the identity is formed. Reflecting the society in which they live, persons typically have multiple identities. Identity theory says that persons' identities are organized in a hierarchy of salience. Identity salience is defined as readiness to act out an identity as a consequence of its properties as a cognitive schema (Stryker and Serpe 1994). An illustration: lecturing is behavior reflecting an identity linked to the role of professor; lecturing one's children is evidence of the salience of a professorial identity. As the illustration implies, identity salience is transsituational; salient identities are carried by persons into situations, affecting those situations. A transsituational concept of identity salience implies the at least partial independence of behavior, including role-related choices, from demands of immediate situations of action.

Cognitive schemata are internalized, stored organizations of information and meanings operating as frames for interpreting experience. A self or identity schema is a cognitive generalization about self that guides the processing of self-relevant information (Markus and Zajonc 1985, 143). In wording more in keeping with a sociologically informed social psychology, identity schemata are cognitive resources for constructing definitions of situations in which persons find themselves.

Identities vary in the number of linked elements they contain (the more elements, the more likely they will emerge from storage, since the more likely some of the elements will be reflected in experiences at hand). They vary as well in fit, the "closeness"—experiential, semantic, syntactic, and so on—of elements to one another (Linville 1987); and they vary in specific meanings incorporated into the elements. Such variation creates variation in how persons holding the schema process and use information. That is, some schemata—highly salient more than less salient identities—create greater sensitivity and receptivity to external, situational cues as well as internal (e.g, emotional responses) cues for behavior reflecting one identity rather than another. Some schemata allow greater retention of and ease in calling up information relevant to one identity rather than another. Some schemata lead persons to define situations in ways invoking one rather than another identity, making more likely one enactment rather than another.

Transsituational concepts of identity and identity salience carry a number of implications. In some (varying) degree responsive to immediate demands of situations, actions are also responsive to identities, in part because salient identities affect definitions of situations. In affecting definitions of situations, they make more probable behavior expressing the identities. Behavioral expressions of an identity serve to verify that one is a particular kind of person; in so doing, they increase the salience of the identity. In brief, then, salient identities can be self-reinforcing and self-enhancing.

They can be self-reinforcing and self-enhancing through a different process. If identities in general are motivations to behave in identity-appropriate ways, salient identities are inherently highly motivational: they strongly move persons to behave in accord with role expectations defining the meaning of the identities. There is reason to think that persons draw a greater measure of self-esteem from performances reflecting salient identities (Ervin and Stryker forthcoming). Since esteem has motivational force, this argues further that persons will seek opportunities to act out the roles underlying salient identities, that they will define a greater variety of situations, appropriately or not, as opportunities to act these roles out, and when possible they will select situations enabling the enactment of salient identities.

Many have noted that identities call for verification or confirmation (see chapter 6; Stryker 1980); and, likely, the higher the salience of an identity, the higher the need for confirmation and the greater the gratification and esteem deriving from confirmation. Implied is that salient identities, whatever the differences between or among them in absolute level of salience, impel—at some level, from great to vanishing degree—behavior in accord with the meanings of these identities. If that is so, identities will compete with one another for expression. Although this is not perhaps a zero-sum game, to the degree that such competition involves identities whose meanings are independent, behavior that reflects one will exclude behavior reflecting another.

Too, although identities may differ widely in salience, they may differ little or not at all. If they are widely disparate, even great situationally induced pressure to behave in accord with the meaning of less salient identities may be overcome. If the salience difference between or among identities is minimal, the demands of the situation per se will be difficult to resist or avoid.

That identities compete for expression and may be variably distant or close in salience suggests that less salient identities can, under particular circumstances, win in competition with more salient identities. An interesting, movement-relevant possibility is hypothesized by Horenczyk (undated), who argues that a less salient identity may get enacted in preference to a more salient identity if the person holding the identities has recently enacted the more salient identity. Using an economy-of-identities analogy and a metaphor of a "banking" system that can store credits earned for role performances expressing identities, he suggests that credits for recent performances of a more salient identity permit persons to behave in terms of the less salient identity, drawing on credits previously earned and banked.

Identities compete for expression, and competition when the identities involved have different meanings can impede the behavioral expression of one or the other. But identities may share meanings as well. To the degree they do, behavior reflecting one will reflect the other. That, presumably, is what takes place in the Catalonian separatist movement in which families and friendship groups are said to nurture the ethnic nationalism underlying that movement (Johnston 1991); and it is presumably an important element in the Palestinian independence movement.

The cognitive and behavioral processes allowing identities to be trans-situational, self-reinforcing, and motivational imply that identities can wield their influence over action independent of relationships that support, or fail to support, the identities. In the short run at least, and potentially in the longer run depending on circumstances such as isolation from countervailing responses of others, identities can become functionally autonomous of the circumstances that give rise to them or affect their salience—they can become functionally independent of commitment. Thus, although identity salience reflects commitment, it cannot be reduced to commitment. It can be expected to have its own, autonomous impact on role-choice behavior; and work seeking to research variation in social movement participation needs to pay attention to both commitment and identity salience.

Variation in movement participation is relevant to research on a wide array of movement topics, from internal organization and dynamics of movements, to the adaptive changes that occur over their lifetime, to their success in achieving their objectives. Thus, at least some social movement researchers ought to consider carrying the arguments of this chapter into their research. Taking identity theory and its concepts seriously imposes stringent data demands on these social movement analysts, demands no existing data set is likely to meet, but the design of future studies may find ways to meet the data demands they make. Should that desideratum prove impossible, sensitivity to the ideas reviewed can still augment researchers' insights into social movement processes and outcomes.

Coda

Social movement members do not participate equivalently or equally in movement activities; this variation is important to many issues in social movement theory and research. We can enhance our general understanding of social movements by making participation differentials among members of movements more comprehensible. To understand such variation, we must recognize the choices movement members face and make; and we must recognize the multiple social groups or networks in which they are typically embedded and the multiple identities linked to positions in groups and networks that underlie those choices. That identity theory; its concepts of identity, identity salience, and commitment; and its vision of the process relating commitment to identity salience and identity salience to role choice enable such recognition has been the burden of this chapter.

Notes

I thank Kent Redding for tolerating my questions, calling attention to relevant literature, forcing me to confront problems in drafts, and being patient as I delayed returning borrowed books.

1. Here, I restrict the term *identity theory* to my own usage; see Stryker (1968, 1980).

2. See Klandermans (1994) and Klandermans and de Weerd, chapter 3, for a view admitting fissures and differentiations within collective identity.

3. But see the account, using a role-based concept of identity, of stability *and* social change, reproduction *and* production, in Serpe (1987) and Stryker and Serpe (1994).

4. This section follows Stryker (1992).

5. Definitional processes central to interactionist thought *are* important, but so are structural constraints.

6. Roles are normative expectations tied to positions in organized groups. Expectations are meanings attached to roles, partly products of culture, partly products of group interaction. Meanings of roles are widely shared, but variation based on subcultures, nongroup interactions, and idiosyncratic experience exists.

7. Commitment in the theory is relational, not cognitive.

References

Blumer, Herbert. 1969. *Symbolic Interactionism.* Englewood Cliffs, N.J.: Prentice-Hall.

Calhoun, Craig, ed. 1994. *Social Theory and the Politics of Identity.* Cambridge, Mass.: Blackwell.

Deaux, Kay. 1996. "Social Identification." In *Social Psychology: Handbook of Basic Principles,* edited by E. Tory Higgins and Arlie W. Kruglanski, 778–98. New York: Guilford.

Ervin, Laurie, and Sheldon Stryker. Forthcoming. "Theorizing the Relationships between Self-Esteem and Identity Theory." In *Extending Self-Esteem Theory and Research: Sociological and Psychological Perspectives,* edited by Timothy Owens, Sheldon Stryker, and Norman Goodman. New York: Cambridge University Press.

Gamson, William A. 1992. "The Social Psychology of Collective Action." In *Frontiers of Social Movement Theory,* edited by Aldon D. Morris and Carol Mueller, 53–76. New Haven: Yale University Press.

Gould, Roger V. 1995. *Insurgent Identities: Class, Community, and Protest in Paris from 1848 to the Commune.* Chicago: University of Chicago Press.

Horenczyk, Gabriel. Undated. "The Actualization of National Identity." Manuscript.

Isaacs, Harold R. 1975. *Idols of the Tribe: Group Identity and Political Change.* Cambridge: Harvard University Press.

Johnston, Hank. 1991. *Tales of Nationalism: Catalonia, 1939–1979.* New Brunswick, N.J.: Rutgers University Press.

Johnston, Hank, Enrique Laraña, and Joseph R. Gusfield. 1994. "Identities, Grievances, and New Social Movements." In *New Social Movements: From Ideology to Identity,* edited by Enrique Laraña, Hank Johnston, and Joseph R. Gusfield, 3–35. Philadelphia: Temple University Press.

Kim, Hyojoung, and Peter S. Bearman. 1997. "The Structure and Dynamics of Movement Participation." *American Sociological Review* 62:70–93.

Klandermans, Bert. 1994. "Transient Identities?: Membership Patterns in the Dutch Peace Movement." In *New Social Movements: From Ideology to Identity,* edited by Enrique Laraña, Hank Johnston, and Joseph R. Gusfield, 168–84. Philadelphia: Temple University Press.

———. 1997. *The Social Psychology of Protest.* Oxford: Blackwell.

Klandermans, Bert, and Dirk Oegema. 1987. "Potentials, Networks, Motivations, and Barriers: Steps toward Participation in Social Movements." *American Sociological Review* 52:519–32.

Klapp, Orrin. 1969. *Collective Search for Identity.* New York: Holt, Rinehart and Winston.

Kornhauser, William. 1962. "Social Bases of Political Commitment: A Study of Liberals and Radicals." In *Human Behavior and Social Process,* edited by Arnold M. Rose, 321–39. Boston: Houghton Mifflin.

Laraña, Enrique, Hank Johnston, and Joseph R. Gusfield, eds. 1994. *New Social Movements: From Ideology to Identity.* Philadelphia: Temple University Press.

Linville, Patricia. 1987. "Self-Complexity as a Cognitive Buffer against Stress-Related Illness and Depression." *Journal of Personality and Social Psychology* 4:663–76.

Markus, Hazel, and Robert B. Zajonc. 1985. "The Cognitive Perspective in Social Psychology." In *The Handbook of Social Psychology,* 3d ed., edited by Gardner Lindzey and Elliot Aronsen, 137–230. New York: Random House.

McAdam, Doug, and Ronnelle Paulson. 1993. "Specifying the Relationship between Social Ties and Activism." *American Journal of Sociology* 99:640–67.

Melucci, Alberto. 1980. "The New Social Movements: A Theoretical Approach." *Social Science Information* 19:199–226.

———. 1985. "The Symbolic Challenge of Contemporary Movements." *Social Research* 52:789–816.

———. 1994. "A Strange Kind of Newness: What's "'New'" in New Social Movements?" In *New Social Movements: From Ideology to Identity,* edited by Enrique Laraña, Hank Johnston, and Joseph R. Gusfield, 101–30. Philadelphia: Temple University Press.

Nagel, Joanne. 1995. "Politics and the Resurgence of American Indian Ethnic Identity." *American Sociological Review* 60:947–65.

Scheff, Thomas. 1994. "Emotions and Identity: A Theory of Ethnic Nationalism." In *Social Theory and the Politics of Identity,* edited by Craig Calhoun, 277–303. Philadelphia: Temple University Press.

Serpe, Richard T. 1987. "Stability and Change in Self: A Structural Symbolic Interactionist Explanation." *Social Psychology Quarterly* 50:44–55.

Somers, Margaret R., and Gloria D. Gibson. 1994. "Reclaiming the Epistemological 'Other': Narrative and the Social Construction of Identity." In *Social Theory and the Politics of Identity,* edited by Craig Calhoun, 337–99. Philadelphia: Temple University Press.

Stryker, Sheldon. 1968."Identity Salience and Role Performance: The Relevance of Symbolic Interaction Theory for Family Research." *Journal of Marriage and Family* 30:558–64.

———. 1980. *Symbolic Interactionism: A Social Structural Version.* Menlo Park, Calif.: Benjamin-Cummings.

———. 1992. "Identity Theory." In *Encyclopedia of Sociology,* edited by Edgar F. Borgatta and Marie L. Borgatta, 871–76. New York: Macmillan.

Stryker, Sheldon, and Richard T. Serpe. 1994. "Identity Salience and Psychological Centrality: Equivalent, Overlapping, or Complementary Concepts?" *Social Psychology Quarterly* 57:16–35.

Tajfel, Henri. 1981. *Human Groups and Social Categories.* London: Academic Press.

Taylor, Verta. 1989. "Social Movement Continuity: The Women's Movement in Abeyance." *American Sociological Review* 54:761–75.

Taylor, Verta, and Nancy E. Whittier. 1992. "Collective Identity in Social Movement Communities: Lesbian Feminist Mobilization." In *Frontiers of Social Movement Theory,* edited by Aldon D. Morris and Carol Mueller, 104–30. New Haven: Yale University Press.

Thoits, Peggy A., and Lauren K. Virshup. 1995. "Me's and We's: Forms and Functions of Social Identities." In *Self and Identity: Fundamental Issues,* edited by Richard Ashmore and Lee Jussim, 106–33. New York: Oxford University Press.

Triandis, Harry C. 1989. "The Self and Social Behavior in Differing Cultural Contexts." *Psychological Review* 96:506–20.

Turner, John C., Michael A. Hogg, Penelope J. Oakes, Stephen D. Reicher, and Maragaret S. Wetherell. 1987. *Rediscovering the Social Group: A Self-Categorization Theory.* Oxford: Blackwell.

Wiley, Norbert. 1994. "The Politics of Identity in American History." In *Social Theory and the Politics of Identity,* edited by Craig Calhoun, 131–49. Cambridge, Mass.: Blackwell.

Zaretsky, Eli. 1994. "Identity Theory, Identity Politics: Psychoanalysis, Marxism, Post-Structuralism." In *Social Theory and the Politics of Identity,* edited by Craig Calhoun, 198–215. Cambridge, Mass.: Blackwell.

2

Identity Work Processes in the Context of Social Movements: Clarifying the Identity/Movement Nexus

David A. Snow and Doug McAdam

One of the central themes running through the literature on social movements during the past decade is the observation that identity is a pivotal concept in attempting to understand movement dynamics. Indeed, one could easily get the impression that identity is the key concept in social movement research today, as one work after another refers to identity politics (Garner 1996; Darnovsky, Epstein, and Flacks 1995; Taylor and Raeburn 1995), contested identities (Taylor 1996), collective identities (Friedman and McAdam 1992; Hunt 1991; Melucci 1989; Taylor and Whittier 1992), insurgent identities (Gould 1995), and identity movements (Gamson 1995). Although this burgeoning literature highlights the relevance of identity-related issues to social movements, there are a number of troublesome tendencies in the literature that muddy rather than clarify our understanding of the identity/movement nexus. These include the tendency to conceptualize the various identity constructs at a cultural or group level; the tendency to ignore the relationship between group-level collective identities and personal identities; the tendency to overlook the literature on identity in social psychology; and the tendency to gloss over the processes through which identities are constructed and maintained at both an individual and collective level. As a result of these tendencies, the growing literature that focuses on the identity/movement connection is characterized by conceptual ambiguity, empirical looseness, and sometimes questionable claims.

Our objective in this chapter is to bring a measure of conceptual and empirical clarity to the identity/movement nexus by elaborating the ways in which personal identities and movement/collective identities are linked processually and by suggesting the implications of those linkages for various movement dynamics and processes. We pursue this objective by first specifying a number of factors that suggest the importance of attending more closely to the connection between individual and collective identities. We then elaborate various identity work processes associated with the development of movement-related identities among participants. Finally, we enumerate a number of issues and questions concerning the relationship between the identity work processes we have elaborated and other dynamic aspects of social movements, examining in some detail the shifts in identity work that tend to characterize different phases of a movement cycle.

The Problem of Identity Correspondence

Although there is no consensual definition of collective identity, examination of most conceptualizations suggests that its essence resides in a shared sense of "one-ness" or "we-ness" among those individuals who compose the collectivity.[1] If a sense of "we-ness" vis-à-vis others is at the core of a collective identity, then such questions as the following beg for clarification: How is it that various individuals come to acquire the shared feelings and cognitions indicative of a collective identity? How is this identity reconciled with other identities that individuals possess? And what is the relationship between this collective identity and action? Gamson insinuates that the answer to such questions resides in the enlargement of "the personal identities of a constituency to include the relevant collective identity as part of their definition of self" (1992, 60). That seems likely. But what are the various means or processes through which this "enlargement of personal identity" occurs? These and related questions allude to what we refer to as the problem of identity correspondence—that is, the alignment or linkage of individual and collective identities and action.

Just as there is no consensual conceptualization of collective identity, so there are no uniformly articulated answers to the problem of identity correspondence. If anything, the issue has been glossed over or inadequately dealt with by the two theoretical traditions that have historically shaped scholarly thinking on the identity/movement nexus. We refer to these two perspectives as the "dispositional" and "structuralist" approaches.

The Dispositional Perspective

The dispositional perspective in social psychology posits a psychofunctional linkage between various personality types or traits and behavioral probabilities or prospects. The core idea is that identifiable social psychological traits or states predispose individuals to make some choices over others and, thus, to pursue some lines of action rather than others. Applied to the social movement arena, this logic holds that movement participants will differ importantly from nonparticipants in terms of various personality and cognitive traits or dispositions. Perhaps the best-known example of this perspective in the study of social movements is the authoritarian personality thesis, which presumes that dogmatic, prejudicial, and insecure individuals are highly susceptible to the appeals of extremist movements (Adorno et al. 1950). Another prominent argument of this genre is the mass society hypothesis, which holds that individuals whose need to belong and urge for meaningful affiliation are not being met elsewhere are especially likely candidates for movement participation (Kornhauser 1959; Nisbet 1954).

More pertinent to our concerns in this chapter is the identity variant of dispositional theory, which suggests that movement participation is driven in large part by various identity considerations or problems. There are essentially two lines of argument: one is the unsatisfactory or spoiled identity thesis; the other is the identity verification thesis. The first, associated closely with the work of Klapp (1969), contends that participants in contemporary movements are engaged in a "collective search for identity" because modern society does not provide sufficient grounding for constituting satisfactory identities. A more finely tuned elaboration of this argument is provided in this volume by Kaplan and Liu (chapter 10). They argue that it is not a generalized, collective groping for identity that undergirds movement participation but a search by individuals with stigmatized or spoiled identities. Consistent with Klapp, Kaplan and Liu add that there is no necessary relationship between the source of one's spoiled identity and the kind of movement they become involved in; rather, any movement will do so long as it provides a more satisfactory identity.

The second argument holds that movements provide people with an opportunity to verify their social identities and that movement participation is thus explicable, at least in part, by the need to validate extant identities. Propounded by Pinel and Swann in this volume (chapter 6), this thesis assumes both fairly stable identities and the correspondence between individual identities and those associated with a movement.

Although both the spoiled identity and verification hypotheses may account for the participation of some movement adherents, it is unreasonable to assume that all or most movement participants are motivated by either of these factors. To assume such a generalized movement motivation flies in the face of the long-standing observation that there is an array of motives associated with movement participation (Turner and Killian 1972;

Zurcher and Snow 1981). In addition, to argue that movement participants are driven primarily by either the need to repair or replace spoiled identities or the need to verify existing ones is to gloss over and trivialize ideological considerations. Additionally, both hypotheses are difficult to reconcile with the malleable and socially constructed character of identities. Summary reviews of movement research as well as studies of various movements clearly indicate that movement participation almost always modifies and sometimes even transforms participant identities, such that movement identities reflect experience in a movement as much as preexisting identities (Hunt and Benford 1994; McAdam 1988; Snow and Machalek 1984; Turner and Killian 1972). Taken together, these critical observations indicate that the problem of identity correspondence is far from resolved by invoking various dispositional explanations.

The Structuralist Perspective

In sharp contrast to the dispositional perspective, structuralists see individual identities as embedded in elements of social structure—specifically, in roles, networks, and groups (Gould 1995; Wellman and Berkowitz 1988). How one is situated in time and space by self and others is structurally given and thus structurally determined. Individuals who are similarly situated structurally—that is, they are incumbents of the same or similar roles or members of the same ethnic, racial, or religious groups, live in the same neighborhood, work in a similar enterprise, and so on—are also likely to have a shared collective identity. Hence the correspondence of individual and collective identity is not particularly problematic because they are essentially isomorphic.[2]

As sociologists, we acknowledge the important structural component of individual and collective identities and the relationship between them. However, we do not regard the structural basis of that relationship as given. Rather, we see it as tenuous and problematic because of the following considerations. First, to assume that similar group memberships or network linkages automatically yield similar identities strikes us as highly questionable. It ignores the long-standing sociological axiom that people can be members of the same group or movement in different ways and with varying degrees of commitment and identification (Etzioni 1975; Kanter 1972; Turner and Killian 1972). Students of religious affiliation and conversion have noted, for example, that people can participate in religious rituals without fully adopting the group's value orientation or identity, or both (Nock 1933; Snow and Machalek 1983). Likewise, students of collective behavior and social movements know that participation can be associated with a variety of motives, only one of which is the correspondence of individual and collective identity. Thus, to infer correspondence between individual and collective identities solely on the basis of membership, affiliation, or participation is empirically suspect.

Another shortcoming with the structural approach to the identity/movement nexus is that it ignores the now well-established finding that identities can vary considerably in their relative salience or centrality. One of the principal contributions of Stryker's role-identity theory (1968, 1980) is the axiom that identities are "ordered into a salience hierarchy" (1980, 60–61), with the consequence that those higher in the hierarchy are more likely to be invoked in a given situation. This suggests that the probability that a particular identity will be salient, and thus invoked in a particular situation, is not automatically determined by its structural footing. Other factors identified as being important determinants of salience include relational commitments (Stryker 1968, 1980), reflected appraisal processes (Burke and Reitzes 1981; Felson 1985), and the congruence between a structurally based role identity and a personal, more idealized identity (Snow and Anderson 1987). These observations suggest that movement identities may be of differential salience for movement participants and that it is therefore empirically and theoretically misguided to presume an automatic link between individual and collective identities or between such identities and engagement in collective action.

We think that identities can also vary in terms of their pervasiveness—that is, in terms of their situational reach or relevance. Some identities can be relevant in many contexts and situations, whereas other identities may be irrelevant to all but one or two situations. Stone's (1966) reformulation of Banton's (1965) tripartite classification of roles into a classification of identities is pertinent here. Thus, Banton's basic roles become basic identities, such as sex and age and even race, ethnicity, and religion in some contexts. These identities typically are widely pervasive in that they are relevant to a broad array of contexts. General identities, based on general roles, such as occupational ones, are relevant to a number of situations but not as broadly generalizable as basic identities. And independent identities, such as swimmer or jogger, are even less pervasive. Thus, identities can vary not only in their salience to interaction in a situation but also in the range of situations to which they are relevant. This is clearly the case with social movements, as we discuss later, as they are likely to vary considerably in terms of the situational pervasiveness or generality of their collective identities. This suggests another dimension of identity that merits consideration when exploring the relationship between individual and collective identities.

The Constructionist Perspective

The above observations clearly indicate that the matter of identity correspondence between individuals and the groups or collectivities with which they are associated is more complex than suggested by purely dispositional or structural analyses. This is hardly a novel observation, of course, as it is one of the cornerstones of the developing constructionist approach to movement collective identity (Hunt 1991; Hunt and Benford 1994; Hunt, Benford, and Snow 1994; Melucci 1989; Schwalbe and Mason-Schrock 1996; Stoecker 1995; Taylor and Whittier 1992). From the vantage point of this perspective, there is considerable indeterminacy between identities and their roots in either personality or social structure. As a result, attention is shifted from the dispositional correlates or structural moorings of identities to their construction and maintenance through joint action, negotiation, and interpretive work. However, to date, relatively little attention has been devoted to the alignment of personal and collective identities. Instead, there has been greater concern with elaboration of the rituals and processes through which collective identities are developed and maintained (Schwalbe and Mason-Schrock 1996; Taylor and Whittier 1992) and with activists' identity talk and how it corresponds with various stages of activism (Hunt and Benford 1994). Although these are clearly important topics of investigation, they do not deal directly or comprehensively with the processes through which personal and collective identities are aligned. Thus, the problem of identity correspondence remains problematic from a constructionist perspective as well.

In light of this lacunae, our objective is to elaborate the various processes through which personal and collective identities are aligned within the social movement arena. We do so not by jettisoning existing dispositional and structural analyses of personal and collective identity but by drawing on concepts and analyses associated with all three perspectives noted above. We begin our analysis by borrowing on the constructionist concept of identity work to capture the various processes relevant to the alignment of personal and movement identities.

Identity Work Processes

The concept of "identity work" was initially used by Snow and Anderson to refer to "the range of activities individuals engage in to create, present, and sustain personal identities that are congruent with and supportive of the self-concept" (1987, 1348). More recently, Schwalbe and Mason-Schrock (1996) have argued that identity work is a group accomplishment as well as an individual one and can therefore be examined at a group or subcultural level.[3] Given this broadened view, they conceptualize identity work as "anything people do, individually or collectively, to give meaning to themselves or others" (Schwalbe and Mason-Schrock 1996, 115), and they then proceed to examine the process whereby groups create the symbolic resources on which the existence of shared identities depend. However, this constitutes only one of three critical problems or processes that fall under the rubric of identity work within the context of social movements. They include (1) the construction of collective identity through the creation of the symbolic resources and boundaries constitutive of collective identity; (2) the problem of identity correspondence as articulated above; and (3) the maintenance of both collective identity and the correspondence of the personal with the collective. As noted earlier, we seek to illuminate the problem of identity correspondence. Specifically, we are interested in the various processes through which identity correspondence occurs, such that a movement's collective identity comes to function among individuals associated with the movement as a significant point of orientation and as motivational springboard to action.[4] Or, to borrow on Goffman's concept of role embracement (1961) and the language of role-identity theory, we ask: How is it that prospective or actual movement adherents come to embrace the role identity associated with a movement, such that personal and collective identity are congruent?

We elaborate two forms of identity work that address the problem of correspondence: identity convergence and identity construction. The previously introduced concepts of identity salience and identity pervasiveness figure prominently in the following discussion, as do the frame alignment processes elaborated by Snow and his colleagues (1986).

Identity Convergence

By identity convergence, we refer to the coalescence of a movement and individuals who already identify with it. In such cases, personal identities are isomorphic or congruent with the collective identity of a movement, such that the existence of a movement provides an avenue for the individual to act in accordance with his or her personal identity. The analytic problem is not that of identity construction or alignment, as the corresponding identities are already in place. Rather, the problem is one of connection and thus the specification of the mechanisms that facilitate the convergence of parallel individual identities with a movement and its collective identity.

Inspection of the literature on movement recruitment and participation suggests that such convergence may be accounted for by two rather different processes: identity seeking and the appropriation of extant solidary networks. Consistent with the previously discussed dispositional perspective, *identity seeking* refers to the process whereby individuals strongly imbued with a particular identity actively search for groups (movements, cults, subcultures) with perspectives and practices consistent with that identity and that allow for its expression. Balch and Taylor (1978) and Straus (1976), among others, have argued that many people who participate in contemporary religious groups and mass therapies are "seekers" in the above sense. In their study of participation in a UFO cult in the 1970s, Balch and Taylor report that the members of the cult were "metaphysical seekers" who defined "their decision to follow the Two" as "a reaffirmation of their seekership . . . as a logical extension of their spiritual quest" (1978, 61). Moreover, they emphasize that it was active seekership and perceived correspondence between the prospective members and the cult, rather than preexisting affective ties, that accounted for the connection between them. We find no reason to take exception with Balch and Taylor's findings, or with the more general contention that some individuals are identity seekers. However, we would argue that identity seekers probably constitute a relatively small number of movement participants and that the convergence of personal and collective identities is rarely due to identity seeking alone.

The *appropriation of existing solidary networks* (hereafter *identity appropriation*) by movement organizers and entrepreneurs can also bring about identity convergence, both relatively quickly and extensively. By solidary networks, we refer to people who not only are linked together structurally in some fashion or another but also share common social relations, a common lifestyle, and a common fate and who therefore are likely to share a common identity. The appropriation of solidary networks is akin to what Oberschall referred to as "bloc recruitment" in relation to movement mobilization (1973, 125–27). He argued, among other things, that such recruitment yields more rapid mobilization because it is not based on the recruitment of solitary individuals.

Subsequent research has found repeatedly that solitary individuals are rarely recruited into social movements, as the bulk of recruitment occurs through preexisting network linkages, both individual and organizational.[5] However, it is unclear what proportion of movement recruitment is based on bloc recruitment or the appropriation of solidary networks versus individual-level recruitment. We do know, however, that a good deal of movement recruitment occurs at the individual level through social networks. Since we learned earlier that shared, salient identities cannot be inferred from shared networks or structural position, caution needs to be exercised so as not to assume that network linkages alone can account for identity convergence. Thus, given the existence of a shared identity among a network of individuals, appropriation of that network is likely to facilitate identity convergence between those prospects and the movement. But in the absence of an extant shared identity, network appropriation alone is unlikely to generate such an identity. However, that is not to suggest that a shared identity may not develop through one or more identity construction processes.

Identity Construction Processes

By identity construction, we refer to the process through which personal and collective identities are aligned, such that individuals regard engagement in movement activity as being consistent with their self-conception and interests. Some variety of identity construction is necessary in all cases in which there is an absence of correspondence between personal identities and movement collective identities. The issue here is not just a matter of structural linkage or connection. In some fashion or another, the personal identities of prospective participants have to be modified so as to enhance the congruence with the movement's collective identity. This fitting or alignment process can vary dramatically, ranging from an adjustment in one's identity salience hierarchy to a thoroughgoing change in one's sense of self.

It thus follows that there are a number of identity construction processes. We have discerned at least four such processes operating in the context of social movements: identity amplification, identity consolidation, identity extension, and identity transformation.

Identity Amplification

Identity amplification involves the embellishment and strengthening of an existing identity that is congruent with a movement's collective identity but not sufficiently salient to ensure participation and activism. Metaphorically, the individual moves from the sidelines to the playing field via the restoration of an existing but previously nonsalient identity. In the language of role-identity theory, a change in the individual's identity salience hierarchy is affected, such that a previously lower-order identity now becomes sufficiently salient to motivate association with and action on behalf of the movement. Note that the identity that has now moved center stage was not foreign to the person's biography. Rather, it may have been a significant, moderately salient, or peripheral identity in one's past. Whatever the case, it has now been elevated to a position of salience in one's hierarchy of identities. Presumably the higher in the hierarchy the individual's movement identity, the stronger the identification with the movement and the more blurred the distinction between personal identity and collective identity.

Identity Consolidation

The process of identity consolidation refers to the adoption of an identity that combines two prior identities that appear to be incompatible because they are typically associated with strikingly different subcultures or traditions, be they political or religious. The phrase appears to have been used first by Gordon (1974), who found it applicable to the "Jesus people" he studied in the 1970s. He distinguished between direct and indirect consolidation. The former, he suggested, involves the adoption of an identity based in part on one that was previously salient in the person's past, as when "a person raised in a Southern Baptist Church, who rejected these beliefs for drugs and perhaps eastern religion," adopts the identity of a Jesus person (Gordon 1974, 166). Indirect consolidation, on the other hand, entails the adoption of an identity that integrates a more recent, intervening one, as when "a person raised as a Catholic, who rejected his Catholicism for the youth culture," becomes a Jesus person (Gordon 1974, 166–67).

Whether this nuanced distinction between direct and indirect consolidation is analytically useful is open to question, but the concept of identity consolidation strikes us as providing analytic purchase in that it directs attention to a pathway to identity correspondence that appears to be distinctive. Further illustration of the process is provided by the more current example of the integration of Christian and psychotherapeutic identities, as has occurred among some evangelicals who now embrace a religious psychotherapy. In such cases, the new identities are not based on the jettisoning of past identities or even on the elevation of a previously marginal identity. Rather, they represent the blending of a past or current salient identity with a new but previously foreign identity.

Identity Extension

This process involves the expansion of the situational relevance or pervasiveness of an individual's personal identity so that its reach is congruent with the movement's. Not only is the individual's personal identity broadened and made more inclusive in terms of its range of relevance, but personal identity and movement collective identity may be indistinguishable for all practical purposes. In such instances, movement adherents are expected to utilize or invoke their movement role identities in virtually all encounters with others relevant to the movement, such that the movement identity comes to function in a fashion akin to a "master status" (Hughes 1945) or "representative role" (Parsons 1951, 100).

Examples abound. Being a "good Christian" is not something that is done just on Sundays within the confines of a church; it extends to the home, to work, to recreation, to all individuals encountered, be they family, friends, acquaintances, or strangers. In a similar vein, members of the Nichiren Shoshu Buddhist movement in America (now referred to as SokaGakkai International) were constantly instructed, during the period in which the first author studied the movement, that whatever they did, whether in the context of family, work, school, or leisure, was to be done with interests or identity of the movement in mind (Snow 1993, 139–55). In the words of one member, "We are expected to behave at all times and in all situations as representatives of the movement, as ambassadors of President Ikeda [their master and leader]." Likewise, in the context of the political arena, Coser, among others, has noted with respect to the Marxist labor movement that "any active member, whether or not he had a leadership role in the organization, was expected to 'represent' the movement to the outside world" (1956, 113–14). And in the rhetoric of the New Left, actual and prospective adherents were continuously reminded that "the personal is political." This, of course, is another way of suggesting, from the standpoint of the movement, that personal identity and collective identity cannot be neatly bifurcated and compartmentalized and that the personal and collective must be merged, or at least one must be enlarged to embrace the other.

The scope of extension can be quite variable across movements, as we will note later. The important point at this juncture is not the variability in identity extension across movements but the fact that it is an important identity construction process that cannot be assumed or explained in terms of the other processes.

Identity Transformation

The three identity construction processes discussed thus far are all linked to a past or current identity. That identity becomes more salient, is consolidated with another one, or is made more pervasive. In some fashion or another, there is a semblance of continuity between the past and the present. In the case of identity transformation, that continuity, that link, is deeply fractured, if not obliterated, with the result being a dramatic change in identity, such that one now sees her- or himself as strikingly different than before.

At the core of this dramatic change is the process described in the conversion literature as "biographical reconstruction." In their review essay on conversion, Snow and Machalek conceptualize it as

> a double-edged process involving the dismantling of the past, on the one hand, and its reconstitution, on the other. Some aspects of the past are jettisoned, others are redefined, and some are put together in ways that would have previously been inconceivable. One's biography is, in short, reconstructed in accordance with [a] new or ascendant universe of discourse and its attendant grammar and vocabulary of motives. (1984, 173)

The outcome of this process of biographical reconstruction is not only a change in perspective and thus in how things are seen but also a change in how one sees oneself and thus a change in identity.

Examples of such dramatic change in perspective and identity are not difficult to find in the religious domain, particularly in the realm of religious movements and cults. But such transformative change in identity is also operative in the political domain. In *The God That Failed,* for example, Crossman (1952) assembled a set of identity-transforming accounts of European intellectuals who converted to communism in the 1930s and then became disillusioned and, so to speak, fell from grace. Although the substantive content of these accounts differs from that of accounts associated with the religious domain, their form is the same. As Arthur Koestler noted regarding his adoption of communism in 1931 as the dominant informing point of view in his life:

> By the time I had finished with *Feuerbach and the State and Revolution,* something had clicked in my brain which shook me like a mental explosion. . . . The whole universe [fell] into pattern like the stray pieces of a jigsaw puzzle assembled by magic at one stroke. There [was] now an answer to every question, doubts and conflicts [were] a matter of the tortured past. (Crossman 1952, 19)

Although the foregoing suggests that identity transformation is not peculiar to any domain of social life, we have not clearly explicated its link to collective identity. We think that connection is reasonably transparent, however. Before individuals become serviceable movement agents—that is, individuals who will act on behalf of and in concert with a movement—it is necessary that their personal identities dovetail with a movement's coll identity. In some cases, this alignment is clearly contingent on the proc of identity transformation.

Implications for Other Movement Processes and Dynamics

Having elaborated the various identity work processes that function to align individual and collective identities, we are now in a position to address a number of questions concerning the relationship between identity work and other dynamic aspects of social movements. Among the various questions one might ask, we think three are particularly important: the first concerns the mechanisms that mediate the forms of identity work described above; the second addresses the question of whether there is a relationship between types of identity work and types of movements; and the third concerns the relationship between identity work processes and movement careers. We briefly highlight the first two questions and then explore the third in some detail.

Mechanisms/Processes Mediating Identity Construction

We noted two basic forms of identity work that address the problem of correspondence between individual identities and movement collective identities: identity convergence and identity construction. The first is not particularly difficult to account for, since it involves either identity seekership on behalf of individuals or the appropriation of solidary networks of shared identities by activists and entrepreneurs. Put simply, those are the mechanisms that account for convergence. In the case of identity construction, however, identification of the various forms or processes—amplification, consolidation, extension, and transformation—does not account for their occurrence. Thus the following question: What are the mechanisms or processes that mediate the various forms of identity construction?

We suspect that identity construction, whatever its form, can be accounted for largely by framing processes, by engagement in collective action itself, or by a combination of both. Framing processes that occur within the context of social movements constitute perhaps the most important mechanism facilitating identity construction processes, largely because identity constructions are an inherent feature of framing activities. As Hunt, Benford, and Snow have noted, "not only do framing processes link individuals and groups ideologically but they proffer, buttress, and embellish identities that range from collaborative to conflictual" (1994, 185). They do this, at a general level, in a fashion consistent with the construction of identities in most contexts—that is, "by situating or placing relevant sets of actors in time and space and by attributing characteristics to them that suggest specifiable relationships and lines of action" (185). At a more concrete level, the construction of identities via framing occurs in the course of identity talk among adherents and activists (Hunt and Benford 1994), when preparing for and giving formal testimony at movement functions, when explaining the movement to others in the course of recruitment and proselytizing activities, when preparing press releases and making public pronouncements, when crafting reports and columns for newspapers, and when adherents are engaged in frame disputes or debates. In each of these interactional contexts, identities are announced or renounced, avowed or disavowed, and embraced or rejected, and the medium is typically framing discourse.

The medium can sometimes be collective action itself, however. The action basis for identity construction can range from bystander observation of a collective event to actual participation motivated by factors other than a shared identity. Illustrative is the experience of sympathetic bystanders coming to identify with the collectivity and to think of themselves in terms of the collectivity because they were bludgeoned by social control agents in the midst of a "police riot" at a protest event. Such happenings function as "demonstration events" inasmuch as they affirm the claims of the movement and thus help to elevate what was a secondary, peripheral, or marginal identity to a position of centrality.

Clearly the foregoing is not an exhaustive accounting of the mechanisms and processes through which identity construction occurs in social movement contexts. But it does suffice to underscore the importance of attending both to the various ways in which individual and collective identities are linked and to the mechanisms and processes that mediate that alignment or correspondence. To gloss over these issues is not only to ignore an important set of movement activities but is also to assume the existence of a reality—a collective identity—that may in fact be empirically tenuous.

Relationship between Identity Work and Movement Types

Since movements can vary dramatically on a number of dimensions—such as the amount of change sought, the locus of change, tactical preferences, organization, and so on—it is reasonable to wonder if some kinds of movements are more likely to be dependent on some kinds of identity work than others. Is there a kind of elective affinity between movement type and type of identity work? We believe there is, although we also suspect that the various identity work processes are probably operative in most movements. Take Promise Keepers, for example. In some instances, identity correspondence or alignment occurs through amplification, as when the identities of father and husband are accented and elevated. In other cases, consolidation may be at work, as when the father identity is consolidated with a born-again, Christian identity. At the same time, we would argue that some types of identity work tend to be dominant or more essential for some types of movements than others. For example, some movements, such as cultish religious ones, like Hare Krishna and the Unification Church (the "Moonies"), tend to be particularly "greedy" in terms of their membership demands and roles.[6] Identity transformation and extension are likely to be particularly critical for these movements. On the other hand, movements that are less greedy and expansive and that tend to be more domain-specific in terms of their reach and objectives are probably more dependent on identity amplification or even identity appropriation. In general, we would suspect that the more culturally foreign a movement, the greedier a movement, and the more politically radical, the more important the identity construction processes and the less important the identity convergence processes.

Such hypotheses, although admittedly provisional, point to additional lines of inquiry that clearly merit investigation and that suggest that a thoroughgoing understanding of collective identity in relation to movements requires more careful investigation than what typically has been the case. At the very least, the foregoing cautions us not to assume that assertions about collective identity in relation to one movement may necessarily apply to another.

Identity Work over the Life Course of a Movement

The third question we address is especially relevant to understanding movement dynamics. The question is: Are certain forms of identity work more important at different stages or points over the life course of a movement? We think the answer is yes. However, we believe it is important to specify the scope conditions that focus and clarify any such answer. In particular, we suspect that the relationship between the various identity work processes and movement careers is likely to vary according to whether the movement is active or is in the "doldrums" and, consistent with the above discussion, by the general type of movement, such as whether it is a public reform movement or a clandestine revolutionary enterprise. In the remainder of this section, we seek to explicate the relationship between identity work processes and movement development by suggesting the kinds of identity work that are most likely to be associated with the three ideal-typical stages in the careers of active, relatively successful, nonrevolutionary movements.

Stage I: Emergence

One of the most consistent findings yielded by empirical research on collective action is that social movements typically emerge out of and are initially dependent on existing organizations or associational networks. Movements as diverse as the Berkeley free speech movement (Heirich 1968), the Civic Forum in Czechoslovakia (Glenn 1997), and the American civil rights movement (McAdam 1982; Morris 1984) developed within established organizations or informal associational networks. Indeed, movements that form in these settings tend to develop very quickly, spread rapidly, and fairly easily overcome the "free-rider problem" that presumably afflicts incipient collective action (Olson 1965).

Why are such indigenously based movements so successful? Part of the answer lies in the host of organizational resources that devolve to the incipient movement through the "sponsoring" organization. But more important, in our view, in explaining the rapid rise and spread of such movements is the form of identity work that defines their emergent mobilization. These movements are able to take off quickly because they are able to appropriate previously established, highly salient collective identities.

Successful movements rarely create compelling collective identities from scratch. Rather, they redefine shared identities within established social settings as synonymous with an emerging activist identity. It is clear, for example, that the civil rights movement grew as rapidly as it did because, in many communities, it was able to appropriate the shared identity of church member and use it as the motivational impetus for protest activity. Descriptive accounts of some of the early church-based campaigns in the movement highlight the importance of these identity appropriation processes.

In his account of the Montgomery bus boycott, Martin Luther King (1958, 76) offers an extended example of this dynamic. Indeed, in the case of most church-based campaigns, it was not so much that movement participants were recruited from among the ranks of active churchgoers as it was a case of church membership itself being redefined to include movement participation as a primary requisite of the role. As another observer of events in Montgomery remarks, "It was [the black church members'] religious duty now not only to go to church, visit the sick, and to pray, but they must attend the mass meetings. To the Negro of Montgomery, Christianity and boycott went hand in hand" (Walton 1956, 19).

Examples of this appropriation of established collective identities by an emerging movement are common in the empirical literature on collective action. As a number of observers have noted regarding the 1964 free speech movement at Berkeley, its rapid growth "can be attributed to its sponsorship by a congeries of existing campus groups. To remain a member in good standing of these groups one had little choice but to conform to the new behavioral expectation: participation in the free speech movement" (Friedman and McAdam 1992, 163; Heirich 1968; Lipset and Wolin 1965). John Glenn (1997) describes a similar instance of identity appropriation in the rise of the Civic Forum movement in Czechoslovakia. There, early on, membership in the independent theater community came to be redefined as synonymous with participation in the movement. The result, as Glenn documents, was the rapid spread of the movement by means of the nationwide network of independent theaters.

These examples contradict the traditional rational choice formulation of the free-rider problem. Movements that seek to mobilize outside established social settings are, indeed, likely to run afoul of the free-rider problem because they lack the mobilizing force of a previously salient collective identity. But this would not appear to be the most common pathway of movement emergence. Rather, many movements tend to develop within established groups/networks through the appropriation of the collective identity and solidary incentives on which the group rests. The threatened loss of the identity and the solidary incentives on which the identity is based is usually sufficient to produce high rates of participation among group members. As a result, the movement is spared the need to provide selective incentives to attract participants. Thus, as long as the movement is rooted within indigenous social settings, appropriating the collective identities and solidary incentives of these settings, the free-rider problem is likely to remain latent.

Stage II: Institutionalization

Eventually, though, most successful movements outgrow their indigenous origins. The organizational locus of the movement passes from established groups or networks to formal social movement organizations (SMOs). Although this transition would seem to be largely inevitable and oftentimes beneficial to the movement, it nonetheless poses a challenge for insurgents. Rooting the movement in formal SMOs means that organizers can no longer trade on the established collective identity and solidary incentives of the indigenous groups/networks in which the movement first developed. This means that identity appropriation ceases to be the most typical or effective form of identity work characteristic of the mature movement. Instead, we suspect that the modal forms of identity work emblematic of the second stage of a successful movement are identity amplification and identity extension. No longer in a position merely to appropriate established collective identities, institutionalized movements, acting through their dominant SMOs, must now engage in targeted recruiting appeals designed to attract new adherents. To do so they typically seek to facilitate either one of two kinds of identity construction. In the first instance, they target potential recruits based on an appeal to a congruent, but not overly salient, individual identity; in the second, they seek to link movement participation to a salient, but narrow, individual identity. In the first case, they are trying to increase the salience of an individual identity that they think will compel participation; in the second they are urging the recruit to recognize the "obvious" congruence between an established salient identity and movement involvement.

The 1964 Mississippi Freedom Summer Project affords an example of an SMO-orchestrated recruitment campaign defined by the two forms of identity work noted above. The Freedom Summer Project was largely orchestrated by a single SMO, the Student Nonviolent Coordinating Committee (SNCC). To achieve its aims of registering black voters and, more generally, dramatizing the systematic denial of civil rights to African Americans throughout the South, SNCC sought to recruit some one thousand primarily white, northern students to come to Mississippi for all or part of the summer of 1964.

Identity amplification and identity extension figured prominently in SNCC's recruitment strategy. Specifically, SNCC targeted four groups of northern college students, seeking, in each case, to compel participation either by heightening the salience of an existing identity (identity amplification) or by extending the behavioral requirements of an already salient individual identity (identity extension). The four targeted groups were liberal campus Christians, "New Leftists," idealistic "Kennedy Democrats," and education majors or other prospective teachers.

To reach these groups, SNCC targeted particular campuses and then, within these campuses, the established organizations that were thought to embody the congruent identities noted above. So recruiting efforts were generally concentrated on those campuses that had active student chapters of New Left organizations (e.g., Students for a Democratic Society [SDS], Friends of SNCC), liberal church groups (e.g., Methodist Student Movement), or Democratic student organizations (e.g., Young Democrats).

To recruit among these target groups, SNCC fashioned a set of specialized appeals tailored to the unique ideational frame of reference peculiar to each. So religious appeals stressing the demands of the "social gospel" in action were used to motivate the liberal Christian community. The New

Left critique of American society formed the basis of the pitch to those in organizations such as SDS or the Friends of SNCC. A third appeal sought to draw teachers into the project by representing it as a kind of "domestic Peace Corps." And the final appeal was to young Democrats, intent on honoring the murdered John F. Kennedy by heeding his call to idealistic action in service to America.

For all the differences in these appeals, the intent in all cases was the same. SNCC sought to frame participation in the project in such way as to compel participation by linking involvement to an already established, if only marginally salient or narrowly defined, individual identity. Interestingly, however, they did so by targeting not individuals per se but rather the ideologically congruent organizations to which they belonged. The strategic wisdom of this approach was revealed by the results of the second author's comparative study of those applicants to the project who did and did not make it to Mississippi that summer. McAdam and Paulsen note that

> neither organizational embeddedness nor strong ties to another volunteer are themselves predictive of . . . activism. Instead, it is a strong subjective identification with a particular identity, *reinforced by organizational* . . . ties, that is especially likely to encourage participation. . . . Our findings . . . argue for a much stronger effect of organizational (or otherwise collective) as opposed to individual ties in mediating entrance into collective action. . . . Ties to individuals may well mediate the recruitment process, but they appear to do so with special force and significance when the tie is embedded in a broader organizational or collective context linking both parties to the movement in question. (1993, 659, 663; emphasis in original)

The example of Freedom Summer makes it clear that some movements that grow beyond their indigenous origins can still recruit effectively by employing different forms of identity work than the singularly efficient identity appropriation on which some emergent movements tend to rely. Indeed, by reaching out to a variety of constituents, as the project organizers did, movements can dramatically expand their geographic and social bases. But the use of targeted recruiting appeals and the creative forms of identity construction on which they depend carries with it a risk as well. By broadening the base of a movement through highly differentiated recruiting appeals, organizers run the risk of sowing the seeds of later factional disputes. As the various histories of the Freedom Summer Project have shown, the entrance of so many disparate elements into Mississippi that summer introduced or exacerbated a host of tensions—race, class, gender, region—into SNCC that almost certainly contributed to its slow decline over the next few years (Carson 1981; McAdam 1988). Thus, SNCC's experience with the Freedom Summer Project underscores an important point germane to the focus of this paper: different forms of identity work (e.g., identity amplification, identity extension) may be linked to different and highly consequential movement dynamics (e.g., the onset of factionalism).

Stage III: General Diffusion

The final stage attained by only the most successful of movements further highlights the ironic trade-off between uncontrolled expansion and a host of dysfunctional movement dynamics. Here we refer to the situation in which movements spread far beyond their initial supporters and basically lose control of the recruitment process and, in essence, enter the public domain. In the U.S. context, examples of such movements would include the women's movement and the antiwar movement of the 1960s and 1970s.

Like the two previous stages, this third stage is also associated with particular forms of identity work. But here a caveat is in order. Although all types of identity work—save identity appropriation—may take place during this third phase of movement development, we want to highlight a specific form of identity work that is increasingly important during this stage and tends, we think, to occasion serious problems for most political movements. We refer to identity seeking.

Unlike other forms of identity work, identity seeking is initiated by the prospective adherent rather than any organizational embodiment of the movement. Sensing that the movement represents a vehicle for the realization of some personally valued identity, prospective recruits seek to affiliate with the struggle.

On the face of it, it would seem that adding this new form of identity work to the movement's recruitment arsenal could only benefit the cause. After all, the movement is now in a position to attract adherents without having to expend much time and energy on recruitment. And, to be sure, certain kinds of benefits do accrue to the movement as a result of identity seeking. When identity seeking becomes a significant phenomenon in a particular movement, we can say that movement has attained a certain "bandwagon" status. And with that status go certain functional benefits. Public opinion polls are apt to reflect widespread popular support for the cause. Low-risk forms of mass protest, such as marches and rallies, are apt to be widely attended, creating the kind of "demonstrati that organizers relish. As these forms of visible support increa seeking is likely to as well, fueling a period of expansion in low-level support and involvement in the movement.

This expansion, however, can foreshadow serious problems as well. Two such problems can be identified. The first is the one we discussed in connection with the kind of SMO-based recruiting that typically fuels movement growth during the institutional stage. As movements grow beyond their localized origins, targeted recruitment tends to bring ever more diverse elements into the struggle, thus expanding the potential for intramovement conflict. Movements that attain the degree of popular support and expansion characteristic of this third and final stage of development are even more vulnerable to the perils of conflict and factionalism. The reason is simple. To the extent that identity seeking becomes an important source of new adherents, the movement's ability to limit access to a narrowly defined constituency has virtually disappeared. Movements, under these circumstances, are less likely to resemble tightly knit and internally cohesive insurgent communities than they are broad, fractious, and increasingly amorphous collections of people who share only the most rudimentary definition of the struggle. The potential for internal conflict in such a situation should be obvious.

There is, however, a second problem, attendant to this stage of the movement, that may well be even more severe than the first. Those movements that have attained the level of popular acceptance we have in mind here are invariably ones that have fashioned a generalized, if amorphous, movement collective identity. Indeed, it is the salience and attractiveness of this collective identity that draws seekers to the movement. The movement's success in fashioning this resonant collective identity, however, poses its own problems. Once a movement has created this kind of generalized collective identity, it can be difficult to control its consumption. In effect,

> the collective identity becomes a public good that all can consume without contributing to its [ongoing] production. For instance, by the mid-1970s, public opinion polls showed that large numbers of women (and some men) identified with or had adopted the identity of "feminist." The very attractiveness of the collective identity had led many to gravitate toward it. But the identification carried with it no obligation to join a feminist organization or to participate in forms

of collective action intended to realize equal rights for women. (Friedman and McAdam 1992, 166–67)

Conclusion

Although interest in the concept of collective identity has grown dramatically among movement scholars in recent years, work in this area remains conceptually muddy at best. In particular, the link between a movement's collective identity and the personal or individual identities of movement adherents has received almost no attention in the literature. Our principal objective in this chapter has been to illuminate this process conceptually by elaborating and differentiating the various identity work processes linking individuals to movements and out of which movement collective identities emerge and evolve over time. Having engaged in this conceptual exercise in the first half of the chapter, we spent the second half exploring the relationship between identity work processes and various movement dynamics, focusing on movement careers. More specifically, we argued that different forms of identity work tend to dominate movement recruitment over time and, more important, that various highly consequential movement dynamics (e.g., factionalism and decline) may well be related to the succession of these identity work processes.

We close on a synthetic note. At the outset of the chapter, we said our goal was to understand better the identity/movement nexus by drawing on the dispositional, structuralist, and constructionist perspectives on identity. However, given the relative lack of attention accorded the last of these perspectives, we have spent most of the chapter elaborating the critical importance of constructionist processes, such as identity work, in mediating the relationship between individual and movement collective identities. But we stand by our earlier assertion that all three perspectives contribute to a more thoroughgoing understanding of the link between personal and collective identities and movement participation. How, then, might these three seemingly disparate perspectives be reconciled? Here we sketch our provisional thinking on the topic.

At a psychological level, we think particular dispositional traits or personality types bear little or no consistent relationship to movement participation. We are, however, inclined to grant considerable importance to general motivational dynamics. For example, we think the work that Swann and others have done on "self-verification" has important implications for an understanding of differential recruitment (see Pinel and Swann, chapter 6 in this volume, and the work they cite). The suggestion is clear: movements that frame their recruiting efforts around appeals to salient self-conceptions are more likely to attract adherents than those that do not.

This psychological tenet has a clear structuralist analog. Those movements that develop within established organizations or associational networks are in a much better position to appropriate the self and identity commitments of significant numbers of people than are movements that seek to recruit isolated individuals. And Swann's work on "self-verification" and Stryker's notion of identity salience help to explain why this is the case. Existing groups and networks afford organizers pools of people whose identity commitments are generally known and therefore available for judicious appropriation.

The ubiquity of these psychological and structural dynamics points again to the pivotal role of constructionist processes in movement participation. That is, there is nothing about a desire for self-verification or the confirmation of a salient identity that necessitates individual activism. Similarly, our network connections can just as easily lead to church attendance, dating, or a change of jobs as movement participation. In short, network structures and general motivational dynamics are generally devoid of specific substantive direction. To understand how affiliation with a specific movement has come to be seen as a vehicle for self-verification, we have to focus on the concrete social processes that have cemented this association in our subject's mind. In the same vein, to understand how network ties encourage activism, we have to know more about the shared meanings that are encoded in those network connections. Networks are powerful shapers of behavior, but a given network could just as easily discourage as encourage activism. It all depends on how the movement comes to be defined within the network and then linked to identities salient to network others. In the absence of these critically important but highly contingent constructionist processes, neither a desire for self-verification nor network integration can tell us much about the identity/network nexus—hence the utility of the constructionist perspective and the need for greater theoretical elaboration and empirical work to tease out the nature, forms, and factors that shape the various identity work processes.

Notes

We would like to thank Victor Gecas, Robert White, and the editors of this volume for their helpful comments.

1. See, for example, the writings of Gamson (1992), Hunt (1991), Melucci (1989), and Taylor and Whittier (1992), for whom a shared sense of "we-ness" is central to their conceptions of collective identity. Even Melucci, whose treatment of collective

identity is perhaps the most slippery, defines it as "an interactive and shared definition" while emphasizing that the "construction of [this] sense of 'we'" is an "on-gong process" (1989, 34, 218).

2. Work reflective of this perspective includes not only that which is avowedly structuralist (Gould 1995) but also much of the work that focuses on cultural politics (see, for example, Darnovsky, Epstein, and Flacks 1995). This latter genre of work sees identities as being anchored in various groupings that can be defined or situated both culturally and structurally, such as gays, lesbians, and feminists. It should also be noted that this structuralist/culturalist approach to collective identity is consistent in some respects with Stryker's role-identity theory (1968, 1980) in sociological social psychology. However, that theoretical linkage is seldom noted in the structuralist/culturalist literature. Moreover, the understanding of identity elaborated by role-identity theory is more complex and nuanced than that which issues from most structuralist/culturalist discussions of collective identity.

3. Identity work also can and does occur beyond the group and subcultural levels. See, for example, Cerulo's analysis of the construction of national identities (1995).

4. The idea that identity can function as an important source of motivation is rooted in Foote's now seminal essay (1951) on identification as a basis for a theory of motivation.

5. For a summary of this extensive literature, see Snow and Oliver (1995, 574–75).

6. See Coser (1967) for an insightful analysis of what he dubbed "greedy organizations."

References

Adorno, T., E. Frenkel-Brunswick, D. J. Levinson, and R. N. Sanford. 1950. *The Authoritarian Personality.* New York: Harper.

Balch, Robert W., and David Taylor. 1978. "Seekers and Saucers: The Role of the Cultic Milieu in Joining a UFO Cult." In *Conversion Careers,* edited by J. Richardson, 43–65. Beverly Hills, Calif.: Sage.

Banton, Michael. 1965. *Roles: An Introduction to the Study of Social Relations.* New York: Basic Books.

Burke, Peter J., and Don C. Reitzes. 1981. "The Link between Identity and Role Performance." *Social Psychology Quarterly* 44:83–92.

Carson, Clayborne. 1981. *In Struggle.* Cambridge: Harvard University Press.

Cerulo, Karen A. 1995. *Identity Designs: The Sights and Sounds of a Nation.* New Brunswick, N.J.: Rutgers University Press.

Coser, Lewis A. 1956. *The Functions of Social Conflict.* New York: Free Press.

———. 1967. "Greedy Organizations." *Archives Europeenes de Sociologie* 8:196–215.

Crossman, Richard, ed. 1952. *The God That Failed.* New York: Bantam.

Darnovsky, Marcy, Barbara Epstein, and Richard Flacks, eds. 1995. *Cultural Politics and Social Movements.* Philadelphia: Temple University Press.

Etzioni, Amitai. 1975. *The Comparative Analysis of Complex Organizations.* New York: Free Press.

Felson, Richard B. 1985. "Reflected Appraisal and the Development of the Self." *Social Psychology Quarterly* 48:71–77.

Foote, Nelson, N. 1951. "Identification as the Basis for a Theory of Motivation." *American Sociological Review* 26:14–21.

Friedman, Debra, and Doug McAdam. 1992. "Collective Identity and Activism: Networks, Choices, and the Life of a Social Movement." In *Frontiers in Social Movement Theory,* edited by A. D. Morris and C. M. Mueller, 156–73. New Haven: Yale University Press.

Gamson, Joshua. 1995. "Must Identity Movements Self-Destruct?: A Queer Dilemma." *Social Problems* 42:390–407.

Gamson, William A. 1992. "The Social Psychology of Collective Action." In *Frontiers in Social Movement Theory,* edited by A. D. Morris and C. M. Mueller, 53–76. New Haven: Yale University Press.

Garner, Roberta. 1996. *Contemporary Movements and Ideologies.* New York: McGraw-Hill.

Glenn, John K. 1997. *Framing Democracy in Eastern Europe: Civic Movements and the Reconstruction of Leninist States.* Ph.D. diss., Department of Sociology, Harvard University.

Goffman, Erving. 1961. *Encounters.* Indianapolis: Bobbs-Merrill.

Gordon, David F. 1974. "The Jesus People: An Identity Synthesis." *Urban Life and Culture* 3:159–78.

Gould, Roger V. 1995. *Insurgent Identities: Class, Community, and Protest in Paris from 1848 to the Commune.* Chicago: University of Chicago Press.

Heirich, Max. 1968. *The Beginning: Berkeley 1964.* New York: Columbia University Press.

Hughes, Everett C. 1945. "Dilemmas and Contradictions of Status." *American Journal of Sociology* 50:353–59.

Hunt, Scott A. 1991. *Constructing Collective Identity in a Peace Movement Organization.* Ph.D.diss., University of Nebraska, Lincoln.

Hunt, Scott A., and Robert D. Benford. 1994. "Identity Talk in the Peace and Justice Movement." *Journal of Contemporary Ethnography* 22:488–517.

Hunt, Scott A., Robert D. Benford, and David A. Snow. 1994. "Identity Fields: Framing Processes and the Social Construction of Movement Identities." In *New Social Movements: From Ideology to Identity,* edited by Enrique Laraña, Hank Johnston, and Joseph R. Gusfield, 185–208. Philadelphia: Temple University Press.

Kanter, Rosabeth M. 1972. *Commitment and Community: Communes and Utopias in Sociological Perspective.* Cambridge: Harvard University Press.

Klapp, Orrin. 1969. *Collective Search for Identity.* New York: Holt, Rinehart and Winston.

King, Martin Luther, Jr. 1958. *Stride toward Freedom.* New York: Harper and Brothers.

Kornhauser, William. 1959. *The Politics of Mass Society.* New York: Free Press.

Lipset, Seymour M., and Sheldon Wolin. 1965. *The Berkeley Student Revolt.* New York: Doubleday Anchor.

McAdam, Doug. 1982. *Political Process and the Development of Black Insurgency, 1930–1970.* Chicago: University of Chicago Press.

———. 1988. *Freedom Summer.* New York: Oxford University Press.

McAdam, Doug, and Ronnelle Paulsen. 1993. "Specifying the Relationship between Social Ties and Activism." *American Journal of Sociology* 99:640–67.

McAdam, Doug, and Dieter Rucht. 1993. "Cross-National Diffusion of Social Movement Ideas." *Annals of the American Academy of Political and Social Science* 528:56–74.

Melucci, Alberto. 1989. *Nomads of the Present: Social Movement and Identity Needs in Contemporary Society.* Edited by John Keane and Paul Mier. Philadelphia: Temple University Press.

Morris, Aldon D. 1984. *The Origins of the Civil Rights Movement.* New York: Free Press.

Nisbet, Robert A. 1954. *The Quest for Community.* New York: Oxford University Press.

Nock, A. D. 1933. *Conversion.* London: Oxford University Press.

Oberschall, Anthony. 1973. *Social Conflict and Social Movements.* Englewood Cliffs, N.J.: Prentice-Hall.

Olson, Mancur. 1965. *The Logic of Collective Action.* Cambridge: Harvard University Press.

Parsons, Talcott. 1951. *The Social System.* New York: Free Press.

Schwalbe, Michael L., and Douglas Mason-Schrock. 1996. "Identity Work as Group Process." *Advances in Group Processes* 13:113–47.

Snow, David A. 1993. *Shakubuku: A Study of the Nichiren Shoshu Buddhist Movement in America, 1960–1975.* New York: Garland Publishing.

Snow, David A., and Leon Anderson. 1987. "Identity Work among the Homeless: The Verbal Construction and Avowal of Personal Identities." *American Journal of Sociology* 92:1336–71.

Snow, David A., and Richard Machalek. 1983. "The Convert as a Social Type." In *Sociological Theory,* edited by Randall Collins, 259–89. San Francisco: Jossey-Bass.

———. 1984. "The Sociology of Conversion." *Annual Review of Sociology* 10:167–90.

Snow, David A., and Pamela E. Oliver. 1995. "Social Movements and Collective Behavior: Social Psychological Dimensions and Considerations." In *Sociological Perspectives on Social Psychology,* edited by Karen S. Cook, Gary Alan Fine, and James S. House, 571–99. Boston: Allyn and Bacon.

Snow, David A., E. Burke Rochford Jr., Steven K. Worden, and Robert D. Benford. 1986. "Frame Alignment Process, Micromobilization, and Movement Participation." *American Sociological Review* 51:464–81.

Stoecker, Randy. 1995. "Community, Movement, Organization: The Problem of Identity Convergence in Collective Action." *Sociological Quarterly* 36:111–30.

Stone, Gregory P. 1966. Review of *Roles: An Introduction to the Study of Social Relations. American Sociological Review* 31: 899.

Straus, Roger. 1976. "Changing Oneself: Seekers and the Creative Transformation of Life Experience." In *Doing Social Life,* edited by J. Lofland, 252–72. New York: Wiley.

Stryker, Sheldon. 1968. "Identity Salience and Role Performance." *Journal of Marriage and the Family* 30:558–64.

———. 1980. *Symbolic Interactionism: A Social Structural Version.* Menlo Park, Calif.: Benjamin-Cummings.

Taylor, Verta. 1996. *Rock-a-By Baby Feminism, Self-Help, and Postpartum Depression.* New York: Routledge.

Taylor, Verta, and Nicole C. Raeburn. 1995. "Identity Politics as High-Risk Activism: Career Consequences for Lesbian, Gay, and Bisexual Sociologists." *Social Problems* 42:352–73.

Taylor, Verta, and Nancy E. Whittier. 1992. "Collective Identity in Social Movement Communities: Lesbian Feminist Mobilization." In *Frontiers in Social Movement Theory,* edited by A. D. Morris and C. M. Mueller, 104–29. New Haven: Yale University Press.

Turner, Ralph H., and Lewis M. Killian. 1972. *Collective Behavior,* 2d ed. Englewood Cliffs, N.J.: Prentice-Hall.

Walton, Norman W. 1956. "The Walking City: A History of the Montgomery Boycott." *Negro History Bulletin* 20:17–20.

Wellman, Barry, and S. D. Berkowitz, eds. 1988. *Social Structures.* New York: Cambridge University Press.

Zurcher, Louis A., and David A. Snow. 1981. "Collective Behavior: Social Movements." In *Social Psychology: Sociological Perspectives,* edited by Morris Rosenberg and Ralph H. Turner, 447–82. New York: Basic Books.

3

Group Identification and Political Protest

Bert Klandermans and Marga de Weerd

Identity, injustice, and agency are three crucial concepts of the social psychology of protest. Of the three concepts, identity has the shortest career in social movement literature. Injustice and agency have a much longer history—be it as relative deprivation, moral indignation, or grievances as far as injustice is concerned; or efficacy, success expectations, or empowerment as far as agency is concerned. As a consequence, the literature on the identity component of collective action frames is still very uneven. Collective identity is seen as a prerequisite of collective action, but in fact it is often not clear what the identity component signifies, how it is conceptualized and operationalized. Most of the writing is theoretical, and hardly any empirical work is done within the social movement domain.

Meanwhile, in European social psychology, social identity became important as a concept. Following the seminal work of Tajfel, European social psychologists saw in the social identity concept an opportunity to make social psychology more social, by taking group membership as a constituent of identity. Social identity was defined as that part of identity that is determined by a person's membership in groups and categories. Within this framework, collective action is seen as one of the identity management strategies. Unlike social movement scholars, social psychologists conducted many empirical studies on the subject, but predominantly in the laboratory with artificial groups.

The two traditions have hardly cross-fertilized each other. This is a matter not only of disciplinary boundaries or different methodological traditions but of a difference in levels of analysis and the complexity of linking those different levels appropriately. Collective identity is a collective belief; social identity, an individual belief. Understanding how the two are connected conceptually is of crucial importance for a proper understanding of the identity component of collective action frames.[1]

In this chapter we attempt to delineate the two conceptualizations of the identity component. We illustrate our arguments with evidence from our study of protest of Dutch farmers against the agricultural policy of national government and the European Union.

Collective Identity

Acting collectively requires some collective identity or consciousness. Admittedly, this is not a groundbreaking observation. For example, studies of the labor movement have always underscored the importance of class consciousness or solidarity for class action. At the same time these studies have also demonstrated that such consciousness does not develop spontaneously.

Melucci (1989) therefore argued that the creation of collective identity is one of the fundamental challenges would-be movement participants face. Collective identity, according to Melucci (1996), is "an interactive and shared definition produced by several individuals (or groups at a more complex level) and concerned with the orientation of action and field of opportunities and constraints in which the action takes place" (44). He conceives of collective identity as a process, because it is constructed and negotiated through a repeated activation of the relationship that links individuals or groups. Central to Melucci's conceptualization are three features: "the continuity of a subject over and beyond variation in time and its adaptations to the environment; the delimitation of this subject with respect to others; (and) the ability to recognize and to be recognized" (45). Much of Melucci's work in the field concerns an attempt to understand how collective identity is constructed and reconstructed. Collective identity, he argues, is a learning process that leads to the formation and maintenance of a unified empirical actor that we can call a social movement (but see chapter 2 in this volume for a critical discussion of this view). It ensures the continuity and permanence of the movement over time and establishes the limits of the actor with respect to its social environment (49).

Taylor and Whittier (1992, 1995), in their attempt to define and operationalize collective identity, emphasize comparable aspects and processes. They define collective identity as "the shared definition of a group that derives from members' common interests, and solidarity" (1995, 172). Like Melucci, they see collective identity as a movement characteristic that is constructed, activated, and sustained through interaction in social movement communities. Thus, they argue, in order to understand collective identity, one must examine that interaction and, especially, the social and political struggle that politicizes identity. These authors' main contribution to the literature on collective identity is an operationalization of the formation of collective identity as consisting of three processes: "(1) the creation of boundaries that insulate and differentiate a category of persons from the dominant society; (2) the development of consciousness that presumes the existence of socially constituted criteria that account for a group's structural position; and (3) the valorization of a group's 'essential differences' through the politicization of everyday life" (1992, 122).

Paradoxically, social psychological research shows time and again that very little is needed for collective identity to be activated. Even the minimal intervention of assigning people randomly to different groups suffices to evoke in-group–out-group dynamics (Hewstone, Stroebe, and Stephenson 1996), and simply priming a "we" schema is enough to activate collective self (Brewer and Gardner 1996). Factors such as similarity in personal characteristics, common fate, and centrality of group membership for one's self-image affect the generation of a collective identity (Gurin and Townsend 1986). And, once formed, groups maintain their collective identity over time by socializing newcomers (Levine and Moreland 1991).

Be this as it may, in order to become the binding element of political protest, collective identity must become politicalized. Yet, in reality, collective identities remain politically neutral most of the time. World championship soccer may increase levels of national identity considerably, but in other than exceptional cases such collective identities do not gain political significance. What, then, does make collective identity politically relevant? The answer to this question given in the literature on social movement participation seems to be the following: collectively defined grievances that produce a "we" feeling *and* causal attributions that denote a "they" that is held responsible for the collective grievances turn routine in-group–out-group dynamics conflictual (Gamson 1992a; Taylor and Whittier 1992). If the out-group is an authority, which is perceived by the in-group to be unjust, encounter with such an authority will rapidly politicize collective identity (Gamson, Fireman, and Rytina 1982; Hirsch 1990), that is, an identity as a group defining itself in opposition against political authorities. This is especially true if authorities appear to be unresponsive to the group's claims or respond in a repressive way (cf. Olivier 1991; Reicher 1996).

Thus, according to social movement literature, causal attributions disseminated by social and political actors give circumstances and social categories their political meaning, which is further confirmed by interactions with authorities. It is this reciprocity of causal attributions and encounters with opponents that produce the potentially explosive mix of shared moral indignation and oppositional consciousness that makes collective identity politically significant. As we will see, social identity theory's account of political protest does not deviate that much from that of social movement literature, except for the fundamental difference that it starts from the perspective of the individual.

Social Identity

"People like to think positively of themselves," write Mummendey et al. (1999) in the opening sentence of their paper on identity management strategies among East Germans a couple of years after the reunification. Indeed, social identity theory (Tajfel and Turner 1986), the theory Mummendey and her students apply, states that people tend to improve a negative identity, maintain a positive identity, and defend a positive identity when it is threatened.[2]

Social identity is that part of a person's self-concept that relates to his or her awareness of belonging to a specific group or category and that has a certain value and emotional meaning.[3] Social identity requires that an individual breaks his or her social environment down into groups and categories and presupposes processes of self-categorization as a member of some categories or groups. The evaluation of the status of these categories or groups result from processes of social comparison, that is, comparison of one's own group with other groups. A perceived favorable status of a category or group compared with that of other groups contributes positively to a person's self-concept.

Social identity theory holds that a perceived negative group status motivates people to engage in identity improvement strategies. Three such strategies are distinguished (Tajfel and Turner 1986): (1) individual attempts to leave the group and to become a member of a more positively evaluated group, (2) collective attempts to improve the group's status, and (3) attempts to redefine the comparison process itself by choosing other reference groups or standards of comparison.

Whether individuals prefer any of these strategies depends, according to social identity theory, on stuctural characteristics of the intergroup situation, namely, the stability versus instability and the legitimacy versus illegitimacy of the relative status of the in-group, and the permeability versus impermeability of group boundaries. Laboratory studies (see Ellemers 1993 for a summary) suggest that permeability of group boundaries reduces in-group identification in low-status groups and makes individual mobility more likely. However, if the low status of one's own group is perceived as unstable and thus improvement of the group's position seems a viable option, in-group identification remains high, and collective strategies are preferred regardless of the permeability of group boundaries. Finally, the perception of group inferiority as illegitimate only seems to matter if the inferior status of one's own group is perceived to be unstable and thus the possibility of successful collective status improvement exists.

Mummendey and her colleagues applied social identity theory in order to understand how East Germans react to their obviously disadvantaged position compared with the West Germans. However, whereas in laboratory experiments one can manipulate the structural characteristics of the situation, in real life they are "core dimensions along which *belief systems* about intergroup relations are systematized" (Mummendey et al. 1999; our emphasis). Tajfel and Turner (1986) conceive of these shared beliefs as varying along a quasi-ideological dimension characterized by two extremes that they refer to as "social mobility" and "social change." Belief systems of social mobility are adhered to by people who feel that it is possible for them to move individually into another group that suits them better; belief systems of social change are adhered to by people who feel that it is difficult to divest themselves of an unsatisfactory, underprivileged, or stigmatized group membership and who as a consequence engage in social movements aiming to change the status quo. Social identity theory predicts that belief systems of social change are more likely to develop when group boundaries are perceived to be impermeable, in other words, when no individual mobility is possible (see also Wright, Taylor, and Moghaddam 1990). But Mummendey et al. emphasize that dominating ideologies and political rhetoric determine the extent to which these beliefs systems are spread and socially shared or controversial in a society.

The evidence these authors present on the East German case concerns the preferences for the identity management strategies distinguished above. Important for our subject is the question of what makes *collective* identity management strategies more likely. The results on that score indicate that perceived legitimacy is the only factor that has a direct impact. Stability and permeability, on the other hand, have a strong indirect influence on the preference for collective strategies by having an impact on in-group identification. In other words, if people perceive the negative group status as stable and the group boundaries as impermeable, their in-group identification strengthens. In its turn, a strong in-group identification together with the perceived illegitimacy of the group's status generates a preference for collective change strategies. The noncollective strategies, on the other hand, all go together with a weak in-group identification resulting from a perception of the intergroup situation as unstable and with permeable group boundaries. Interestingly, perceptions of legitimacy versus illegitimacy are irrelevant in this context. In other words, if they expect that the situation will change, people do not seem to care too much about the legitimacy or illegitimacy of a negative group status.[4]

Mummendey et al. hypothesized—in line with social identity theory—a mediating role of in-group identification between perceived characteristics of the intergroup situation on the one hand and the preference for identity management strategies on the other. In fact, in the East German case in-group identification turned out to be a much more important mediator than hypothesized. Indeed, it explained most of the differential preference for collective and noncollective strategies. Kelly (1993) and Major (1994), coming from a different angle (the status of women in society), arrive at the same conclusion. On the basis of their discussions of factors fostering collective action strategies in response to inequality, they conclude that group identification is indispensable for such action. The importance of social identity theory for our discussion is that it emphasizes that for an individual collective action is only one of the possible identity improvement strategies and that group identification is a crucial factor in the choice between strategies.

Group Identification

In a way, it is surprising that group identification has not been proposed more often as a concept relevant for protest behavior, as its significance is so obvious. Without group identification there can be no group deprivation, according to Major (1994), and she is perfectly right. Group comparisons are made only for groups with whom one identifies (see also Tajfel and Turner 1986). On the basis of our previous discussion we can now add that without group identification there can be no preference for collective action strategies. That raises, of course, the question of which groups people identify with and which of all those group identifications become politically relevant. People belong to all kinds of groups: the unemployed, car owners, female, soccer fans, red haired, residents from the same neighborhood, Europeans, and so on. They do not identify with most of them, and if they do, this identification usually remains politically irrelevant.

Of course, the question is usually not that open and can be reduced to that of to what extent do people identify with the specific group or category of relevance for our research questions. Moreover, people's social behavior often tells us about categories with which they do and do not identify. In a discussion of social identity and political involvement, Andrews (1991) makes the distinction between voluntary and involuntary group membership. Gender, age, race, nation, and social class are examples of involuntary groups. The awareness of belonging to such a group need not evoke any positive or negative feelings. Membership in a voluntary group, on the other hand, is self-chosen, and these choices do tell something about how someone sees her- or himself. One can emphasize involuntary group membership (such as a Surinam in the Netherlands who becomes a member of a Surinam association) or negate or even deny it (for example, an elderly person who refuses to become a member of a union of the elderly). Whether involuntary group membership becomes politically relevant depends, according to Andrews, on the political orientation of the person involved.

Group Identification as the Link between Collective and Social Identity

Obviously, collective identity and social identity are related concepts. However, they refer to different aspects of group life. To put it simply: collective identity concerns cognitions shared by members of a single group, whereas social identity concerns cognitions of a single individual about his or her membership in one or more groups. Indeed, collective identity is a characteristic of a group and involves more than one individual; social identity is a characteristic of an individual and usually involves more than one group. In sum, then, although they are related, collective identity and social identity are concepts at different levels of analysis, and this distinction is important if we are to conceptualize the identity component of collective action frames properly.

In an essay entitled "The Social Psychology of Collective Action," Gamson (1992b) takes a similar stand. In Gamson's eyes some of the key questions of social movement literature involve the mesh between self and society, which he sees as characteristic social psychological questions. More specifically, he argues that collective identity concerns the mesh between the individual and cultural systems. According to Gamson, part of the reason why social movement literature on collective identity is so vague is its tendency to blur individual and cultural levels. Gamson holds that "the locus of collective identity is cultural; it is manifested through the language and symbols by which it is publicly expressed. We know collective identity by the cultural icons and artifacts displayed by those who embrace it. To measure it one would ask people about the meaning of labels and other cultural symbols, not about their personal identity" (60).

Indeed, collective identity concerns shared beliefs. Thus its study must meet the same requirements as that of any kind of shared belief, that is, distinguishing properly between the collective and individual levels of analysis. Elsewhere (Klandermans 1997), the first author made the distinction between the *social construction* of collective beliefs, which is the process of the formation of collective beliefs at the group level, and the *appropriation* of collective beliefs, which is the process of the formation of the idiosyncratic remakes of those beliefs at the individual level. Similarly, one must distinguish the social construction of collective identity at the group level from the appropriation of collective identity at the individual level. We hold that group identification can be defined as the counterpart of collective identity at the individual level. To put it another way, no collective identity of a group can be constructed without individual members who identify with the group. To be sure, individuals may identify with a cause without identifying with groups or organizations that work for the cause. But that, in our view, does not constitute collective identity. After all, collective identity is defined here as a group characteristic, as beliefs shared by members of a group. Group identification can be assessed in all kinds of ways, but any operationalization of group identification will refer somehow to what it means to an individual to belong to the group in point and will thus implicitly or explicitly refer to the pride of being a member of the group, to the symbols, the values, the fate shared by the group members.[5]

At the same time, identification with a group is a building block of a person's social identity. As a rule, one's social identity is construed from his or her identifications with different groups. After all, an individual is a member of and identifies with more than one group, for example, farmers, Catholics, a family, a soccer club, and so on. This does not mean that we cannot fruitfully study identification with a single group. On the contrary, as long as our research questions concern the status of that specific group or, alternatively, collective action on behalf of it, studying group identification makes perfect sense. Yet social identity theory draws our attention to the fact that a group member belongs to other groups as well and that the group we are investigating may not even be the group with which he or she identifies most strongly. In fact, as argued, someone may even deny group membership.

Although they concern two separate matters, social identity and collective identity do coincide, because people who share a collective identity tend to share group memberships as well. For example, in the Netherlands in the heyday of pillarization it was part of the collective identity of Catholics to vote for the Catholic party, to be a member of a Catholic labor union or a Catholic women's or farmer's organization, and so on. As a consequence, the social identities of Catholics overlapped to a large extent.

Indeed, more generally the literature on such phenomena as multiorganizational fields, pillarization, or working-class communities suggests that people from identical walks of life tend to share memberships in all kinds of groups and organizations. This is something that has not been researched extensively in collective or social identity literature as far as we know, but it is certainly true that many overlapping memberships exist between movement organizations (Della Porta and Rucht 1995; Klandermans 1997).

Levels of Analysis

A group's collective identity can be studied in its own right by examining such phenomena as the group's symbols, rituals, beliefs, and the values its members share. An individual's identification with a group can be studied in its own right as well by examining the individual's beliefs, sentiments, commitment to the group, use of symbols, participation in rituals, and so on. The latter will always be an idiosyncratic remake of the former, and that has important epistemological consequences. By investigating individual beliefs we may be able to assess some distribution of levels of group identification in more or less detail, but that will never tell us all about the group's collective identity. On the other hand, by studying a group's rituals, symbols, or articles of faith we may be able to describe the group's collective identity, but that does not tell us much about an individual's level of group identification. Yet the two are tightly intertwined; in fact, they are two sides of the same coin. Those who are interested in the identity component of collective action frames are, of course, free to study the subject at either the individual or the collective level, or both; however, it is important that they keep in mind the different levels of analysis. The remainder of this chapter focuses on the individual level and thus concentrates on group identification as a factor influencing an individual's preference for collective action strategies to improve negative group status. The group we concentrate on are Dutch farmers. More specifically, we are interested in the question of to what extent Dutch farmers identify with their professional group and whether such identification fosters participation in collective action on behalf of the farmers. Collective action participation presupposes the existence of grievances, of feelings of injustice. But both social movement theory and social identity theory hold that participation in collective action requires in addition some level of group identification.

In the past years Dutch farmers, like farmers in most European countries, have suffered serious setbacks, either because of measures taken by their national governments, or because of the agricultural policy of the European Union, or because of both. Cuts in the European Union's agricultural funds, tensions between agricultural and environmental policy, measures to confine manure surpluses, and so on have increased the social and political pressure on farmers tremendously. Our own research provides evidence that farmers feel that they do not get what they deserve, that society does not appreciate their contribution, and that the future of their profession is at risk. In short, farmers feel that their professional group has acquired a negative status compared with that of other occupational categories and that they do not deserve such a status (Klandermans et al. 1999).

Theoretically, such a negative group status—social movement literature would refer to it as relative group deprivation—is assumed to weaken group identification. On the other hand, group identification is supposed to mediate between such grievances and collective action participation in response to it. As a consequence, and because Dutch farmers *are* experiencing a negative group status, we hypothesize that identification with the professional group among these farmers will stimulate collective action participation.

A brief note on methods: between fall 1993 and fall 1995 we interviewed a sample of 168 Dutch farmers three times. The sample was drawn from the farming population in four farming communities. Face-to-face, computer-assisted interviews were conducted by trained interviewers at the respondents' homes. The interviews lasted on the average one hour. The timing of the interviews was such that important agricultural measures and responses by the farming community could be expected. The samples interviewed resulted from random samples drawn by a commercial data bank. Our first interview round started with a response rate of 35 percent; response rates for the next two interviews were 74 percent and 81 percent, respectively. Although 35 percent as a response rate is low, it is not really problematic, as we are predominantly interested in comparisons of the answers of the same group of respondents at three points in time.

The age of the respondents ranged from eighteen to sixty-nine years (average forty-six). All but six of the interviewees were male. Fourteen percent of the respondents owned large farms, 57 percent had farms of moderate size, and the remaining 30 percent had small farms. One-fifth were dairy farmers, two-fifths arable farmers, and two-fifths had mixed farms. Approximately one-third of the farmers described their farms as successful, one-third as not successful, and one-third was undecided in this respect.

Group Identification among Dutch Farmers

We attempted to assess group identification among Dutch farmers in a variety of ways (table 1). First, we asked farmers about in-group identification. More than 90 percent of the farmers said they identified with other Dutch

Table 1. Group Identification among Dutch Farmers, 1993–1995 (percentages)

	1993	1994	1995
In-group identification	94.6	—	93.5
Out-group differentiation	72.0	—	72.0
Participation in farmers' organizations			
No member	9.5	13.7	11.9
Member not active	38.1	39.3	44.0
Active member	31.5	25.6	28.0
Officeholder	20.8	21.4	16.1
Level of identification			
Regional	92.8	95.8	97.0
National	85.1	88.7	89.9
European	45.3	54.8	58.3
Occupational pride			
Farmer again	62.5	61.9	61.3
Stay farmer	54.8	58.4	56.5
Permeability of group boundaries	32.1	31.5	32.1

farmers, a percentage that remained fairly stable over the two-year period. Ninety percent of our respondents did not change their mind at all.

Second, we assessed out-group differentiation. As social identity literature emphasizes, identification always has these two aspects, identification with the in-group and differentiation from the out-group. Social identity is defined in terms of both the groups to which someone belongs and the groups to which someone does not belong. Seventy-two percent of our respondents said they felt more committed to farmers than any other occupational group. Interestingly, although the overall percentages at the two points in time are exactly the same, close to 30 percent of the respondents changed their mind in either direction. In-group identification and out-group differentiation seem to be two separate aspects of group identification, as the correlations between the two factors are low (.03 and .16). By simply adding the two we combined in-group identification and out-group differentation into one measure of group identification ranging from 2 (low) to 4 (high). This measure is used in our further analyses.

Following our reasoning concerning voluntary group memberships, we also asked about membership in farmers' organizations. To reiterate, membership in a farmers' organization is interpreted as an act that underscores a person's identification with farmers as a category. As far as membership per se is concerned, the findings confirm our results regarding in-group identification. Approximately 90 percent of the respondents are members of a farmers' organization. However, a much lower percentage (approximately 50 percent) are active as a member either by taking part in meetings or by holding some office in the organization. These activity levels are fairly stable, as the correlations between activity levels at the three points in time demonstrate (t1xt2:.66, t1xt3:.59, t2xt3:.70).

We then asked our respondents to distinguish between farmers in their region, those in the country, and those in the European Union. The reasoning behind this question was that identification may take place at different levels of inclusion. In line with social identity theory, we assumed that identification would be highest at the lowest level of inclusion and lowest at the highest level of inclusion. Farmers in the European Union are a far less concrete category with which it is more difficult to identify than farmers in the region, with whom one can have direct contact on a regular base. On the other hand, agricultural policy is defined at the European level in an increasing degree. It is conceivable that, as a consequence, European farmers as a category are becoming more and more salient. It is, therefore, worth investigating to what extent circumstances have imposed a collective identity on farmers in Europe.

As expected, we found much higher levels of identification at the less inclusive levels: percentages beyond 90 for regional farmers, close to 90 for national farmers, and around 50 for farmers in the European Union. Identification at the national level is correlated to identification at both the regional and the European level (correlations ranging from .30 to .60), whereas identification at the regional level is correlated only weakly to identification at the European level (correlations ranging from .16 to .23). Interestingly, although over the years levels of identification have gone up for all three levels, those for the European Union have increased the most. Apparently, circumstances have strengthened identification with the professional group but most so at the European level. We will return to this.

Two more aspects of group identification were assessed. First, we attempted to measure occupational pride. We asked our respondents whether they would become farmers again were they allowed to choose anew, and whether they would stay farmers even if the money they were making was hardly beyond subsistence level. A substantial proportion of the farmers (around 60 percent) answered both questions in the affirmative. These percentages did not change much over time. Indeed, people hardly changed their mind in this respect, as the autocorrelations of a combined measure demonstrate (t1xt2:.62, t1xt3:.54, t2xt3:.70). Then we asked how easy it would be for them to find another job. As discussed, in social identity theory permeability of group boundaries, that is, how easy it is to change groups, is an important factor, not only as a determinant of group identification but also as a determinant of identity management strategies. Impermeable group boundaries supposedly encourage collective action. Therefore, estimates of how easy it would be to find another job are an important aspect of the definition of the situation. A large proportion of our respondents feel they would not be able to find another job or are uncertain about it. About 30 percent estimate that it would (probably) not be difficult for them to find another job if they were to quit farming. These percentages are fairly stable at both the group level and the individual level (t1xt2:.57, t1xt3:.59, t2xt3:.66).

These different aspects of group identification are relatively independent of one another. Occupational pride and perceived permeability of boundaries are not related to any of the other aspects of group identification. As in-group identification is defined in terms of farmers in the Netherlands, it will not come as a surprise that it has the highest correlation with identification at the national level (.29 and .35), higher than identification at the regional (.06 and .18) or European level (.23 and .22). The behavioral component of group identification, participation in farmers' organization, bears only weak relationships with the cognitive indicators.

The picture that emerges from these findings suggests strong and stable in-group identifications among Dutch farmers, both cognitive and behavioral. Yet the findings also allude to a few distinctive patterns and interesting transformations. Although the farmers all identify strongly with the in-group, especially if it is defined as regional or national farmers, it is also clear that not every respondent is equally active in farmers' organizations. It is also clear that farmers differ in terms of the extent to which they distance themselves from other occupations. Moreover, although at the group level little change in out-group differentiation seems to have taken place, analyses at the individual level reveal a fair amount of change. Our respondents also showed a wide variation in their estimates of the openness of other occupations in case they leave farming. And finally, over the two years that we have collected data, a strengthening of in-group identification seems to have taken place, especially as far as identification with European farmers is concerned.

Protest Participation among Dutch Farmers

Protest participation was registered in two different ways. We assessed the intention to take part in four forms of collective action that were part of the

Table 2. Protest Intention and Participation among Dutch Farmers, 1993–1995

	1993	1994	1995
Intention to participate	2.85[a]	2.74[a]	2.79[a]
Protest participation	—	10.7%	16.7%
Affected by manure policy	—	11.0%	25.0%
Not affected by manure policy	—	10.3%	4.4%

Correlations

	Intention in 1993	Intention in 1994	Intention in 1995	Part[b] 1994	Part[b] 1995
Intention in 1993	—				
Intention in 1994	.69	—			
Intention in 1995	.71	.76	—		
Part 1994[b]	.23	.24	.18	—	
Part 1995[b]	.29	.37	.37	.31	—

[a]On a scale from 1 (no intention to participate at all) to 5 (intention to participate in any action).
[b]Part 1994 = participation in 1994; Part 1995 = participation in 1995.

repertoire or considered to be so—demonstrations, blockades, symbolic actions (such as dumping manure on the doorsteps of the Ministry of Agriculture), refusal to pay taxes. We asked for each of these action forms whether respondents would participate if they were to disagree completely with an agricultural measure or with agricultural policy in general. Throughout the three surveys about half of our respondents was prepared to take part in demonstrations, symbolic actions, or tax refusals. Blockades were less popular, but still a quarter to one-third were prepared to participate in such actions. The answers to these questions were combined into a scale from 1 (no intention to participate at all) to 5 (intention to participate in any action). In addition, we asked whether in the past year respondents took part in any collective action directed at agricultural measures or policy (table 2).

Action preparedness remains reasonably high over the years. It is also fairly stable at the individual level, as the correlations between intention scores in the three interviews indicate. Action preparedness does predict action participation, even two years later. Action participation increased considerably between 1994 and 1995. This increase in participation is completely due to the conflict between farmers and the Ministry of Agriculture over manure surpluses. Among those farmers who are somehow involved in the manure problem, an increase in protest participation from 11 to 25 percent was observed, whereas among the remaining farmers protest participation dropped from

10.3 to 4.4 percent. In other words, the protesting population changed in composition in response to a change in conflict matter. Interestingly, action preparedness as assessed in the years before could predict which farmers would take part in these protests and which would not, although not a full 100 percent.

Group Identification and Action Preparedness

We conducted regression analyses to assess whether identity measures accounted for variance in action preparedness. Indeed, group identification, both cognitive and behavioral, plays an important role in the explanation of action preparedness. The more farmers identify with their occupational category and the more they distance themselves from other occupational categories, the more they are prepared to participate in collective action. Whether identification occurs at the regional, national, or European level is less relevant, as is occupational pride. But permeability of group boundaries—in other words, how difficult it is to find another job—is important, even though this is opposite to what social identity theory would predict. The easier it is in the eyes of our respondents to find another job, the *more* prepared they are to take part in collective action to improve the status of their group (table 3).

Table 3 presents the results of three regression analyses. The first one concerns action preparedness as assessed in 1993. Group identification, permeability of group boundaries, and participation in farmers' organizations each contribute to the explanation of the intention to take part in collective action. As mentioned, action preparedness is fairly stable. Thus, it does not come as a surprise that action preparedness in 1993 is the best predictor of action preparedness in 1994. Nevertheless, in 1994 permeability of group boundaries does add significantly to the variance already explained. In 1995, again action preparedness in the year before explains most of the variance, but group identification and participation in farmers' organizations in addition contribute significantly. Thus, factors related to group identification (cognitive, behavioral, alternatives) do have a significant impact on action preparedness not only initially but as time goes by. In fact, in 1995, in addition to the impact it has directly, group identification contributes indirectly via action preparedness in the years before.

Group Identification and Action Participation

Group identification appears to have a direct impact on action participation as well. Table 4 presents the results of two logistic regression analyses with action participation in the year passed as the dependent variable. In 1994,

Table 3. Group Identification and Action Preparedness among Dutch Farmers, 1993–1995: Regression Analyses (OLS)

	Action Preparedness in		
	1993	1994	1995
Action preparedness			
In 1993		.670 (.055)	
In 1994			.714 (.052)
Group identification			
In 1993	.304 (.151)		
In 1995			.313 (.098)
Permeability of boundaries			
In 1993	.144 (.052)		
In 1994		.136 (.039)	
Participation in organizations			
In 1993	.210 (.038)		
In 1995			.140 (.057)
Intercept	1.04 (.580)	.493 (.183)	−.52 (.348)
R^2	.100	.512	.625
Number of cases	168	168	168

Note: Numbers in parentheses are standard errors.

Table 4. Group Identification and Protest Participation among Dutch Farmers, 1994 and 1995: Logistic Regression Analyses

	Participation in	
	1994	1995
Action preparedness		
In 1993	.814 (.282)	
In 1994		1.128 (.319)
Protest participation		
In 1994		1.422 (.615)
Group identification		
In 1993		1.385 (.691)
Participation in organization		
In 1994		.536 (.257)
Intercept	−4.7 (1.01)	−13.0 (3.10)
−2 log likelihood	104.791	109.621
Number of cases	168	168

Note: Numbers in parentheses are standard errors.

action participation is plainly determined by action preparedness as measured in 1993. Group identification does not have any impact on protest participation, not directly in any case. Indirectly it has, of course, via the impact of action preparedness on action participation. Protest participation in 1995, however, is a different story. In addition to action participation in the year before and action preparedness as measured in 1994, group identification adds significantly to the explanation of action participation. Obviously, not only was 1995 a turbulent year in that it brought an increase in farmers' protest, but more than the years before, such protest gave testimony of a collective identity, as the increased impact of group identification on action preparedness and protest participation demonstrates.

A Note on Causality

An interesting question that continues to occupy movement scholars is, of course, whether group identification produces participation or rather participation produces group identification. There are plausible arguments for both types of reasoning. Our panel design makes it possible to shed light on this question. Interestingly, the answer to this question differs for action preparedness and participation.

Table 5 provides the cross-lagged correlations of group identification and action preparedness and participation. Action preparedness in 1993 is a better predictor of group identification in 1995 than group identification in 1993 is of action preparedness in 1995. This suggests that action preparedness intensifies group identification, rather than group identification intensifying action preparedness. On the other hand, group identification in 1993 is a better predictor of participation in 1995 than participation in

Table 5. Cross-Lagged Correlations of Group Identification, Action Preparedness, and Action Participation among Dutch Farmers, 1993 and 1995

		Group Identification	
		1993	1995
Action preparedness	1993	.16	.34
—	1995	.16	.39
Action participation	1993	.04	.08
—	1995	.20	.17

1994 is of group identification in 1995. This suggests that identification produces participation, rather than the other way around.

In fact, the pattern is more complicated. After all, action preparedness is a powerful predictor of action participation, while action participation reinforces action preparedness. Hence, what remains are factors that reinforce one another. Action preparedness reinforces group identification. Group identification in its turn fosters action participation, which again strengthens action preparedness.

Determinants of Group Identification

Group identification (cognitive and behavioral) and perceived permeability of boundaries appear to be determinants of action preparedness, though the latter in an unexpected way. We want to follow the track one step further by asking: Who are those farmers who identify with their occupational group and feel that alternatives to farming are available? Interestingly, evidence suggests that it is farmers from larger farms who are younger and better educated, have an interest in politics, and are better informed and more knowledgeable about agricultural politics. Let us unpack this observation a bit more.

Especially in 1995, group identification is related to farm size and to political interest and knowledge (7 significant correlations on a total of 7; average correlation .22; correlations ranging from .18 to .31). Among the better-educated, politically interested, and informed farmers, this concerns more often identification with farmers at the national and European levels (32 significant correlations on a total of 42; average correlation .19; correlations ranging from .09 to .36).

Participation in farmers' organizations is related to farm size and level of education and political interest and knowledge (22 significant correlations on a total of 24; average correlation .24; correlations ranging from .14 to .41).

Perceived permeability of group boundaries, finally, is related to age and education. Farmers who are younger and better educated are more often convinced that they can easily find another job if they were to quit farming (correlations with age: .53, .53, and .54; correlations with level of education: .18, .22, .22).

Altogether, these correlations suggest that it is the most ready and able who identify with their occupational group and thus engage in collective action. This is, of course, fully in line with what resource mobilization theory would suggest. Protest seems to be staged by resourceful people. But our data suggest that it is resourcefulness translated into group identification that makes the difference.

Conclusions

In this chapter we have made the theoretical distinction between collective identity, social identity, and group identification. Collective identity was defined as a group characteristic, social identity as an individual characteristic, and group identification as the link between the two. From both social identity theory and social movement theory it was derived that group identification is a necessary condition for protest participation.

By way of illustration, empirical evidence on group identification among Dutch farmers was presented. Obviously, Dutch farmers identified strongly with their occupational group, the most with farmers in the region and the least with European farmers. Yet in-group identification with farmers at the European level did increase, which may signify a growing salience of categorization as a European farmer. In that regard it is important that higher levels of education and political interest and knowledge strengthen identification at the European level. This suggests that identification at a higher level of abstraction requires higher levels of political consciousness.

Over the three interviews we observed an increased participation in protest. More detailed analyses revealed that this was completely due to resistance against the government's policy regarding manure surpluses. As a consequence, the protesting population changed, but more important, correlations between group identification and protest participation increased. This we interpreted as indicating the growing salience and political relevance of an identity as farmer.

To those who believed in the usefulness of action preparedness as an indicator of protest participation, it must be comforting that intentions could predict participation even two years ahead. Others may argue that the correlation was never higher than .37. It is important to see that group identification adds to the impact of intention. Apparently, group identification not only raises the preparedness to participate but also makes people carry out their intentions. Not accidentally, participation in a farmers' organization plays a significant role in that regard. Presumably, this is a matter not only of identification but of being involved in mobilization networks as well.

As expected theoretically, group identification fosters protest participation (both action intention and actual participation). Interestingly, it is outgroup differentiation, more than in-group identification, that has an impact on action preparedness or participation. Even more interesting and certainly counter to the predictions of social identity theory is the finding that permeability of group boundaries stimulates action participation. Further analyses suggest that this is a matter of moral strength. Farmers' protest seems to be staged by a self-conscious group of farmers, who, rather than feeling stuck in a declining industry, are fighting to be able to continue a profession of which they are proud.

Notes

1. Surprisingly absent in both literatures is Stryker's identity theory (1980 and chapter 1 in this volume). Identity in that theoretical framework refers to self-cognitions tied to roles and through roles to positions in organized social relationships. Although it differs from social identity in that the latter refers to a group or category as a whole, role identity obviously, like social identity, is an individual belief.

2. Note that Swann and his collaborators (chapter 6, this volume) provide evidence suggesting that sometimes people seek confirmation of a negative self-view.

3. Social identity theory uses group and category as synonyms. In so doing it elides a fundamental distinction in Stryker's identity theory. In fact, social identity theory often operationalizes social identity as identification with a group rather than identification with a category, thus focusing on identities that, according to identity theory, are more salient. Indeed, much of social identity theory research concerns *salient* identities, but much less attention is given to what makes identities salient, a crucial question in the context of identity theory (Stryker 1987).

4. This finding diverges from those stemming from laboratory studies within the social identity framework but is in line with what one would predict on the basis of Folger's (1986) elaboration of relative deprivation theory (see Klandermans 1997 for a detailed discussion of the injustice component of collective action frames).

5. Group identification is akin to commitment to the group. This is confirmed by the way Mummendey et al. (1995) operationalized the concept. Therefore, a look at commitment literature is useful, as Kelly and Breinlinger (1996) demonstrate. Indeed, in the context of a study of participation in the labor movement, Kelly and Breinlinger operationalize group identification as commitment to the union.

References

Abrams, Dominique, and Nick Emler. 1991. "Self-Denial as a Paradox of Political and Regional Social Identity: Findings from a Study of 16- and 18-Year-Olds." *European Journal of Social Psychology* 22:279–365.

Andrews, Molly. 1991. *Lifetimes of Commitment: Aging, Politics, Psychology.* Cambridge: Cambridge University Press.

Barling, Julian, Clive Fullagar, and Kevin E. Kelloway. 1992. *The Union and Its Members: A Psychological Approach.* New York: Oxford University Press.

Brewer, Marilynn B. 1991. "The Social Self: On Being the Same and Different at the Same Time." *Personality and Social Psychology Bulletin* 17:475–82.

Brewer, Marilynn B., and Wendi Gardner. 1996. "Who Is This 'We'?: Levels of Collective Identity and Self-Representations." *Journal of Personality and Social Psychology* 71:83–93.

Brewer, Marilynn B., and Michael Silver. 1997. "Group Distinctiveness, Social Identity, and Collective Mobilization." Paper presented at the conference "Self, Identity, and Social Movements," Indianapolis, April 17–20.

Della Porta, Donatella, and Dieter Rucht. 1995. "Left-Libertarian Movements in Context: A Comparison of Italy and West Germany, 1965–1990." In *The Politics of Social Protest: Comparative Perspectives on States and Social Movements,* edited by J. Craig Jenkins and Bert Klandermans, 229–73. Minneapolis: University of Minnesota Press.

Ellemers, Naomi. 1993. "The Influence of Socio-Structural Variables on Identity Management Strategies." In *European Review of Social Psychology,* edited by Wolfgang Stroebe and Miles Hewstone, 4:27–58. Chichester, England: Wiley.

Folger Robert. 1986. "A Referent Cognition Theory of Relative Deprivation." In *Relative Deprivation and Social Comparison: The Ontario Symposium,* edited by James M. Olson, C. Peter Herman, and Mark P. Zanna, 4:33–56. Hillsdale, N.J.: Lawrence Erlbaum.

Gamson, William A. 1992a. *Talking Politics.* Cambridge: Cambridge University Press.

———. 1992b. "The Social Psychology of Collective Action." In *Frontiers in Social Movement Theory,* edited by Aldon D. Morris and Carol McClurg Mueller, 53–76. New Haven, Conn.: Yale University Press.

Gamson, William A., Bruce Fireman, and Steve Rytina. 1982. *Encounters with Unjust Authorities.* Homewood, Ill.: Dorsey Press.

Gurin, P., and A. Townsend. 1986. "Properties of Gender Identity and Their Implications for Gender Consciousness." *British Journal of Social Psychology* 25:139–48.

Hewstone, Miles, Wolfgang Stroebe, and Geoffrey Stephenson. 1996. *Introduction to Social Psychology: A European Perspective.* Oxford: Blackwell.

Hirsch, Eric L. 1990. "Sacrifice for the Cause: The Impact of Group Processes on Recruitment and Commitment in Protest Movements." *American Sociological Review* 55:243–54.

Kelly, Caroline. 1993. "Group Identification, Intergroup Perceptions, and Collective Action." In *European Review of Social Psychology,* edited by Wolfgang Stroebe and Miles Hewstone, 4:59–83. Chichester, England: Wiley.

Kelly, Caroline, and Sara Breinlinger. 1996. *The Social Psychology of Collective Action.* Basingstoke, England: Taylor and Francis.

Klandermans, Bert. 1990. "Linking the 'Old' and the 'New': Movement Networks in the Netherlands." In *Challenging the Political Order: New Social and Political*

Movements in Western Democracies, edited by Russell J. Dalton and Manfred Kuechler, 122–36. Cambridge, England: Polity Press.

———. 1997. *The Social Psychology of Protest.* Oxford: Blackwell.

Klandermans, Bert, Marga de Weerd, Maria Costa, and Jose-Manuel Sabucedo. 1999. "Injustice and Adversarial Frames in a Supranational Political Context: Farmers' Protest in the Netherlands and Spain." In *Social Movements in a Globalizing World,* edited by Hanspeter Kriesi, Donatella della Porta, and Dieter Rucht, 134–47. London: Macmillan.

Levine, John M., and Richard L. Moreland. 1991. "Culture and Socialization in Work Groups." In *Perspectives on Socially Shared Cognition,* edited by Lauren B. Resnick, John M. Levine, and Stephanie D. Teasley, 257–79. Washington, D.C.: American Psychological Association.

Major, Brenda. 1994. "From Social Inequality to Personal Entitlement: The Role of Social Comparisons, Legitimacy Appraisals, and Group Membership." *Advances in Experimental Social Psychology* 26:293–355.

McAdam, Doug, John McCarthy, and Mayer N. Zald. 1996. *Comparative Perspectives on Social Movements: Political Opportunities, Mobilizing Structures, and Cultural Framing.* Cambridge: Cambridge University Press.

Melucci, Alberto. 1989. *Nomads of the Present: Social Movements and Individual Needs in Contemporary Society.* London: Hutchinson Radius.

———. 1996. *Challenging Codes: Collective Action in the Information Age.* Cambridge: Cambridge University Press.

Mummendey, Amelie, Andreas Klink, Rosemarie Mielke, Michael Wenzel, and Matthias Blanz. 1999. "Socio-Structural Characteristics of Intergroup Relations and Identity Management Strategies: Results from a Field Study in East Germany." *European Journal of Social Psychology* 29:259–86.

Olivier, Johan L. 1991. "State Repression and Collective Action in South Africa, 1970–84." *South African Journal of Sociology* 22:109–17.

Reicher, Steve D. 1996. "The Battle of Westminster: Developing the Social Identity Model of Crowd Behaviour in Order to Explain the Initiation and Development of Collective Conflict." *European Journal of Social Psychology* 26:115–34.

Stryker, Sheldon. 1980. *Symbolic Interactionism: A Structural Version.* Menlo Park, Calif.: Benjamin-Cummings.

———. 1987. "Identity Theory: Developments and Extensions." In *Self and Identity: Sociological Perspectives,* edited by Krysia Yardley and Terry Honess, 89–104. London: Wiley.

Tajfel, Henri, and John C. Turner. 1986. "The Social Identity Theory of Intergroup Behaviour." In *The Social Psychology of Intergroup Relations,* edited by S. Worchel and W. G. Austin, 7–24. Monterey, Calif.: Brooks/Cole.

Taylor, Verta, and Nancy E. Whittier. 1992. "Collective Identity in Social Movement Communities: Lesbian Feminist Mobilization." In *Frontiers of Social Movement Theory,* edited by Aldon D. Morris and Carol Mueller, 104–30. New Haven: Yale University Press.

———. 1995. "Analytical Approaches to Social Movement Culture: The Culture of the Women's Movement." In *Social Movements and Culture,* edited by Hank Johnston and Bert Klandermans, 163–87. Minneapolis/London: University of Minnesota Press/UCL Press.

Turner, John C. 1987. *Rediscovering the Social Group: A Self-Categorization Theory.* Oxford: Blackwell.

Wright, Stephen C., Donald M. Taylor, and Fathali M. Moghaddam. 1990. "Responding to Membership in a Disadvantaged Group: From Acceptance to Collective Protest." *Journal of Personality and Social Psychology* 58:994–1003.

Part II
Theoretical and Conceptual Developments

Personal Identity

4

Value Identities, Self-Motives, and Social Movements

Viktor Gecas

The concept of identity has become a fertile ground for understanding collective behavior, personal experience, and the relationship between self and society (see Baumeister 1986 and Weigert 1983 for historical overviews). *Identity* generally refers to who or what one is. But the terms in which this issue is addressed vary considerably, giving rise to a diversity of meanings.[1]

Social psychological approaches to identity have emphasized its situated or locational character. Stone's (1962) influential conceptualization views identity as locating a person in social space by virtue of the relationships and memberships that it implies. This social space is typically viewed as a social structural space, that is, as a relatively enduring pattern of social arrangements or interrelationships within a particular group, organization, or society as a whole. The units or elements constituting these social structures give rise to several important types of identities and are the bases for several identity theories: role identity (Stryker 1980 and chapter 1 in this volume) focuses on the location of individuals within various role systems (e.g., occupational roles, family roles); group identity, dealing with group memberships and intergroup relations (e.g., ethnic groups, minority groups, gangs), has been the focus of the social identity theories of Tajfel (1981) and Turner (1985); and collective identity (Melucci 1995), dealing with shared self-definitions in the service of a collective effort, has recently emerged as a focus within the social movements literature (Pichardo 1997).

These social structural contexts are indeed important sources of identity, critical to self-definitions, social interaction, and the maintenance of the social order. But they are not the only social sources of identity. Values and value systems constitute another important location for identities, but one that has been relatively neglected by identity theorists, despite Turner's (1968) suggestive observation that "the self-conception starts with values and aspirations, and continues to be represented in value and aspiration terms" (97) and Smith's (1963) discussion of the importance of "self-values" as components of self-definition as well as standards individuals use for self-evaluation. Identities anchored in values and value systems are important elements of self-conception, perhaps among the most important, since values give meaning, purpose, and direction to our lives.

In principle, any self-characterization (e.g., wishes, desires, achievements, roles, values, attitudes) can be considered in identity terms, as Rosenberg's (1979) definition of self-concept suggests. But some elements of self-conception are sociologically more important than others. A strong case has already been made for the importance of role identities, by Stryker (1980, 1987) and others identified with identity theory, linking individuals with social structures. Similarly, group identities are structurally important in that they provide a basis for in-group identification and solidarity and affect the nature of intergroup relations. I believe an equally strong case can be made for the importance of value identities, in linking individuals to cultural systems and to social groups or collectivities with similar value identities, as is typically the case in social movements.

There is certainly an overlap between value-based identities and identities grounded in social relationships and group memberships, since most role identities and group identities have value components. We may value our group memberships and role identities, incorporating these into our value systems. Furthermore, some role identities and group identities are associated with specific values. Most institutional role identities have value components. For example, physicians are expected to value life, ease suffering, show compassion; professors are expected to value knowledge and learning; and parents should love and care for their children. In addition, group memberships may imply certain values, such as loyalty, self-sacrifice, and solidarity. In short, values pervade most aspects of our lives, and few identities of any type are value-neutral.

However, there are important differences in emphasis and orientation between value-based identities and identities based primarily on roles or group memberships. Value-based identities are more transcendent than are identities based on roles or even on most group memberships. That is, they are less situation-bound, typically relevant across a range of diverse situations. The value domain as the locational context for identities places a greater emphasis on culture than on social structure, and on the moral context of identities.[2] C. Taylor (1989, 27), a philosopher, underscores the essential link between identity and morality when he writes: "To know who you are is to be oriented in moral space, a space in which questions arise about what is good and bad, what is worth doing and what is not, what has meaning and importance for you and what is trivial and secondary." Taylor also suggests that identities constitute an important basis for one's sense of authenticity as well as one's self-esteem and self-efficacy. I argue in this chapter that identities based on values have special relevance for a social psychological understanding of social movements, since the value systems and ideologies associated with social movements have identity implications affecting members' commitment and sense of authenticity.

The Nature of Values and Value-Based Identities

In general, values are defined as conceptions or beliefs about desirable modes of conduct or states of being that transcend specific situations, guide decision making and the evaluation of events, and are ordered by relative importance (Rokeach 1973; Schwartz and Bilsky 1990; Shamir 1990). Values serve as standards by which to live, as well as goals for which to strive.[3] In both senses they demand something of the person, which may involve pain, self-sacrifice, and certainly effort. The consequence of acting in accordance with one's values, Shamir (1990) observes, is not a sense of pleasure but rather a sense of affirmation attained when the person abides by his or her moral commitments. Values tend to be relatively enduring (more so than attitudes and preferences) and relatively transituational (more so than roles). They are important elements of culture providing meaning, purpose, and direction to the participants in that culture.

Even though values, defined as beliefs, are primarily cognitive, they are emotionally charged. People feel pride and satisfaction in the affirmation of their values, guilt and shame in not living up to their values, and anger or fear when their values are threatened. These emotional concomitants of values are part of the motivational force of values and value systems.

Rokeach (1973, 1979) provides the most extensive social psychological treatment of values. He distinguishes between two types of values: "instrumental" and "terminal," reflecting the familiar distinction between means and ends or goals.[4] Instrumental values consist of such characteristics or traits as "honest," "brave," "responsible" (there are eighteen of these in Rokeach's measure). Terminal values include such concepts as "freedom," "equality," "pleasure," "a world of beauty." A person's value system, according to Rokeach, is a hierarchy of these values based on their relative importance.[5]

Despite its conceptual appeal, the distinction between "instrumental" and "terminal" values is not always clear-cut. Values designated as means (instrumental) can become ends (terminal) and vice versa, as Schwartz and Bilsky (1990) point out. Furthermore, some terminal values (e.g., pleasure) may become instrumental to other terminal values (e.g., happiness), and some instrumental values can become ends served by other instrumental values. So the distinction between instrumental and terminal values blurs on closer examination. Yet it is useful for our purposes to distinguish between these two types of values, although not necessarily with the labels Rokeach provides. We can distinguish between values emphasizing desired qualities of characters or personality (the "instrumental" group) from those emphasizing desired social or personal conditions (the "terminal" group). These give rise to two types of value identities discussed below.

Although Rokeach did not deal explicitly with identities, and only in a limited way with self-concept via the self-esteem motive, his value scheme can easily be adapted to the notion of value-based identities. All that is required is that individuals conceive of themselves in terms of the values they hold. In the same manner in which roles become the basis for role identities, commitment to values and conceptions of oneself in terms of one's values are the basis for value identities. Values such as "freedom" and "equality" become the value identities: "I am a person who stands for freedom and equality." It should also be mentioned that value identities, like other identities, are not restricted to self-attributions. They may also involve attributions made by others, as in "labeling" and "altercasting." These types of identity attributions and misattributions may involve negative as well as positive identities. Negative identity labels, of course, are more likely to be contested or denied by those so labeled.

Value identities, as elements of self-definition, can refer to desired personal qualities and desired social conditions. Elsewhere I used the concept "character identity" (Gecas and Mortimer 1987) to refer to value-based identities that are typically expressed as character traits such as "honest," "brave," "compassionate." Character identities emphasize the kind of person one is, whereas role identities and collective identities specify what one is. There is, however, a connection between character identities and role identities. Some role identities become infused with value connotations or come to imply certain character traits (e.g., the "compassionate nurse," the "devoted mother," the "brave soldier"). There may also be a self-selection factor in that certain kinds of people, possessing certain instrumental values, seek out roles associated with these values. However, character identities, even if originally associated with particular role identities, can be more diffuse and less situation-specific than are role identities.

Even though character identities are less situation-specific than are role identities, they are enacted, contested, and affirmed within specific situations. In fact, the symbolic interactionist emphasis on negotiating identities in social interactions is most appropriate to these character identities. It is this aspect of self-concept that individuals are most likely to strive to protect in their self-presentations and impression management activities (Goffman 1959). Interactionist discussions of "accounts" (Scott and Lyman 1968) and "disclaimers" (Hewitt and Stokes 1975) focus on the kinds of explanations, justifications, and excuses that people use for the sake of presenting self as a certain kind of person—a competent and morally acceptable person.

For most people, character identities constitute an important basis for self-evaluation because of their relevance for assessments of competence and morality. Rokeach built these two dimensions into his discussion of instrumental values and stated that the "ought" character of values (i.e., that we *ought* to act this way or to follow these principles) is mostly applicable to those instrumental values concerning morality than to those concerning competence. This may be an overly restrictive view of "moral values," since morality is also relevant to various terminal values, especially when they are part of political or religious ideologies. For example, values such as "equality," "freedom," and "salvation" have strong moral implications for those committed to these values and value identities. To falter or fail in the pursuit of these values, therefore, is to falter morally.

However, the interconnections between values, self, and morality are more complicated than this discussion suggests. The extent to which values and value identities serve as guides for moral behavior depends, among other things, on one's general moral orientation. Distinguishing between the "justice orientation" guiding Kohlberg's (1981) theory of moral development and the "care orientation" guiding Gilligan's (1982) moral theory, Kristiansen and Hotte (1996) suggest that the relationship between one's values and one's moral behavior is strongest when one's moral orientation is based on justice rather than on care, since the former emphasizes general values and principles as a guide to moral behavior and the latter puts more emphasis on situational contingencies and interpersonal concerns. A parallel argument is offered by Markus and Kitayama (1991) in their analyses of the difference between individuals with self-schemata that are "independent" versus those whose self-schemata are "interdependent"—values and value identities are more likely to serve as guides to moral behavior for those with "independent self-construals" than for those with "interdependent selves." Other factors may also affect the strength of these relationships, such as level of moral development, clarity of one's values and self-conceptions, degree of value conflict and ambivalence (see Kristiansen and Hotte 1996 and Murray 1993 for discussions of these issues).

Whereas instrumental values characterize a person's dispositions and character traits, terminal values and the identities based on them are more general and abstract expressions of goals and desired states of being. Values such as "world peace," "a comfortable life," "freedom," and "equality" are examples of terminal values from Rokeach's measure. They signify, as Rokeach maintained, desired goals or end states of being. But they also signify more: they signify the ideological grounding of the individual in the form of political, religious, or philosophical doctrines. That is, they are more likely to be found within *systems* of values and beliefs (Williams 1979). They characterize the moral or political or philosophical stand that persons take and in terms of which define themselves. This view is similar to C. Taylor's (1989) conception of identity as a moral stand: "To know who I am is to know where I stand." The power and importance of this category of values lie in their systemic properties, particularly in the form of ideologies and theologies.[6]

Identity and Ideology

Ideology refers to a body of doctrine, a system of values and beliefs, a set of myths and symbols of a social group or a social movement, which provide group members with a common vocabulary for understanding their world and justifications either for maintaining it or for changing it. Ideologies, as Warren (1990) argues, have a wide range of identity implications, such as telling individuals who they are, where they fit into the social hierarchy, who is a member of a community and who is not, how they relate to authority, and what kind of power and dignity they possess and providing a moral framework for social relations and individual experience.

The identity implications of ideologies are broader than the value identities ideologies provide. They may also provide important role identities and membership or collective identities as well as a worldview integrating these various elements. The power and persistence of ideologies, even when they seem to be working against the self-interests of those who hold them, are in the identities and values they provide for the self. These value-based identities give meaning, purpose, and direction to individuals, thereby motivating individuals to maintain and protect their ideologies. This is most evident under conditions of threat. Religions, especially fundamentalist religions, are among the most inclusive ideologies. They provide their members with an extensive system of values and principles to live by, a set of group symbols and rituals to maintain the various identities in systems of relationships in this world and thereafter, and various defenses against threat to the ideology. A good illustration can be found in Zygmunt's (1970) study of Jehovah's Witnesses who have been able to maintain and affirm their collective identity even in the face of numerous prophetic failures (predicting the end of the established world order). In fact, under conditions of external threat, members may become even more committed to their ideologies.

Ideologies are important contexts for the maintenance of value identities. But there is a negative side to ideologies as well for self and society. Ideologies may help to sustain the self, but sometimes at the expense of interpersonal tolerance, understanding, and growth. As Gouldner (1976) and Warren (1990) observe, the maintenance of one's ideology, especially politically or religiously extreme ideologies, involves considerable self-delusion and selective perception. To the extent that ideology becomes the grounding of identity, a person's being becomes contingent on the maintenance of that ideology and thus sets limits on the capacity to change oneself or the ideology (Warren 1990, 47). Self-identity is gained through ideologies, but sometimes at the expense of a capacity for choice. The more rigid and absolutistic the ideology, the more likely these negative consequences for the self. Yet ideologies are important for social order and even more important for social movements and social change.

Collective Identities, Value Identities, and Social Movements

With the rise of what has come to be called the "new social movements" (e.g., feminism, environmentalism, and peace activism, as opposed to the older class-based social movements), self-concept concerns have moved into the foreground, mainly in the form of "collective identity" (see Pichardo 1997 and Snow and Oliver 1995 for reviews). Melucci (1995) suggests that the construction of a collective identity is the most important task of a social movement and a key element in understanding its dynamics. For Melucci, collective identity is an evolving definition that group members have of themselves and their social world, one that emerges out of the joint actions of group members, and it is central to the development of the group's goals, strategies, and field of action (Snow and Oliver 1995, 558–89). V. Taylor (1989, 771) provides a concise definition of collective identity in her studies of women's movements: "Collective identity is the shared definition of a group that derives from its members' common interests and

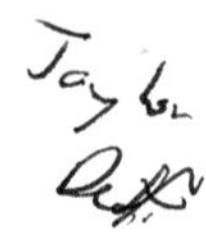

solidarity." Gamson (1992, 55) suggests the following conceptualization, based on his studies of the equal rights movement, women's movement, and the New Left: "Collective identity concerns the mesh between the individual and cultural systems. More specifically, the question is how individuals' sense of who they are becomes engaged with a definition shared by coparticipants in some effort at social change."

There are two key elements that emerge out of these definitions of collective identity: (1) group members' sense of themselves as part of a group—a sense of "we"; and (2) a cognitive framework or political consensus that specifies goals, means, and fields of action. The first is the membership component, focusing on definition of self as part of a social group. This is similar to Tajfel's (1981) and Turner's (1985) discussions of "social identity" and "self-categorization" as the basis for in-group and out-group relations (but see chapter 3 in this volume for a discussion of the differences between social identity and collective identity). The second component emphasizes the cultural and ideological framework of the collective identity, the shared values, definition of the situation, and plan of action. As part of their general definition of the political situation, group members attribute their discontent to structural, cultural, or systemic causes rather than to personal failings or individual deviance (Taylor and Whittier 1992, 114). Out of these definitions and attributions notions of justice and injustice take shape, and strategies of political action develop. This is the locus of value identities for members of a social movement.

Value identities are embedded within collective identities as key elements within the ideologies of social movements. In fact, a social movement is typically identified as representing and advocating one or a few specific values, such as "equality," "liberty," "pro-life," "pro-choice," "pro-environment." Such values as integral parts of a movement's ideology become important aspects of members' self-definitions, of their value identities, with implications for individuals' commitment to the social movement. They may even provide the moral foundation for a person's self-conception (in C. Taylor's [1989] sense of the moral self). This is evident in White and Fraser's (chapter 15, this volume) description of the Republican Sinn Féin movement in Ireland. This movement for political freedom from British rule is described in moral as well as political terms. Members' commitment to the Republican Sinn Féin movement is a commitment to value identities with strong moral (almost religious) overtones. Failure to live up to the requirements and expectations imposed by these collective and value identities is viewed as a moral failure.

Value Identities, Self-Motives, and Commitment to Social Movements

In one sense, value identities provide an obvious basis for members' commitment to a social group or movement. To the extent that group members are committed to the values constitutive of the group's ideology, define themselves in terms of these values, and think of these values as true or right, they are likely to be committed to the group or movement and its goals. This is what Kanter (1972) calls moral commitment in her three-category typology—commitment based on the beliefs and values for which the group stands.

However, how do people become committed to a group's values and develop self-conceptions or identities based on those values? There could be many reasons, such as instrumental or utilitarian attachments to a group; the development of affective bonds with group members (Kanter's other two types of commitment), which then lead to adoption of the group's values and ideology; processes of socialization; or identification with and persuasion by a charismatic leader. These may all be differentially important for members of a group. But there is also another set of processes relevant to value-identity commitment. These processes constitute the motivational dynamics of the self-concept and are referred to as self-motives. It is this connection that I consider a bit further.

Elsewhere (Gecas 1986, 1991) I have argued for the importance of three self-motives as the motivational foundation of the self-concept: self-esteem, self-efficacy, and authenticity. The self-esteem motive refers to the motivation to view oneself favorably and to try to maintain or enhance a favorable evaluation of oneself. The self-esteem motive is the basis for a number of contemporary theories in social psychology (see Gecas and Burke 1995 for a review). Self-efficacy is the motivation to perceive oneself as a causal agent in one's environment, as efficacious and competent. The deficit, and typically undesirable condition, of self-efficacy is experienced as powerlessness, helplessness, or inferiority. Authenticity refers to the individual's strivings for meaning, coherence, and significance. It deals with assessments of what is real and what is false with regard to oneself and suggests that individuals are motivated to experience themselves as meaningful and real. It also implies that individuals strive for congruence between their self-values and their behavior, since lack of congruence leads to feelings of inauthenticity (Erickson 1995; Gecas 1991). These self-motivations imply that by virtue of having a self-concept the individual is motivated to maintain a favorable assessment of it, to conceive of self as efficacious and consequential, and to experience it as meaningful and real.

Value identities are relevant to all three of these self-motives. Character identities, or identities based on what Rokeach called instrumental values, are sources of much of our self-esteem and self-efficacy, since these value identities are typically cast in terms of morality and competence. Value identities referring to general goals and end states are the basis of much of our feeling of authenticity. Being true to one's values and principles is being true to oneself in a fundamental way. Conversely, discrepancies between one's value identities and one's behavior result in feelings of inauthenticity. Of course, violations of valued character identities could also result in feelings of inauthenticity. To the extent that a social movement can sustain or enhance these self-motives (self-esteem, efficacy, and authenticity) via the ideology and value identities that it provides, it increases member loyalty and commitment to the social movement.

The extent to which these value-based self-motives are mobilized in the service of a social movement's goals depends in large part on the leadership of the social movement. Such mobilization is more likely to occur when the leadership is charismatic. A charismatic leader leads by force of personality and the perception that he or she symbolizes or personifies the values and goals of the social movement. Charismatic leaders are able to transform the needs and interests of followers from self-interest to collective interests by virtue of their moral authority, their appeals to collective values and goals, and their reliance on symbolic inspirational and emotion-arousing activities (House, Spangler, and Waycke 1991; Shamir, House, and Arthur 1993). President John F. Kennedy's admonition "Ask not what your country can do for you, but what you can do for your country" and Martin Luther King's "dream" of a future America in which racial equality had been achieved inspired millions of citizens to work for noble causes.

Charismatic leaders succeed in mobilizing group members because they are able to (and they are successful to the extent that they are able to) tap into the self-concepts of the followers. Group goals are transformed into moral imperatives and connected to value identities; the performance of even mundane tasks in the service of group goals is conceptualized as a reflection of members' character identities and elevated in value; collective efficacy is associated with personal efficacy and worth. By recruiting the self-concepts of group members, increasing the salience of collective identities and values, linking behaviors and goals to these identities and values, charismatic leaders motivate followers through the creation of personal commitment (Shamir, House, and Arthur 1993). In short, charismatic leaders increase the intrinsic value of effort and group goals by linking them to valued aspects of members' self-concepts, thereby harnessing the motivational forces of self-worth, self-efficacy, and authenticity.

Research on commitment to social movements would benefit from greater attention to self-motives, especially those deriving from value identities. Of the three, self-efficacy has received the most attention from social movements scholars, especially as related to political activism. Research on political activism suggests that high self-efficacy combined with perceptions of system unresponsiveness or low trust in the political system generates not only resentment but also efforts at political change (see Gecas 1989 and Snow and Oliver 1995 for reviews). Paige (1971), for example, found that those who participated in the Newark riots of 1967 tended to score high on self-efficacy but low on political trust. Concerted political action may also depend on perceptions of the group's or movement's efficacy, or what Bandura calls "collective efficacy" (1986, 449–52). Collective efficacy refers to members' judgments about their group's capabilities to engage in successful political action. Collective efficacy can be expected to affect personal efficacy of group members. In addition, participation in political activism may itself increase feelings of personal and collective efficacy, especially if the actions are successful, thereby increasing members' commitment to their group and to their cause. In general, research and theory suggest that persons are more likely to become committed to groups that strengthen their sense of efficacy (Gecas 1989; Lawler 1992).

The self-esteem motive, which is ubiquitous in most areas of social psychology, is relatively absent in studies of social movements (but see chapters 9 and 10 in this volume). However, its relevance for members' involvement with and commitment to a social movement is fairly obvious. We would expect that group involvement that increases members' self-esteem, that makes members feel good about themselves, also increases their commitment to the group. Some evidence for this expectation can be found in the work of Tajfel and his colleagues on social identity theory (see Hogg and Abrams 1990), which suggests that identification with a group (in-group) leads to the development of favorable stereotypes of group members and unfavorable stereotypes of out-group members. This tendency to form favorable and unfavorable attitudes based on group membership, social identity theory suggests, is a function of the self-esteem motive. This line of theory and research suggests that members' commitment to their group is a function of the self-esteem they derive from group membership.

Authenticity is the least visible self-motive, either here or anywhere else in social psychology. However, it has great potential in helping us to understand the social psychology of social movements and the basis of members' commitment. Authenticity based on value identities connects individuals with the moral and ideological systems of groups and movements. Indeed, it may be the most important basis of commitment to a group. I propose that to the extent that value identities derived from a group's moral and ideological framework provide group members with meaning, purpose, and significance, thereby contributing to members' sense of authenticity, members' commitment to the group increases. There are a few related strands within social psychology that seem to resonate with the authenticity motive. Steele's (1988) work on "self-affirmation" and Swann's (1983; chapter 6, this volume) on "self-verification" bear a resemblance to the self-authenticity motive in that they emphasize motivational processes that affirm or verify valued aspects of the self-concept. There is a difference in emphasis, however. The emphasis in "self-affirmation" and "self-verification" conceptualizations is on the extent to which the external environment (i.e., other people) supports or affirms or verifies a particular aspect of a person's self-concept and the consequences of this environmental response for individual well-being and interpersonal relations. The emphasis in the "authenticity motive" is on the need or motivation to act in accordance with one's true self and on the consequences of not doing so (i.e., inauthenticity). Related concerns with individuals' search for meaning and purpose, and the cultural systems of meanings and values from which these derive, are more integral to the authenticity motive than they are to the self-affirmation and self-verification motives.

Values, and the identities based on them, are motivationally important because they are directly relevant to the self's motivational system composed of self-worth, self-efficacy, and self-authenticity. The success of a social movement depends to a large extent on its ability to commit followers to the value identities it provides in pursuit of the movement's goals.

Conclusion

Political conflicts in modern society, as Goldstein and Rayner (1994) observe, are increasingly centered on issues of identity. This is certainly evident in the various nationalistic, ethnic, and tribal conflicts around the world, involving clashes between group or collective identities. It is also increasingly evident in political conflicts within modern societies, especially as expressed in the "new social movements." These identity conflicts are more likely to be value-based. The concept of value-based or value identities underscores the social psychological aspects of these conflicts grounded in philosophical and ideological differences.

It could be argued that the value identities provided by social movements have a clarity and forcefulness that is lacking in most other aspects of modern society. With the decline of religion and tradition, Baumeister

(1991) and others (e.g., Weigert 1991) maintain, values have become problematic in modern society and moral issues less clear-cut. Consequently, identities based on equivocal values may also be problematic. Some of the appeal of social movements in modern times might be the clarity of the values and value identities they provide.

Value identities, although overlapping with role identities and collective identities, point in a somewhat different direction than these other identity constructs. They place greater emphasis on the cultural and moral context of self-definitions and provide the terms within which concepts of justice and injustice take shape. As such, they also have a direct bearing on one's sense of authenticity and inauthenticity depending on the congruence between one's value identities and one's actions. Shame and guilt can be viewed as the emotional consequences of a lack of congruence between value identities, especially those dealing with character-relevant values, and behavior. It is uncertain whether people act in accordance with their value identities and the moral obligations they imply because of the sense of authenticity or affirmation they derive from such action or because of fear that not acting this way would result in feelings of guilt or shame (Shamir 1990). But either as "pull" factors or as "push" factors, value identities constitute powerful motivations for individuals, constituting some of the most important elements of the self-concept.

Notes

1. A common distinction in the literature on identity is between "personal identity" and "social identity." The former emphasizes the construction or development of a unique, integrated sense of self and is associated with the work of Erik Erikson (1959) and other developmental psychologists. The latter is characteristic of social psychological approaches emphasizing the multiplicity of identities that individuals possess by virtue of their group memberships and role relationships. This is somewhat of an arbitrary distinction, since all identities are social in that they are all products of social and symbolic processes. Yet there is some merit in this distinction. "Identity" involves both commonality (e.g., membership) and differentiation (distinctness). "Social identities" are more likely to emphasize commonalities, in the form of group memberships or categorical identifications; "personal identities" are more likely to emphasize idiosyncratic or unique characteristics, such as personal name, unique experiences, or biographies. But these are matters of degree rather than kind, since social identities in their configuration result in "unique" self-concepts and much of our personal biographies consist of experiences within our various social identities.

2. This is not to deny the relevance of situational factors in the *enactment* of values and morality. Research on bystander intervention in helping behavior (Latane and

Darley 1970) as well as Milgram's (1974) studies of conformity are testimony to the power of situational factors in affecting morally charged behaviors.

3. This conception of value as a type of belief contrasts with the economic conception of value as a calculation of the worth or utility of an object in use or exchange (see Ball-Rokeach and Loges 1992).

4. The distinction between "instrumental" and "terminal" values is a common feature of value definitions (see, for example, Braithwaite and Law 1985). This, of course, is not the only basis for distinguishing values. Another common distinction is individualistic/collectivistic values.

5. Whether the structure of one's values is hierarchical in a linear sense, as Rokeach maintained, is a matter of dispute. A case could be made for a pattern of overlapping clusters of values, since many values exist within systems (e.g., ideologies), with the clusters perhaps arranged in a loose hierarchy.

6. Rokeach did not go very far in this direction, focusing instead on specific values and their relative rankings. He did, however, take an interesting step in the direction of values and ideologies by proposing a two-value model of political ideology based on the values of freedom and equality. By juxtaposing freedom and equality, each on a continuum from high desirability to low desirability, four value combinations are created describing four major political orientations: socialism = equality high + freedom high; communism = equality high + freedom low; fascism = equality low + freedom low; and capitalism = equality low + freedom high. This is a simple but interesting typology. Each of these general political orientations or ideologies is, of course, composed of more than just these two values in their positive and negative forms (see Braithwaite 1994 for an elaboration of this scheme). However, since Rokeach was much less interested in ideologies than he was in specific values, he did not move very far in the direction of value systems or in exploring specific ideologies. These, however, constitute important moorings for our value identities, especially those value identities referring to desired social conditions or end states.

References

Ball-Rokeach, Sandra J., and William E. Loges. 1992. "Value Theory and Research." In *Encyclopedia of Sociology*, edited by E. F. Borgatta and M. L. Borgatta, 2222–28. New York: Macmillan.

Bandura, Albert. 1986. *Social Foundations of Thought and Action: A Social Cognitive Theory.* Englewood Cliffs, N.J.: Prentice-Hall.

Baumeister, Roy F. 1986. *Identity: Cultural Change and the Struggle for Self.* New York: Oxford University Press.

———. 1991. *Meanings of Life.* New York: Guilford Press.

Braithwaite, Valerie A. 1994. "Beyond Rokeach's Equality-Freedom Model: Two-Dimensional Values in a One-Dimensional World." *Journal of Social Issues* 50:67–94.

Braithwaite, Valerie A., and H. G. Law. 1985. "Structure of Human Values: Testing the Adequacy of the Rokeach Value Survey." *Journal of Personality and Social Psychology* 49:250–63.

Erickson, Rebecca J. 1995. "The Importance of Authenticity for Self and Society." *Symbolic Interaction* 18:121–44.

Erikson, Erik H. 1959. "Identity and the Life Cycle." *Psychological Issues* 1:1–171.

Gamson, William. 1992. "The Social Psychology of Collective Action." In *Frontiers in Social Movement Theory,* edited by A. D. Morris and C. M. Mueller, 53–76. New Haven: Yale University Press.

Gecas, Viktor. 1986. "The Motivational Significance of Self-Concept for Socialization Theory." In *Advances in Group Processes,* edited by E. Lawler, 3:131–56. Greenwich, Conn.: JAI Press.

———. 1989. "The Social Psychology of Self-Efficacy." *Annual Review of Sociology* 15:291–316.

———. 1991. "The Self-Concept as a Basis for a Theory of Motivation." In *The Self-Society Dynamic: Cognition, Emotion, and Action,* edited by J. A. Howard and P. L. Callero, 171–87. New York: Cambridge University Press.

Gecas, Viktor, and Peter J. Burke. 1995. "Self and Identity." In *Sociological Perspectives on Social Psychology,* edited by K. S. Cook, G. A. Fine, and J. S. House, 41–67. Boston: Allyn and Bacon.

Gecas, Viktor, and Jaylan T. Mortimer. 1987. "Stability and Change in the Self-Concept from Adolescence to Adulthood." In *Self and Identity: Perspectives across the Lifespan,* edited by T. Honess and K. Yardley, 265–86. London: Routledge and Kegan Paul.

Gilligan, Carol. 1982. *In a Different Voice.* Cambridge: Harvard University Press.Goffman, Erving. 1959. *The Presentation of Self in Everyday Life.* New York: Doubleday and Co.

Goldstein, Jonah, and Jeremy Rayner. 1994. "The Politics of Identity in Late Modern Society." *Theory and Society* 23:367–84.

Gouldner, Alvin. 1976. *The Dialectic of Ideology and Technology.* New York: Oxford University Press.

Hewitt, John P., and Robert Stokes. 1975. "Disclaimers." *American Sociological Review* 40:1–11.

Hogg, Michael A., and Dominic Abrams. 1990. "Social Motivation, Self-Esteem, and Social Identity." In *Social Identity Theory: Constructive and Critical Advances,* edited by D. Abrams and M. A. Hogg, 30–47. New York: Harvester.

House, Robert J., D. Spangler, and J. Waycke. 1991. "Personality and Charisma in the U.S. Presidency: A Psychological Theory of Leadership Effectiveness." *Administrative Science Quarterly* 36:364–96.

Kanter, Rosabeth. 1972. *Commitment and Community: Communes and Utopias in Sociological Perspective.* Cambridge: Harvard University Press.

Kohlberg, Lawrence. 1981. *The Philosophy of Moral Development.* San Francisco: Harper and Row.

Kristiansen, Connie M., and Alan M. Hotte. 1996. "Morality and the Self." In *The Psychology of Values: The Ontario Symposium,* edited by C. Seligman, J. M. Olson, and M. P. Zanna, 8:73–105. Mahwah, N.J.: Lawrence Erlbaum.

Latane, Bib, and John M. Darley. 1970. *The Unresponsive Bystander: Why Doesn't He Help?* New York: Appleton.

Lawler, Edward J. 1992. "Affective Attachments in Nested Groups: A Choice-Process Theory." *American Sociological Review* 57:327–39.

Markus, Hazel R., and S. Kitayama. 1991. "Culture and the Self: Implications for Cognition, Emotion, and Motivation." *Psychological Review* 98:224–53.

Melucci, Alberto. 1995. "The Process of Collective Identity." In *Social Movements and Culture,* edited by H. Johnston and B. Klandermans, 41–63. Minneapolis: University of Minnesota Press.

Milgram, Stanley. 1974. *Obedience to Authority.* New York: Harper and Row.

Murray, Thomas H. 1993. "Moral Reasoning in Social Context." *Journal of Social Issues* 40:85–200.

Paige, J. M. 1971. "Political Orientation and Riot Participation." *American Sociological Review* 36:810–20.

Pichardo, N. A. 1997. "The New Social Movements: A Critical Review." *Annual Review of Sociology* 23:411–30.

Rokeach, Milton. 1973. *The Nature of Human Values.* New York: Free Press.

———. 1979. *Understanding Human Values: Individual and Societal.* New York: Free Press.

Rosenberg, Morris. 1979. *Conceiving the Self.* New York: Basic Books.

Schwartz, Shalom H., and Bilksy, Wolfgang. 1990. "Toward a Theory of the Universal Content and Structure of Values: Extensions and Cross-Cultural Replications." *Journal of Personality and Social Psychology* 58:878–91.

Scott, Marvin B., and Sanford Lyman. 1968. "Accounts." *American Sociological Review* 33:46–62.

Shamir, Boas. 1990. "Calculations, Values, and Identities: The Sources of Collectivistic Work Motivation." *Human Relations* 43:313–32.

Shamir, Boas, R. J. House, and M. B. Arthur. 1993. "The Motivational Effects of Charismatic Leadership: A Self-Concept Based Theory." *Organizational Science* 4:577–94.

Smith, M. Brewster. 1963. "Personal Values in the Study of Lives." In *The Study of Lives,* edited by R.W. White, 124–43. New York: Atherton Press.

Snow, David A., and Pamela E. Oliver. 1995. "Social Movements and Collective Behavior." In *Sociological Perspectives in Social Psychology,* edited by K. S. Cook, G. A. Fine, and J. S. House, 571–90. Boston: Allyn and Bacon.

Steele, Claude. 1988. "The Psychology of Self-Affirmation: Sustaining the Integrity of the Self." *Advances in Experimental Social Psychology* 21:261–302.

Stone, Gregory P. 1962. "Appearance and the Self." In *Human Behavior and Social Processes,* edited by A. M. Rose, 94–116. Boston: Houghton Mifflin.

Stryker, Sheldon. 1980. *Symbolic Interactionism: A Social Structural Version.* Menlo Park, Calif.: Benjamin-Cummings.

———. 1987. "Identity Theory: Developments and Extensions." In *Self and Identity: Psychological Perspectives,* edited by K. Kardley and T. Honess, 89–104. New York: Wiley.

Swann, William B., Jr. 1983. "Self-Verification: Bringing Social Reality into Harmony with the Self." In *Psychological Perspectives on the Self,* edited by J. Suls and A. G. Greenwald, 2:33–66. Hillsdale, N.J.: Lawrence Erlbaum.

Tajfel, Henri. 1981. *Human Groups and Social Categories.* Cambridge: Cambridge University Press.

Taylor, Charles. 1989. *Sources of the Self.* Cambridge: Harvard University Press.

Taylor, Verta. 1989. "Social Movement Continuity: The Women's Movement in Abeyance." *American Sociological Review* 54:761–75.

Taylor, Verta, and Nancy Whittier. 1992. "Collective Identity in Social Movement Communities." In *Frontiers in Social Movement Theory,* edited by A. D. Morris and C. M. Mueller, 104–29. New Haven: Yale University Press.

Turner, John C. 1985. "Social Categorization and the Self-Concept: A Social-Cognitive Theory of Group Behavior." In *Advances in Group Processes: Theory and Research,* edited by E. J. Lawler, 2:77–121. Greenwich, Conn.: JAI Press.

Turner, Ralph H. 1968. "Self-Conception in Social Interaction." In *The Self in Social Interaction,* edited by C. Gordon and K. J. Gergen, 93–106. New York: Wiley.

Warren, Mark. 1990. "Ideology and the Self." *Theory and Society* 19:599–634.

Weigert, Andrew J. 1983. "Identity: Its Emergence within Sociological Psychology." *Symbolic Interaction* 6:183–206.

———. 1991. *Mixed Emotions.* Albany: State University of New York Press.

Williams, Robin M., Jr. 1979. "Change and Stability in Values and Value Systems: A Sociological Perspective." In *Understanding Human Values,* edited by M. Rokeach, 15–46. New York: Free Press.

Zygmunt, Joseph F. 1970. "Prophetic Failure and Chiliastic Identity: The Case of Jehovah's Witnesses." *American Journal of Sociology* 75:926–48.

5

Self-Change in Social Movements

K. Jill Kiecolt

A recurring theme in research on social movements is the self-transformation that may occur through participation: "individual identities are brought to movement participation and changed in the process" (Johnston, Laraña, and Gusfield 1994, 12; also Klapp 1969; Turner 1969). How much existing or nascent identities motivate individuals' participation, how much identities change, and how central identity change is to movement goals vary by type of movement (Johnston, Laraña, and Gusfield 1994; Turner 1991). Nevertheless, "a task of all social movements" is to get participants to incorporate the movement's collective identity into their self-definition (Gamson 1992a, 60).

Self-transformation also has been studied as an individual endeavor, by psychological social psychologists, clinical psychologists, psychiatrists, and sociologists. Interest in the topic has increased along with the belief that self-change over the entire life course is possible (Dannefer 1984; Demo 1992; Lerner and Busch-Rossnagel 1981), desirable, and even mandatory. People are urged to acquire culturally favored qualities such as high self-esteem and self-efficacy, to cast off undesirable identities such as "victim," and to improve their appearance (e.g., Meyer 1986; Starker 1989). Perhaps as a result, much research on intentional self-change is concerned with how people effect self-improvement by changing personality traits, identities, appearance, and behavior. Researchers have studied the antecedents of self-change (e.g., Ebaugh 1988; Gurin 1990; Kiecolt 1994; Prochaska, DiClemente, and Norcross 1992; Thoits 1985); structural supports for self-change such as voluntary self-help groups (Wuthnow 1994) and the popular self-help literature (Starker 1989); and the process of self-change (e.g., Cantor and Kihlstrom 1987; Curtis and Stricker 1991; Gurin 1990; Howard 1991; Markus and Wurf 1987; Prochaska, DiClemente, and Norcross 1992).

In this chapter I draw on theory and research on the self-concept to suggest ways in which the self-concept may change through participation in social movements. I begin by reviewing literature on the self-concept that relates to self-change. Following that, I describe six types of change in the self-concept, provide some examples of these types of change in social movements, and then outline the mechanisms by which social movements may bring about self-concept change.

Identity and the Self-Concept

Studying identity as it is constructed and changed by social movements requires understanding the self-concept. The self-concept refers to the stable, relatively enduring idea of self (Turner 1987). It includes identities and personal attributes or traits. Identities are internalized role designations (Stryker and Serpe 1994), social categories that carry prescriptions for acting, thinking, and feeling. Identities are organized hierarchically (Stryker 1987) according to their psychological centrality (their subjective importance) and their salience (how readily they are invoked in situations) (Stryker and Serpe 1994).

Traits and attributes are adjectives (e.g., "assertive") and adverbs (e.g., "confidently") that describe the ways in which people enact their identities or roles. Some general attributes, such as introversion versus extroversion, extend across identities as "more or less pervasive styles of relating to the external world" (Stryker 1987, 100). Other attributes accompany particular identities or clusters of identities (Reid and Deaux 1996). For example, a person may be more "caring" as a friend than as a boss. Like identities, attributes also vary in centrality to persons' self-concepts and by how readily they are invoked.

Self-Concept Change

Self-concept change involves changing some aspect of one's self-concept: identities, attributes, or both. The change can be intentional or unintentional. If intentional, self-change is an "effort to construct a particular kind of self" (Turner 1987, 125). In most cases, persons are bringing their self-conception as well as their self-images, or situated selves, into line with an "ideal self" or "ought self" (Higgins, Klein, and Strauman 1987). For example, a person may cast off a self-conception as ineffectual. If the change is unintentional, persons may discover that they are changing or realize that they have changed (more on this later) in a more or less desirable direction.

Regardless of whether self-concept change is intentional or unintentional, it involves making a change that becomes habitual enough that persons do not easily revert to a former view of self or unthinkingly act as they used to. Thus "persons must change their behavior as well as their attitudes and beliefs, the changes in behavior must matter to self and others, and the changes in self-conception and behavior must persist" (Kiecolt 1994, 50). How long the changes persist is, of course, an empirical question (Klandermans 1994).

Self-concept change can take various forms. A first category of self-concept change involves changes in a person's hierarchy of identities, on which identities or attributes are ranked in terms of psychological centrality or salience (Stryker 1987). Mortimer, Finch, and Kumka (1982) have identified three types of changes in one's hierarchy of identities. First, *structural change* occurs when identities are either added or discarded. For example, one might add an identity such as "activist" or discard an undesirable identity such as "victim" (Ebaugh 1988; Fein 1990). Second, *level change* involves change in the importance of a role identity or in the level of an attribute, without a change in their ranking. For example, one's identity as an activist might become more important as one becomes more involved in a social movement organization, but its importance relative to other identities would not change. Finally, *ipsative change* refers to a change in the ranking of one's role identities or in "the relative strength of behavioral dispositions" (Mortimer, Finch, and Kumka 1982, 270). That is, some identities or traits become more prominent (higher ranking) than others. For example, one's identity as an activist might become more central or salient than one's identity as a hobbyist, or one might become more "involved" than "complacent." Thus, ipsative change might entail developing some identities or traits at the expense of others.

A second general category of self-concept change involves change in the *meanings* of an identity. Numerous researchers have asked what identities mean to people, by discovering their associated attributes or how they rate on more general dimensions such as evaluation, power, and activity (e.g., Deaux 1991; Heise 1979; Hoelter 1985). Most recently, Simon (1997) defines the meaning of an identity as beliefs about its content, specifically what competent performance of the identity entails. Three aspects of the content of identities or roles are especially pertinent to self-change in social movements. First, *functionality* refers to what can be accomplished through a role: satisfaction with a role should increase with incumbents' beliefs about what they can accomplish through the role (Turner and Colomy 1988). Second, *representation* refers to the image projected by the role. Images may be predominantly positive or negative. At the individual level, persons' images of an identity, such as "peace activist," might become more positive or negative.[1] Third, the *perceived interconnectedness* of identities (Simon 1997) may change. Simon (1997), for example, examines whether men and women view their work roles as part of their family roles. With respect to social movements, we might ask whether people define an identity (e.g., church member) as including the role of activist. Cognitively, interconnectedness partly entails associating a cluster of attributes with more than one identity. Reid and Deaux (1996, 1085) give an example in which the identities of "activist," "advocate," and "atheist" share the attributes "skeptical," "concerned," and "not satisfied." In summary, if persons change their appraisal of the functionality or the representation of one of their identities, or of the interconnectedness of their identities, their self-concept has changed.

Examples of Self-Concept Change in Social Movements

What types of identities are involved in social movements? Gamson (1992b, 84) views collective identities as "three embedded layers": an *organizational* activist identity that is specific to one social movement organization; a broader, *movement* activist identity; and perhaps a *solidary group* identity based on social categories such as ethnicity, class, gender, and community of residence. As Gamson (1992b) points out, the layers may be separate: people may identify with women, but not with the feminist movement or with any particular organization. This layering of movement-related identities is important to keep in mind.

The evidence suggests that participation in social movements can change the self-concept, in any of the six ways (changes in identity hierarchies and meanings) described above. Perhaps most important, *structural change* occurs when people acquire identities as activists (Fantasia 1988; Kelly and Breinlinger 1996), such as "civil rights advocates, minutemen, ecumenicists, conservationists, or feminists" (Turner and Killian 1987, 340). (Snow and McAdam [chapter 2, this volume] term this type of change "identity transformation.") Participants' movement identities may persist decades after their initial involvement, as McAdam (1989) finds with civil rights activists. Similarly, Klandermans (1994) identifies "shifters," peace movement activists who "had a lifelong history as activists" and who later joined other movements. (In Gamson's [1992b] terms, shifters had movement activist identities as well as organizational activist identities.)

Acquiring an activist identity may lead to acquiring other identities as well. Gibbs (1982), the leader of the movement to relocate residents of the Love Canal area, mentions that many women who were active in the struggle became involved in other community organizations afterward. Conversely, as people acquire new activist identities and spend time on movement activities, they may also relinquish identities (e.g., Girl Scout leader) they no longer have time to maintain (Fantasia 1988).

Second, *level change,* a change in the level of an attribute or in the salience or psychological centrality of identities, also may occur from movement involvement. One of the most important and often described types of level changes is increased self-efficacy or a sense of empowerment (Kelly and Breinlinger 1996). Social movements afford opportunities for action, which, if successful, can increase activists' sense of self-efficacy (Turner and Killian 1987). For example, Merrill Proudfoot, a white Protestant minister, became transformed "from an anxious but sympathetic bystander to a confident and determined activist through the medium of participation" in lunch-counter sit-ins (1962; cited in Turner and Killian 1987, 341). Activists' increased self-efficacy is often visible to others as well. Fantasia (1988, 166) quotes a respondent describing participants in union organizing: "Most of the girls have become much more independent . . . and free-thinking, using their heads."

Level change also occurs when identities related to a movement become more psychologically central or salient. Such identities can either be solidary group identities or organizational or movement activist identities. For example, the feminist movement has sought to get women to identify themselves as women and to recognize their common fate in order to raise group consciousness (Evans 1979; Gurin and Townsend 1986). In one of the few studies to measure changes in the psychological centrality of identities, Kelly and Breinlinger (1996) find that degree of self-identification as an activist increases over time, in their case, with involvement in women's movement groups in Britain.

Finally, participation in social movements can cause level change by diminishing the salience or centrality of other identities that compete with movement participation. Several accounts of women's participation in union organizing, strikes, or social movements suggest that their identities as homemakers become less salient as their movement involvement increases (Fantasia 1988; Kelly and Breinlinger 1996; Kingsolver 1995).

Third, ipsative change entails a change in the *ranking* of identities or in the relative strength of attributes. (This is akin to Snow and McAdam's [chapter 2, this volume] term "identity amplification.") Although to my knowledge ipsative change has not been measured quantitatively in connection with social movements, numerous instances of it appear in accounts of social movement participation, especially among women. In their case, the identity of activist overtakes family or recreation identities (Fantasia 1988; Gibbs 1982).

Movements can also effect changes in what identities mean to participants. To reiterate, this refers to the "personal [movement] identities" that individuals hold, rather than to the "collective identities" (Hunt and Benford 1994) that movement organizations and participants construct at the cultural level through framing (Gamson 1992a; Melucci 1989; Snow and Oliver 1995).[2] At the individual level, participants change their beliefs about what constitutes an identity and redefine themselves accordingly (Gamson 1992a).

First, social movement participants can change their appraisal of the *functionality* of an identity, or what they believe they can accomplish through it. Movements seek to increase the perceived functionality of an organizational or movement activist identity in order to mobilize participation. The layering of movement identities is important: Some movements that involve a solidary group identity, such as the lesbian feminist movement, must also convince participants that the solidary group identity is low in functionality, that it is deprived of its fair share of power or influence (Gurin and Townsend 1986; Snow and Oliver 1995; Turner and Killian 1987). This combined change (increased functionality of an activist identity, decreased functionality of a solidary group identity) is central to the development of group consciousness (Gurin and Townsend 1986).

In contrast, other social movements that involve a solidary group identity seek to increase the perceived functionality of that identity. The mythopoetic or men's movement (Schwalbe 1996), for example, has enlarged the definition of *man* to include both "masculine" and "feminine" qualities. Schwalbe quotes Paul Boynton (1991; in Schwalbe 1996):

> Within our "deep masculine" we will find the good things that we've been searching for. We will find our ability to be benevolent, courageous, decisive and appropriately aggressive. We will find enthusiasm, loyalty and energy. We will discover a spiritual dimension that gives our lives a sense of meaning. We will find that we are fully capable of nurturing, protecting, and grieving. We can feel joy, appreciate beauty, experience wonder, and live our lives with spontaneity. (123)

Sometimes activists' appraisals of functionality of a particular movement activist identity decline over time, perhaps because movement campaigns are not succeeding. For example, Kelly and Breinlinger (1996) find that longer participation in women's groups is associated with less optimism concerning achieving social change. Similarly, Hunt and Benford (1994) quote a former Nebraskans for Peace activist:

> I've lost energy. I'm not energized like I was. The meetings, the sacrifices I've made, no evidence of progress, all that—it adds up. It wears on you until you're burned out. . . . I'll still be involved but not like I am now. I still believe what we're doing is important and that we do make progress, painfully slow progress. (509)

Activists, however, may appraise one movement activist identity as ineffectual, but not others, as in Klandermans's (1994) finding that peace movement activists left to join other movements.

Second, participation can change the *representation* of an identity by getting participants to associate a more favorable image with it. The civil rights movement's promotion of black pride, for example, led black adherents to define their ethnic identities in more positive terms. Men in the mythopoetic movement seek to remake "man" into a positive moral identity and to define themselves accordingly (Schwalbe 1996, 108). Usually a movement defines a positive in-group identity for itself and ascribes a negative identity to an out-group (Blumer 1953, cited in Turner and Killian 1987; Turner 1991), as part of establishing boundaries (Taylor and Whittier 1992). At the individual level, defining one's own group favorably and an out-group unfavorably is a component of group consciousness (Gurin and Townsend 1986).

Finally, participation in social movements can change the *perceived interconnectedness* of identities. For example, many members of the Coalition of Labor Union Women see their identities as feminists and as union members as inextricably linked (chapter 14, this volume).

In his study of environmental activists, Lichterman (1996) identifies two types of social movement organizations: "communitarian" and "personal." Although not phrased as such, these are two ways in which participants' identities may be interconnected. In the more familiar communitarian form, social movements strive to get participants to define an organizational or movement activist identity as part of a solidary identity around which the movement is organized, such as "ethnic group" or "community member." Such social movement organizations (SMOs) often recruit participants from existing, nonmovement organizations and then "redefine existing roles within established organizations as the basis of an emerging activist identity" (Friedman and McAdam 1992, 163). In the civil rights movement, participants redefined their identities as church members to include the identity of "activist" (Friedman and McAdam 1992, 163). In the antitoxics movement, in a mostly black SMO that Lichterman (1996) calls Hillviewers Against Toxics (HAT), activists recruit members on the basis of their community and ethnic identities: "'HAT is community people who are getting the community involved,'" one recruiter explained, thus "associating HAT's needs with those of the (black) community as a whole" (105). (Snow and McAdam [chapter 2, this volume] term this type of self-change "identity appropriation.")

In "personalism," the newer form of interconnectedness, activist identities do not grow out of common solidary group identities. Rather, activists participate as individuals—"personal agents of social change" (Lichterman 1996, 34). At least in the environmental movement, they resemble Klandermans's (1994) "shifters," with strong movement identities but weaker ties to particular SMOs. Yet more than "communitarian" activists, they bring a "politicized self" into their occupational, family, and leisure roles. They try to make minor decisions (which toothpaste to buy) as well as long-term life choices (which job to take) that are consistent with their movement activist identity. (This type of interconnectedness is akin to Snow and McAdam's [chapter 2, this volume] term "identity extension.") Perhaps the greater the involvement in a social movement, the more interconnected are activist and other identities.

Self-Concept Change in Social Movements

Before proposing how the self-concept can change by participating in social movements, two points need to be made. First, self-concept change in social movements is not usually sudden. Nevertheless, sudden and lasting self-concept change can sometimes occur: Martin Luther King Jr., sitting alone at his kitchen table, "underwent a profound spiritual transformation" (Garrow 1987, 442) that left him with lifelong "feelings of companionship [with God], of self-assurance, and of mission" (442). Less dramatically, Hunt and Benford (1994) describe several accounts in which peace movement activists credited personal events with changing their consciousness. One activist suddenly became a pacifist after getting a low number in the draft. By most accounts, however, self-concept change in social movements usually occurs gradually, from interaction over time.

> I think often to hear something once is kind of a light-bulb moment . . . but unless one hears it many, many times, it may not be something that we incorporate into our lives. So awareness is one thing and incorporation is another. (respondent quoted in Wuthnow 1994, 311–12)

Second, social movements vary by how deliberately they try to change participants' identities. Identity change is a central goal of some movements but merely a by-product of others (Taylor and Whittier 1992). At one extreme are therapeutic or spiritual movements, which aim to improve participants' psychological well-being rather than effect political change (Klapp 1969; Schwalbe 1996; Turner and Killian 1987). For example, two central goals of the mythopoetic or "men's" movement (Schwalbe 1996) are to affirm and define participants' identities as men and to help them feel better about themselves. Other movements, such as the lesbian feminist movement and the civil rights movement, aim to change participants' identities as well as challenge institutionalized power structures (Morris 1992; Taylor and Whittier 1992, 105). Still other movements work for political change and only seek to change participants' self-concepts by fostering an activist identity. I assume that self-concept change is a by-product rather than the primary goal of most social movements (Hunt, Benford, and Snow 1994).

How Social Movements Change the Self-Concept

How does self-concept change occur through participation in social movements? I propose a model based on the "social structure and personality" framework (House 1981). In this model, shown in figure 1, aspects of the social structure and culture of movements influence the self-concept via more "proximate influences" that operate in interaction and that in turn impinge on psychological processes. The model gives examples of the various levels of variables that researchers need to identify: (1) pertinent characteristics of the structure and culture of social movements, as well as of their social context; (2) aspects of social movement interaction, since individuals' identities are created, negotiated, and sustained through interaction (Gamson 1992a; Hunt and Benford 1994; Klandermans 1992; Melucci 1989; Snow and Oliver 1995; Taylor and Whittier 1992); and (3) psychological processes (House 1981). In the following sections I discuss internalization as a psychological process by which self-concept change occurs, sketch some types of interaction in which internalization is especially likely to occur, and then suggest some characteristics of social movements that may foster self-concept change.

Psychological Processes of Self-Concept Change: Internalization

Beginning with the most proximate influence, an important psychological process through which the self-concept changes is internalization. In internalization, people change their self-concepts in accordance with their behavior. Internalization can occur in two ways (Tice 1992). First, individuals whose

Figure 1. Model for self-concept change in social movements

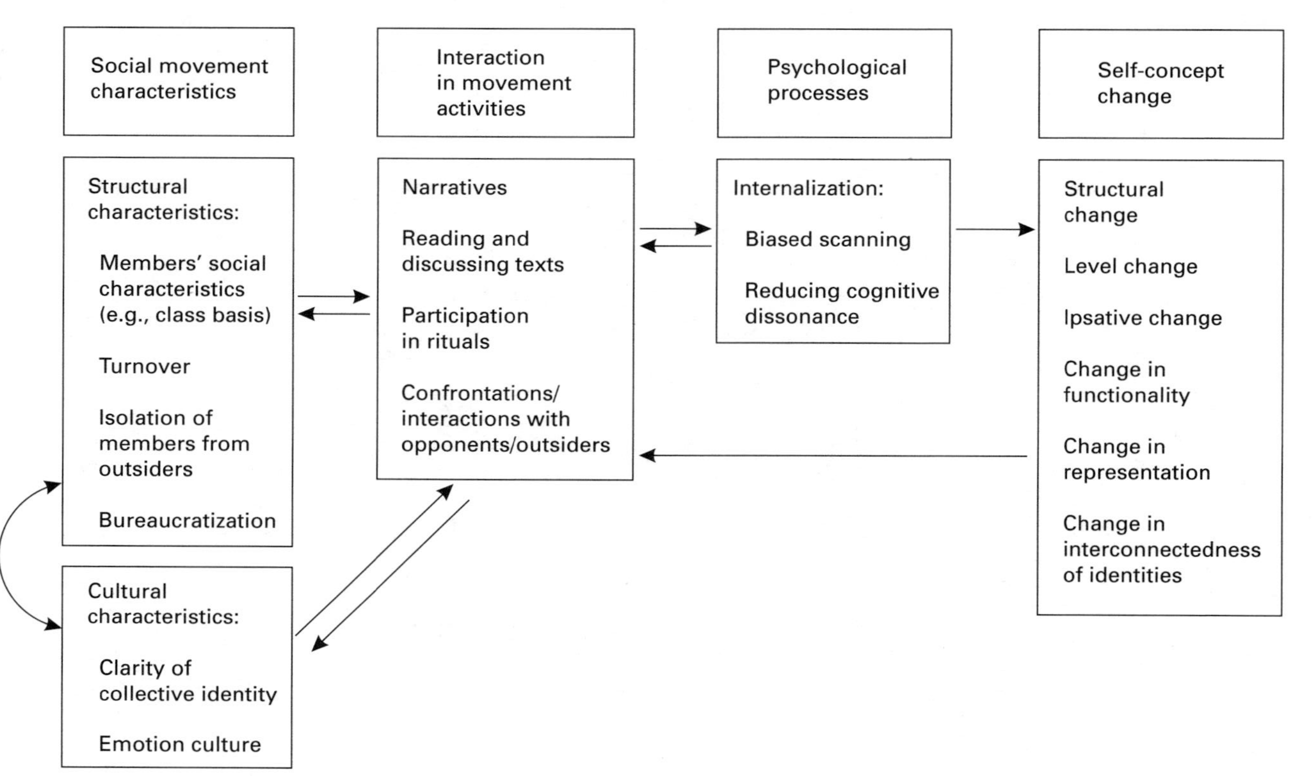

behavior is inconsistent with their self-concept can change their self-beliefs in order to reduce *cognitive dissonance.* Second, the self-concept can change as a result of *biased scanning,* in which one's "behavior directs attention toward certain aspects of the self-concept, and so self-evaluations shift in the direction of the salient cognitions" (Tice 1992, 436). Experiments to investigate biased scanning induce subjects to enact behavior that is congruent with a particular self-concept (e.g., extraversion). Afterward, subjects' self-descriptions tend to migrate in the direction of their behavior. Thus behavior enacted because of social influence, as well as behavior people initiate, can lead to self-concept change. Importantly, internalization from biased scanning is greater after public behavior, in which subjects know that other people are observing them, than after private behavior (Tice 1992). The notion of biased scanning implies that an identity or attribute must already be part of one's self-concept if it is to be made more salient. Thus, persons probably must have a nascent movement-related identity in order for the self-concept to change from participation.[3]

What happens in social movements to elicit efforts to reduce cognitive dissonance or to direct attention toward particular aspects of the self-concept? With regard to *cognitive dissonance,* the literature on social movements contains numerous accounts of participants who found themselves doing things they could never have imagined beforehand and who consequently changed their beliefs about themselves. For example, Lois Gibbs (1982), who successfully led the movement to relocate the residents of the Love Canal area permanently, describes herself as a "housewife" who was "painfully shy." Nevertheless, despite her discomfort in talking to strangers, she solicited public support and government funds for relocation because of her conviction that pollution from Love Canal was causing needless personal tragedy (birth defects, illness, and death) for her and her neighbors' families.

> From a woman who had skipped a day of school when she had to present a book report, Lois became the spokeswoman and political strategist for a thousand families in Niagara Falls. She conducted meetings, gave press conferences, confronted officials, negotiated with the governor and his representatives, appeared on national television, testified before Congress, addressed college classes, and was recognized by the President of the United States for her efforts. (xiv)

Like Gibbs, many social movement participants change their self-conceptions to fit their new, hard-won skills and abilities as "organizers, speakers, and activists" (Kelly and Breinlinger 1996, 115; see also Evans

1979; Fantasia 1988; Gibbs 1982). As one of Fantasia's (1988) respondents, a licensed practical nurse who was active as a union organizer, recalls:

> I think a lot of us grew a lot through it. We did things we never thought we were capable of before. We went and talked to management, made our . . . needs clear, which I (ten years ago) probably would have sat back and said, "I can't do that, I'm just a lowly LPN." But it really strengthened us. (176–77)

Participation in social movements also may change the self-concept through biased scanning, as participants direct their attention to particular aspects of the self-concept as they interact. Biased scanning is the psychological process that occurs in connection with *identity work* (Snow and Anderson 1987): "anything we do, alone or with others, to establish, change, or lay claim to meanings as particular kinds of persons" (Schwalbe 1996, 105). As individuals, we do identity work in every interaction. In social movements, people also do collective identity work, to define the meaning of a collective identity. Through interaction, participants "help each other define what they are as a kind of people" (105). Specifically, participants build their personal identities in the direction they desire; impute a collective identity to an SMO or movement, as well as to its antagonists; and demonstrate to themselves and to others that their personal identities are aligned with the SMO's or movement's collective identity (Hunt and Benford 1994, 493; Schwalbe 1996).

The question then becomes, in what kinds of interaction are movement participants likely to do identity work? Based on previous work (Schwalbe 1996; Wuthnow 1994), I sketch four kinds of interactions in social movements—narrative, texts, ritual, and confrontations/interactions with movement opponents or outsiders—in which identity work often occurs.

How Interaction in Movements Effects Self-Change: Identity Work

Narrative

Possibly the most common source of identity work is narrative. As participants of social movements interact, they tell stories about themselves and their experiences. "Raw experience is often difficult to remember; it needs to be organized in our own minds for us to know what it means. Having to tell a story in a group forces people to organize their experience" (Wuthnow 1994, 312). People also tell stories in order to make sense of their experiences (Baumeister and Newman 1994).

In telling stories about themselves, social movement participants wittingly or unwittingly direct attention to particular aspects of their and others' self-concepts. Of course, participants in social movements tell stories about themselves on many occasions. Stories are like daytime soap operas; each development can be understood only in the context of previous episodes (Wuthnow 1994). The effect of storytelling on identity is cumulative: "People in groups do not simply tell stories—they become their stories" (Wuthnow 1994, 301). What a person chooses to share in a group becomes more important to that person's identity. The reason is that, to a group, a storyteller's identity is that presented in his or her story, and the group treats the person accordingly. The group's affirmation of this identity reinforces and legitimates it. And through the familiar dynamic of reflected appraisals (Rosenberg 1979), "that process in itself can have a significant impact on the way in which individuals think about themselves" (Wuthnow 1994, 301).

The stories that peace movement activists tell, for example, not only accent features of the self-concept but also recount instances of self-concept change (Hunt and Benford 1994, 492–93). Four themes are prominent: (1) stories of "becoming aware" of an injustice foster an activist identity by associating participants with heroes, heroines, and allies and by dissociating them from villains; (2) stories of "becoming active" describe how participants were recruited; (3) stories of "becoming committed" tell of greater involvement and identification with a movement; and (4) stories of "becoming weary" tell of negative experiences that led activists to stop participating. Social movements may deliberately use stories of becoming aware, becoming active, and becoming committed in order to promote identity change in the direction of the movement's collective identity. For example, presaging consciousness-raising in the feminist movement, organizers in the Students for a Democratic Society (SDS) opened meetings by talking about their backgrounds and how they became radicalized, and they then encouraged others to do likewise. Evans (1979) quotes SDS vice president Carl Davidson as saying:

> You'd be astonished at the reception this gets, when people realize they aren't alone, that the failures and problems they ascribed to themselves stem in large part from the society in which they live and the images of themselves they accepted from society.(175)

The group then interprets the stories collectively. Moreover, participants also tell stories about their movement, reinforcing their collective identity. As Wuthnow (1994) notes, purely personal stories do not substitute for stories about collective experiences.[4]

Texts

Social movements commonly produce and draw on writings. These texts provide "templates for interpreting the meaning of personal experiences" (Wuthnow 1994, 311); people may relate the stories or principles in texts to their personal lives. By affirming collective identities, texts foster identity change. For example, in the lesbian feminist community in the 1980s, "national newspapers such as *Off Our Backs,* national magazines such as *Outlook,* publishing companies . . . and a variety of journals and newsletters" helped to create and reaffirm a distinct lesbian feminist identity (Taylor and Whittier 1992, 112).

Similarly, Schwalbe (1996) describes how the men in the mythopoetic movement use texts in performing identity work: they draw on Jungian psychology as popularized by movement leaders (e.g., Robert Bly) in books, newsletters, newspapers, and small magazines (37). These works define men's identity in favorable terms. As one article proclaimed, "It's Good TO BE A Man!" In local men's groups, men use the ideas in texts to interpret other men's experiences and help them construct their identities. The men also read, write, listen to, and discuss poetry that affirms their identities as particular kinds of men.

Rituals

Social movement organizations also can effect change in participants' self-concepts through rituals. Social movements develop rituals (Blumer 1953, cited in Turner and Killian 1987), "symbolic enactment[s] of values, beliefs, or feelings" that are usually private and invisible (Schwalbe 1996, 81). Rituals such as the annual lesbian feminist "Take Back the Night" marches against violence (Taylor and Whittier 1992, 120) and gay rights parades celebrate "special occasions, such as the birthdays of their heroes and anniversaries of their heroes' great trials" (Turner and Killian 1987, 338). Movements may develop "special signs and gestures" by which members recognize one another, as well as their own songs, such as "We Shall Overcome" (Turner and Killian 1987, 338). The mythopoetic men in Schwalbe's (1996) study use ritual extensively in doing identity work: dancing, drumming, chanting, and "radical rituals," such as a sweat lodge ritual.

Through rituals, participants in a social movement reaffirm their common values and align their personal and collective identities. Schwalbe (1996) finds that the mythopoetic men deliberately use "radical rituals" to effect desired changes in themselves (81) and that such rituals can actually change participants' views of themselves. He quotes a participant who felt more assertive as a result:

> It's partially therapy but also working in men's stuff, the mythopoetic stuff, that has made me feel more like a growler. The nonrational experience by the lake or in the sweat lodge also made me feel that if my life was threatened that I could probably act like a beast. You know, I could be a beast and protect. I might die in the process, but I wouldn't shrink. (116)

Confrontation/Interaction with Movement Opponents or Outsiders

Narratives, texts, and rituals are by-products of a movement rather than main movement activities. Moreover, they may involve only movement participants. When participants engage in activism, however, such as when they march in demonstrations or try to recruit new members, they must deal with opponents or outsiders. Whenever movement participants interact with opponents or outsiders, they are likely to do identity work. Such interactions draw participants' attention to their movement-related identities by emphasizing the distinctions between the in-group ("us") and the out-group ("them").

Movement Characteristics That Foster Self-Change

What aspects of the structure and culture of social movements promote self-change? As figure 1 shows, structural characteristics of social movements can be aggregated from members' characteristics, or they can be global characteristics. For example, movements vary in participants' isolation from contacts with outsiders. Identity theory (chapter 1, this volume) would predict that isolation from contacts that support previous, nonmovement identities should make identity change congruent with a movement's collective identity more likely. To take another example, Lichterman (1996) finds that the class basis of social movement organizations influences the type of interconnectedness of identities that participants adopt. Environmental movement organizations that draw members mostly from the broad professional middle class tend to foster "personal" interconnectedness (see above), whereas organizations that draw more from blue-collar occupations tend to foster a "communitarian" movement identity. Class membership also is associated with the degree of discussing "group process" in meetings (Lichterman 1996). Thus class membership also may affect self-concept change indirectly, to the extent that attention to group process entails doing identity work.

Studies of the "culture" of social movements are fairly recent, and many aspects remain to be specified. Nevertheless, numerous features of social movement culture may influence self-concept change. Two features are (1) the clarity of social movement identities and (2) emotion cultures. First, movements vary in how clearly they articulate a collective identity. This analysis has assumed that social movements clearly articulate positive identities for participants. But Gamson (1995) finds that not all social movements seek to construct a clear collective identity. Instead, a movement may try to "blur and deconstruct group categories, and to keep them forever unstable" (Gamson 1995, 393). A loose set of groups subsumed under the label of "queer politics" rejects stable self-definitions as gay or lesbian. Based on this phenomenon, Gamson questions whether movements must construct stable collective identities in order for collective action and social change to occur. We might also ask: In such a movement, what kinds of collective identities do movement adherents incorporate into their own self-definitions? In what ways do adherents' self-concepts change, and how stable are the changes?

In other cases, a movement may paint an unfavorable image of its antagonists without delineating a favorable image of its adherents. Marshall (1993, 13–14) finds that the antifeminist organization Concerned Women for America characterizes feminists in quite derogatory terms ("extreme," "selfish," and "defiant") but that it does not articulate women participants' positive qualities as women or even as homemakers and parents. As a result, she argues, the antifeminist movement has not fully exploited its potential "for creating a new self-affirming identity" (14). Perhaps participants in this movement do not perceive much overlap between their movement identity and their solidary group identities, but how the clarity of a collective identity affects self-concept change remains to be investigated.

Second, the "emotion culture" of movements may influence the extent and type of self-change. Emotion culture refers to the movement's feeling rules and expression rules, which specify the emotions that individuals should feel and express in given situations, respectively (Hochschild 1983; Taylor 1995). Emotions both predate and arise in social movements. Social movements seek to manage negative emotions such as anger, shame, and fear by channeling them into "feelings conducive to protest and activism" (Taylor 1995, 229). Movements also frame organization, movement, and solidary identities favorably so that participants will feel positive emotions—pride, self-efficacy, and authenticity—in connection with those identities (chapter 12, this volume; Taylor 1995). People may change their self-concept in order to stop feeling negative emotions or to continue to feel

the positive emotions that accompany a more desirable self-concept (Kiecolt 1994). Consequently, the more successfully a movement's emotion culture manages negative emotions and evokes positive ones, the more that participants' personal identities may change to become more aligned with the movements' collective identity and the more salient that identity may be.

Conclusion

This analysis has described six ways in which the self-concept may change through participation in social movements. Three of these involve changes in hierarchies of identities or traits, or both, and three involve changes in the meanings of identities. The "social structure and personality" framework (House 1981) is useful for elucidating the mechanisms by which social movements can bring about such self-concept change. In the model based on this framework shown in figure 1, aspects of social movement structure and culture (e.g., emotion culture) influence the kinds of interactions respondents have. Four types of interactions that foster self-concept change are narratives (Hunt and Benford 1994; Wuthnow 1994), texts (Schwalbe 1996), ritual (Schwalbe 1996; Taylor 1995), and confrontations/interactions with opponents and outsiders. Most proximately, cognitive dissonance and biased scanning (Tice 1992) are two psychological processes that encourage self-concept change.

Completely elaborating a "social structure and personality" model (House 1981) requires considering not only how social movements change the self-concept but also how self-change influences the structure and culture of social movements. To give two examples, a heightened sense of efficacy is likely to increase members' participation (Kelly and Breinlinger 1996), which could in turn increase the size of a movement and its chances for success. Second, based on identity theory (chapter 1, this volume), greater interconnectedness of movement and other identities could reduce turnover of members. Alternatively, if interconnectedness of identities increases the likelihood of intimate contact with persons outside the movement, it might lessen the movement's influence on members and increase turnover.

Future research still needs to answer Turner and Killian's (1987, 238) question: What determines the kind of personal transformation, that is, self-change, that adherents undergo as a result of participating in a social movement? And what determines the extent of self-change? The model shown in figure 1 needs much more elaboration in order to answer these questions. In addition to the movement-level variables discussed in this analysis, numerous other aspects of social movements may matter. Certain characteristics of respondents and their social context (e.g., their social network) may be important (McAdam 1989; Snow and Oliver 1995). More aspects of interaction in social movements also need to be identified. As Piliavin and Callero's (1991) work on acquiring a blood donor identity shows, aspects of participants' experiences or interactions matter. In the case of social movements, participating in successful collective efforts may be crucial for increasing self-efficacy. Other psychological processes aside from internalization that are associated with self-change need to be delineated, and the aspects of social movements and persons' interactions within them that activate these psychological processes need to be specified. Formulating a comprehensive theory is outside the scope of this analysis, but many of the variables and links may already have been suggested by previous work in social movements and social psychology.

Notes

I thank the editors of this volume, Rachel Parker-Gwin, and Dale Wimberley for helpful comments and suggestions.

1. Functionality and representation are similar to the power and evaluation dimensions of an identity (e.g., Heise 1979; Hoelter 1985).

2. To clarify, some social identity theorists use the term *personal identities* to refer to personality traits that differentiate a person from others. They would term the individual movement identities described here as *social identities* (e.g., Reid and Deaux 1996), specifically, *relational identities,* which derive from interpersonal relationships, or *collective identities,* which derive from membership in social categories (e.g., Brewer and Gardner 1996).

3. Since people usually try to verify their self-conceptions (e.g., chapter 6, this volume), they would resist aligning their own identities with discrepant collective identities (Hunt and Benford 1994). Social movements may accentuate similarities between extant identities and movement identities in order to recruit members (Snow and McAdam, chapter 2, this volume).

4. Stories don't have to be true to succeed as identity work. Thus stories can serve as indicators of people's mental maps, but not necessarily as accurate representations of events.

References

Baumeister, Roy F., and Leonard S. Newman. 1994. "How Stories Make Sense of Personal Experiences: Motives That Shape Autobiographical Narratives." *Personality and Social Psychology Bulletin* 20:676–90.

Brewer, Marilyn B., and Wendi Gardner. 1996. "Who Is This 'We'?: Levels of Collective Identity and Self Representations." *Journal of Personality and Social Psychology* 71:83–93.

Cantor, Nancy, and John F. Kihlstrom. 1987. *Personality and Social Intelligence.* Englewood Cliffs, N.J.: Prentice-Hall.

Curtis, Rebecca C., and George Stricker, eds. 1991. *How People Change Inside and Outside Therapy.* New York: Plenum Press.

Dannefer, Dale. 1984. "Adult Development and Social Theory: A Paradigmatic Reappraisal." *American Sociological Review* 49:100–116.

Deaux, Kay. 1991. "Social Identities: Thoughts on Structure and Change." In *The Relational Self: Theoretical Convergences in Psychoanalysis and Social Psychology,* edited by Rebecca C. Curtis, 77–93. New York: Guilford Press.

Demo, David H. 1992. "The Self-Concept over Time: Research Issues and Directions." *Annual Review of Sociology* 18:303–26.

Ebaugh, Helen Rose Fuchs. 1988. *Becoming an Ex: The Process of Role Exit.* Chicago: University of Chicago Press.

Evans, Sara. 1979. *Personal Politics: The Roots of Women's Liberation in the Civil Rights Movement and the New Left.* New York: Vintage Books.

Fantasia, Rick. 1988. *Cultures of Solidarity: Consciousness, Action, and Contemporary American Workers.* Berkeley: University of California Press.

Fein, Melvyn. 1990. *Role Change: A Resocialization Perspective.* New York: Praeger.

Friedman, Debra, and Doug McAdam. 1992. "Identity Incentives and Activism: Networks, Choices, and the Life of a Social Movement." In *Frontiers in Social Movement Theory,* edited by Aldon D. Morris and Carol Mueller, 156–73. New Haven: Yale University Press.

Gamson, Joshua. 1995. "Must Identity Movements Self-Destruct?: A Queer Dilemma." *Social Problems* 42:390–407.

Gamson, William. 1992a. "The Social Psychology of Collective Action." In *Frontiers in Social Movement Theory,* edited by Aldon D. Morris and Carol Mueller, 53–76. New Haven: Yale University Press.

———. 1992b. *Talking Politics.* Cambridge: Cambridge University Press.

Garrow, David J. 1987. "Martin Luther King, Jr., and the Spirit of Leadership." *Journal of American History* 74:438–47.

Gibbs, Lois Marie. 1982. *Love Canal: My Story.* Albany: State University of New York Press.

Gurin, Joel. 1990. "Remaking Our Lives." *American Health* 9:50–52.

Gurin, Patricia, and Aloen Townsend. 1986. "Properties of Gender Identity and Their Implications for Gender Consciousness." *British Journal of Social Psychology* 25:139–48.

Heise, David R. 1979. *Understanding Events.* London: Cambridge University Press.

Higgins, E. Tory, Ruth L. Klein, and Timothy J. Strauman. 1987. "Self-Discrepancies: Distinguishing among Self-States, Self-State Conflicts, and Emotional

Vulnerabilities." In *Self and Identity: Psychosocial Perspectives,* edited by Krysia Yardley and Terry Honess, 173–86. New York: Wiley.

Hochschild, Arlie Russell. 1983. *The Managed Heart: Commercialization of Human Feeling.*

Berkeley: University of California Press.

Hoelter, Jon W. 1985. "The Structure of Self-Conception: Conceptualization and Measurement." *Journal of Personality and Social Psychology* 49:1392–1407.

House, James S. 1981. "Social Structure and Personality." In *Social Psychology: Sociological Perspectives,* edited by Morris Rosenberg and Ralph H. Turner, 525–61. New York: Basic Books.

Howard, Judith A. 1991. "From Changing Selves toward Changing Society." In *The Self-Society Dynamic,* edited by Judith A. Howard and Peter Callero, 209–37. Cambridge: Cambridge University Press.

Hunt, Scott A., and Robert D. Benford. 1994. "Identity Talk in the Peace and Justice Movement." *Journal of Contemporary Ethnography* 22:488–517.

Hunt, Scott A., Robert D. Benford, and David A. Snow. 1994. "Identity Fields: Framing Processes and the Social Construction of Movement Identities." In *New Social Movements: From Ideology to Identity,* edited by Enrique Laraña, Hank Johnston, and Joseph R. Gusfield, 185–208. Philadelphia: Temple University Press.

Johnston, Hank, Enrique Laraña, and Joseph R. Gusfield. 1994. "Identities, Grievances, and New Social Movements." In *New Social Movements: From Ideology to Identity,* edited by Enrique Laraña, Hank Johnston, and Joseph R. Gusfield, 3–35. Philadelphia: Temple University Press.

Kelly, Caroline, and Sara Breinlinger. 1996. *The Social Psychology of Collective Action: Identity, Injustice, and Gender.* London: Taylor and Francis.

Kiecolt, K. Jill. 1994. "Stress and the Decision to Change Oneself: A Theoretical Model." *Social Psychology Quarterly* 57:49–63.

Kingsolver, Barbara. 1995. "Holding the Line: Women in the Great Arizona Mine Strike of 1983." In *Sociology: Exploring the Architecture of Everyday Life: Readings,* edited by David M. Newman, 322–35. Thousand Oaks, Calif.: Pine Forge Press.

Klandermans, Bert. 1992. "The Social Construction of Protest and Multiorganizational Fields." In *Frontiers in Social Movement Theory,* edited by Aldon D. Morris and Carol Mueller, 77–103. New Haven: Yale University Press.

———. 1994. "Transient Identities?: Membership Patterns in the Dutch Peace Movement." In *New Social Movements: From Ideology to Identity,* edited by Enrique Laraña, Hank Johnston, and Joseph R. Gusfield, 168–84. Philadelphia: Temple University Press.

Klapp, Orrin E. 1969. *Collective Search for Identity.* New York: Holt, Rinehart, and Winston.

Lerner, Richard, and Nancy A. Busch-Rossnagel. 1981. "Individuals as Producers of Their Development: Conceptual and Empirical Bases." In *Individuals as Producers of Their Development: A Life-Span Perspective,* edited by Richard Lerner and Nancy A. Busch-Rossnagel, 1–36. New York: Academic Press.

Lichterman, Paul. 1996. *The Search for Political Community: American Activists Reinventing Commitment.* Cambridge: Cambridge University Press.

Markus, Hazel, and Elissa Wurf. 1987. "The Dynamic Self-Concept: A Social Psychological Perspective." *Annual Review of Psychology* 38:299–337.

Marshall, Susan E. 1993. "Social Movement Organizations and Group Consciousness: The Paradox of Women's Antifeminism." Paper presented at the annual meeting of the American Sociological Association.

McAdam, Doug. 1989. "The Biographical Consequences of Activism." *American Sociological Review* 54:744–60.

Melucci, Alberto. 1989. *Nomads of the Present: Social Movements and Individual Needs in Contemporary Society.* Philadelphia: Temple University Press.

Morris, Aldon D. 1992. "Political Consciousness and Collective Action." In *Frontiers in Social Movement Theory,* edited by Aldon D. Morris and Carol Mueller, 351–73. New Haven: Yale University Press.

Mortimer, Jeylan, Michael Finch, and Donald Kumka. 1982. "Persistence and Change in Development: The Multidimensional Self-Concept." In *Life-Span Development and Behavior,* edited by Paul B. Baltes and Orville G. Brim Jr., 4:263–312. New York: Academic Press.

Piliavin, Jane Allyn, and Peter L. Callero. 1991. *Giving Blood: The Development of an Altruistic Identity.* Baltimore: Johns Hopkins University Press.

Prochaska, James O., Carlo C. DiClemente, and John C. Norcross. 1992. "In Search of How People Change: Applications to Addictive Behaviors." *American Psychologist* 47:1102–14.

Reid, Anne, and Kay Deaux. 1996. "Relationship between Social and Personal Identities: Segregation or Integration?" *Journal of Personality and Social Psychology* 71:1084–91.

Rosenberg, Morris. 1979. *Conceiving the Self.* New York: Basic Books.

Schwalbe, Michael. 1996. *Unlocking the Iron Cage: The Men's Movement, Gender Politics, and American Culture.* New York: Oxford University Press.

Simon, Robin W. 1997. "The Meanings Individuals Attach to Role Identities and Their Implications for Mental Health." *Journal of Health and Social Behavior* 38:256–74.

Snow, David A., and Leon Anderson. 1987. "Identity Work among the Homeless: The Verbal Construction and Avowal of Personal Identities." *American Journal of Sociology* 92:1336–71.

Snow, David A., and Pamela E. Oliver. 1995. "Social Movements and Collective Behavior: Social Psychological Dimensions and Considerations." In *Sociological*

Perspectives on Social Psychology, edited by Karen S. Cook, James S. House, and Gary Alan Fine, 571–99. Boston: Allyn and Bacon.

Starker, Stephen. 1989. *Oracle at the Supermarket: The American Preoccupation with Self-Help Books.* New Brunswick, N.J.: Transaction.

Stryker, Sheldon. 1987. "Identity Theory: Developments and Extensions." In *Self and Identity: Psychosocial Perspectives,* edited by Krysia Yardley and Terry Honess, 89–104. London: Wiley.

Stryker, Sheldon, and Richard T. Serpe. 1994. "Identity Salience and Psychological Centrality: Equivalent, Overlapping, or Complementary Concepts?" *Social Psychology Quarterly* 57: 16–35.

Taylor, Verta. 1995. "Watching for Vibes: Bringing Emotions into the Study of Feminist Organizations." In *Feminist Organizations: Harvest of the New Women's Movement,* edited by Myra Marx Ferree and Patricia Yancey Martin, 223–33. Philadelphia: Temple University Press.

Taylor, Verta, and Nancy Whittier. 1992. "Collective Identity in Social Movement Communities: Lesbian Feminist Mobilization." In *Frontiers in Social Movement Theory,* edited by Aldon D. Morris and Carol Mueller, 104–29. New Haven: Yale University Press.

Thoits, Peggy A. 1985. "Self-Labeling Processes in Mental Illness: The Role of Emotional Deviance." *American Journal of Sociology* 91:221–49.

Tice, Dianne M. 1992. "Self-Concept Change and Self-Presentation: The Looking-Glass Self Is Also a Magnifying Glass." *Journal of Personality and Social Psychology* 63:435–51.

Turner, Ralph H. 1969. "The Theme of Contemporary Social Movements." *British Journal of Sociology* 20:390–405.

———. 1987. "Articulating Self and Social Structure." In *Self and Identity: Psychosocial Perspectives,* edited by Krysia Yardley and Terry Honess, 119–32. New York: Wiley.

———. 1991. "The Dynamics of Collective Identity: Alberto Melucci and Social Movement Theory." Paper presented at the annual meeting of the Society for the Study of Symbolic Interaction.

Turner, Ralph H., and Paul Colomy. 1988. "Role Differentiation: Orienting Principles." *Advances in Group Processes* 5:1–27.

Turner, Ralph H., and Lewis M. Killian. 1987. *Collective Behavior.* Englewood Cliffs, N.J.: Prentice-Hall.

Wuthnow, Robert. 1994. *Sharing the Journey: Support Groups and America's New Quest for Community.* New York: Free Press.

Social and Collective Identity

6

Finding the Self through Others: Self-Verification and Social Movement Participation

Elizabeth C. Pinel and William B. Swann Jr.

Brooks Hatlin spent most of his life in Maine's Shawshank federal penitentiary. There he endured conditions that were shocking even by the harsh standards of American prisons; beatings and rapes punctuated an atmosphere of unrelenting terror and despair. Yet as horrifying as his prisoner identity was, Brooks couldn't live without it. When, after thirty-five years, he was finally released, he slipped into a dark despair that culminated in suicide.

Why did Brooks's release from the brutality of life at Shawshank precipitate his suicide? The screenwriter of *The Shawshank Redemption* implies that Brooks embraced death because he could not cope with the uncertainty and unpredictability of life as a free man. Apparently, being abruptly released after a long incarceration shook the very foundation of his belief system. Hopelessly confused and distraught, Brooks had lost a sense of who he was. His life had consequently become meaningless, devoid of purpose, and, from an existential perspective, terrifying. As another former inmate put it upon his release: "All I want is to be back where things make sense. Where I won't have to be afraid all the time" (Darabont 1995).

Brooks's despair in the wake of an objectively positive change in his life is not simply the stuff of which movies are made. The affinity for familiar identities may even cause victims of horrific experiences to cling to identities that are, from an outsider's perspective, extremely negative. Witness the ambivalence of a former victim of sexual abuse named Janice as she left her former identity behind:

> I was giving up a person who was really a very viable, powerful, self-reliant human being. There were a lot of positive things about those negative aspects of my personality. And I didn't want to give them up. Maybe it wasn't the best way of coping, but at least I was used to it. I felt incredibly vulnerable having to let go in order to make the room to create a new person. In what void would I be thrown if I let go of this stuff? I felt like a raw muscle walking around for a long time. (Bass and Davis 1988, 62)

The reactions of Brooks and Janice illustrate how people can become thoroughly wedded to identities that are, in some sense, nonoptimal. Why do people become wedded to such identities?

Self-Verification Strivings

Some have suggested that the familiarity of long-standing self-views explains people's commitment to them. Steinem (1996) comments that

> change, no matter how much for the better, still feels lonely at first—as if we were out there on the edge of the universe with wind whistling past our ears—because it doesn't feel like home. Old patterns, no matter how negative and painful they may be, have an incredible magnetic power—because they do feel like home. (38)

We suggest that the allure of "old patterns" and the identities associated with them resides in a deep-seated need for self-verification. Self-verification theory (Swann 1983) begins with the assumption that self-views guide people's behaviors, enable people to predict the reactions of others, and organize people's conception of reality (e.g., Mead 1934). Because people rely on their self-views to serve these vital functions, and because only stable self-views can serve these functions effectively, people work to confirm their self-views (e.g., Aronson 1968; Secord and Backman 1965; Swann 1996). For people wanting to predict and control their worlds, then, self-verifying evaluations are what the purr of the automobile is to the driver or the roar of the jet engine is to the pilot: a signal that all's as it should be.

Research suggests that the desire for self-verification is exceedingly general. It does not matter whether people's self-views are positive or negative, well founded or misplaced; as soon as people become confident of their self-views, they work to confirm them and strive to refute information that disconfirms them.

Given its pervasiveness, the desire for self-verification should apply to one's social identities (e.g., working woman, gay man) as well as one's individual self-views (e.g., ambitious person, loyal person). As such, the self-verification perspective could shed light on several issues concerning social movements: why people join, stay in, and leave social movements; what makes social movements succeed or fail; and how participation in social movements makes changing one's self-views possible and even likely.

To provide a flavor of how and why people strive for self-verification, we begin with a review of recent research on self-verification processes. Throughout this review, we pay particular attention to self-verification strivings among people with negative self-views because for these people (in contrast to people with positive self-views) self-verification theory makes predictions that are distinct from those made by self-enhancement theory (Greenwald 1980; Jones 1973; Kaplan 1975; chapter 10 in this volume). Whereas self-enhancement theory argues that people with negative and positive self-views alike have a basic need to feel good and loved and therefore prefer positive evaluations, self-verification theory assumes that people with negative self-views prefer negative evaluations.

Forms of Self-Verification

An especially important form of self-verification occurs when people choose partners who see them as they see themselves, thereby creating social environments that support their self-views. In one study, for example, people with positive and negative self-views chose whether to interact with an evaluator who had a favorable or unfavorable impression of them. The percentages in table 1 show that people with positive self-views preferred favorable partners and that people with negative self-views preferred unfavorable partners (e.g., Swann, Stein-Seroussi, and Giesler 1992).

More than a dozen replications in different laboratories using diverse methodologies have provided converging evidence that people with negative self-views seek negative feedback and interaction partners (for a review, see Swann 1996). Both males and females display this propensity to an equal degree, whether the self-views in question are fixed or mutable, specific (intelligent, sociable, dominant) or global (worthy or worthless person). Not surprisingly, people are particularly likely to seek self-verifying evaluations if their self-views are extreme and firmly held (e.g., Pelham and Swann 1994; Swann and Ely 1984; Swann, Pelham, and Chidester 1988). Clinically depressed persons, for example, are more likely to seek negative evaluations than people with low self-esteem, presumably because depressives are more convinced that they are worthless (Giesler, Josephs, and Swann 1996). Moreover, receiving confirmation of one's self-views seems to be inherently gratifying. For instance, people with negative self-views prefer

Table 1. Choice of Interaction Partner as a Function of Participants' Self-View

	Percentage Choosing Favorable Partner	Percentage Choosing Unfavorable Partner
Participant's Self-View:		
Positive	72	28
Negative	22	78

Note: The chi-square test of independence conducted on these data was statistically significant, χ^2 (1, N = 81) = 20.25, p = .001.

interacting with people who have evaluated them negatively when presented with the alternative of participating in a different experiment (Swann, Wenzlaff, and Tafarodi 1992). This research suggests that people choosing negative, self-verifying feedback are not just doing so to *avoid* overly positive partners.

People's efforts to verify their negative self-views should not be confused with masochism. Rather than savoring unfavorable evaluations (as one might expect of masochists), people with negative self-views seem intensely ambivalent about such evaluations. While choosing a negative evaluator, one person with low self-esteem noted:

> I like the [favorable] evaluation but I am not sure that it is, ah, correct, maybe. It sounds good, but [the unfavorable evaluator] . . . seems to know more about me. So, I'll choose [the unfavorable evaluator]. (Swann, Stein-Seroussi, and Giesler 1992, anonymous research participant)

Note how the thoughts that give rise to such ambivalence seem to emerge sequentially. On receiving and categorizing positive feedback, people are immediately drawn to it, regardless of their self-views. A preference for self-verifying feedback emerges only later, once people access their self-views and compare them with the feedback (for a further discussion of the mechanisms that seem to underlie self-verification effects, see Swann and Schroeder 1995).

If, despite their attempts to acquire self-verifying feedback, people receive repeated doses of feedback that challenges their self-views, they become anxious (Swann, Pinel, and Tafarodi 1997) and take steps to remedy the situation (Swann, Wenzlaff, and Tafarodi 1992). They may, for instance, strive to make others recognize them for the persons they believe themselves to be. In one study, people who suspected that their interaction partner perceived them as being more or less likable than they saw themselves took steps to bring their partner's evaluation into harmony with their self-views, even if this meant lowering the partner's evaluation (e.g., Swann and Read 1981). Such compensatory activity may immunize people's self-views against self-discrepant feedback. In another study, people who had an opportunity to "set a disconfirming evaluator straight" were less likely to change their self-views than people who received no such opportunity (e.g., Swann and Hill 1982).

Should the foregoing strategies fail to produce self-verifying worlds, people may withdraw, physically or psychologically, from relationships in which they receive disconfirming feedback. For example, Swann, De La Ronde, and Hixon (1994) found that people were less intimate with spouses who perceived them more (or less) favorably than they perceived themselves than were people married to verifying spouses (see also De La Ronde and Swann 1998; Ritts and Stein 1995).

If withdrawal is unfeasible, people may construct the illusion of self-confirming worlds by "seeing" more support for their self-views than actually exists. Thus, people with positive and negative self-views alike spend the longest time looking at evaluations that they expect will confirm their self-views (e.g., Swann and Read 1981). In a similar vein, people recall more incidental information about experimental tasks in which they receive self-confirmatory rather than self-discrepant feedback (Crary 1966). Other research suggests that self-conceptions channel the type as well as the amount of feedback people recall: just as people with positive self-views remember more favorable than unfavorable statements that have been made about them, people with negative self-views remember more unfavorable than favorable statements (e.g., Swann and Read 1981).

Moreover, if attentional and memorial processes are not enough to insulate people against self-discrepant evaluations, people may nullify such evaluations by selectively dismissing them. Consistent with this claim, people feel more confident in the perceptiveness of evaluators whose appraisals confirm their self-conceptions (e.g., Shrauger and Lund 1975). In conjunction with the processes outlined above, such selective dismissal of challenging feedback may systematically skew people's perceptions of reality, such that they conclude that their social worlds are far more supportive of their self-views than they actually are.

On the surface, the findings reviewed in this section seem to clinch the argument that people with negative self-views seek verification of those self-views. Yet it may be premature to take the choices of people with negative self-views at face value. Perhaps what appears to be a quest for self-verification may actually reflect a desire for praise and adulation that, ironically, goes awry.

The Ironic Perspective on Self-Verification

Whereas self-verification theorists assume that people with negative self-views seek confirmation for those self-views to promote feelings of predictability, control, and coherence, proponents of the ironic perspective on self-verification assume that such behaviors actually reflect efforts to gain praise in a roundabout way (see Baumeister 1989; Coyne 1976; Coyne et al. 1987; Horney 1939). The ironic perspective has gained some support from past research. For example, people sometimes seem to engineer obstacles to their success so that they will have a ready excuse should they fail. In one of the first empirical demonstrations of such "strategic self-handicapping," Berglas and Jones (1978) offered people who had either positive or negative performance expectancies a "performance-enhancing" or "performance-debilitating" drug. As predicted, participants who expected to fail were more likely to choose the drug that would clinch their failure (see also Baumgardner and Levy 1988; Rhodewalt and Hill 1995).

Evidence of strategic self-handicapping helps legitimize the notion that behaviors that some researchers have attributed to self-verification strivings may actually reflect ironic attempts to attain positive evaluations. This interpretation becomes less plausible, however, in light of the results of a "think-aloud" study in which participants stated their reasons for their choice of interaction partner (Swann, Stein-Seroussi, and Giesler 1992). The procedure paralleled that used in earlier studies of participants' choice of interaction partners, except that participants thought out loud into a tape recorder as they chose an evaluator with whom to interact. As in the earlier work, most people with positive self-views chose the favorable evaluator, and most people with negative self-views chose the unfavorable evaluator.

Swann, Stein-Seroussi, and Giesler (1992) were most interested in what the self-verifiers—those people with negative self-views who chose unfavorable partners and those people with positive self-views who chose favorable partners—said as they chose a self-verifying partner. Consistent with self-verification theory, the overriding concern seemed to be the fit between the partner's evaluation and what participants knew to be true of themselves. One participant explained: "That's just a very good way to talk about me. Well, I mean, after examining all of this I think [the unfavorable evaluator] pretty much has me pegged (anonymous research participant)." Another declared: "I don't like the conflicting opinion of what I actually think."

Self-verifiers in the think-aloud study also voiced a concern with getting along with the evaluators during the forthcoming interaction. Participants wanted their interactions to unfold in a predictable, orderly manner. One person reasoned: "Seeing as he knows what he's dealing with we might get along better . . . so I think I'll have an easier time getting along with [the unfavorable evaluator] (anonymous research participant)." Another participant shared these thoughts: "[The unfavorable evaluator] seems like a person I could sort of really get along with."

In sum, the results of the think-aloud study support the assumptions underlying self-verification theory by showing that participants were concerned with both how well the evaluations fit with their self-views and how well they would get along with the evaluator. This is not to say that people never choose relationship partners for ironic reasons. In fact, some participants did express a desire for a negative partner so that they could bring that person to like them (and thus prove to their partner their true worth). Nevertheless, the only people who offered this reason for choosing a negative partner were people with *positive* self-views—people with negative self-views never mentioned it. As such, the attempt to "win converts" and, in so doing, receive positive feedback via an ironic route cannot explain why people with negative self-views sought self-verifying partners.

It seems, then, that the desire for self-verification offers the best explanation of the tendency for people with negative self-views to seek negative feedback. Apparently, people's verification needs influence their choice of interaction partners, their information-processing activities, and their reactions to self-discrepant feedback (for a review, see Swann 1996). Furthermore, when asked why they seek self-verifying evaluations, people voice concerns that are strikingly consistent with the self-verification perspective (e.g., Swann, Stein-Seroussi, and Giesler 1992).

Nevertheless, virtually all past research on self-verification has focused on people's desire to stabilize their *individual* self-views (i.e., those self-views that set them apart from others). However, people do not just define themselves in relation to other people; they also define themselves as members of social groups. We argue that such social identities are functionally similar to individual self-views (for similar perspectives see Brewer 1991; Smith and Henry 1996; Turner et al. 1994). As such, people should be just as motivated to verify their social identities as they are to verify their individual self-views.

Recognizing that self-verification strivings manifest themselves at the level of social identities could have several implications for research and theorizing on social movements because participants in social movements are typically bound together by a common social identity (cf. chapter 2, this volume). In the remainder of this chapter, we highlight these implications by (1) reviewing research consistent with the claim that self-verification processes occur at the level of social identities and (2) elucidating the link between the need for self-verification and social movement participation.

The Verification of Social Identities

Although we know of no one who has set out explicitly to determine whether self-verification processes extend to social identities (however, see Abrams and Hogg 1988 and Hogg and Abrams 1990 for related ideas), the results of several laboratory investigations (e.g., Branscombe and Wann 1994; Brown et al. 1999; Crocker and Luhtanen 1990) and ethnographic studies (Braginsky, Braginsky, and Ring 1969; Metcalf 1976) are consistent with this notion. Take, for example, research on people's evaluations of their various social identities (dubbed "collective self-esteem" by Crocker and Luhtanen 1990; Luhtanen and Crocker 1992). Crocker and Luhtanen (1990) have observed that people's levels of collective self-esteem moderate their displays of intergroup bias such that people with high levels of collective self-esteem display it but people with low levels of collective self-esteem do not (for related findings, see Crocker et al. 1987; Seta and Seta 1992). These findings harken back to evidence that people with positive self-views but not people with negative self-views perceive their actions and themselves through rose-colored glasses (e.g., Swann and Read 1981; Swann et al. 1987).

Studies of the effects of threatening people's social identities also suggest that self-verification strivings extend to social identities. For instance, Branscombe and Wann (1994) recruited participants who did or did not identify strongly with the United States and exposed them to either an original or a modified film clip from *Rocky IV.* In the original clip, Rocky Balboa (the North American hero in the Rocky films) wins a boxing match against Ivan Drago (the Soviet competitor); in the modified clip Rocky loses to Ivan. Participants who reported identifying strongly with the United States derogated people from the Soviet Union after seeing Rocky lose to Ivan. Assuming that the participants who identified strongly with the United States had a positive social identity (this is a relatively safe assumption, given the moderate, positive correlation between importance of one's group identification and collective self-esteem; see Luhtanen and Crocker 1992), their response to the threat may well have reflected a need to verify that social identity (see Swann and Hill 1982; Swann, Wenzlaff, and Tafarodi 1992).

Because Branscombe and Wann's (1994) participants presumably had high collective self-esteem (Luhtanen and Crocker 1992), however, their findings could also be attributed to a desire for positive evaluations. Conceivably, participants who were threatened by Rocky's loss derogated the Russians to restore their wounded self-esteem and not to verify their self-views as citizens of the United States. Thus, although consistent with a self-verification perspective, Branscombe and Wann's (1994) findings can also be understood as reflecting positivity strivings.

Although Branscombe and Wann's (1994) participants may have been acting out of a need for self-verification or positivity, recent research indicates that the need for self-verification, independent of the need for positivity, does indeed influence the extent to which people display intergroup bias. Brown et al. (1999) posited that stable self-views, worldviews, and beliefs about others all foster feelings of predictability and coherence. They thus reasoned that the feelings of unpredictability and confusion brought on by challenges to one type of belief (e.g., worldviews) could be compensated for by shoring up seemingly unrelated beliefs (e.g., self-views or beliefs about others). This led to the prediction that people whose worldviews have been threatened and who subsequently receive confirmation for their self-views will feel relatively little need to shore up their feelings of predictability, coherence, and control by acting on their evaluations of other people (see Steele 1988 for a related methodology). In contrast, people who receive no alternative means of restoring predictability, coherence, and control after their worldviews have been challenged should feel compelled to shore up those feelings by acting on their beliefs about other people. Note that if people's desire for predictability, coherence, and control underlies this effect, it should occur even if, following a threat to their worldview, people received confirmation of a *negative* self-view.

To test this reasoning, Brown et al.'s (1999) participants read either innocuous newsbriefs (e.g., ibuprofen and aspirin are the two most commonly used over-the-counter painkillers) or newsbriefs that threatened their worldviews (e.g. 25 percent of mothers and 28 percent of fathers surveyed said they would sever all connections with their nuclear family if offered a million dollars to do so). Some participants then received verification for a negative self-view while others did not. Participants, all of whom scored high on a measure of homophobia, then had an opportunity to derogate an out-group member—a gay man. When participants' beliefs about the world were threatened and they received no subsequent self-verification, they responded by derogating the gay man. However, when participants' worldviews were threatened and they then received verification for their self-views (which, in this case, were negative), they tended to refrain from derogating the gay man. Apparently, the act of confirming a negative self-view served to reinstate psychological coherence for the previously threatened participants, and they thus felt little need to restore coherence by derogating an out-group member.

Until now our discussion of self-verification and social identities has focused on identities that most people perceive as positive. Consistent with the self-verification perspective, however, people also cling to social identities that are negative (i.e., identities that are devalued by the larger society). Consider Metcalf's (1976) study of Navajo women who moved to urban settings so that they could enjoy improved educational and financial opportunities. When they arrived in the city, these women found that they were required to give up their traditional dress, language, and customs. This caused them to feel uprooted and cut off from the "true selves" they left behind on their reservations, so much so that they dreamed of returning to their reservations, despite the hardships they knew awaited them there.

Longtime residents of mental hospitals show a similar reluctance to shed identities that many people would consider negative. Braginsky, Braginsky, and Ring (1969) observed that, whereas residents who had been in the hospital for a short period attempted to convince the staff that they had recovered, those who had been in the hospital for an extended period actually feigned mental disorder. Presumably, these long-term residents had become so accustomed to viewing themselves as psychologically disordered that they took steps to remain in a context in which they would receive further confirmation for this identity.

In short, the research literature suggests that people are just as motivated to verify their social identities as they are to verify their individual self-views. Moreover, like individual self-views, social identities give rise to information-processing biases that make people's worlds seem more verifying than they actually are (e.g., Crocker and Luhtanen 1990; Crocker et al. 1987; Seta and Seta 1992). Similarly, people respond to threats to their social identities and individual self-views alike by striving to reaffirm these self-views (Branscombe and Wann 1994). Furthermore, evidence that verifying people's individual self-views can forestall such compensatory responses (Brown et al. 1999) suggests that such responses stem, in part, from people's need for predictability and control (see Solomon, Greenberg, and Pyszczynski 1991 for a similar perspective). Finally, evidence that people cling tightly to social identities that are less than optimal (e.g., Braginsky, Braginsky, and Ring 1969; Metcalf 1976) suggests that the verification of social identities does not just occur for the purpose of maintaining positive social identities.

If, as we have suggested, self-verification strivings cause people to cling to their social identities, we should find evidence of verification strivings in the literature on social movements. We highlight relevant research and theorizing in the next section.

Social Movements and Self-Verification

The repeated demonstrations of people's preference for verifying partners over nonverifying partners (for a review, see Swann 1996) suggest that the need for self-verification regularly influences people's choice of interaction partners. It follows that people's self-verification needs may play a role in their decision to join social movements.

Consistent with this hypothesis, people seem most attracted to social movements that are associated with identities that match their own identities (e.g., Hunt and Benford 1994; chapter 2, this volume). For instance, when asked why he joined Nebraskans for Peace, a leader of the movement remarked: "I suppose it was because it seemed an intelligent group, caring. It presented a global outlook and local too. These are important to me personally so I felt comfortable" (Hunt and Benford 1994, 495).

Laboratory investigations corroborate these observations. For example, Ellemers, van Knippenberg, and Wilke (1990) provided participants with success or failure feedback about their individual abilities and success or failure feedback about their (assigned) group's abilities. Their interest was in discovering the groups with which people would identify most when there was a possibility of switching groups. Compared with unsuccessful people assigned to unsuccessful groups, successful people assigned to unsuccessful groups identified more strongly with the successful out-group than with their own group. This finding is particularly suggestive given research demonstrating that strong in-group preferences emerge even when groups are randomly determined (e.g., Oakes and Turner 1980; Tajfel and Turner 1986). Apparently, the compatibility between one's self-views and the group's identity overrides the powerful tendency to prefer the in-group.

Of course, a fit between one's self-views and a movement identity does not guarantee social movement participation (e.g., Klandermans and Oemega 1987; McAdam and Paulsen 1993). Even the most committed activists probably join only a handful of the movements with which they identify. What else determines movement participation? And, in the case of people who identify with several movements, what makes them commit themselves more to one movement than another?

Research on self-verification provides an answer to these questions. Recall that people with low self-esteem who are clinically depressed show more of a preference for confirmatory feedback than do people who merely have low self-esteem (Giesler, Josephs, and Swann 1996). Furthermore, people are more likely to seek out confirmatory feedback for those self-views of which they are certain than for those of which they are uncertain (Swann et al. 1998). Together, these findings indicate that self-verification strivings are particularly pronounced for self-views that are extreme or firmly held (see also Pelham and Swann 1994; Swann and Ely 1984; Swann, Pelham, and Chidester 1988). It follows, then, that people who have a firmly held self-view relevant to a given social movement will be most likely to participate in that movement.

A similar argument appears in the writings of both Stryker (chapter 1, this volume) and McAdam and Paulsen (1993). These authors have suggested that *identity salience* (i.e., the extent to which one's social ties require that one be committed to that identity; see Stryker 1968) determines how likely people are to participate in social movements. In support of this argument, McAdam and Paulsen (1993) observed that individuals who both possessed a self-view that aligned with the goals of the 1964 Mississippi Freedom Summer Project and belonged to an organization that reaffirmed that self-view were those most likely to follow through with their plans to participate in the project. Similarly, Gurin and Townsend (1986) observed a positive correlation between the extent to which women think about being a woman and the extent to which they believe women must work collectively to fight for women's rights.

Of course, for many people, the decision to join a social movement is heavily influenced by the active recruitment of movement participants. And, not surprisingly, the most successful movement organizers use the self-verifying properties of the social movement to lure recruits. As Snow and McAdam (chapter 2, this volume) point out, movements ranging from the civil rights movement to the free speech movement at Berkeley successfully recruited new participants by highlighting the compatibility of the movement identity with the identities of the potential recruits. Similarly, Snow et al. (1986) observed that social movement organizations that appeal to people's values elicit more support and participation than ones that do not. It appears, then, that sensitivity to people's self-verification needs can reap substantial dividends in the form of additional recruits.

Another approach to unraveling the mystery of why people join social movements is to examine why they sometimes leave particular movements. The data seem to suggest that people withdraw from social movements when their continued participation would frustrate their self-verification needs. Consider White and Fraser's (chapter 15, this volume) analysis of the people who broke from Provisional Sinn Féin to form Republican Sinn Féin. These people regarded the concessions that Provisional Sinn Féin was making to the British government as evidence that it were "selling out" and not acting true to the "cause." In short, these people broke off from Provisional Sinn Féin because their continued involvement would have meant belonging to a movement whose identity conflicted with their own.

Roth's (chapter 14, this volume) discussion of the mini movements subsumed by the Coalition of Labor Union Women (CLUW) similarly suggests that continued involvement in social movements hinges on the consistency between the movement identity and the self-views of its participants (see also Hunt and Benford 1994). Roth writes of one woman who quit the CLUW when the other members violated her expectation that members should be assertive to the point of being argumentative. In the woman's words: "Everybody agreed to everything. It was like a convention of the Stepford Wives. It was like surreal, it was so weird." Apparently, just as people are less committed to their marriages when their spouses frustrate their verification needs (De La Ronde and Swann 1998; Ritts and Stein 1995; Swann, De La Ronde, and Hixon 1994), so too do they become less committed to social movements that fail to provide them with self-verification.

At first blush, our claim that people leave social movements that frustrate their verification needs might seem inconsistent with evidence that people sometimes undergo noticeable self-change as a result of their involvement in social movements (chapter 5, this volume; McAdam 1989). After all, if people's self-views have changed as a result of their social movement involvement, they must have encountered some self-discrepant information along the way. Why didn't such self-discrepant information prompt people to leave the movement? More generally, if people have such a strong affinity for their stable self-views, why do they sometimes remain in situations that cause them to change their self-views?

An answer to these questions emerges when one considers the nature of the self-concept change produced by movement participation. In such circumstances, people rarely undergo radical changes in self-definition; rather, their new self-views often represent a natural extension of the old. For example, the people who ultimately participated in the 1964 Mississippi Freedom Summer Project were already committed to peace and racial equality when the project started (McAdam and Paulsen 1993); participating in the project merely intensified their commitment (McAdam 1989).

"Changing" in this way surely would not require substantial changes to one's firmly held self-views and therefore would not interfere with the need for self-verification.

Of course, sometimes people do undergo more severe forms of self-change as a result of their movement participation (e.g., chapter 5, this volume). Change of this sort only seems to occur, however, after substantial identity work. Such work involves (a) making sense of one's past in terms of the new self-view one is trying to achieve and (b) reaffirming one's new self-view through group activities. This process is painfully slow, with participants "rebounding" during the early stages. In short, the more dramatic forms of self-change that result from movement participation do not occur quickly; considerable amounts of time must be spent nourishing the new identities and integrating them with people's preexisting beliefs about themselves (see also Kiecolt 1994).

Our analysis of the change in self-definition that people sometimes undergo as a result of social movement involvement fits quite nicely with research indicating that people respond favorably to self-discrepant feedback when it is provided in the context of verifying feedback. For example, Trope and Neter (1994) observed that people tolerate self-discrepant information that could lead to self-improvement only after being assured through self-verifying evaluations that their self-views were accurate.[1] Similarly, people enjoy improvements to their psychological health after receiving veridical personality feedback, presumably because such feedback consists of a combination of verifying and novel information (Finn and Tonsager 1992).

One implication of our discussion of change through social movement participation is that, if attempts at change do not occur through a process that addresses people's self-verification needs, people will flee. Why? Why does change become more likely if it is couched in a verifying context?

One possibility is that, because stable self-views provide people with the feelings of predictability, coherence, and control (Swann 1996), sudden shifts in their self-views leave people in a world where suddenly nothing makes sense. Consistent with this analysis, when people shift identities, they frequently experience "reality shock"—a rough transition period during which they distrust their interpretations of reality (cf. Fein and Nuehring 1981). In addition, people become anxious and confused when they receive unexpected evaluations that they cannot explain away, even when such evaluations are positive (Pinel and Swann 1998). From this perspective, it is no wonder that participants who perceive radical discrepancies between their self-views and the movement identity often leave the movement.

Summary and Closing Remarks

This chapter was designed to highlight some of the implications of self-verification theory for understanding the why and the who of social movement participation. We began with the assumption that self-verification strivings manifest themselves in the way people structure, interpret, and react to their experiences and that this motive extends to all classes of self-views, whether those self-views happen to be positive or negative and whether they are unique to an individual or shared with others. This led to the hypothesis that people's desire for self-verification should express itself in their social movement activities. Indeed, self-verification strivings seem to play a role in people's decision to join social movements (Gurin and Townsend 1986; Hunt and Benford 1994; McAdam and Paulsen 1993; Snow et al. 1986; chapters 1 and 2, this volume), in what happens to them as a result of their participation (chapters 5 and 12, this volume; McAdam 1989), and in their decision to leave social movements (Hunt and Benford 1994; chapters 14 and 15, this volume).

Of course, we recognize that the role played by self-verification strivings in social movement participation depends, in part, on the nature of the movement. Movement participation aimed at transforming society's views of a particular group (e.g., the women's movement; the civil rights movement; the postpartum movement) might be more influenced by self-verification strivings than participation in movements with goals that cross group lines (e.g., the nuclear disarmament movement or the environmental movement). Likewise, the influence of self-verification might be more pronounced in ethnic nationalist movements, in which participants are born with the identity embodied by the movement, than in new social movements, wherein participants align their identity with that of the movement (see Johnston 1994).

We also acknowledge that many motives other than the desire for self-verification may influence movement-related processes. For instance, the decision to join and remain in social movements could be influenced by people's perceptions of whether the movement will achieve its goal (although see Klandermans and Oemega 1987), the sheer size of the movement (chapter 2, this volume), or their search for meaning (chapter 4, this volume).

Despite general agreement that multiple motives play a role in social movement participation, some researchers argue that the desire for positivity dominates all other potential motives (see chapters 9 and 10, this volume). This perspective, we believe, cannot accommodate several findings in the social movement literature. To be sure, many movements do have the explicit goal of raising the esteem in which their members are held by nonmembers (e.g., chapter 12, this volume), but not all do. In fact, some movements have the converse goal of humbling their participants. Consider the transformation this member of the Nichiren Shoshu Buddhist movement underwent as a result of his participation:

> Before joining Nichiren Shoshu I blamed any problems I had on other people or on the environment. It was always my parents, or school, or society. But through chanting I discovered the real source of my difficulties: myself. Chanting has helped me to realize that rather than running around blaming others, I am the one who needs to change. (Snow et al. 1986, 474)

Such examples seem difficult to understand in terms of Kaplan and Liu's (chapter 10, this volume) model: it seems odd that people seeking positivity would get involved and remain in a movement designed to underscore their flaws.

An equally poignant example of a social movement phenomenon that poses difficulties for the positivity perspective comes from Taylor's (chapter 13, this volume) observations of the postpartum support group movement. Women who join this movement wish to make it known that new mothers rarely conform to the idealized image portrayed in the media. Rather than loving their newborns right off the bat, young mothers experience much ambivalence toward their newborns. Sometimes, the negative feelings escalate to the point where mothers are moved to hurt their newborns physically.

This is a largely unspoken reality that people intent on cultivating positive self-views should want to hide. But instead, those women involved in the postpartum movement work to bring society's impressions of them into line with their negative self-views: they want to change the image of the young mother from a positive to a negative one! We do not know of a theoretical perspective other than self-verification that provides a parsimonious account for this behavior.

Coda

Wherever one looks, people are struggling for their voice to be heard, whether they are trying to educate others about their racial or ethnic identity, disseminate their social values, or promote the agenda of a special-interest group. The result is a chaos of variegated interests in which people are thrust into competition with one another: men against men; women against women; employee against employer; race against race; and social class against social class.

Although the causes of this state of affairs are complex, we believe that people's efforts to verify their conceptions of themselves play a central role: When people join social movements, one of their prepotent concerns is to receive validation for important aspects of themselves. Paradoxically, in seeking to identify with others, people are striving to be themselves.

Note

1. Although Trope and Neter (1994) did not actually measure their participants' self-views, because the distribution for self-esteem is negatively skewed (Taylor and Brown 1988), we can safely assume that positive feedback verified the self-views of most of Trope and Neter's participants.

References

Abrams, Dominic, and Michael A. Hogg. 1988. "Comments on the Motivational Status of Self-Esteem in Social Identity and Intergroup Discrimination."*European Journal of Social Psychology* 18:317–34.

Aronson, Elliot. 1968. "A Theory of Cognitive Dissonance: A Current Perspective." In *Advances in Experimental Social Psychology,* edited by Leonard Berkowitz, 4:1–34. New York: Academic Press.

Bass, Ellen, and Laura Davis. 1988. *The Courage to Heal: A Guide for Women Survivors of Child Sexual Abuse.* New York: Harper & Row.

Baumeister, Roy. 1989. "The Optimal Margin of Illusion." *Journal of Social and Clinical Psychology* 8:176–89.

Baumgardner, Ann H., and Paul E. Levy. 1988. "Role of Self-Esteem in Perceptions of Ability and Effort: Illogic or Insight?" *Personality and Social Psychology Bulletin* 14:429–38.

Berglas, Stephen, and Edward E. Jones. 1978. "Drug Choice as a Self-Handicapping Strategy in Response to Noncontingent Success." *Journal of Personality and Social Psychology* 36:405–17.

Braginsky, Benjamin M., Dorothea D. Braginsky, and Kenneth Ring. 1969. *Methods of Madness: The Mental Hospital as a Last Resort.* New York: Holt, Rinehart and Winston.

Branscombe, Nyla R., Daniel L. Wann. 1994. "Collective Self-Esteem Consequences When a Valued Social Identity Is on Trial." *European Journal of Social Psychology* 24:641–57.

Brewer, Marilyn B. 1991. "The Social Self: On Being the Same and Different at the Same Time." *Personality and Social Psychology Bulletin* 17:475–82.

Brown, Ryan, Jennifer K. Bosson, Cary Booker, and William B. Swann Jr. 1999. "Psychological Coherence and the Interplay among World-Views, Self-Views, and Outgroup Derogation." Manuscript.

Coyne, James C. 1976. "Toward an Interactional Description of Depression." *Psychiatry* 39:28–40.

Coyne, James C., Ronald C. Kessler, Margalit Tal, Joanne Turnbull, Camille B. Wortman, and John F. Greden. 1987. "Living with a Depressed Person." *Journal of Consulting and Clinical Psychology* 55:347–52.

Crary, William G. 1966. "Reactions to Incongruent Self-Experiences." *Journal of Consulting Psychology* 30:246–52.

Crocker, Jennifer, and Riia Luhtanen. 1990. "Collective Self-Esteem and Ingroup Bias." *Journal of Personality and Social Psychology* 58:60–67.

Crocker, Jennifer, Leigh L. Thompson, Kathleen M. McGraw, and Cindy Ingerman. 1987. "Downward Comparison, Prejudice, and Evaluations of Others: Effects of Self-Esteem and Threat." *Journal of Personality and Social Psychology* 52:907–16.

Darabont, Frank. 1995. *The Shawshank Redemption: The Shooting Script.* New York: Newmarket Press.

De La Ronde, Chris, and William B. Swann Jr. 1998. "Partner Verification: Restoring Shattered Images of Our Intimates." *Journal of Personality and Social Psychology* 75:374–82.

Ellemers, Naomi, Ad van Knippenberg, and Henk Wilke. 1990. "The Influence of Permeability of Group Boundaries and Stability of Group Status on Strategies of Individual Mobility and Social Change." *British Journal of Social Psychology* 29:233–46.

Fein, Sara B., and Elane M. Nuehring. 1981. "Intrapsychic Effects of Stigma: A Process of Breakdown and Reconstruction of Social Reality." *Journal of Homosexuality* 7:3–13.

Finn, Stephen E., and Mary E. Tonsager. 1992. "Therapeutic Impact of Providing MMPI-2 Feedback to College Students Awaiting Therapy." *Journal of Psychological Assessment* 4:278–87.

Giesler, R. Brian, Robert. A. Josephs, and William. B. Swann Jr. 1996. "Self-Verification in Clinical Depression: The Desire for Negative Evaluation." *Journal of Abnormal Psychology* 105:358–68.

Greenwald, Anthony G. 1980. "The Totalitarian Ego: Fabrication and Revision of Personal History." *American Psychologist* 35:603–18.

Gurin, Patricia, and Aloen Townsend. 1986. "Properties of Gender Identity and Their Implications for Gender Consciousness." *British Journal of Social Psychology* 25:139–48.

Hogg, Michael A., and D. Abrams. 1990. "Social Motivation, Self-Esteem, and Social Identity." In *Social Identity Theory: Constructive and Critical Advances,* edited by Dominic Abrams and Michael A. Hogg, 28–41. New York: Springer-Verlag.

Horney, Karen. 1939. *New Ways in Psychoanalysis.* New York: Norton.

Hunt, Scott A., and Robert D. Benford. 1994. "Identity Talk in the Peace and Justice Movement." *Journal of Contemporary Ethnography* 22:488–517.

Johnston, Hank. 1994. "New Social Movements and Old Regional Nationalisms." In *New Social Movements: From Ideology to Identity,* edited by Enrique Laraña, Hank Johnston, and Joseph R. Gusfield, 267–86. Philadelphia: Temple University Press.

Jones, Stephen C. 1973. "Self- and Interpersonal Evaluations: Esteem Theories versus Consistency Theories." *Psychological Bulletin* 79:185–99.

Kaplan, Howard B. 1975. "The Self-Esteem Motive and Change in Self-Attitudes." *Journal of Nervous and Mental Disease* 161:265–75.

Kiecolt, K. Jill. 1994. "Stress and the Decision to Change Oneself: A Theoretical Model." *Social Psychology Quarterly* 57:49–63.

Klandermans, Bert, and Dirk Oegema. 1987. "Potentials, Networks, Motivations, and Barriers: Steps towards Participation in Social Movements." *American Sociological Review* 52:519–31.

Luhtanen, Riia, and Jennifer Crocker. 1992. "A Collective Self-Esteem Scale: Self-Evaluation of One's Social Identity." *Personality and Social Psychology Bulletin* 18:302–18.

McAdam, Doug. 1989. "The Biographical Consequences of Activism." *American Sociological Review* 54:744–60.

McAdam, Doug, and Ronnelle Paulsen. 1993. "Specifying the Relationship between Social Ties and Activism." *American Journal of Sociology* 99:640–67.

Mead, George H. 1934. *Mind, Self, and Society.* Chicago: University of Chicago Press.

Metcalf, Ann. 1976. "From Schoolgirl to Mother: The Effects of Education on Navajo Women.: *Social Problems* 23:535–44.

Oakes, Penelope J., and John C. Turner. 1980. "Social Categorization and Intergroup Behaviour: Does Minimal Intergroup Discrimination Make Social Identity More Positive?" *European Journal of Social Psychology* 10:295–301.

Pelham, Brett W., and William B. Swann Jr. 1994. "The Juncture of Intrapersonal and Interpersonal Knowledge: Self-Certainty and Interpersonal Congruence." *Personality and Social Psychology Bulletin* 20:349–57.

Pinel, Elizabeth C., and William B. Swann Jr. 1998. "The Cognitive-Affective Crossfire Revisited: Affective Reactions to Self-Discrepant Feedback." Manuscript in preparation.

Rhodewalt, Frederick, and S. Kristian Hill. 1995. "Self-Handicapping in the Classroom: The Effects of Claimed Self-Handicaps on Responses to Academic Failure." *Basic and Applied Social Psychology* 16:397–416.

Ritts, Vicki, and James R. Stein. 1995. "Verification and Commitment in Marital Relationships: An Exploration of Self-Verification Theory in Community College Students." *Psychological Reports* 76:383–86.

Secord, Paul F., and Carl W. Backman. 1965. "An Interpersonal Approach to Personality." In *Progress in Experimental Personality Research,* edited by Brendan Maher, 2:91–125. New York: Academic Press.

Seta, Catherine E., and John J. Seta. 1992. "Observers and Participants in an Intergroup Setting." *Journal of Personality and Social Psychology* 63:629–43.

Shrauger, J. Sidney, and Adrian Lund. 1975. "Self-Evaluation and Reactions to Evaluations from Others." *Journal of Personality* 43:94–108.

Smith, Eliot R., and Susan Henry. 1996. "An In-Group Becomes Part of the Self: Response Time Evidence." *Personality and Social Psychology Bulletin* 22:635–42.

Snow, David A., E. Burke Rochford, Steven K. Worden, and Robert D. Benford. 1986. "Frame Alignment Processes, Micromobilization, and Movement Participation." *American Sociological Review* 51:464–81.

Solomon, Sheldon, Jeff Greenberg, and Thomas Pyszczynski.1991. "Terror Management Theory of Self-Esteem." In *Handbook of Social and Clinical Psychology: The Health Perspective,* edited by C. R. Snyder and Donelson R. Forsyth, 162:21–40. New York: Pergamon Press.

Steele, Claude M. 1988. "The Psychology of Self-Affirmation: Sustaining the Integrity of the Self." In *Advances in Experimental Social Psychology,* edited by Leonard Berkowitz, 21:261–302. New York: Academic Press.

Steinem, Gloria. 1996. *Revolution from Within: A Book of Self-Esteem.* Boston: Little, Brown.

Stryker, Sheldon. 1968. "Identity Salience and Role Performance." *Journal of Marriage and the Family* 30:558–64.

Swann, William B., Jr. 1983. "Self-Verification: Bringing Social Reality into Harmony with the Self." In *Social Psychological Perspectives on the Self,* edited by J. Suls and A. G. Greenwald, 2:33–66. Hillsdale, N.J.: Lawrence Erlbaum.

———. 1996. *Self-Traps: The Elusive Quest for Higher Self-Esteem.* New York: Freeman.

Swann, William B., Jr., Jennifer K. Bosson, Brett W. Pelham, and Elizabeth C. Pinel. 1998. "Self-Certainty and Self-Verification." Manuscript in preparation.

Swann, William B., Jr., Chris De La Ronde, and J. Gregory Hixon. 1994. "Authenticity and Positivity Strivings in Marriage and Courtship." *Journal of Personality and Social Psychology* 66:857–69.

Swann, William B., Jr., and Robin J. Ely. 1984. "A Battle of Wills: Self-Verification versus Behavioral Confirmation." *Journal of Personality and Social Psychology* 46:1287–1302.

Swann, William B., Jr., John J. Griffin, Steven C. Predmore, and Bebe Gaines. 1987. "The Cognitive-Affective Crossfire: When Self-Consistency Confronts Self-Enhancement." *Journal of Personality and Social Psychology* 52:881–89.

Swann, William B., Jr., and Craig A. Hill. 1982. "When Our Identities Are Mistaken: Reaffirming Self-Conceptions through Social Interaction." *Journal of Personality and Social Psychology* 43:59–66.

Swann, William B., Jr., Brett W. Pelham, and Thomas R. Chidester. 1988. "Change through Paradox: Using Self-Verification to Alter Beliefs." *Journal of Personality and Social Psychology* 54:268–73.

Swann, William B., Jr., Elizabeth C. Pinel, and Romin W. Tafarodi. 1997. Unpublished manuscript.

Swann, William B., Jr., and Stephen J. Read. 1981. "Self-Verification Processes: How We Sustain Our Self-Conceptions." *Journal of Experimental Social Psychology* 17:351–72.

Swann, William B., Jr., and Daniel G. Schroeder. 1995. "The Search for Beauty and Truth: A Framework for Understanding Reactions to Evaluations." *Personality and Social Psychology Bulletin* 21:1307–18.

Swann, William B., Jr., Alan Stein-Seroussi, and R. Brian Giesler. 1992. "Why People Self-Verify." *Journal of Personality and Social Psychology* 62:392–401.

Swann, William B., Jr., Richard M. Wenzlaff, and Roman W. Tafarodi. 1992. "Depression and the Search for Negative Evaluations: More Evidence of the Role of Self-Verification Strivings." *Journal of Abnormal Psychology* 101:314–71.

Tajfel, Henry, and John C. Turner. 1986. "The Social Identity of Intergroup Behavior." In *Psychology of Intergroup Relations,* 2d ed., edited by S. Worchel and W. G. Austin, 7–24. Chicago: Nelson-Hall.

Taylor, Shelley E., and Jonathan D. Brown. 1988. "Illusion and Well-Being: A Social Psychological Perspective on Mental Health." *Psychological Bulletin* 103:193–210.

Trope, Yaacov, and Efrat Neter. 1994. "Reconciling Competing Motives in Self-Evaluation: The Role of Self-Control in Feedback Seeking." *Journal of Personality and Social Psychology* 66:646–57.

Turner, John C., Penelope J. Oakes, S. Alexander Haslam, and Craig McGaraty. 1994. "Self and Collective: Cognition and Social Context." *Personality and Social Psychology Bulletin* 20:454–63.

7

Group Distinctiveness, Social Identification, and Collective Mobilization

Marilynn B. Brewer and Michael D. Silver

Tajfel's theory of social identity and its recent extensions (Tajfel 1982; Tajfel and Turner 1986; Turner et al. 1987) is, above all, a theory of how cognitive representations of the self provide the critical link between individual and collective behavior. In this respect, social identity theory shares many of the goals and assumptions of identity theories in general (Hogg, Terry, White 1995). The unique aspect of Tajfel and Turner's theory is its emphasis on the sense of self that is derived from membership in large, dispersed social categories (including sex, ethnicity, religion, nationality) and the sociocognitive processes that underlie such identification.

In the Tajfel-Turner framework, group identification is a product of self-categorization—a cognitive representation of the self as an embodiment of a more inclusive category, accompanied by an awareness of similarity, in-group identity, and shared fate with others who belong to that category.[1] Most important, group identification is characterized as a depersonalized self-representation, "a shift towards the perception of self as an interchangeable exemplar of some social category and away from the perception of self as a unique person" (Turner et al. 1987, 50). It is this depersonalization (which is not to be confused with more negative concepts such as "deindividuation" or "dehumanization") that accounts for a wide range of collective behaviors. As Hogg, Terry, and White (1995) put it:

> Depersonalization of the self is the basic process underlying group phenomena—for example, social stereotyping, group cohesion and ethnocentrism, cooperation and altruism, emotional contagion and

> empathy, collective behavior, shared norms, and the mutual influence process. . . . Through depersonalization, self-categorization effectively brings self-perception and behavior into line with the contextually relevant in-group prototype, and thus transforms individuals into group members and individuality into group behavior. (261)

The concept of depersonalized self-categorization in effect makes group processes independent of interpersonal processes of attraction, influence, and compliance (Hogg 1996). As a consequence, group identification and collective action are not constrained by group size or dispersion. When a social identity is engaged, a shared understanding of group attributes, norms, and goals (the group "prototype") is sufficient to produce uniformity of behavior and purpose among those who share that social identity. In this sense, social identification can be viewed as a group resource that is critical to the ability of the group to mobilize collective action among its members or to recruit group members into a social movement. Thus, understanding how, when, and why large numbers of those who belong to a particular social category adopt that category membership as an important social identity is essential to predicting and explaining collective movements.

Selecting Social Identities and the Theory of Optimal Distinctiveness

Although research derived from the theories of social identity and self-categorization has gone a long way toward elaborating the sociocognitive bases of group identification and its consequences for group behavior, the determinants of the strength and importance of particular social identities remain somewhat elusive. According to self-categorization theory, the salience of specific social identities is highly context-specific; both the selection and the form taken by social identities are the product of a complex social dynamic, influenced by their meaningfulness within a given social (intergroup) context (Turner et al. 1987). The theory does not provide a basis for predicting what properties of groups or of individuals might account for more chronic or cross-situational levels of social identification with particular groups. Yet some provision for extending social identities across time and place would seem to be necessary to account for sustained collective action.

Using social identity theory as a point of departure, Brewer's (1991) theory of optimal distinctiveness was developed to provide one account of the motivations underlying group identification that would acknowledge the dynamic nature of social identification and at the same time provide for chronically high levels of identification with specific groups. The theory postulates that social identification is derived from the opposing forces of two universal human motives—the need for *inclusion and assimilation* on the one hand and the need for *differentiation* from others on the other.

Optimal distinctiveness theory assumes that group identification has motivational and functional origins that are deeply rooted in our evolution as a social species. The desire for belonging associated with the need for inclusion motivates immersion in social groups—the larger and more inclusive the grouping, the more this motive is satisfied. The need for differentiation operates in opposition to the need for immersion as represented in the drive for individuation and personal identity. As group membership becomes more and more inclusive, the need for inclusion is satisfied, but the need for differentiation is activated; conversely, as inclusiveness decreases, the differentiation need is reduced, but the need for assimilation is activated.

Although personality, socialization, and cultural values may produce individual differences in the relative strength of the needs for inclusion and differentiation, the model postulates that the presence of opposing processes is universal. According to the model, the two opposing motives produce an emergent characteristic—the capacity for social identification with distinctive groups that satisfy both needs simultaneously. The need for inclusion/belonging is met within the in-group; the need for differentiation, by distinctions between in-group and out-groups. Thus, unlike theories that account for group identification strictly in terms of the need for belonging alone, optimal distinctiveness theory assumes that the need for inclusion is naturally moderated by an opposing need for differentiation that regulates group identification processes.

The dynamic interplay that gives rise to optimal social identities provides a model for understanding how properties of specific social groups and the needs and motivations of particular individuals might interact to determine levels of social identification. In order to engage member identification and loyalty, groups must have explicit, agreed-on rules of inclusion and of exclusion that define clear boundaries between in-group and out-groups. On the one hand, effective groups must have defined criteria for group membership that meet needs for secure inclusion and belonging on the part of those who satisfy those criteria. At the same time, the criteria must be sufficiently delineated and exclusive to meet members' needs for differentiation and distinctiveness. *Shared distinctiveness* is the group property that is most likely to engage high levels of attachment and identification with a given social group or category.

Group leaders or spokespersons must be sensitive to both social motives in their appeals to group members. Mobilization efforts that appeal to highly inclusive values at the expense of distinctiveness are likely to fail, as are efforts that raise excessively high standards of membership allegiance that threaten members' needs for secure inclusion. Social identification will be highest for those groups that make members feel they are valued and representative members of an exclusive category. Thus, optimal distinctiveness theory provides a general model for understanding the formation, maintenance, and fission of social movements.

The Causes and Consequences of Social Identification

The model represented in figure 1 uses optimal distinctiveness theory as a starting point for a general model of the relationships between individual and group attributes, group identification, and the mobilization of collective action. In the first step of the model, optimal distinctiveness predicts how group characteristics and individual needs will interact to engage group identification processes. In effect, the model hypothesizes that the match between the group's inclusiveness and boundedness (exclusion rules) and the relative strength of the individual's needs for assimilation versus differentiation will determine whether the group provides an optimal social identity for that individual. Successful groups must meet both needs to some extent, assuring that those who are "in" feel securely included and at the same time sufficiently distinct from those who are "out." Groups that set the threshold of acceptance too high are not likely to attract a sufficient number of members, but setting the threshold too low will not satisfy members' need for differentiation. In the latter case, the group may contain a large number of nominal members but few who are strongly identified.

Assimilation and Differentiation Needs as Determinants of Group Identification

In general, groups that are distinctive by virtue of minority status or clarity of defining features will be more likely to engage high levels of social identification on the part of their members than groups that are large or amorphous. Consistent with this hypothesis, a large number of experiments on intergroup discrimination support the hypothesis that in-group favoritism varies with relative group size, such that members of minority groups exhibit more in-group preference and bias than members of majority groups (Mullen, Brown, and Smith 1992).

Although minority status per se satisfies group members' needs for distinctiveness, in many contexts minority size is correlated with various forms

Figure 1. Model of group identification and collective action

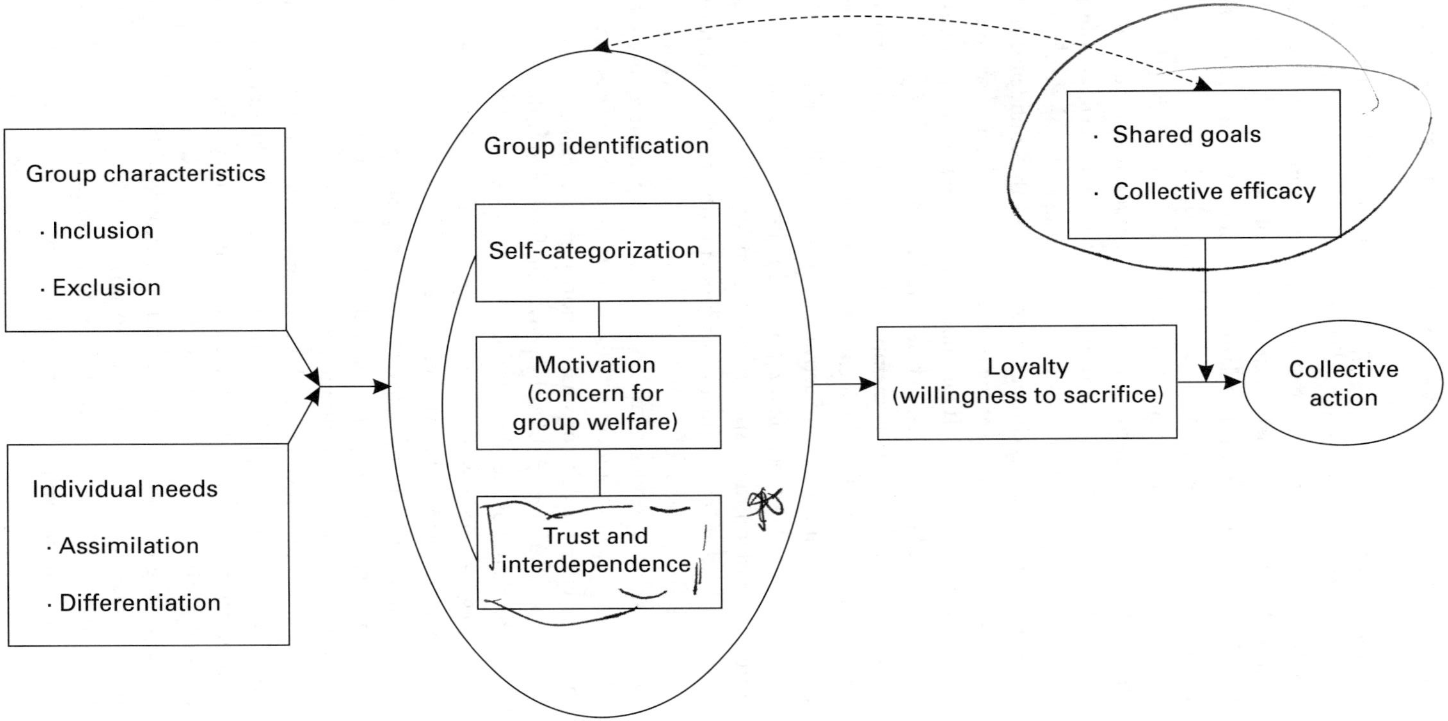

Group characteristics

· Inclusion

· Exclusion

Individual needs

· Assimilation

· Differentiation

Group identification

Self-categorization

Motivation (concern for group welfare)

Trust and interdependence

Loyalty (willingness to sacrifice)

· Shared goals

· Collective efficacy

Collective action

of disadvantage in terms of group power, status, and other resources. Thus, it is often the case that group distinctiveness competes with other social needs, such as self-enhancement, social status, and power, as sources of group identification. When status differentials are at stake, group characteristics will interact with the relative strength of these needs at the individual level to determine strength of social identification.

An experiment reported in Brewer, Manzi, and Shaw (1993) demonstrated that activation of the need for differentiation can moderate the relative impact of in-group size and in-group status on social identification. In this experiment, an initial state of deindividuation was subtly created in some of the participants through a novel use of the confidentiality instructions that were introduced at the outset of the experimental session. The person was given an arbitrary ID number in the context of written instructions that emphasized that the researchers were "not interested in [the participant] as an individual but as a member of the college student population." Immersion in such a broadly inclusive category was expected to overindulge the need for assimilation and activate the need for differentiation.

Following the depersonalization induction, subjects were given a dot estimation task on the basis of which (ostensibly) they were assigned to the category of either "overestimator" or "underestimator." Further instructions informed group members that more than 80 percent of college students were classified as underestimators but only 20 percent as overestimators. Thus, assignment to underestimator/overestimator categories meant assignment to a large majority or small minority group, respectively. In addition, group status was manipulated by providing further information about relative performance of members of the two categories on a difficult ability test. One category was purported to average well above the midpoint in performance on the test while the other averaged below the midpoint. The status manipulation was fully crossed with group size, to produce conditions involving high status majority, low status majority, high status minority, and low status minority in-group membership.

In-group identification in this experiment was assessed by participants' ratings of their in-group on evaluative traits such as kindness, trustworthiness, and warmth. The results were consistent with predictions derived from optimal distinctiveness theory about the relative effects of group size and status on in-group identification. Under control conditions, both group status and majority size contributed to positive valuations of the in-group. Under the deindividuated conditions, however, participants valued minority group membership more than majority categorization, regardless of group status.

The findings of this initial experiment confirm that even disadvantaged or low-status groups can engage group identification if they fulfill members' joint needs for inclusion and differentiation. If the premises of optimal distinctiveness theory are correct, then arousing *either* the drive for differentiation or the drive for assimilation/inclusion should make membership in distinctive groups more important to the individual. This hypothesis was supported by results of an experiment by Pickett (1996) in which drive states were manipulated by having participants selectively recall memories of situations in which they had felt excessively distinctive from everyone else or recall and think about situations when they had felt excessively similar to others. (Participants in a control condition were asked simply to think about the last two movies they had seen.)

Following the rumination task, all participants were moved into a separate phase of the experiment in which they were given a list of thirty-two social categories of various sizes (e.g., males, females, honors students, fraternity members, left-handed people) and asked to indicate, for each, whether they were a member of that category and to rate how important (on a five-point scale) their membership (or nonmembership) in that group was to them. As predicted from optimal distinctiveness theory, subjects who had participated in the excessive similarity or differentiation rumination conditions rated group memberships overall as more important (M = 2.65) than subjects in the control condition (M = 2.45).[2]

Group memberships were further distinguished on the basis of relative size. From the list of thirty-two groups, Pickett identified the ten most common categories (i.e., those identified as membership groups by a large proportion of the respondents) and the ten least common categories. The relative importance of membership or nonmembership in common and distinctive categories varied systematically as a function of rumination condition. Compared with control subjects, participants in the excessive similarity condition placed greater importance on their membership in relatively distinctive groups (and their nonmembership in some common groups). Participants in the excessive distinctiveness condition, however, assigned less importance to their distinctive group memberships compared with more common group memberships. In a later conceptual replication of this experiment, using a different method to arouse assimilation and distinctiveness motives, Silver (1997) also found that arousal of different need states affected participants' degree of social identification with distinctive group memberships.

These experimental findings support the assumptions of optimal distinctiveness theory that arousing needs for inclusion or differentiation enhances the importance of social identities that meet these needs and that the strength of social identification is a function of the interaction between the inclusiveness of the social group and the relative strength of needs for assimilation and distinctiveness at the individual level (as depicted in figure 1). In these laboratory studies, inclusion and differentiation needs were activated by instructions from an experimenter, but one can readily imagine real-world contexts in which these motives become differentially salient (e.g., participation in rallies or mass gatherings that make group inclusiveness particularly salient, political speeches that appeal to in-group–out-group distinctiveness). Thus, although some group identifications are chronically important, the strength of identification can be influenced by immediate context.

Psychological Consequences of Social Identification

As a depersonalized self-categorization, group identification involves a transformation of the sense of self from the individual "I" to the collective "we." In effect, the boundaries of the self are redefined to include others who share the relevant category membership. This transformation has cognitive, motivational, and affective manifestations.

At the most basic level, group identification is a cognitive recategorization, with consequences for the perception of others as a function of whether they belong to the in-group category or not. According to the principle of category accentuation, perceived similarities among members of the same category are enhanced while perception of differences between categories are exaggerated (Tajfel 1969). Hence, commonalities with fellow in-group members are more important than intragroup differences when social identification is salient. Once this commonality is engaged, the meaning of "self-interest" is transformed to the group level. When identification is strong, outcomes for the group as a whole (or those for other members of the in-group) have a hedonistic impact on the individual group member, even when his or her own outcomes are not directly affected. When social identification is engaged, group welfare becomes a part of the rational calculus by which an individual evaluates the costs and benefits of intended actions and potential outcomes.

One way to assess the importance that an individual attaches to group outcomes is to observe how the person behaves when faced with a conflict between opportunities to benefit the self at the expense of group welfare and opportunities to sacrifice self-interest for the sake of the collective. Social dilemmas are classes of social situations (such as resource conservation and contributions to public goods) that pose such choices between immediate individual gain and long-term collective outcomes (Messick and Brewer 1983). A laboratory analogue of scarce-resource dilemmas has been designed to test conditions under which individuals will voluntarily restrain their own consumption from a common resource pool in order to preserve the resource for the group as a whole (Messick et al. 1983). In this laboratory paradigm, the common resource is a pool of points, each with monetary value, and the collective is a group of six or more individuals who share access to this resource pool. Members of the group act independently and anonymously, with no visual contact or communication with other participants in the collective.

In a series of experiments using this paradigm, Kramer and Brewer (1986) found that responses to depletion of the collective resource were significantly affected by the level of social identification that had been made salient in the context. Individuals were more likely to exercise restraint to conserve an endangered collective resource when a common social identity among users of the resource pool had been made salient than when no superordinate group identification had been provided. Furthermore, the level of restraint on personal consumption increased as the severity of the resource crisis intensified. Participants' voluntary self-sacrifice was not mediated by normative expectations or beliefs about what other group members were likely to do. (In fact, in one experiment, subjects in the high social identification condition sacrificed more when feedback from the experimenter indicated that other members of their group were failing to conserve—in an apparent attempt to compensate for the selfishness of the others.) Instead, the findings appear to reflect a transformation of social motives whereby an individualistic self-interested orientation is matched or superseded by the motivation to maximize joint or collective interests.

In addition to affective attachments to the group as a whole, group identification transforms the affective ties among group members. Shared group identity increases perceptions of interdependence and common fate. Most important, it increases the willingness to trust the intentions and motives of fellow group members. Kramer, Brewer, and Hanna (1996) have argued that identity-based trust is one of the most important psychological mechanisms underlying collective action. Because social identities are depersonalized, trust in fellow in-group members is conferred in the absence of any prior history of reciprocal benefits or obligations. Presumptive actions predicated on trust are often necessary to resolve the dilemma of trust versus distrust that would otherwise immobilize large organizations. Since both indiscriminate trust and indiscriminate distrust are costly, mutually recognized group boundaries serve to delineate the limits of risk. Shared social identities define bounded communities of mutual trust and obligation.

From Group Identification to Collective Action

Thus far we have discussed group identification at the level of the individual and the individual's attachment to particular social group memberships. The question still remains how individuals come to develop shared group identifications that lead to collective identities. Returning to the model represented in figure 1, the cognitive, motivational, and affective transformations associated with group identification are all presumed to contribute to group *loyalty,* defined here as the willingness of group members to exert effort, pay costs, or sacrifice personal benefits on behalf of the group as a whole. One way to represent this relationship is to think of loyalty as the action potential associated with a particular social identity. Because loyalty has its bases in the mutual effects of the cognitive, motivational, and affective components of social identification, there should be a direct, positive correlation between the strength of members' identification with a particular group and group loyalty.

We found support for this relationship in the results from a small survey of group memberships among Ohio State University students. As part of the survey, students were asked to complete scales of social identification and loyalty with respect to three groups to which they belonged—Americans, Ohio State University students, and a subgroup (e.g., honors students, fraternity members, Republicans) that they had personally identified as a membership group. The three groups were selected to represent different levels of inclusiveness for college students in the United States. The group identification measure was a ten-item scale adapted from Mael and Tetrick's (1992) Scale of Identification with a Psychological Group, which includes items such as "When someone criticizes this group, it feels like a personal insult," and "When I talk about this group, I usually say 'we' rather than 'they,'" each rated on a four-point scale from "strongly disagree" to "strongly agree."

The group loyalty measure was developed specifically for this study based on responses obtained in an earlier student survey to an open-ended question on what it means to be loyal to groups to which one belongs. Responses to this survey item were content analyzed and used to construct an eight-item scale of willingness to pay costs (e.g., donate time and effort to group, organize activities, risk life fighting for the group) and stand up for the group (e.g., defend the group publicly, wear group symbols). (See Silver 1997 for full scale information.)

Table 1. Mean Identity and Loyalty Ratings for Three Target In-Groups (n = 323)

Target Group	Identity Rating	Loyalty Rating
Americans	19.37	18.82
Ohio State University students	17.06	16.68
Subgroup	20.72	19.24

Note: N = 323. Possible identity scores ranged from 0 to 30. Possible loyalty scores ranged from 0 to 32.

Strength of identification and loyalty were assessed separately for each of the three social groups. Mean ratings of identification and loyalty obtained from analyses of 138 student questionnaires are reported in table 1. As expected, both identification and loyalty were highest for the distinctive subgroup identified by each student as a significant membership group. Ratings for the two more inclusive categories, however, reflected the type of group rather than relative group size. National identity engaged higher ratings of identification and loyalty than university identity for most students.

More important, the intercorrelations between strength of group identification and loyalty among the three groups provided evidence for both convergent and discriminant validity of the measures (see table 2). The bivariate correlations italicized in table 2 document the significant positive relationship between strength of social identification and loyalty within each of the three groups. (The relatively low correlations among these measures between groups indicate that this relationship is not simply an artifact of methods factors.) Finally, the finding that correlations between reported loyalty to superordinate groups, such as Americans and Ohio State University students, and loyalty to more specific subgroups were generally positive (ranging from .35 to .47) indicates that most students do not perceive their loyalties to be in conflict with one another. At least at the level of reported willingness to serve and make sacrifices for one's meaningful group identities, loyalty is apparently not a zero-sum commodity.

Although these results support the predicted interrelationship between social identification and willingness to make sacrifices on the group's behalf, the link between social identification and mobilization of collective action is not necessarily a direct one. The aggregate level of group loyalty among members of a social category constitutes a group resource in the form of mobilization potential. Converting that potential into coordinated group

Table 2. Correlations among Identity and Loyalty Ratings for Three Target In-Groups

	Identity Ratings			Loyalty Ratings		
	Americans	OSU Students	Subgroup	Americans	OSU Students	Subgroup
Identity ratings						
Americans	—					
OSU students	.51	—				
Subgroup	.38	.35	—			
Loyalty ratings						
Americans	*.57*	.35	.29	—		
OSU students	.27	*.60*	.22	.51	—	
Subgroup	.14	.10	*.63*	.40	.36	—

Note: N = 323. OSU = Ohio State University.

action depends on a number of convergent processes that are linked to, but not fully determined by, group identification at the individual level. Additional sociocognitive variables such as shared fate, collective goals and values, and beliefs that collective action can be effective may be necessary catalysts for the conversion of group identification into group mobilization.

The Role of Social Identification in Perceived Injustice

As a basis for collective movements, group identification theory is often contrasted with more individualistic accounts of the motivations underlying participation in collective action, including relative deprivation theory (Runciman 1966). Taylor and McKirnan's (1984) five-stage model of intergroup conflict, for instance, assumes that personal experiences of deprivation relative to one's aspirations are a necessary precursor to group consciousness and perceptions of intergroup discrimination and conflict.

Social identity theory, on the other hand, assumes that feelings of relative deprivation can be experienced at the group level even in the absence of personal experiences of deprivation or discrimination. Group identification entails a shift in social comparison from the interpersonal to the intergroup level. When social identification is high, group members become less concerned with comparisons between their own individual outcomes and those of other individuals and more concerned with the status or outcomes of their group compared with those of other groups. Since intergroup differences are generally more pronounced and unambiguous than interpersonal comparisons, perceptions that one's group has been disadvantaged or discriminated against tend to be stronger than feelings of personal deprivation or discrimination (Taylor et al. 1990).

Intergroup social comparison is fundamental to Tajfel and Turner's (1986) social identity theory of social change (see also Reicher 1996). As a basis for collective self-esteem, social identification induces a desire to see the in-group in a positive light, to achieve a sense of "positive distinctiveness" in comparison to relevant out-groups. But group members are also sensitive to the realities of the in-group's position in a larger intergroup context. When the in-group's position is at the lower end of a status or power hierarchy, the recognition of the in-group's relative low status conflicts with the need for positive distinctiveness.

According to Tajfel and Turner (1986), there are several alternative routes that the individual member of a low-status group might take to redefine the situation and resolve the conflict. One route is that of social mobility, whereby the individual dissociates himself or herself from the social category and pursues membership in a higher-status group. A second method is that of social creativity, whereby group members find alternative bases for intergroup comparison in which the in-group can be evaluated more positively than the higher-status out-groups. The third route is social change, whereby group members seek to alter the status system itself in order to improve the relative position of the ingroup.[3] Only the social change orientation is associated with collective action.

Heightened awareness of collective relative deprivation has consistently been found to be related to in-group loyalty, perceived injustice, and willingness to engage in collective protest, with or without the experience of personal relative deprivation (Foster and Matheson 1995; Grant and Brown 1995; Guimond and Dube-Simard 1983; Kelly 1993). However, perception of group deprivation alone is also not sufficient to account for collective action (e.g., Gurney and Tierney 1982). Strength of social identification and collective relative deprivation operate interactively to produce the potential for collective action. Measures of social identification and perceived relative deprivation considered separately do not strongly predict activism, but the joint effect of both is a significant predictor (Hinkle et al. 1996).

The relationship between group identification and feelings of collective deprivation is clearly a two-way street. On the one hand, group identification enhances sensitivity to intergroup comparisons that underlie perceptions of relative disadvantage. On the other hand, beliefs in collective victimization enhance group members' awareness of shared experience that serves to coalesce group boundaries and enhances social identification. This leads to the somewhat paradoxical outcome that levels of group identification, commitment, and loyalty are positively correlated with beliefs that the in-group is disadvantaged or stigmatized (Abrams and Emler 1992; Mlicki and Ellemers 1996). In effect, the greater the personal cost associated with maintaining group membership, the greater the level of commitment and loyalty that is attached to that social identity (see Hirschman 1970 for a similar perspective). Again, it is the joint effect of identification and relative deprivation that enhances the mobilization potential of group identities.

The Role of Social Identification in Shared Goals and Values

At a more general level, the effects of perceived collective relative deprivation can be classified as one manifestation of the effects of shared goals or values on group action. Redress of shared injustice is apparently a powerful group goal, but similar mobilization effects can be achieved by other goals and values, such as protecting group privileges or changing social policies, if and when such goals are held in common by members of the group. Social identification plays a role in achieving such commonality of values and purposes among social category members.

Social identification makes individuals more sensitive to group norms as a guide to attitudes and behavior. According to self-categorization theory (Turner et al. 1987), group identification involves a process of self-stereotyping whereby the individual seeks to assimilate to a prototypic representation of those characteristics, behaviors, and attitudes that define the in-group's distinctive identity. The desire to be a good group representative or a securely included group member motivates conformity and increases susceptibility to intragroup social influence (Abrams and Hogg 1990). Thus, social identification processes may underlie the general finding that persuasive messages from in-group sources are more effective than messages attributed to an out-group source. Individuals are more likely to change in the direction advocated by an in-group message and are more motivated to process such messages carefully and in depth. Hogg (1996) has suggested that this increased processing is motivated by the assumption that in-group messages will provide information on in-group norms and hence are highly self-relevant. To the extent that members of a social category selectively process in-group messages and ignore or dismiss out-group messages, intragroup influence will contribute to uniformity of attitudes and behavioral norms within groups and differentiation from out-groups. This process then feeds back to enhance in-group homogeneity, intergroup distinctiveness, and, ultimately, increased social identification.

The Role of Social Identification in Collective Efficacy

From an expectancy-value perspective (Klandermans 1984), individual beliefs that collective action can be effective in producing change (and that change is possible) are a critical factor for motivating participation in collective movements. Indeed, studies of the effects of social identification and collective relative deprivation have also shown that beliefs in the efficacy of collective action moderate the relationship between group identification and activism—when identification and relative deprivation are high, collective efficacy beliefs increase the intention to participate in collective action or protest (Abrams and Emler 1992; Hinkle et al. 1996).

These studies also demonstrate, however, that perceptions of collective efficacy alone do not contribute directly to willingness to engage in collective action but do so only in combination with shared identity and salient common goals. As Kelly (1993) points out, the belief that collective action is possible and effective is a subjective judgment that is itself subject to social influence and social identification processes. The kind of individual cost-benefit calculations implied by expectancy-value theory may be relatively important as determinants of social action among individuals who are low in social identification but become less directly involved when social identification is salient and the stakes are high.

A study of trade union activism (cited in Kelly 1993) provided support for the proposition that the effects of expectancy beliefs vary as a function of level of social identification and the costs of group loyalty. In this study, members of a British trade union rated their willingness to engage in a number of activist behaviors that varied in their potential cost to the individual in terms of visible commitment to the union movement. For behaviors that were relatively easy or low cost, behavioral intentions were jointly determined by value-expectancy evaluations of the goal of the action, collectivist orientation, and level of group identification with the union. For more difficult forms of action, however, only level of identification proved to be a significant predictor of activist intentions. As Kelly (1993) suggests, activism at this level may be intimately tied to the meaning of identification itself.

Conclusion

The purpose of this review has been to document that group identification not only provides the motivational underpinnings for group loyalty and potential collective action but also enters into a system of positive feedback loops with other variables that influence collective action. Throughout the model illustrated in figure 1, group-level variables interact with individual processes in a system of mutual causal relationships. Individual needs and group characteristics interact to engage social identification processes, which in turn shape perceptions of collective deprivation, injustice, common goals, and collective efficacy. But each of these in turn influences the group characteristics of shared distinctiveness that engage high levels of social identification among group members. The intimate link between cognitive representations of the self and representations of the collective that is inherent to this conceptualization of group identification may well be the sine qua non of collective action.

Notes

The program of research described in this chapter was supported in part by funding from the National Science Foundation (Grant No. SBR-955514398) and by a seed grant from the Midwest Consortium for International Security Studies.

1. The term *group identification* (or *social identification*) is used throughout the remainder of this chapter in a manner that is consistent with the definitional distinctions

made by Klandermans and de Weerd (chapter 3, this volume) between social identity, group identification, and collective identity.

2. This mean difference was statistically significant, $F(1,193) = 5.34, p < .05$.

3. See chapter 3 in this volume for a discussion of various factors that might be involved in selecting among these alternative routes.

References

Abrams, Dominic, and Nicholas Emler. 1992. "Self-Denial as a Paradox of Political and Regional Social Identity: Findings from a Study of 16- and 18-Year-Olds." *European Journal of Social Psychology* 22:279–95.

Abrams, Dominic, and Michael A. Hogg. 1990. "Social Identification, Self-Categorization, and Social Influence." In *European Review of Social Psychology,* edited by Wolfgang Stroebe and Miles Hewstone, 1:195–228. Chichester, England: Wiley.

Brewer, Marilynn B. 1991. "The Social Self: On Being the Same and Different at the Same Time." *Personality and Social Psychology Bulletin* 17:475–82.

Brewer, Marilynn B., Jorge Manzi, and John S. Shaw. 1993. "In-Group Identification as a Function of Depersonalization, Distinctiveness, and Status." *Psychological Science* 4:88–92.

Foster, Mindi D., and Kimberly Matheson. 1995. "Double Relative Deprivation: Combining the Personal and Political." *Personality and Social Psychology Bulletin* 21:1167–77.

Grant, Peter R., and Rupert Brown. 1995. "From Ethnocentrism to Collective Protest: Responses to Relative Deprivation and Threats to Social Identity." *Social Psychology Quarterly* 58:195–211.

Guimond, Serge, and Lisa Dube-Simard. 1983. "Relative Deprivation Theory and the Quebec Nationalist Movement: The Cognition-Emotion Distinction and the Personal-Group Deprivation Issue." *Journal of Personality and Social Psychology* 44:526–35.

Gurney, Joan, and Kathleen Tierney. 1982. "Relative Deprivation and Social Movements: A Critical Look at Twenty Years of Theory and Research." *Sociological Quarterly* 23:23–47.

Hinkle, Steve, Lee Fox-Cardamone, Jule Haseleu, Rupert Brown, and Lois Irwin. 1996. "Grassroots Political Action as an Intergroup Phenomenon." *Journal of Social Issues* 52(1): 39–51.

Hirschman, Albert O. 1970. *Exit, Voice, and Loyalty: Responses to Decline in Firms, Organizations, and States.* Cambridge: Harvard University Press.

Hogg, Michael A. 1996. "Intragroup Process, Group Structure, and Social Identity." In *Social Identifications: The Developing Legacy of Henri Tajfel,* edited by W. Peter Robinson, 65–93. Oxford: Butterworth-Heinemann.

Hogg, Michael A., Deborah Terry, and Katherine White. 1995. "A Tale of Two Theories: A Critical Comparison of Identity Theory with Social Identity Theory." *Social Psychology Quarterly* 58:255–69.

Kelly, Caroline. 1993. "Group Identification, Intergroup Perceptions, and Collective Action." In *European Review of Social Psychology,* edited by Wolfgang Stroebe and Miles Hewstone, 4:59–83. Chichester, England: Wiley.

Klandermans, Bert. 1984. "Mobilization and Participation: Social Psychological Expansions of Resource Mobilization Theory." *American Sociological Review* 49:583–600.

Kramer, Roderick M., and Marilynn B. Brewer. 1986. "Social Group Identity and the Emergence of Cooperation in Resource Conservation Dilemmas." In *Psychology of Decisions and Conflict,* vol. 3, *Experimental social dilemmas,* edited by Henk Wilke, David Messick, and Christie Rutte, 205–30. Frankfurt: Verlag Peter Lang.

Kramer, Roderick M., Marilynn B. Brewer, and Benjamin Hanna. 1996. "Collective Trust and Collective Action: The Decision to Trust as a Social Decision." In *Trust in Organizations,* edited by Roderick Kramer and Tom Tyler, 357–89. Thousand Oaks, Calif.: Sage.

Mael, Fred A., and Lois E. Tetrick. 1992. "Identifying Organizational Identification." *Educational and Psychological Measurement* 52:813–24.

Messick, David M., and Marilynn B. Brewer. 1983. "Solving Social Dilemmas: A Review." In *Review of Personality and Social Psychology,* edited by Ladd Wheeler and Philip Shaver, 4:11–44. Beverly Hills, Calif.: Sage.

Messick, David M., Henk Wilke, Marilynn B. Brewer, Roderick Kramer, Patricia Zemke, and Layton Lui. 1983. "Individual Adaptation and Structural Changes as Solutions to Social Dilemmas." *Journal of Personality and Social Psychology* 44:294–309.

Mlicki, Pawel P., and Naomi Ellemers. 1996. "Being Different or Being Better? National Stereotypes and Identifications of Polish and Dutch Students." *European Journal of Social Psychology* 26:97–114.

Mullen, Brian, Rupert Brown, and Colleen Smith. 1992. "Ingroup Bias as a Function of Salience, Relevance, and Status: An Integration." *European Journal of Social Psychology* 22:103–22.

Pickett, Cynthia L. 1996. "Distinctiveness Motives and Their Effects on Perceived Group Membership Importance and the Accessibility of Ingroup and Outgroup Traits." Master's thesis, Ohio State University, Columbus.

Reicher, Stephen. 1996. "Social Identity and Social Change: Rethinking the Context of Social Psychology." In *Social Identifications: The Developing Legacy of Henri Tajfel,* edited by W. Peter Robinson, 317–36. Oxford: Butterworth-Heinemann.

Runciman, Walter G. 1966. *Relative Deprivation and Social Justice: A Study of Attitudes to Social Inequality in Twentieth Century England.* Berkeley: University of California Press.

Silver, Michael D. 1997. "Group Loyalty and Group Identification: The Initial Development and Evaluation of a New Measure of Group Loyalty." Master's thesis, Ohio State University, Columbus.

Tajfel, Henri. 1969. "Cognitive Aspects of Prejudice." *Journal of Social Issues* 25:79–97.

———, ed. 1982. *Social Identity and Intergroup Relations.* Cambridge: Cambridge University Press.

Tajfel, Henri, and John C. Turner. 1986. "The Social Identity Theory of Intergroup Behavior." In *Psychology of Intergroup Relations,* edited by S. Worchel and W. Austin, 7–24. Chicago: Nelson-Hall.

Taylor, Donald M., and David J. McKirnan. 1984. "A Five-Stage Model of Intergroup Relations." *British Journal of Social Psychology* 23:291–300.

Taylor, Donald M., Stephen C. Wright, Fathali M. Moghaddam, and Richard N. Lalonde. 1990. "The Personal/Group Discrimination Discrepancy: Perceiving My Group, but Not Myself, to Be a Target for Discrimination." *Personality and Social Psychology Bulletin* 16:254–63.

Turner, John C., Michael A. Hogg, Penelope Oakes, Stephen Reicher, and Margaret Wetherell. 1987. *Rediscovering the Social Group: A Self-Categorization Theory.* Oxford: Basil Blackwell.

8

Contemplating Collectivism

Kay Deaux and Anne Reid

Individualism, a fundamental assumption in many of social psychology's models, is gradually yielding to alternative conceptions of the ways in which people relate to other people and other groups. In various forms, collectivism is emerging as a concept of interest. For some social scientists, this emphasis is hardly new. Sociological social psychologists, for example, have always been more tuned to the influence of societies and systems (Stryker 1997). Similarly, social psychologists in Europe have traditionally paid more attention to the collective aspects of human behavior. These voices, as well as an increasing roster of investigators and theorists within the United States (e.g., Markus and Kitayama 1994; Schweder and Bourne 1984; Triandis 1995), are pushing for a recognition and an analysis of collectivism in social life.

Enthusiasm for pursuit of the collective is probably greater than consensus as to what the concept entails. The term has been used across a full range of psychological phenomena, from individual attitudes to cultural values. In this chapter, we review some of these conceptions and uses. In particular, we analyze collectivism in terms of the levels of analysis represented (Doise 1986).

As an alternative to both the individual and cultural levels, we propose a group-specific conception of collectivism that is both more amenable to social psychological theorizing and more useful in exploring the links between social identity and social movements. We introduce a new measure of collectivism, developed as a multifactored scale that assesses theoretically relevant aspects of group-focused collective values. Finally, we consider the implications of this conceptual approach for studying social movements.

Prevailing Conceptions of Collectivism and Individualism

Collectivism, for the most part, has been studied at one of two levels: that of the society or culture and that of the individual. We review research in each of these areas briefly to establish contrast points for our own group-specific approach.

Individualism and Collectivism as Cultural Concepts

The current popularity of collectivism as a way of characterizing cultures can be traced most readily to the work of Hofstede (1980). Surveying employees of a large multinational corporation in forty different countries, Hofstede pointed to four key dimensions that differentiated the average scores of the workers in each country. One of these dimensions, a contrast between individualistic and collectivistic work values, became the reference point for numerous cross-cultural investigations in the ensuing years. The actual measurement of collectivism shifted, from items that focused primarily on the relationship between a worker and the organization to more varied and sometimes more general settings, but the concept of a cultural level of collectivism maintained its appeal to many.

Hofstede's ordering of countries along the dimension of collectivism produced not unexpected results. The United States emerged as the most individualistic of the forty countries surveyed, followed closely by Australia, Britain, and Canada. The collective end of the dimension was anchored by countries that included Venezuela, Colombia, and Pakistan. Hofstede further buttressed his arguments on the role of collectivism by demonstrating significant correlations between individualism and such economic indicators as gross national product (GNP) and occupational mobility.

A more extended project exploring cultural differences in collectivism is represented in the work of Triandis (1972, 1995). Initially using the United States and Greece to illustrate the contrast between individualistic and collective cultures, Triandis and his colleagues assessed citizens of numerous countries and found orderings similar to that of Hofstede. In Triandis's terms, this difference can be characterized in the following way: "Individualists give priority to personal goals over the goals of collectives; collectivists either make no distinctions between personal and collective goals, or if they do make such distinctions, they subordinate their personal goals to the collective goals" (Triandis 1989, 509).

Behavioral implications of these cultural differences in collectivism, although the subject of considerable speculation, have rarely been tested. More often, investigators have been content to demonstrate correlations between collectivism/individualism and other personality measures. Hofstede (1980), for example, reported a significant correlation between the need for affiliation and individualism, a link that presumably reflects the greater need for individualists to create friendships whereas collectivists have more ready-made networks. (See Triandis 1995 for summaries of other correlates.) Some behavioral evidence is provided by Wheeler, Reis, and Bond (1989). Comparing Chinese students in Hong Kong with U.S. students in Rochester, New York, these investigators used an interaction record technique to assess the number and type of social interactions that students had. As they predicted, based on assumed differences between a collectivist and an individualist culture, the Chinese students reported fewer but longer interactions and had more interactions that focused on tasks or group activities.

Despite its apparent cachet, collectivism as a concept for distinguishing among cultures is not without problems. Hypothesized cultural differences are most often tested at the level of individual attitudes. Concepts such as subjective culture and cultural syndrome, offered as the theoretical means of linking the cultural level of belief to the individual unit of behavior, have not been well developed. Nor has much attention been given to subcultural variations that may exist within a country. Indeed, writers often seem to assume a homogeneity that is unlikely to be true.

For an analysis of social movements, subcultural variations would seem far more likely to offer explanatory potential than would the larger-scale country differences. Social movements, almost by definition, initially involve a minority group within the culture that emphasizes the differences between itself and others in the society on key issues and that pushes for some change in the status quo. Further, it is not clear that differences in collectivism are the major source of variation between countries. As Kashima and his colleagues have recently shown, when individualistic characteristics of agency and assertiveness are assessed separately from collectivism, the former account for more variation than does the latter (Kashima et al. 1995).

Individualism and Collectivism as Individual Differences

Triandis has argued that it is important to maintain a distinction between the psychological and cultural levels of collectivism (Triandis et al. 1985). To highlight this distinction, he coined the terms *allocentric* and *idiocentric* to refer to people who think and act in a collectivist and an individualist manner, respectively. To assess the psychometric properties and correlates of measures of allocentrism and idiocentrism, Triandis et al. (1985) conducted three studies with students in the United States. Many of the predicted relationships were found: for example, higher allocentrism was associated with positive evaluation of cooperation and equality, and idiocentrism correlated significantly with measures of need achievement and alienation (although the correlations were relatively low).

A somewhat similar proposal for individual differences in the ways in which people construe their relationships with others is offered by Singelis (1994). Using Markus and Kitayama's (1994) theoretical analysis of independent and interdependent selves, Singelis developed a scale that assessed the two separate dimensions. As a means of validation, he compared samples of Asian Americans and Caucasian Americans. He also assessed reactions to an attribution scenario to confirm his prediction that people high in interdependence would be more likely to attribute cause to the situation. In this case, both the individual-level response and the cultural-level group are used to validate the individual-level measure.

The Terrain between Culture and Persons

As studies of collectivism and individualism accumulate, some investigators have felt the need to explore the implications of the concepts at some midrange level, using a unit of analysis that is larger than the individual but smaller than a country. Rhee, Uleman, and Lee (1996), as one example, make a distinction between kin and nonkin groups. The former are defined in terms of family units, including parents, children, and other relatives; nonkin groups include friends, neighbors, and work groups. Exploring this distinction in three cultural groups—Koreans, Asian Americans, and European Americans—Rhee and colleagues found that the two manifestations of individualism were most dissimilar for European Americans. In other words, individualism expressed in terms of one's family group does not predict individualism in the context of nonkin such as neighbors and friends. Among both Koreans and Asian Americans, the two forms of individualism were strongly related. When collectivism was considered, assessed as a separate dimension, the patterns for kin and nonkin were moderately similar for all three groups.

Separating issues related to the immediate family from other kinds of groups is an important step. Families and relationships are likely to have some important features that other kinds of groups do not have (Brewer and Gardner 1996; Deaux et al. 1995). At the same time, it should be noted that the nonkin items selected by Rhee, Uleman, and Lee (1996) cover a fairly limited range and primarily focus on either friends or neighbors, domains that would generally fall within the realm of personal relationships.

Hui (1988) also suggested that it was important to consider different kinds of collectives and used several different target groups in his assessment of individualism and collectivism (spouse, parents, kin, neighbor, friend, and co-worker). Again, most of these targets are forms of interpersonal relationships. Matsumoto, Kudoh, and Takeuchi (1996) assessed individualism and collectivism among Japanese and Americans, testing two different populations within each country (working adults and university students) and using four different reference groups (specifically, family, close friends, colleagues, and strangers). Somewhat unexpectedly, they found that Japanese were *less* collectivist than Americans. More to the point, they found substantial variation in collectivism scores as a function of reference group. Students, for example, were more collectivist toward friends than families, whereas working adults were more collectivist within their families. On the basis of these and other findings, Matsumoto and colleagues argue that a simple cultural level of analysis assumes more homogeneity within culture than is in fact the case. Changes in reference group, as well as more global cultural changes across time, will alter the level of collectivism that any individual endorses.

Questioning the Level of Analysis

In considering collectivism, we need to think more carefully about levels of analysis. As Doise (1986) articulates so well, social psychologists can address social phenomena at one of several levels of analysis, ranging from the intrapersonal to the cultural. At each level, different phenomena are the focus of interest, and different assumptions are made (sometimes explicitly, sometimes not). As noted, investigators have typically considered collectivism at the level of the culture or at the level of the individual. We raise two issues with regard to these conceptualizations.

First, although the concept may be framed in terms of one level of analysis, for example, collectivism as a characteristic of cultures, the assessment of the concept and related outcomes can occur at a different level of analysis, as in the measurement of individual differences in general collectivist tendencies or as a criterion of interpersonal conversation. These "level crossings" need to be recognized and their implications explored.

Second, we suggest that the analysis of collectivism would be enriched by considering more fully the level of analysis between that of the culture and that of the individual. In between these two poles is the area that, for many social psychologists, is most familiar and most tractable, namely, the group. To explain group-coordinated action or collective movements, this intermediate level of analysis would seem the most appropriate. It is in this space that social movements develop, and it is through these groups that the individual links to the larger cultural context.

Both of these issues are elaborated on in table 1, which presents our analysis of perspectives on collectivism, focusing on the level of the initial conceptualization, the method of assessment, and the outcomes or criteria of interest, as they are realized at the level of culture, group, or individual.

Conceptual analyses of collectivism, most prominent in the work of Triandis (1995) and his colleagues, are generally formulated in terms of cultures, following the initial lead of Hofstede (1980), or as a disposition of the individual. Thus the conceptual unit of analysis is either a country or a person. Collectivism considered as a group-level concept is a rarity. One exception to this statement, however, is the work of Brown, Hinkle, and their colleagues within the framework of social identity theory (Brown et al. 1992; Hinkle Brown 1990). In trying to understand some inconsistent patterns of in-group versus out-group favoritism, these authors suggested that groups may vary in important respects, leading some groups to use intergroup comparison as a means of maintaining social identity while others do not. One of the two dimensions they proposed to distinguish between groups is individualism and collectivism, relying on the theoretical formulations and empirical work of Hofstede and Triandis.

Additional evidence supporting different degrees of collectivism at the group level comes from Deaux et al. (1985). In assessing people's judgments of the place that various forms of social identity occupy in a multidimensional space, these investigators isolated a dimension of individualism/collectivism on which identities differed. Religious and ethnic groups, as an example, were viewed as more collective in their orientation; occupations were seen as more individualistic.

Three levels of assessment can also be defined. A societal-level index might be a content analysis of some media product of the culture, such as popular literature or children's textbooks. Alternatively, one could gather data from individuals but use the culture as the focus of the questions. For example, one might ask how collective a person feels toward the society as a whole. Assessment of collectivism at the group level would reflect a group production, such as a founding document of group principles. As in the case of culture, one could also obtain measures from individuals but use the specific group as the focus of questions about collective tendencies. Finally, at the individual level of analysis, individuals could be asked about their general tendencies toward collectivism, independent of group or culture.

Similarly, the outcomes or criteria posed in the research can be considered at each of the three levels of analysis. Cultural-level outcomes might be

Table 1. Three Levels of Analysis Associated with Collectivism

Level of Analysis	Initial Conceptualization	Method of Assessment	Outcomes of Interest
Cultural	Collectivism is a characteristic of cultures. Some cultures, e.g., China, are more collective than others, e.g., the United States.	Measurement of cultural variation in collectivism, e.g., (a) content analysis of a culture's popular media for themes of collectivism or (b) individually administered questionnaires that take the country as the point of reference.	Differences between cultures high and low in collectivism in cultural outcomes such as gross national product, crime rates, human rights record, openness of borders.
Group	Collectivism is a characteristic of social groups. Some groups, e.g., the Citadel, are more collective than others, e.g., the American Sociological Association.	Measurement of group variation in collectivism, e.g., (a) content analysis of group charters and mission statements for themes of collectivism or (b) individually administered questionnaires that take the group as the point of reference.	Differences between groups high and low in collectivism in group outcomes such as success in achieving group goals, tendency to unite in the face of adversity.
Individual	Collectivism is a characteristic of individuals. Some people, e.g., allocentrics, are more collective than others, e.g., idiocentrics.	Measurement of individual variation in collectivism, e.g., individually administered questionnaires that assess general attitudes toward collective activity.	Differences between individuals high and low in collectivism in individual outcomes such as preferred style of reward allocation and attributions of causality.

economic indicators, such as GNP, or political policies and legislation aimed at benefiting the society as a whole. Group-level outcomes would be framed in terms of the particular group agenda: in the case of a labor movement, for example, the outcome might be frequency of strikes or protest rallies. At the individual level, the consequences of collectivism have included cooperative behavior, social interaction, and the expression of romantic love.

In practice, both the assessment of collectivism and the chosen outcomes most often fall at the individual level of analysis. Thus, for example, although Hinkle and Brown (1990) argue for differences *between groups* in level of collectivism versus individualism, empirically they assessed individual differences in individualism and collectivism *within* a group. Similarly, the original work of Hofstede (1980) and the more recent work of Triandis (1995) both rely on individually administered questionnaires to assess the collectivism of (members of) a country. The same focus on the individual is evident when one considers the range of criterion variables that have been investigated. Often investigations deal with the relationship between measures of collectivism and some other personality variable, such as need for affiliation (Hofstede 1980). Other individual behaviors that have been studied include feelings of romantic love (Dion and Dion 1991) and the number and length of social interactions that a person has in a day (Wheeler, Reis, and Bond 1989). In only a few cases has the cultural-level construct of collectivism been linked to cultural-level outcomes, as Hofstede (1980) did in reporting GNP data.

It seems clear that the analysis of collectivism would benefit from more extensive development of measures that tap the cultural and group levels of analysis. Particularly for the study of social movements, attention needs to be directed to those group-level indicators of collectivism that might gauge the success or failure of a social movement.

Consideration of table 1 also suggests the need to think carefully about which levels are represented in one's analysis of collectivism and whether there is a consistency from conceptualization through assessment and outcome. To cross levels of analysis is not necessarily to commit a fatal flaw. Such crossing does, however, pose a greater challenge to the investigator to account for the causal mechanisms that might link the predictor to the criterion. If, for example, a culture is conceptualized as collective, how is it that individuals in that culture come to have stronger needs for affiliation within the family unit? Would those needs extend to other relationships or groups, and if not, why? Do the social representations (Moscovici 1988) in the culture need to be analyzed more carefully for the message that they are conveying and that are in turn expressed by individuals? Alternatively, if the individual is high in collectivity, are there any limits on the contexts in which collectivism will be expressed or enacted? These are the kinds of questions that we, as well as others, need to address when we move between levels of analysis.

A New View of Collectivism

Dissatisfied with existing conceptualizations of collectivity, we have been working on a project that theorizes and assesses collectivism at the level of group membership. Still a work in progress, our research nonetheless is suggesting promising directions for bringing a more social psychological perspective to the concept of collectivism.

Conceptualizing Collectivism as a Group Concept

The initial assumption that guides our work is that collectivism can, and indeed should, be conceptualized as a way of identifying with a particular group membership. Rather than viewing collectivism as a property that characterizes a culture as a whole or as a traitlike feature of individuals, we suggest that collectivism can be defined in reference to specific social identifications and group memberships (a level of analysis that is more suitable to discussing the implications for social movements).

We also assume, in contrast to most analyses at either individual or cultural levels, that collectivism at the group level is dynamic rather than static. This assumption of fluidity suggests that the collectivism of a group (or of a member's orientation toward that particular group) can change over time or under different circumstances. Consciousness-raising is one example of a technique used to increase collective identification of members with a group. Key events in a group's history, such as Stonewall for the lesbian and gay community or the Million Man March for African American men, can also affect the collectivism level of the group as a whole.

Working Assumptions

In developing a scale to measure group-based collectivism, we began with three working assumptions: (1) conceptualizing collectivism as a unipolar construct; (2) assessing group-level collectivism by asking individuals how collective they feel toward the group; and (3) treating collectivism as group-specific rather than generic.

Collectivism as a Unipolar Construct

Conceptions of individualism and collectivism initially assumed a single dimension, anchored by individualism at one end and collectivism at the other. Gradually, however, this bipolar assumption is giving way to a two-dimensional model (Kagitcibasi and Berry 1989; Oyserman 1993). Both Oyserman (1993) and Triandis (1995), for example, now propose separate items to measure collectivism and individualism. Evidence in support of a two-dimensional model comes both from studies that correlate the two independent scales and from some limited studies of predictive validity (see Kashima et al. 1995; Oyserman 1993; Torres 1996).

Given the evidence for the conceptual independence of individualism and collectivism, one can then question whether both factors are equally appropriate for the study of group-based collectivism. Our interest is in the degree to which collectivism is associated with group-related actions. Thus it is the strength of collectivism, as associated with a particular group identification, that should be most predictive of actions taken or not taken. Whether individuals (or groups) are high on individualism would, theoretically, predict quite different behaviors and ones unlikely to be related to group action or social movements. In measurement terms, a low score on collectivism would thus not be interpreted as relating in any way to individualism but would only indicate the relative absence of collective tendencies.

The Individual as Unit of Measurement

As noted in table 1, two alternatives are available to the investigator who is concerned with group levels of collectivism. In one, the unit of measurement is some group product, such as a group charter. In the second alternative, data are gathered from individuals, but the focus of the data collection is the group rather than a general individual disposition.

The distinction between this strategy and the more typical procedures followed in assessing cultural collectivism is an important one. In the typical study of culture, scales are administered to individuals who respond to questions concerning their general feelings about collectivism, with questions ranging in focus from family to friends to individual habits. It is then assumed that the average of these individual dispositions can be used as an index of the collectivism of the culture. In contrast, what we advocate here is a measure that, while asking individuals for their attitudes, focuses those attitudes on a specific group membership. As a result, the obtained average is based on scores that share a common reference point, namely, the social group of interest.

Specific versus Generic Group Membership

A third and closely related assumption is that collectivism should be assessed in terms of specific group memberships rather than some general feelings toward groups in general. We suggest that people can be collective in their attitudes toward some groups and not others. Similarly, within a given culture or society, some groups may show high degrees of collectivism, whereas other groups in that same culture may have little collective character.

Work by Reid (1998) supports these assumptions of specificity and variability. First, she finds that levels of collectivism vary, depending on the group in focus. In general, religious groups (e.g., Catholic, Christian, Jewish) were high in collectivism, but occupation and hobby groups such as student and computer programmer were relatively low in collectivism. Second, if collectivism is group-specific, as we argue, then a person's collectivism score with reference to one group to which they belong should not be predictive of his or her collectivism toward another membership group. This assumption is also supported by her data. People's level of collectivism toward their ethnic or religious group, for example, did not predict level of collectivism toward an occupation or hobby group membership.

Developing a Group-Specific Measure of Collectivism

To create a pool of items for our measure of collectivism, we looked first at existent scales, in particular those developed by Triandis and his colleagues, and selected items that had respectable loadings. In addition, we created a number of items ourselves, primarily with the intent of covering aspects of collective behavior that we felt had been neglected in previous measures but that were part of social psychological theorizing on collectivity. Examples of these areas include a belief in common fate, behavioral involvement with others who share an identity, reliance on norms of the group, and affective connections to others in the group.

We also believed it was important to develop items that would be applicable to virtually any group. This strategy is in contrast to many existing scales of collectivism, which include items referring to specific types of group membership (often loaded heavily on family and friendship items). On the one hand, we wanted items general enough that they could appropriately describe any group membership; on the other hand, we wanted each item to specify the particular group that was of interest in a given investigation.

We solved this dual need by developing a set of items that, in their general form, did not refer to any particular type of group or relationship. At the same time, by using a "fill in the blank" format, we could adapt the questionnaire to any specific need. An example of an item on the scale is "I prefer to spend my free time with other _____s", with the blank completed as appropriate for a particular study.

Figure 1. Sample items from the Identity-Specific Collectivism Scale (ISCOL)

Factor 1: Social identity
Being a ___ is central to who I am.
I am glad to be a ___.

Factor 2: Common fate
When ___ do well, I feel good.
The success of ___ as a group is more important than my own personal success.

Factor 3: Discomfort with the collective
I feel uneasy with other ___s.
Even though I'm a ___, I do not feel particularly connected to other ___s.

Factor 4: Behavioral involvement
My most rewarding friendships are with other ___.
I am more likely to help a ___ than I am to help someone who is not a ___.

Factor 5: Standards and goals
___ have a set of standards that I feel I must live by.
I tend to share the same opinions as other ___s.

Factor 6: Emotional attachment
I feel a common bond with other ___s.

The items were administered to a sample of more than four hundred people, varying in ethnicity and gender, with reference to different identity groups. The results were then subjected to an exploratory factor analysis, using a principal components analysis with oblimin rotation. The number of factors was determined by examination of eigen values and scree plot, as well as theoretical concerns. On the basis of this analysis, we now have a thirty-six-item scale of collectivism, further divided into six distinct factors. Figure 1 lists the six factors, with sample items from each.

Taken as a set, these six factors appear to capture much of the theoretical turf considered in discussions of the collective aspects of social identification. For example, the factors of emotional attachment and behavioral involvement correspond quite closely to Stryker's concepts of affective commitment and interactive commitment, respectively. Several of the factors appear to have clear relevance for a person's willingness to engage in social movements: a belief in common fate, the adoption of standards and goals, and behavioral involvement with other members of the group all could support collective action.

These six factors can be rather easily grouped into the time-honored triad of cognitive, affective, and behavioral domains. Cognitive aspects of collectivity are stressed in the social identity factors and in goals and standards, two themes that are central to self-categorization and social identity accounts of collectivity. Two other factors, emotional attachment and discomfort with the collective (scored in a reverse direction), tap emotional aspects of collectivity. And finally, common fate and behavioral involvement suggest more action orientation. Although there is some overlap in individual items, the tripartite division makes some sense. In future work, we will explore the predictive power of these subfactors as well as the total scale.

It is worth noting that social identity is, in this measure, a component of collectivism. In other analyses, we consistently find moderate to high correlations between the strength of social identification and collectivism. Theoretically, the relation between these two concepts is of considerable interest. Although social identification would seem to be a necessary component of collectivism, the reverse is not necessarily true. A person can, we believe, strongly identify with a category or group without pursuing the collective possibilities of that identification.

With much of the basic psychometric work now completed, we next move into the realm of group behavior. The potential connections between collectivism and social action can be tested at one of two levels and ideally at both. First, we can ask whether an individual's group-specific level of collectivism is predictive of his or her willingness to engage in collective action on behalf of the group. Second, we can pose a similar question between groups, that is, whether groups whose members on the average are more collective will be more apt to engage in collective action and more successful when they do so.

Identity, Collectivism, and Social Movements

From the perspective of an individualist psychology, collective action has always been somewhat suspect. Most commonly, collective action is described in terms of deindividuation, lowered self-regulation, a sacrifice of rationality for emotion, and similar processes, all of which convey a clear value position that group action is somehow morally irresponsible and to be resisted. LeBon is one of the earliest proponents of this viewpoint, and his influence can still be detected. Yet if the beginning point of analysis is one that recognizes the person as a socially defined being and self-definition as in part shaped by group memberships and social identifications, then the prospect of collective action takes a quite different tone.

Investigators within the tradition of social identity theory, and in particular Reicher (1982, 1987), have been clear and convincing in their arguments for this altered vantage point. People in a crowd or a collective act in terms of a common social identification. One of the processes involved as individuals identify with a collective entity is what Turner (1982) has termed *referent informational influence.* Within this term he includes a variety of subprocesses, including self-categorization and the learning of stereotypical in-group norms. Most of these processes deal with the cognitive aspects of social identification, that is, how we acquire beliefs about our group and in turn develop and modify beliefs about ourselves, and indeed are represented in the two cognitive factors that emerged in our analysis.

Cognitive categorization is not enough, however, either to explain the full process of social identification at the individual level, much less the phenomena that constitute social movements. Both affective and behavioral domains need to be brought into the discussion (Deaux 1996). In the measure of collectivism that we are developing, key components include emotional attachment, comfort with the collective, behavioral involvement, and perceptions of common fate.

Sorting out terminology is an important task for investigators in this area. Models offered by Brewer and Silver (chapter 7, this volume) and by Klandermans and de Weerd (chapter 3, this volume), for example, cover compatible territory but not necessarily with the same labels for concepts. Similarly, the six factors of collectivism that we have identified overlap with the tripartite distinction of Klandermans and de Weerd. The shared definitions implied by our factor of norms and standards, for example, seem to fit with their definition of collective identity; in addition, their definition of group identification invokes collective action, which is suggested by our subscales of common fate and behavioral involvement. Brewer and Silver's measure of group loyalty, which correlates highly with a measure of group identification, is another piece of this not yet fully specified nomological network.

Beyond terminology, there are important issues concerning level of analysis, to which a number of the authors in this volume (Klandermans and de Weerd, Snow and McAdams) refer. As we diagram in figure 1 of this chapter, there are important shifts in the concepts or predictors, the level of measurement, and the outcomes of choice as we move from the cultural to the group to the individual level of analysis. Far too little attention has been given to these shifts in the empirical literature in social psychology.

Table 2. Links between Collectivism and Social Movements at Different Levels of Analysis

Level of Analysis	Implications for Social Movements
Culture	Cultures high in collectivism stress the importance of status hierarchies, set strict norms and standards for members, and emphasize the greater good relative to individual human rights. Social movements may be less likely in collective cultures than in cultures relatively low in collectivism.
Group	Social movements at the group level are framed in terms of the particular group agenda, e.g., frequency of strikes among a group of auto workers, rallies staged by a feminist organization, boycotts organized by animal rights group. More collective groups may be more likely to initiate, maintain, and successfully elicit social action from members.
Individual	Social movements are played out at the individual level, e.g., tendency to participate in protests, boycotts, rallies, and fund drives on behalf of one's in-groups. More collective individuals may be more likely to participate in social actions initiated by their groups.

Collectivism implies an emphasis on group cohesion, common fate, distinction from out-groups, and shared norms and standards. As such, higher levels of collectivism should be associated with greater social action on behalf of and on the part of the in-group. As the level of analysis shifts from a cultural to an individual focus, so too does the precise way in which collectivism can be linked to social movements and action. Table 2 presents a framework for considering these different ways of looking at collectivism.

Consideration of collectivism at the cultural level, in terms of countries or perhaps clearly defined subcultures within a country, would lead one to focus on large-scale, broad-based social movements. Within a collective country, one might expect to see a greater concern for the social good and the development of policies to support the population at large. Additionally, to the extent that international relations become a focus, one might look to areas such as war, border protection, and trade policies and sanctions. In each case, countries high in collectivism should be more likely than countries low in collectivism to engage in behaviors that protect and favor their country over others. We might also speculate, however, that if the level of collectivism for the country was very high, social movements by smaller groups within the larger culture might be less apt to develop than when the cultural level of collectivism was lower.

At the group level, the impact of collectivism on social movements would depend on the specific group's agenda. Groups high in collectivism may be more likely to act as a unit to achieve their common goals, as compared with groups low in collectivism. Thus, highly collective groups would be more likely to encourage membership participation in such group actions as strikes, rallies, protests, and boycotts. Groups low in collectivism would be less likely to promote such actions and less successful in arousing membership support.

Collectivism at the individual level describes a general disposition. On the one hand, one might assume that people high in collectivism would be more engaged in collective forms of interaction at all levels of inclusiveness, from the culture to the one-to-one relationship. Such a conception, although suggested by some models, nonetheless presents problems. For example, Triandis and his colleagues suggest that the highly collective individual will be more devoted to the in-group (primarily family) but will be less likely to identify with other potential in-groups outside the family context. One also might question how the person high in generic collectivity would resolve potential conflicts among competing in-groups. These are issues that future research needs to address.

In developing our measure of collectivism, we define the concept at a group level of analysis, in contrast to the cultural or individual levels of previous work. To pursue this strategy, it is not unreasonable to assume that a group's average collectivism score, *if* based on *group-specific* measures of collectivism, is a useful proxy for assessing the collective orientation of that group. However, this assumption needs to be tested in the context of group rather than individual actions. In order for collectivism, conceptualized at the level of the group, to have utility for the study of social movements, we, like other investigators before us, need to consider levels of analysis more carefully.

An understanding of developmental sequence is also key to a comprehensive analysis of collectivism and social movements. In chapter 2, Snow and McAdams describe their version of the identity construction process. In a similar manner, we need to embed our notion of collectivism in a theoretical pathway. It is possible, for example, that collectivism is a kind of emergent property, developing after initial categories are chosen and commitments are made. In other work, we (Deaux et al. 1999) have examined the functions that social identifications serve for individuals. Some of these are individual satisfactions (e.g., knowing the self better, providing a basis of social comparison), and others are dependent on a group or intergroup context (e.g., cooperation, intergroup competition). We speculate that some of these functions may be initial motivations for joining a group and that others may emerge as a group agenda, taken on only after identification with the group has solidified. Longitudinal studies are needed to provide support for these hunches.

How and why collectivism emerges, at both individual and group levels, is an issue of tremendous importance. A full understanding of group action (whether for good or harm) demands that we look both to the individual and to the group—and, even more important, at the theoretical paths between these levels. For us, group-focused collectivism is one promising route to explore these issues.

Note

Some of the research reported in this chapter was supported by a grant from the National Science Foundation (BNS-9110130) awarded to the first author. Many City University of New York graduate students were involved in this research, but in particular we want to recognize the contributions of Kim Mizrahi and Barton Poulson. We are also grateful to Sheldon Stryker and to members of the CUNY Identity Research Seminar for their very helpful comments on an earlier version of this chapter.

References

Brewer, Marilynn B., and Wendi Gardner. 1996. "Who Is This 'We'?: Levels of Collective Identity and Self Representations." *Journal of Personality and Social Psychology* 71:83–93.

Brown, Rupert, Steve Hinkle, Pamela G. Ely, L. Fox-Cardamone, Pamela Maras, and L. A. Taylor. 1992. "Recognizing Group Diversity: Individualist-Collectivism and Autonomous-Relational Social Orientation and Their Implications for Intergroup Processes." *British Journal of Social Psychology* 31:327–42.

Deaux, Kay. 1996. "Social Identification." In *Social Psychology: Handbook of Basic Principles,* edited by E. Tory Higgins and Arie W. Kruglanski, 777–98. New York: Guilford.

Deaux, Kay, Anne Reid, Kim Mizrahi, and Dave Cotting. 1999. "Connecting the Person to the Social: The Functions of Social Identification." In *The Psychology of the Social Self,* edited by Tom R. Tyler, Rod Kramer, and Oliver John, 91–113. Mahwah, N.J.: Lawrence Erlbaum.

Deaux, Kay, Anne Reid, Kim Mizrahi, and Kathleen A. Ethier. 1995. "Parameters of Social Identity." *Journal of Personality and Social Psychology* 68:280–91.

Dion, Karen K., and Kenneth L. Dion. 1991. "Psychological Individualism and Romantic Love." *Journal of Social Behavior and Personality* 6:17–33.

Doise, Willem. 1986. *Levels of Explanation in Social Psychology.* Cambridge: Cambridge University Press.

Hinkle, Steve, and Rupert Brown. 1990. "Intergroup Comparisons and Social Identity: Some Links and Lacunae." In *Social Identity Theory: Constructive and Critical Advances,* edited by Dominic Abrams and Michael A. Hogg, 48–70. New York: Springer-Verlag.

Hofstede, Geert. 1980. *Culture's Consequences: International Differences in Work-Related Values.* Beverly Hills, Calif.: Sage.

Hui, C. H. 1988. "Measurement of Individualism-Collectivism." *Journal for Research in Personality* 22:17–36.

Kagitcibasi, C., and John Berry. 1989. "Cross-Cultural Psychology: Current Research and Trends." *Annual Review of Psychology* 40:493–531.

Kashima, Yoshihisa, Susumu Yamaguchi, Uichol Kim, Sang-Chin Choi, Michele J. Gelfand, and Masaki Yuki. 1995. "Culture, Gender, and Self: A Perspective from Individualism-Collectivism Research." *Journal of Personality and Social Psychology* 69:925–37.

Markus, Hazel R., and Shinobu Kitayama. 1994. "A Collective Fear of the Collective: Implications for Selves and Theories of Selves." *Personality and Social Psychology Bulletin* 20:568–79.

Matsumoto, David, Tsutomu Kudoh, and Sachiko Takeuchi. 1996. "Changing Patterns of Individualism and Collectivism in the United States and Japan." *Culture and Psychology* 2:77–107.

Moscovici, Serge. 1988. "Notes toward a Description of Social Representations." *European Journal of Social Psychology* 18:211–50.

Oyserman, Daphna. 1993. "The Lens of Personhood: Viewing the Self and Others in a Multicultural Society." *Journal of Personality and Social Psychology* 65:993–1009.

Reicher, Stephen. 1982. "The Determination of Collective Behavior." In *Social Identity and Intergroup Relations,* edited by Henri Tajfel, 41–83. Cambridge: Cambridge University Press.

———. 1987. "Crowd Behavior as Social Action." In John C. Turner, Michael A. Hogg, Penelope J. Oakes, Steve D. Reicher, and Margaret Wetherell, *Rediscovering the Social Group: A Self-Categorization Theory,* 171–202. Oxford: Blackwell.

Reid, Anne. 1998. "Validation of ISCOL: An Identity Specific Measure of Collectivism." Ph.D. diss., City University of New York.

Rhee, Eun, James S. Uleman, and Hoon Koo Lee. 1996. "Variations in Collectivism and Individualism by Ingroup and Culture: Confirmatory Factor Analysis." *Journal of Personality and Social Psychology* 71:1037–54.

Schweder, Richard A., and E. Bourne. 1984. "Does the Concept of the Person Vary Cross-Culturally?" In *Culture Theory: Essays on Mind, Self, and Emotion,* edited by Richard A. Schweder and Robert A. LeVine, 158–99. Cambridge: Cambridge University Press.

Singelis, Theodore M. 1994. "The Measurement of Independent and Interdependent Self-Construals." *Personality and Social Psychology Bulletin* 20:580–91.

Stryker, Sheldon. 1997. "In the Beginning There Is Society: Lessons from a Sociological Social Psychology." In *The Message of Social Psychology: Perspectives on Mind in Society,* edited by Craig McGarty and S. A. Haslam, 315–27. Oxford: Blackwell.

Torres, Ana. 1996. "Exploring Group Diversity: Relationship between Identification and Ingroup Bias." Ph.D. diss., University of Kent.

Triandis, Harry C., ed. 1972. *The Analysis of Subjective Culture.* New York: Wiley.

———. 1989. "The Self and Social Behavior in Differing Cultural Contexts." *Psychological Review* 96:506–20.

———. 1995. *Individualism and Collectivism.* Boulder, Colo.: Westview Press.

Triandis, Harry C., Kwok Leung, Marcelo J. Villareal, and Felicia L. Clack. 1985. "Allocentric versus Idiocentric Tendencies: Convergent and Discriminant Validation." *Journal of Research in Personality* 19:395–415.

Turner, John C. 1982. "Towards a Cognitive Redefinition of the Social Group." In *Social Identity and Intergroup Relations,* edited by Henri Tajfel, 15–40. Cambridge: Cambridge University Press; Paris: Editions de la Maison des Sciences de l'Homme.

Wheeler, Ladd, Harry T. Reis, and Michael Harris Bond. 1989. "Collectivism-Individualism in Everyday Social Life: The Middle Kingdom and the Melting Pot." *Journal of Personality and Social Psychology* 57:79–86.

Self and Self-Esteem

9

Self-Concept as a Force in Social Movement Involvement

Timothy J. Owens and Pamela J. Aronson

Our chapter is organized around two interrelated concerns or goals, each with the express purpose of linking aspects of self-esteem and identity to the impetus to become involved in social movements. The first and main concern seeks to extend and connect social identity (SI) and collective identity (CI) to what we refer to here as "individual self-esteem" (ISE) and "social self-esteem" (SSE) and, in so doing, bring these literatures to bear on social movement participation. Since we are chiefly concerned with describing how ISE and SSE may be implicated in social movement activism, we do not detail the identity theory roots of our ideas. Other chapters in this volume, particularly in Part I, explore identity theories in depth. However, in order to assist the reader in following our argument and the rationale behind it, we provide a very basic overview of the role the two identities listed above play in our theory. Our second concern anchors self-esteem and social movement participation in perceptions of fairness and justice. Before we discuss our two main objectives, however, and present illustrations and our specific hypotheses, an overview of social movements and their social psychology will help put our ideas in the broader context to which they are directed.

Background

An Overview of the Social Psychology of Social Movements

Although social movements are generally defined quite broadly, to include such diverse events and organizations as revolutions, public interest lobbies, and religious movements, they most frequently refer to political reform movements (McAdam, McCarthy, and Mayer 1988). In such social movements, groups of people or social movement organizations develop and utilize particular ideologies, goals, strategies, and tactics to alter the political arena. Recent research increasingly focuses on the social psychology of social movements, including such issues as the social context in which meaning construction occurs, the definition of the actor, and the cultural context of the social movement (Mueller 1992). These approaches are the most relevant in our consideration of identity, self-esteem, and social movement participation.

Research on individuals' impetus to become involved in social movements has taken both microstructural and individual approaches. Microstructural accounts stress that the primary reason for involvement is one's structural location, which makes participation relatively easy and pulls the individual into the social movement. This includes prior contact with other movement participants, membership in other organizations, a history of prior activism, and "biographical availability," which is the absence of personal constraints (such as family responsibilities) that increase the costs of participation (McAdam, McCarthy, and Mayer 1988). Many of these reasons are supported by examples from the civil rights (McAdam 1988) and women's movements (Evans 1979; Freeman 1983; Taylor and Whittier 1992).

More individualistic approaches to activism have explained involvement in either psychological, attitudinal, or rational choice terms. Psychological accounts have focused on character traits or states of mind that lead to participation. For example, the theory of relative deprivation claims that "it is an unfavorable gap between what a person feels he or she is entitled to and what, in fact, they are receiving that encourages activism" (McAdam, McCarthy, and Mayer 1988). Attitudinal explanations posit that activism grows out of a strong sense of support for the goals of the social movement. Lastly, rational choice accounts argue that individuals are rational actors who judge and act on the potential benefits and costs of participation. In this view, collective identities act as "selective incentives" that motivate participation (Friedman and McAdam 1992).

One prominent concern within the social psychological approach to social movements is the development of collective identity, which seeks to explain movement emergence as the link between micro and macro levels. In many accounts, the construction of collective identity is itself a reason for involvement. As Gamson (1992a) puts it: "Participation in social movements frequently involves an enlargement of personal identity for participants and offers fulfillment and realization of self" (56). Thus, for Gamson (1992a), collective identity is the enlargement of an individual's identity to include the collective, the "we," and this process positively affects the self. Solidarity, which involves an individual's identification with and commitment to a social movement, is also a key ingredient (Gamson 1992a). Third, Gamson (1992a) defines consciousness as the way in which the meanings that individuals attribute to social situations become a shared definition and contain the possibility for collective action. This involves the adoption of a social movement's collective action frame, which links the individual participant with the social movement organization's "interpretative frameworks" (Snow and Benford 1992; Snow et al. 1986).

One component of the collective action frame that relates to our discussion of self-esteem and perceived injustice is the "injustice component" (Gamson 1992b). Gamson (1992b, 7) defines this as "moral indignation expressed in the form of political consciousness." An injustice collective action frame is linked to people's beliefs about conditions that have made them suffer hardship or loss (Gamson 1992b); it may lead to collective mobilization when people stop tolerating the past rules and norms that previously structured their lives (Flacks 1988). Flacks (1988) labels this internal struggle "liberation consciousness" inasmuch as it requires a break with past cognitive structures. Group identity alone is not a sufficient propellant. Rather, liberation consciousness develops when people begin to doubt the moral rightness of their accustomed subordination and begin to formulate new demands, which correspond to new identities (Flacks 1988).

A concept analogous to the "injustice component" is the "belief in a just world" thesis (BJW). In contrast to the injustice component, BJW falls within the "stratification beliefs" research tradition and is rarely cited in the social movements literature. It is premised on the assumption that humans are motivated to believe that people generally get what they deserve based on their actions or moral qualities and that by behaving "responsibly" and "properly" people can generally avoid personal troubles (Kluegel and Smith 1986). One consequence of the adoption of this belief is the use of "fate control," whereby people in unfortunate circumstances (e.g., the poor, victims of misfortune, AIDS sufferers, and Holocaust victims) are derogated and assumed personally responsible for their problems. Lerner (1980) argues that the belief that unfortunate circumstances are the result of flawed moral character or conduct allows some to sustain the conclusion that "people get what they deserve and deserve what they get." We would consequently assert that people guided by the "justice component" would be unlikely to subscribe strongly to the "belief in a just world." Conversely, those who acknowledge the possibility of an unjust world—at least for some groups and people—would be more open to the possibility of engaging in collective action either directly or indirectly to redress the problem. If they identified with the oppressed group, the probability of action should be magnified.

Theoretical Orientation

In this section we lay the theoretical groundwork for our effort to link social movement activism to identity, self-esteem, and justice. We begin with an overview and elaboration of our key theoretical concepts: social identity, collective identity, social self-esteem, and individual self-esteem.

Linking Identity and Self-Esteem to Social Movement Participation

Social Identity

It is taken axiomatically that the human mind classifies and categorizes those parts of reality that enter into its experience. This rich and varied cognitive tapestry begins in infancy when the individual starts being labeled, classified, and pigeonholed into socially defined categories (e.g., Indian, Hindu, Punjabi, girl) and continues throughout one's life course (e.g., naturalized American, Californian, grandmother, matriarch, Legionnaire). These categories eventually constitute the individual's social identity. We view social identity in two broad ways, one stemming from the sociological strain of labeling theory represented by Goffman (1963) and the other from European social psychology represented by Tajfel (1981). In the sociological sense, one's social identity is derived from the groups, statuses, and categories to which individuals are *socially recognized* as belonging. It is one of their labels. The world thus encounters the individual, and vice versa, in varying categorical terms: WASP, nun, American Indian, homeless person, and so on. This can be illustrated by recent comments reported in the *New York Times* by the United States ambassador to Switzerland, Madeleine Kunin, about being Jewish in Switzerland versus the United States (Sciolino 1997). In her 1985 inaugural speech as governor of Vermont, Kunin willingly mentioned several of her social identities: the first *woman* to serve as governor in that state as well as the third *Democrat* since the Civil War and the second governor of *European birth.* Mentioning that she was also the first *Jewish* governor did not occur to her (Sciolino 1997, A3). However, she recently lamented that her social identity as a Jew is invoked constantly by the Swiss press: "In Switzerland my Jewishness is more visible [than in the United States], shall we say" (A3).

Social identity in the sense used by psychological social psychologists (Tajfel and Turner 1986) comes at the issue not so much as the imposition of an identity from the outside (as in labeling) but as a cognitive tool used by individuals to partition, categorize, and order their social environment and their place in it. SI theory starts by assuming the primacy of the mind and considers social identity

> that *part* of an individual's self-concept which derives from his knowledge of his membership in a social group (or groups) together with the value and emotional significance attached to that membership. . . . The assumption is made that, however rich and complex may be the individuals' view of themselves in relation to their surrounding world . . . *some* aspects of that view are contributed by the membership of certain social groups or categories. Some of these memberships are more salient than others; and some may vary in salience in time as a function of a variety of social situations. (Tajfel 1981, 255)

Not only do people take in the overall cultural evaluations of groups (e.g., status, prestige, worth), but they also vary in the degree of legitimacy they afford those cultural evaluations. Taylor's (1996) study of women in a postpartum depression self-help group is illustrative. She shows that the women in her study perceive a high degree of general stigma for the ambivalent and sometimes hostile and even homicidal feelings they have had toward their newborns. Through identity politics of the woman's self-help movement, Taylor shows that postpartum depression self-help is a social movement of political resistance and social change. Many of the mothers take solace in the movement's attempts to delegitimize the perceived opinions of a male-dominated medical establishment that the women believe denigrates such feelings and labels them—and by extension the women in the group—as abnormal and perhaps wicked. Thus, a person might well see and understand the lower standing and possible contempt of his or her group from the culture's point of view but attach little, if any, legitimacy to that evaluation.

Collective Identity

CI holds a somewhat subordinate place in our theory but merits brief mention. According to Melucci (1989), collective identity is a process by which a set of individuals interact to create a shared identity or consciousness. Unlike social identity, which is an individual-level concept that has social and cultural roots, collective identity is a distinctly group-level concept referring to how a group identifies itself. (In a sense, social identities are to individuals what collective identities are to groups.) Consequently, CI is derived from the group's own self-identification. If one wanted to study the collective identity of Teamsters for a Democratic Union, for example, one would have to go to the TDU members directly. However, in order to understand a person's social identity as a TDU member and union reformer, the investigator would do best to measure not only how the TDU member evaluates his or her TDU identity and its relative importance but also how he or she perceives how relevant *others* evaluate and judge it.

Our main focus is on social identity. However, we acknowledge that SI and CI can be linked in meaningful ways to action. A group's collective identity work—or the work of others in shaping a group's identity—can be deduced by individuals and incorporated into their social identity and ultimately, perhaps, their self-concept. Once it is so incorporated, the probability for action predicated on one's identity comes into play (Stryker 1980).

Social Self-Esteem

In the broadest sense, SSE may be defined as a generally held attitude toward the worth or esteem of a particular group, category, or collectivity.[1] (For simplicity, we henceforth use "group" to mean collectivity or category.) SSE begins with a person's perception of a society's or culture's general attitude toward and evaluation of the worth or esteem of a group to which he or she belongs or identifies. The closer an individual identifies with a particular group (whether an actual member or not), the more he or she will likely experience some degree of pride or shame in the group's SSE. When these evaluations are perceived as legitimate and the SSE is relatively high, the individual will tend to see his or her identification with the group as a source of satisfaction and perhaps contentment. When the SSE is low and the group's boundary is relatively permeable, many individuals will likely attempt to move to another, more highly evaluated group or distance themselves from the disesteemed identity, particularly if the legitimacy of the evaluation is accepted. An illustration would be the phenomenon of "passing" among some light-skinned blacks (Williams 1995). When the group's boundaries are relatively impermeable, the perceived SSE is low, and the evaluation is deemed illegitimate, the group may engage in collective behavior aimed at (1) changing the evaluation criteria used to compare one group with another; (2) finding or promoting a more distinctively positive evaluation criteria; or (3) seeking a different group with which one is compared (Thoits and Virshup 1997). We argue that it is the latter case (i.e., perceptions of low SSE, illegitimacy, and perhaps relative impermeability) coupled with generally high individual self-esteem that constitutes the fertile ground from which the seed of social movement activism may grow.

Individual Self-Esteem

ISE is employed here in the way typically found in the broader self-esteem literature (Rosenberg 1979), namely, the sense of esteem or disesteem existing or occurring within the individual self or mind, or a positive attitude toward the self as an object. Like the self-concept generally, ISE arises out of and is shaped by the groups, networks, and social situations in which the individual participates (Owens 1992) and the roles he or she assumes or relinquishes (Owens, Mortimer, and Finch 1996). And even though ISE resides in the individual's mind, it largely results from the *relations* people have in the world around them. As used in the present context, ISE is linked to Owens's (1993) notion of two-dimensional positive and negative global self-esteem or composed of *generally* self-denigrating or *generally* self-confirming attitudes toward the self.

Linking Self-Esteem and Social Justice to Social Movement Participation

Our second theoretical concern grounds self-esteem in conceptions of fairness and justice. This idea is partly influenced by recent arguments that some people with high self-esteem may be provoked to violence when affronted (Baumeister, Smart, and Boden 1996). However, we turn the discussion in a different direction by examining the impetus (or lack thereof) to become involved in a social movement by investigating the interplay between one's ISE and the sense that some group or category (not necessarily one to which a person actually belongs) is the victim of unfair treatment or injustice.[2] We specifically postulate that people with high positive self-esteem who couple that with a heightened sense of social justice or fairness will be drawn into social movements at higher rates than those with high positive self-esteem but little or no sense of or interest in social justice or fairness (or a person who subscribes to the belief in a just world). In other words, for a person whose high positive self-esteem is coupled with a salient social conscience, becoming involved in a social movement may approach an imperative to maintaining that high positive self-esteem—thus motivating the individual toward action—in contrast to a person with high positive self-esteem who, for whatever reason, does not have a salient social conscience that is also psychologically central to his or her self-system. The latter person with high self-esteem may use that trait to build a career or amass fame and fortune rather than attend to larger issues such as economic, social, or environmental justice.

To summarize, we make two contentions stemming from our premise that it is not so much people with low self-esteem who get involved in social movements as it is people with high self-esteem. First, there will be an increased probability of becoming active in a social movement among those who perceive a disjuncture between their personal feelings of high positive

ISE and their perception of the low esteem others generally confer on a social identity of importance to them. Second, there will be an increased probability of becoming a social movement activist among those who perceive that a group or collectivity—especially one with which they identify but do not necessarily belong to—is treated unjustly or unfairly. As the two gaps widen, a cause for the disjuncture may be sought and fought, thus mobilizing people around a common perceived threat or enemy.

Scope Conditions, Illustrations, and Hypotheses

In this section, we provide examples from various social movements to illustrate the links between self-esteem, injustice, and social movement participation. These are intended as examples only; they are not offered as proofs of the nature of such processes. The examples are followed by specific hypotheses that vary in complexity. We view these hypotheses as directions for future research in the areas of self-esteem and the impetus to become involved in social movements. In seeking such a link, we must, of necessity, implement certain scope conditions. We turn to them first.

Scope and Conditions

Scope Condition 1

First and foremost, we lay no claim to explaining all manner of social movement participation. Rather, we confine our inquiry to the impetus to and probability of becoming involved in a social movement, particularly those movements aimed at redressing perceived collective grievances or perceived injustices, not simply to oneself, but to some group or collectivity with which one identifies.[3] We further assume that these grievances are perceived as chronic rather than acute. The first assumption recalls, in part, McCarthy and Zald's (1977) recommendation—amplified by Gamson (1990)—to move the study of social movements away from an emphasis on deprivation and grievances in favor of a more macro and rationalistic view embodied in resource mobilization theory. Rather than framing participation in social movements as a reaction to social disorganization mounted by the uprooted, alienated, and disorganized (Gamson 1990), we seek to link activism to those people characterized by relatively high levels of self-esteem who would not ordinarily be characterized as psychologically or emotionally needy or at risk. Furthermore, we acknowledge the importance of recent trends that view social movements as a link between micro and macro levels. For the purposes of this chapter we choose to focus on the micro processes behind recruitment to and retention in social movements. However, regardless of one's level of indignation, we recognize the potential importance of social networks and preexisting organizations in enabling one to move from grievance to action (McAdam 1988; Morris 1981; White 1989). Finally, distinguishing between acute and chronic grievances or injustices is important because we are focusing on those who perceive some kind of systematic or structural disadvantage of long duration, rather than those reacting to an acute or temporal injustice or grievance resulting in swift collective behavior in the form discussed by Le Bon (1960), such as a riot or "charging of the gates."[4]

Scope Condition 2

We confine our discussion of the self to one aspect, self-esteem, and specifically positive general self-esteem (Owens 1993). Consequently, our class of movement participant would not ordinarily be perceived by self or others as a misfit, a marginal person, or someone seeking self-transformation, that is, seeking belongingness or purpose through social movement participation, or what some refer to as an irrational motive (Ferree 1992). Rather, the class of participant described here may be quite rational in his or her motivation and may come to feel impelled to act out of two forms of self-interestedness. First, action is not so much predicated on a *search* for self-esteem as it is on a motivation to *maintain* one's positive self-regard (Swann, Stein-Seroussi, and Giesler 1992; Taylor and Brown 1988). In short, inaction may constitute a threat to one's self-esteem via a diminished perception of positive ISE. Second, and related to the first, one may be motivated to act through a perceived disjuncture between one's high positive self-esteem and the recognition that a group or collectivity with which one identifies is somehow thwarted, disesteemed, or "wrongfully" labeled as inferior or deviant (Kitsuse 1979). In this case one quite rationally seeks to rehabilitate the image of one's group or to see that the perceived injustices to it are reduced or eliminated. We posit, therefore, that some people with high self-esteem will be motivated to action in order to keep their high attitudes toward their ISE consonant with their perceptions of the worth, esteem, and justice afforded to groups to which they identify—or, their social identity. This strategy of self-verification (Swann, Stein-Seroussi, and Giesler 1992; Riley and Burke 1995) may thus embody a good deal of self-interestedness.

Scope Condition 3

We view high positive self-esteem as a perhaps necessary though not sufficient motive in transforming a person from being concerned, disgruntled, or outraged to being an activist—especially an early or first mover (Williamson 1975). As we argue later, the linkage between self-esteem and social movement participation flows through and is bonded by one's social identity.

The Relationship between Self-Esteem and Social Movement Participation

We set out here to illustrate how a *divergence* between one's self-esteem and the perceived esteem afforded a group or collectivity with which one identifies can serve as a significant motivator in social movement participation. The point may be demonstrated by interview quotes from a study of women active in a local chapter of the League of Women Voters during the 1950s and 1960s and those active in a local chapter of the National Organization for Women (NOW) during the 1970s and early 1980s. This study examined the political and feminist identities of women activists and found that these identities are influenced by the historical context in which these women came of political age, as well as transformative events in individuals' personal history (see Aronson 2000 for more information). In general, these women appear to have high positive self-esteem and became active in their respective organizations after becoming aware of the devaluation and discrimination women faced during these time periods. Those active in the league were all housewives when they joined the organization in the 1950s and 1960s. Their primary reason for joining was to be able to use their skills and intellectual talents to move beyond their limited world of children and housework, which was the expectation and reality for most middle-class women during this period. However, as we also argue, they were motivated to become involved because their high individual self-esteem did not comport with their perceived low social self-esteem.

For example, one activist held many leadership positions in her local league chapter during the 1950s and 1960s. She expressed high self-regard both in these activities and in several statements about her experiences, in which she sounded confident and had faith in her own abilities:

> So I was in charge of that, and the organization was quite well organized. . . . We ran a very important operation.
>
> I was very very successful.
>
> So it was very easy for me . . . to work. I was doing a good job. I didn't have to worry.
>
> I mean this sounds kind of boastful, but by that time I really knew the system.
>
> I read that proposal and it just caught my attention and I said, oh, I can do this with one hand tied behind my back.

This activist explained that her reason for involvement was to move her own life beyond the limited roles set for women in that era. As she put it,

> The things that made me want to be involved is [sic] I wanted to feel I was having part of the action, I was having some influence on my life, on more than just voting.
>
> It provided me with the intellectual stimulation which I needed. And it put me in touch with another world other than the world of children and housework.

Other women expressed similar motivations for involvement. For example, another league activist said:

> My husband used to joke about my League activity. He described those of us that were doing this as "psychically unemployed." . . . You know, he meant we had good brains and abilities and . . . there's just so much of the time that you can talk to the kids. . . . So, that was really, I guess, really what it was about.

These examples suggest that these activists sought to bridge the gap between how they felt about themselves (i.e., educated, competent, effective, and intelligent) and the roles generally available to women of that era. Although the housewife role was not necessarily disesteemed in the larger culture, the limited nature of women's possibilities illustrates a general societal perception that women's capabilities were limited, and these women sought to change this through their own participation. In the vernacular of this chapter, the women were acting to close the gap between their ISE and their perceived SSE vis-à-vis women. That is, these women became active in the league not simply because they saw women's talents and skills being devalued and limited in general but because they themselves experienced this disesteem of women's capabilities. However, they gave value to their own talents and skills. This suggests that such personal experience may be likely to lead to involvement in particular social movements.

Another activist, who joined NOW in the late 1960s, held several organizational leadership roles and was heavily involved in the organization's public speaking campaign. Suggesting her high positive self-esteem, she would often speak to somewhat hostile groups about women's issues, directly challenging their beliefs about women's roles. She calls herself an "early war horse," illustrating the difficulty of many of the situations she faced. She expressed several concerns about the social self-esteem of women during that period. Speaking about one of these experiences, she said:

> I can remember one of the most blatant forms of sex discrimination to me went on in physics class. It's possible that variations of this go on in all kinds of science classes, all over the place, still do. But in that one the idea was that if there are any girls in this class they will sit in the corner in the back of the room where none of the equipment works. And we don't throw it away, we just throw it back there, 'cause then there's the illusion that they have the equipment.

Her experience with sexism, the disesteem accorded to women in that period, pushed her to become involved in the women's movement. This example represents another case in which someone experienced a gap between her own positive ISE and the social esteem of a group with which she identified. It appears that this gap helped lead this activist to social movement participation.[5]

We turn now to our first two specific hypotheses derived, in part, from the illustrations and our desire to incorporate the self in social movement involvement.

Hypothesis 1: Simple Bivariate

As self-esteem increases, the probability of participating in a social movement increases.

As a direct link, we could posit the following simple relationship:

M1: Self-esteem + Social movement participation.

The merit of such a model is that it draws on the notion that people with high self-esteem tend to be more prosocial and have better social and psychological well-being than those with low self-esteem (Owens 1993). People with high self-esteem also tend to perceive themselves as more efficacious and competent. If true, people with high self-esteem should exhibit more involvement in social movements, an arguably prosocial (in terms of trying to effect social change) and frequently demanding endeavor. The model's limitation is that although an association may exist, it is likely weak, since social movement involvement is far more complex than this simple model suggests (White 1989).

Instead, we argue the merit of considering two elaborated models, both of which draw on or incorporate aspects of identity theory discussed above to illustrate how self-esteem may be an important, though overlooked, social force in the recruitment to and participation in social movements.[6] In the next two models we specifically posit a *divergence thesis* in which the gap between one's self-esteem and the perceived esteem and justice accorded a group or collectivity with which one identifies serves as a significant motivator in social movement participation.

Hypothesis 2: Individual Self-Esteem versus Social Self-Esteem and Social Movement Participation

As the divergence between positive individual self-esteem (ISE) and social self-esteem (SSE) increases, the greater the likelihood an attempt will be made to reduce the gap by participating in an appropriate social movement (SMA).

We expect ISE and SSE to affect participation in two ways. First, an increase in the divergence between ISE and SSE, for a given level of ISE, will increase the probability of participation. Second, the lower the person's ISE for a given level of divergence (ISE-SSE), the lower the probability of participation. Assuming a categorical dependent variable (acted in a social movement vs. didn't act), this can be modeled with logit or probit as follows:

$$M2_a\text{: } \Pr(\text{SMA}) = \Lambda[B_0 + B_1(\text{ISE-SSE}) + B_2\text{ISE}],$$

where Λ is the cumulative density function for the logistic distribution and B_0 is the intercept. B_1 indicates the effect of divergence, while B_2 reflects the effect of ISE. Thus, as the divergence between one's positive individual self-esteem (ISE) and one's social self-esteem (SSE) increases, so does the likelihood that an attempt will be made to reduce the gap by participating in an appropriate social movement (SMA). The use of "appropriate" is intentional, since we explicitly distance ourselves from the notion that people found in the above condition will seek involvement in *any* social movement in an attempt to reduce the perceived gap (which would contradict our assumption of rationality). Consequently, by "appropriate" we mean social movements directed, in part, toward improving the low esteem that one perceives others generally confer on a group—and thus a social identity—important to the individual. It must further be acknowledged that one might want to reduce the gap but network demands elsewhere or the lack of resources may make direct involvement extremely difficult. Finally, a plausible alternative to $M1_a$ would be:

$$M2_b\text{: } \Pr(\text{SMA}) = \Lambda(B_0 + B_1(\text{ISE-SSE}) + B_2\text{ISE} + B_3\text{ISE}^2),$$

where $B_3\text{ISE}^2$ would allow for the inclusion of a more radical curve depicting the probability of action or Pr(SMA).

While the "gap" may be felt substantively as a form of cognitive dissonance, self-concept theory suggests that individuals are highly motivated to protect and maintain their self-pictures, particularly through the motives of self-esteem and self-consistency (Owens 1993). Briefly, the self-esteem motive induces people to think as well of themselves as possible. Many self theorists regard this as a universally dominant motive (Kaplan 1975). If true, the person with high positive self-esteem (and the self-perceived internal resources that come with it) would, we assert, be especially motivated to mount some form of action to bring his or her social self-esteem into alignment with his or her individual self-esteem.

It should be noted, however, that people may take other routes to attempt to reduce the gap. For example, some may reduce the importance of and their commitment to a particular social identity. Others might express their disgruntlement but do little to resolve the problem actively—in other words, complain but do nothing. It could alternatively be argued that when a person with high positive individual self-esteem adopts a personal identity (in the sense demonstrated by Stryker in chapter 1 in this volume) that begins to converge with a social identity, the person will be motivated to act on the coalescing identity. This action may take at least two forms. First, one may participate in a social movement charged with actively supporting the identity against perceived threats outside the immediate collectivity. Second (although not necessarily mutually exclusive of the first), the individual may seek or discover a subgroup or subculture that allows him or her to act on his or her personal identity (or coalescing identity) in a network or collectivity doing the same. This alternative route may or may not be activist in the sense of overtly promoting or advancing the identity outside the newfound clique. The individual may be content to commingle and interact with people expressing a similar identity or doing similar "identity work" (Snow and Anderson 1987).

The Relationship between Self-Esteem, Perceived Social Injustice, and Social Movement Participation

We now consider cases in which someone with high positive individual self-esteem and a high sense of justice or fairness experiences chronic injustice toward a group with whom he or she has a salient social identity. Our examples suggest that these situations may lead to social movement involvement. The first example comes from Farrell Dobbs's (1972) account of his radicalization and eventual deep involvement in the depression-era union movement, especially the events surrounding the bloody and protracted 1934 Teamsters Strike in Minneapolis. Although Dobbs makes no specific reference to his self-esteem, we may surmise it was high. This is especially true given the feelings of self-confidence and efficacy he exhibited in the summer of 1932 by quitting a secure and well-paid job as a junior executive at the Omaha office of Western Electric and moving his wife and two young daughters to Minneapolis. He writes that he and his wife, Marvel, planned to use his executive severance pay of several hundred dollars to get a small business started in Minneapolis.

> Once it was under way Marvel would take over the management. I would then go to the University of Minnesota to study political science and law, hopefully to become a judge and dispense some justice. When our finances permitted, Marvel would also enter the university so that eventually we could act as a team in carrying out our new course. (19)

His budding activism, which eventually led him to be a major actor in the pre–World War II American labor movement (prior to the Communist purges) and socialist politics into the 1970s, was catalyzed with a 1931 newspaper picture of the Japanese shelling of Shanghai and his involvement in labor force reduction meetings at Western Electric in 1932. Concerning the Chinese incident, he writes:

> [The] working-class quarter . . . had been reduced to a mass of rubble by Japanese artillery, but the wealthy district stood unscathed. As a worker I felt instinctive sympathy for my Chinese counterparts who had been attacked so brutally. It made me feel that something was basically wrong with a world in which such a terrible thing could happen. (18)

The eventual journey to the union movement—and activism—began a year later when he was asked to attend a meeting with Western Electric's division superintendent and his district supervisors. Dobbs writes:

> By that time the post-1929 economic depression had become severe and a session was held to compile a list of employees for a general layoff. Among those named was John Staley, a worker who had been with the company a long time and who would soon be eligible for retirement under the company's stingy pension plan. The points were made that his layoff would enable the company to keep a younger, more productive worker and save some pension money later on. Because I had worked with John and drank with him [prior to Dobbs's promotion to management he was a switchboard installer with Staley], he was more than just a name to me. What was being done to him filled me with revulsion. It became clear that they were trying to make a tool out of me through their training and I wanted no part of it. (18)

Turning to the women activists, one NOW member described the chronic injustices she encountered in the 1960s.

> So, something so basic as having NO plumbing in your building that women were allowed to use, UGH! It was very dramatic one by one to come across these women with these outrageous obstacles to doing daily life. . . . But the worst of it was that female employees who went to get their pay, cash pay, for a lot of relatively low skill labor, [which] was very common . . . [were] shown a slip showing it had already been picked up.
>
> . . . The sequence was husband, father, brother, woman. They all had, in that descending sequence, the right to claim her wages. . . . So imagine how many people had a right to your wage first, UGH! So by the time the issue was people keeping their original name, or keeping marital name, I think I was probably at the shouting stage with impatience after having heard all these really grinding basic issues, and then for someone to have a preference for [keeping their original name] and to be told that . . . the law doesn't allow it!!

This activist directly cited injustice as a reason for her involvement. When asked the importance of being involved in the women's movement, she responded:

> Not ignoring the unfairness. If we're going to stand here and address the question of "is this question fair? FAIR?!!" Punitive, and obstacle ridden and outrageous and wasteful—it's completely unfair!! Can it be made better? Well, nothing is going to change if people don't make an effort.

Similarly, another activist appears to have positive ISE and a sense of injustice about the ways women were treated during this time period. She ran for public office, a seemingly risky step and a sign of her high ISE. Her sense of injustice about the ways women were treated stemmed from her personal experiences. Despite her tremendous community involvement, she recounted a time when someone suggested that her husband run for office instead of her:

> And yet [a public official] turned and said to my husband, "Why don't you run for school board?" I can remember, it was just infuriating!!

However, she decided to run for office and, in fact, got elected. She described her feelings about the election, and about her position once she got elected, as follows:

> They never called me until it was all over. . . . That was another one of those cliques, the double standards—the men were called immediately to come down and watch the recount and I wasn't, even though I was clearly one of the top contenders.
>
> I really came quickly to the understanding that the men on the administration simply didn't hear my voice. It's not that I have a quiet voice. I do NOT have a quiet voice, but I would say something, and they would just continue the conversation. Somebody would bring up the same topic as if it was their own idea, and I realized that they simply weren't hearing me. . . . They didn't respond to my question at all, and that was a real consciousness raiser. I had gotten elected to the school board with the understanding that I was a co-equal.

This example suggests that feelings of injustice are often tied to personal experiences, and this can be a powerful motivator to become involved in a social movement. Social movement participants can be high ISE people who are confronted by a case of injustice toward a group with which they identify. Involvement in the social movement is directed at righting the wrong inflicted on that group. This is reflected in a comment by another women's movement activist:

> The rules were just totally different [for men's and women's dorms], and I hadn't really thought about it. All these flags started coming up, and I started to realize the unfairness of it all, that women really didn't have the same opportunities. And that became important to me, important enough that I was willing to spend a lot of my time to try to make things better.

In summary, these examples illustrate that high positive self-esteem, coupled with experiences with chronic injustice toward a group with which one has a salient social identity, can lead to social movement participation. It should be noted that although belonging to the group or having it as a social identity would undoubtedly facilitate participation in a social movement aimed at righting an injustice, neither is a necessary or sufficient precursor to action. The operant precondition is that the individual must *identify* with the group or have the group as one of his or her salient social identities. Moreover, activation in this case will be especially conditional on one's access to movement participants or movement recruitment appeals via one's social networks. McAdam's (1988) account of the recruitment of northern college students to Freedom Summer's drive to end American apartheid is illustrative.

The self, justice, and social movement nexus is codified in our third and last hypothesis.

Hypothesis 3: Individual Self-Esteem versus Perceived Social Injustice and Social Movement Participation

When a person with high positive individual self-esteem (ISE) and a high sense of justice or fairness (Justice) becomes aware of gross or chronic injustice (CIj) toward a group with which he or she has a salient social identify (SI), the higher is his or her probability of becoming a social movement activist (SMA).

This hypothesis could be expressed most simply as the product of the variables such that a zero on any particular variable (ISE, J, CIj, or SI) would negate the probability of SMA. Alternatively, one might cast it as a type of value-added model (Smelser 1962). In a hypothetical value-added model, as each factor was sequentially included in the model, the probability of social movement action would increase. For example, we might start with ISE and SSE, move to Justice, then add CIj*SI to obtain Pr(SMA). However, both of these models are stringent interpretations of the third hypothesis and would likely be untenable. For purposes of discussion one might consider Model 3, below, more defensible.

$$\text{M3: } \Pr(\text{SMA}) = \Lambda[B_0 + B_1(\text{CIj*SI}) + B_2\text{ISE} + B_3\text{CIj} + B_4\text{Justice}],$$

where once again Λ is the cumulative density function for the logistic distribution and B_0 is the intercept. B_1 indicates the joint effect of perceptions of chronic injustice toward a group with which one has a salient identity, and B_2 reflects the effect of ISE, B_3 reflects the effect of CIj, and B_4 reflects the effect of Justice.

Conclusion

Despite a plethora of work, advances in self-esteem research have rarely extended to macro phenomena, such as social movements, thus blocking a linkage of potential benefit to both literatures. It was the goal of this chapter to help establish such a link by positing three general models. As conceived here, self-esteem and social movement participation are linked not only directly but also indirectly. As the most basic and direct link, we argued an admittedly weak case that individual self-esteem alone was sufficient to propel individuals toward movement activism (hypothesis 1). Two elaborated models were posed to rectify this oversimplification of ISE's presumed causal role in social movement participation. In the first elaboration we argued the merits of a discrepancy function. In this view, as the disparity between one's positive ISE and one's SSE widens, people's motivation to engage in an appropriate social movement will increase (hypothesis 2). Second, we argued that perhaps a concern for general social justice coupled with a perception of chronic injustice toward some group with which one has a salient social identity is also necessary to generate movement activism (hypothesis 3). The later hypotheses are posed as directions for future research on self-esteem and social movement participation.

The major caveat we identified in our chapter is the need to bound our inquiry by a series of scope conditions. The conditions speak not only to the self-concept literature but also to the social movement literature. Thus, although we acknowledge that some may see only meager utility in the so-called dispositional perspective on social movement participation (see chapter 2 in this volume), people's self-attitudes do, in fact, have an appreciable impact on their behaviors generally (Mecca, Smelser, and Vasconcellos 1989; Scheff and Retzinger 1992; Simmons and Blyth 1987) and, we argue, the impetus to be a social movement activist particularly.

Very little in the social movements literature that we reviewed has incorporated self-level variables in earnest (save various chapters in this volume), but that is not a sign of the weakness or irrelevance of the self-concept in activism. Rather, it is a sign that the literature on the self needs to engage the social movements literature, and vice versa, so the self occupies a more prominent place in explaining why—on an individual level—people become movement activists, what they get out of activism, and why (from the standpoint of the self) they stay or leave. The importance of networks and "biographical availability" in recruitment to and retention in social movements is certainly warranted and is by no means incompatible with the views expressed here. However, the role of the self, we argue, must also find its way in the discussion.

Notes

For feedback on an earlier version the authors are grateful to Bert Klandermans and Scott Long.

1. Luhtanen and Crocker (1992) have also explored this connection with respect to collective self-esteem, a much broader conceptualization than ours. We prefer the term *social self-esteem* because the term *collective self-esteem* is problematic inasmuch as it blurs important conceptual distinctions while also making the unit, and level, of analysis questionable.

Our use of *group* does not necessarily follow the typical sociological meaning of the term (e.g., an ongoing interaction among a set of individuals). Instead, we follow Tajfel's (1981, 254) usage: "a cognitive entity that is meaningful to the individual at a particular point of time."

2. A case in point is a former leader of the Native American Solidarity Council (NASC), a group of whites who in the late 1970s and early 1980s moved into predominantly American Indian neighborhoods with the express purpose of befriending the Native American community and working with it on issues of social justice. One of the leaders, J. M., was by all accounts a woman with high self-esteem who fought not only against white injustice toward Indians but also against Native American suspicion of her group's true motives (Owens 1980).

3. A counterexample may be found in social movements or organizations aimed at increasing or improving one's spirituality, sense of self, or belongingness, such as many of the groups and people reported in Zablocki's (1980) study of urban communes.

4. See Myers (1997) for an examination of the long-term structural and economic grievances generally underpinning many race riots in the 1960s. The South-Central Los Angles race riots in 1992 following the first police verdict in the Rodney King beating, although representative of a long-simmering rage over perceived legal injustices, would nevertheless be illustrative of an acute response by an emotionally aroused collectivity to a perceived temporal outrage.

5. The activism of reputed Mafia don Joseph Colombo in the Italian-American Civil Rights League (IACRL) is another case in point. Colombo founded the IACRL ostensibly to elevate the stature and esteem of Italian Americans and to instill ethnic pride (i.e., social self-esteem and collective self-esteem, respectively). On June 29, 1970, Colombo led a fifty-thousand-person IACRL rally in Manhattan's Columbus Circle, which included Governor Nelson Rockefeller, an honorary member of the IACRL (Osterlund and Royle 1993). Although we have no hard evidence of Colombo's self-esteem, published reports of his comportment and demeanor suggest a man with considerable self-regard and confidence who was motivated or perhaps driven to improve the perceived low esteem of a group from which he derived an important social identity—Italian American. (His passion for the IACRL eventually resulted in an assassination attempt by New York mobsters fed up with his activism.)

6. A reasonable third elaborated hypothesis, not explored in the present chapter, is the relation of personal identity esteem versus social identity esteem in social movement participation. That is, active involvement in a social movement characterized by a collectivity with a given social identity may occur in order to protect personal role identities to which very high esteem is attached. This appears to be the case for some people's involvement in the pro-choice movement, in which limitations on abortion are viewed as attacks on esteemed gender-related identities (Luker 1984). What would be of considerable theoretical and practical interest is the specification of the set of conditions, both social structural and social psychological, that account for apparently diverse relationships of esteem attached to social identities and esteem attached to personal identities (see chapter 2 in this volume with respect to this aim).

References

Aronson, Pamela J. 2000. "The Development and Transformation of Feminist Identities under Changing Historical Conditions." In *Advances in Life Course Research: Self and Identity through the Life Course in Cross-Cultural Perspective,* edited by T. J. Owens. Stamford, Conn.: JAI Press.

Baumeister, Roy F., Laura Smart, and Joseph M. Boden. 1996. "Relation of Threatened Egotism to Violence and Aggression: The Dark Side of High Self-Esteem." *Psychological Review* 103:5–33.

Dobbs, Farrell. 1972. *Teamster Rebellion.* New York: Nomad Press.

Evans, Sara. 1979. *Personal Politics: The Roots of Women's Liberation in the Civil Rights Movement and the Left Movement.* New York: Vintage Books.

Ferree, Myra Marx. 1992. "The Political Context of Rationality: Rational Choice Theory and Resource Mobilization." In *Frontiers in Social Movement Theory,* edited by A. D. Morris and C. M. Mueller, 29–52. New Haven: Yale University Press.

Flacks, Richard. 1988. *Making History: The American Left and the American Mind.* New York: Columbia University Press.

Freeman, Jo. 1975. *The Politics of Women's Liberation.* New York: Longman.

———. 1983. *Social Movements of the Sixties and Seventies.* New York: Longman.

Friedman, Debra, and Doug McAdam. 1992. "Collective Identity and Activism: Networks, Choices, and the Life of a Social Movement." In *Frontiers in Social Movement Theory,* edited by A. D. Morris and C. M. Mueller, 156–73. New Haven: Yale University Press.

Gamson, William. 1990. *The Strategy of Social Protest.* 2d ed. Belmont, Calif.: Wadsworth Publishing Co.

———. 1992a. "The Social Psychology of Collective Action." In *Frontiers in Social Movement Theory,* edited by A. D. Morris and C. M. Mueller, 53–76. New Haven: Yale University Press.

———. 1992b. *Talking Politics.* New York: Cambridge University Press.

Goffman, Erving. 1963. *Stigma: Notes on the Management of Spoiled Identity.* Englewood Cliffs, N.J.: Prentice-Hall.

Kaplan, Howard B. 1975. *Self-Attitudes and Deviant Behavior.* Pacific Palisades, Calif.: Goodyear.

Kitsuse, John I. 1979. "Coming Out All Over: Deviants and the Politics of Social Problems." *Social Problems* 28:1–13.

Kluegel, James R., and Eliot R. Smith. 1986. *Beliefs about Inequality.* New York: Aldine de Gruyter.

Le Bon, Gustave. 1960. *The Crowd: A Study of the Popular Mind.* New York: Viking Press.

Lerner, Melvin J. 1980. *The Belief in a Just World: A Fundamental Delusion.* New York: Plenum.

Luhtanen, Riia, and Jennifer Crocker. 1992. "A Collective Self-Esteem Scale: Self-Evaluations of One's Social Identity." *Personality and Social Psychology Bulletin* 18:302–18.

Luker, Kristin. 1984. *Abortion and the Politics of Motherhood.* Berkeley: University of California Press.

May, Elaine Tyler. 1988. *Homeward Bound: American Families in the Cold War Era.* New York: Basic Books.

McAdam, Doug. 1988. *Freedom Summer.* New York: Oxford University Press.

McAdam, Doug, John McCarthy, and Zald Mayer. 1988. "Social Movements." In *Handbook of Sociology,* edited by Neil Smelser, 695–737. Newbury Park, Calif.: Sage.

McCarthy, John D., and Mayer N. Zald. 1977. "Resource Mobilization in Social Movements: A Partial Theory." *American Journal of Sociology* 82:112–34.

Mecca, Andrew M., Neil J. Smelser, and John Vasconcellos, eds. 1989. *The Social Importance of Self-Esteem.* Berkeley: University of California Press.

Melucci, Alberto. 1989. *Nomads of the Present: Social Movements and Individual Needs in Contemporary Society.* Edited by John Keane and Paul Mier. Philadelphia: Temple University Press.

Morris, Aldon. 1981. "Black Southern Sit-In Movement: An Analysis of Internal Organization." *American Sociological Review* 46:744–67.

Mueller, Carol McClurg. 1992. "Building Social Movement Theory." In *Frontiers in Social Movement Theory,* edited by A. D. Morris and C. M. Mueller, 3–25. New Haven: Yale University Press.

Myers, Daniel J. 1997. "Racial Rioting in the 1960s: An Event History Analysis of Local Conditions." *American Sociological Review* 62:94–113.

Osterlund, David, and David Royle. 1993. *Target Mafia.* New York: Osterlund Co. and David Royle Productions in association with Arts & Entertainment Networks. 250 minutes, videocassettes.

Owens, Timothy J. 1980. "Identity, Ideology, and Political Action in a Radical Veterans Group." Manuscript, Department of Sociology, University of Minnesota.

———. 1992. "The Effect of Post–High School Social Context on Self-Esteem." *Sociological Quarterly* 33:553–77.

———. 1993. "Accentuate the Positive—and the Negative: Rethinking the Use of Self-Esteem, Self-Deprecation, and Self-Confidence." *Social Psychology Quarterly* 56:288–99.

———. 1994. "Leaving Home before Marriage: Ethnicity, Familism, and Generational Relationships." *Contemporary Sociology* 23:702–3.

Owens, Timothy J., Jeylan T. Mortimer, and Michael D. Finch. 1996. "Self-Determination as a Source of Self-Esteem in Adolescence." *Social Forces* 74:1377–404.

Riley, Anna, and Peter J. Burke. 1995. "Identities and Self-Verification in the Small Group." *Social Psychology Quarterly* 58:61–73.

Rosenberg, Morris. 1979. *Conceiving the Self.* New York: Basic Books.

Scheff, Thomas J., and Suzanne M. Retzinger. 1992. *Emotions and Conflict: Shame and Rage in Destructive Conflicts.* Thousand Oaks, Calif.: Sage.

Sciolino, Elaine. 1997. "'A Careful Dance' for U.S Envoy in Switzerland." *New York Times,* October 4, A3.

Simmons, Roberta G., and Dale A. Blyth. 1987. *Moving into Adolescence: The Impact of Pubertal Change and School Context.* New York: Aldine de Gruyter.

Smelser, Neil J. 1962. *Theory of Collective Behavior.* New York: Free Press.

Snow, David A., and Leon Anderson. 1987. "Identity Work among the Homeless: The Verbal Construction and Avowal of Personal Identities." *American Journal of Sociology* 92:1336–71.

Snow, David A., and Robert Benford. 1992. "Master Frames and Cycles of Protest." In *Frontiers in Social Movement Theory,* edited by A. D. Morris and C. M. Mueller, 133–55. New Haven: Yale University Press.

Snow, David A., Brook Rochford Jr., Steve Worden, and Robert Benford. 1986. "Frame Alignment Processes, Micromobilization, and Movement Participation." *American Sociological Review* 51:464–81.

Stryker, Sheldon. 1980. *Symbolic Interactionism: A Social Structural Version.* Menlo Park, Calif.: Benjamin-Cummings.

Swann, William B., Jr., Alan Stein-Seroussi, and R. Brian Giesler. 1992. "Why People Self-Verify." *Journal of Personality and Social Psychology* 62:392–401.

Tajfel, Henri. 1981. *Human Groups and Social Categories: Studies in Social Psychology.* Cambridge: Cambridge University Press.

Tajfel, Henri, and J. C. Turner. 1986. "The Social Identity Theory of Intergroup Behavior." In *Psychology of Intergroup Relations,* 2d ed., edited by S. Worschel and W. Austin, 7–24. Chicago: Nelson-Hall.

Taylor, Shelley E., and Jonathon D. Brown. 1988. "Illusion and Well-Being: A Social Psychological Perspective on Mental Health." *Psychological Bulletin* 103:193–210.

Taylor, Verta. 1996. *Rock-a-by Baby: Feminism, Self-Help, and Postpartum Depression.* New York: Routledge.

Taylor, Verta, and Nancy E. Whittier. 1992. "Collective Identity in Social Movement Communities: Lesbian Feminist Mobilization." In *Frontiers of Social Movement Theory,* edited by A. D. Morris and C. M. Mueller, 104–30. New Haven: Yale University Press.

Thoits, Peggy A., and Lauren K. Virshup. 1997. "Me's and We's: Forms and Functions of Social Identities." In *Self and Identity: Fundamental Issues,* edited by R. D. Ashmore and L. Jussim, 1:106–33. New York: Oxford University Press.

White, Robert W. 1989. "From Peaceful Protest to Guerilla War: Micromobilization of the Provisional Irish Republican Army." *American Journal of Sociology* 94:1277–302.

Williams, Gregory Howard. 1995. *Life on the Color Line: The True Story of a White Boy Who Discovered He Was Black.* New York: Dutton.

Williamson, Oliver E. 1975. *Markets and Hierarchies, Analysis and Antitrust Implications: A Study of the Economics of Internal Organization.* New York: Free Press.

Zablocki, Benjamin David. 1980. *Alienation and Charisma: A Study of Contemporary American Communes.* New York: Free Press.

10

Social Movements as Collective Coping with Spoiled Personal Identities: Intimations from a Panel Study of Changes in the Life Course between Adolescence and Adulthood

Howard B. Kaplan and Xiaoru Liu

Numerous explanations of participation in social movements have been proposed. Among these are models that account for motivation to participate in terms of spoiled (stigmatized) personal identities.

Stigmatized Identities and Social Movements: A Partial Explanation of Participation in Collective Coping

The dynamic relationship between stigmatized identities and participation in social movements may be thought of as consisting of four interrelated processes: the experience of self-devaluing circumstances; the development of a stigmatized identity and differentiation from nonstigmatized others; the anticipation and experience of the self-enhancing implications of participation in social movements; and the decision to choose to participate in particular social movements (figure 1).

Self-Devaluing Experiences and Stigmatized Personal Identities

The attributes and experiences contributing to a stigmatized personal identity may include deviant behaviors, membership in objectionable groups, physical stigmata, or past experiences (such as having been institutionalized) that are intrinsically disvalued or from which objectionable qualities may be inferred. It is not always a single trait or experience that stigmatizes an individual. Often, stigmatization is the cumulative consequence of a history of failing to possess desirable attributes and evoking rejecting responses from conventional membership groups. Some rejecting responses are secondary to deviant adaptations, as when society punishes crimes

Figure 1. Causal model of the relationship between self-devaluing experiences and disposition to participate in collective movements

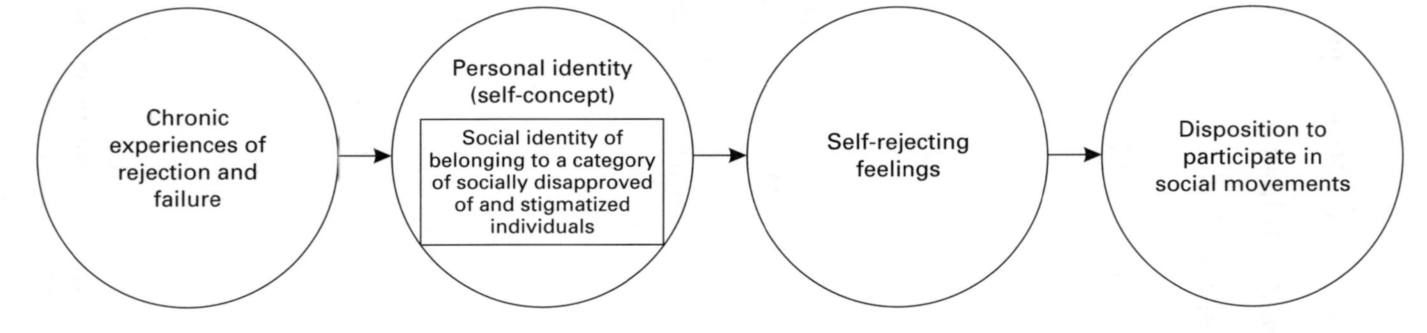

motivated by the failure to accomplish what is expected. The end result is a self-perception of possessing a stigmatized personal identity, perceiving oneself as stigmatized and as the object of collective stigmatization.

Stigmatized and Nonstigmatized Social Identities

Personal identity, as used here, refers to general self-perception as a successful or unsuccessful member of salient conventional groups. Success is measured by having the qualities admired within the group, evoking positive responses from group members, and evaluating oneself positively as a consequence of perceiving oneself as a successful group member. Not being a successful member of salient conventional membership groups is reflected in the opposite being the case. Personal identity becomes a *social identity* when it reflects psychological group membership, holding cognitive representations of self as identical to or interchangeable with other members of the group on dimensions characterizing, defining, or stereotypical of the group (Hogg and Turner 1987, 148).

Self-perception as generally rejected and a failure according to conventional standards is not ordinarily thought of as a social identity apart from the specific bases (such as group memberships) of one's self-evaluation. We argue that pervasive perception of self-rejection, rejection by others, and self-perceived failure compose a general self-attributed identity as belonging to a category of persons who are outcasts from the conventional world. This social identity and consequent negative self-feelings motivate actions rendering the stigmatized identity acceptable and the conventional socio-normative system objectionable. Membership groups in which experiences of rejection and failure lead to a self-attributed stigmatized identity become defined as an out-group as part of a self-protective stance according to which the conventional normative system is itself rejected as invalid. The collective movements one becomes a part of or to which one aspires become positive reference points for self-evaluation. In short, pervasive experiences of rejection and failure in membership groups lead to a social identity that distinguishes between the category of the stigmatized and the unspoiled conventional world and to a feeling of apartness drawing the distinction between stigmatized and conventional others.

Anticipated Self-Enhancing Outcomes

Individuals become disposed to participate in social movements as adaptations to stigmatized social identities. Participation in social movements consciously or unconsciously is intended to enhance self-attitudes and assuage the distress associated with self-attributed negative identity. Projected self-enhancing outcomes may be mediated by concomitants of participation in social movements. First, participation in social movements may provide a new set of intrinsically valued normative standards the individual attempts to approximate (including the fact of participation). If the individual adopts the new system of values, previously stigmatizing personal attributes now become the basis for self-approval, and in any case approximating the new personally endorsed values provides a basis for self-approbation. Second, at the same time, participation in the social movement signifies rejection of the conventional standards according to which the individual judged him- or herself to be a failure and the object of rejection. Rejecting those standards, individuals no longer feel compelled to devalue themselves for having failed to approximate those standards. Third, in addition to the intrinsic gratification achieved by approximating now valued standards, persons enjoy self-enhancing indications of approval and other rewards from fellow protesters. Fourth, the social movement, to the extent that it is successful, may lead to a redistribution of rewards defined as valuable by both the members of the protest movement and the members of more favored social categories heretofore enjoying a greater share of these rewards. Fifth, effective participation in a movement may increase a person's sense of self-efficacy and so increase overall positive self-evaluation. The sense of personal efficacy that frequently derives from participation in a movement is nicely illustrated by people with disabilities who developed oppositional consciousness as a result of participating in rallies (Groch 1994).

Selection of Social Movements

The social movement literature suggests that individuals whose identity is threatened will participate in a social movement promising to obviate that threat. Generally, it is expected that the movement will be formally relevant to the aspect of the self-concept that is threatened and to the nature of the threat. If one's national identity is threatened, then the person is disposed to affiliate with movements dedicated to the restoration of national honor (Skinner 1994). If perceived devaluation of one's ethnic status threatens one's overall self-evaluation, then the person will be inclined to join an ethnic movement that will enhance that aspect of social identity (Thomson 1995). When being gay is the basis of threats to self-acceptance, the individual affiliates in such a way as to "renegotiate the boundaries and definitions of . . . [his or her] religious identity to include a positive valuation of homosexuality" (Thumma 1991, 333). This chapter explores the hypothesis that having a spoiled identity, regardless of the particular basis of that identity, will dispose individuals to participate in social movements that may or may not be manifestly relevant to the perceived source of one's devalued self-image. Participants in some movements may vary widely in the nature of their stigmatization and have in common only that they perceive themselves as stigmatized. Individuals whose sources of self-devaluation are quite diverse may yet be potential participants in any particular social movement. We do not assume that the collective identity that characterizes a social movement is based on homogeneous experiences and characteristics (Groch 1994). Rather, the core of a social movement may only initially share such an identity and experiences. Numerous adherents of the movement's ideology may be the heterogeneous result of a variety of life histories having nothing in common save that they reflect personal experiences of chronic rejection and failure. The collective action provides the potential for self-enhancement, but the ideology underlying the movement is in no way formally related to the precise bases of the experiences of self-rejection and failure. Out of diverse life histories the several adherents focus on a single issue that comes to symbolize their commonality with the original core of the movement sharing the experience of oppression and the oppositional consciousness that derives from the separate experience of rejection and failure and is intended to guide the struggle of the group "to undermine, reform, or overthrow a system of domination" (Morris 1992, 363). Association with the collective movement may have no connection with the source of one's own self-rejection other than that the movement represents an effective invalidation of the conventional standards according to which one was rejected and rejected him- or herself.

The proposition that experiences of rejection and failure in membership groups and concomitant self-attributed negative social identity are associated with participation in social movements rests on the point of view that various social movements are functionally equivalent routes to the resolution of personal needs (Hoffer 1951; Klapp 1969; Zurcher and Snow 1981, 452). In short, a movement may serve as a means for enhancement of separate bruised identities. How individuals who perhaps have little in common besides the pervasive experience of rejection and failure come to ally with one another or with preexisting social movements, whether initially through interpersonal communication (Gamson 1992; Hunt and Benford 1994; Snow and Anderson 1987) or later through actual participation in protest activities (Klandermans 1984; Taylor and Whittier 1992), is not germane in this discussion. However, it is hypothesized that, through whatever mechanism, individuals who have traveled different paths from experiences of rejection and failure in conventional membership groups collectively identify with a category of the stigmatized and are disposed to participate in and identify with any of a variety of social protest actions that have in common the reflection of resentment of the conventional world from which their self-perceptions of failure and rejection derived.

This model derives from a general theory of deviant behavior and is consistent with a tradition in the social movement literature that was prevalent in the 1950s and 1960s, fell out of favor in the 1970s, and began to attract attention again in the 1980s.

Theoretical Foundation

The general theory asserts that the summary motive for behavior is the attainment, maintenance, or restoration of positive self-attitudes (Kaplan 1975, 1980, 1984, 1986, 1995, 1996). In the course of the normal socialization process, one learns to value the possession of particular attributes, the performance of certain behaviors, and particular experiences that are the outcome of the purposive or accidental responses of others toward one. These attributes, behaviors, and experiences are the basis for the individual's feelings of self-worth. If the person is unable to evaluate himself or herself positively, then the person will be motivated to behave in ways that will increase feelings of self-worth and decrease the feelings of psychological distress that are associated with self-rejecting attitudes. If a person perceives an inability to achieve the attributes, perform the behaviors, and enjoy the experiences he or she has been taught to value as the basis for overall positive self-evaluation through conventional behavior, than that person will be motivated to behave in deviant ways that offer promise of gaining a feeling of self-worth.

Normally, conventionally approved self-protective or self-enhancing mechanisms function to maintain personally acceptable levels of self-approval. Normative self-protective or self-enhancing responses (stimulated by the need for positive self-feelings), however, may be frustrated by a number of circumstances. Although individuals may be motivated to so behave as to attain the personal attributes, perform the behaviors, and become the object of socially desirable responses, they might be unable to do so as a result of any or all of a number of more or less long-standing circumstances, such as socially ascribed or constitutionally given deficits, the inability to conform to multiple sets of applicable but conflicting expectations, and lack of resources.

The frustration of the normative self-protective or self-enhancing responses increases the experience of self-devaluation. Nevertheless, the person's outcomes are so intimately tied to the conventional order that the individual continues to be emotionally invested in conventional socializing agents and the evaluative standards internalized in the course of the socialization experience, including those that define the acceptability of self-enhancing or self-protective mechanisms. However, should the individual's experience of self-rejecting feelings be so intense, continuous, and pervasive in the person's current life space because the range of normative responses proves to be ineffective either in reducing the experience of self-rejection or in forestalling the continuation of self-rejecting feelings, the definition of what constitutes acceptable self-protective and self-enhancing responses may change. The range of responses within the individual's limits of acceptability (and, at the same time, within the socially defined limits of acceptability) that have proved to be ineffective in the past and threaten to be futile in the future with regard to restoring the experience of positive self-feelings and reducing the experience of negative self-feelings ceases to be attractive to the individual. The individual, consciously or unconsciously, seeks and becomes aware of alternative mechanisms that fall beyond the limits of what were once personally acceptable standards of behavior and that offer the promise of reducing the experience of self-rejecting feelings.

This theoretical orientation is applicable to the explanation of participation in social movements insofar as social movements reflect contranormative attempts to subvert the conventional structure, and participation may be motivated by the need to attain or restore self-acceptance on the part of individuals who are characterized by pervasive self-rejecting feelings as a result of chronic experiences of rejection and failure in conventional membership groups. Participation in social movements may enhance self-attitudes or protect against self-rejecting experiences by indicating rejection of the conventional standards according to which one is judged to have failed, for example, by defining participation as intrinsically worthy, by redefining stigmatizing attributes or social identities in more positive terms, by successfully attaining goals that have positive self-evaluative significance goals that were previously unattainable, by enjoying a sense of self-efficacy that accompanies such success, or by approximating a newly valued set of normative standards and so earning positive evaluations from those who share these standards and from oneself, the individual who has adopted the standards as self-evaluative criteria. Once the person becomes committed to the standards of the movement, the newly adopted standards become salient self-evaluative criteria; and failures to approximate those standards evoke negative self-attitudes and negative responses from others in the movement.

Social Movement Literature

The present model is in the tradition of explaining participation in social movements in terms of individual-level psychological processes, a tradition most apparent in the 1950s and 1960s. Largely dismissed in the 1970s (see the introductory chapter, this volume), the explanation of social protest participation in terms of individual-level processes experienced something of a resurgence in the 1980s.

The 1950s and 1960s studies have been collectively characterized as the classical model (McAdam 1982) according to which social movements are most immediately influenced by some disruptive psychological state that is the consequence of some sort of structural strain. Social movements represent adaptations through which disruptive psychological states are assuaged. In our model, the disruptive psychological state relates to negative self-feelings that are the consequence of severe and prolonged self-devaluing circumstances from many or all of a variety of sources.

The rejection of individual-level constructs as explanations for social movement participation has been attributed to the tendency of earlier accounts to portray participants as suffering from spoiled identities (Hoffer 1951) or identity deficits (Klapp 1969; Kornhauser 1959) and to the dominance of organizational and political perspectives in the 1970s (Snow and Oliver 1995, 588). Regarding the former influence, although there is no necessary connection between the general proposition that psychological dispositions or needs render people susceptible to the appeal of social movements, on the one hand, and psychopathology, on the other hand, such explanations have been taken to imply that participants in social movements are necessarily psychologically deficient in some way (Snow and Oliver 1995, 578).

McAdam (1982) suggests that the acceptability of the position that individual discontent is a proximate cause of social movements was contingent on the need of liberal academics to discredit antidemocratic movements under consideration in the 1950s. However, this position, along with its implications of irrationality associated with participation in social movements, fell out of favor with the emergence of left-wing protest movements favorably received in liberal academic circles.

For these reasons (the presence of alternative explanations and the coupling of individual-level explanations with the stigma of psychopathology) and others, theoretical orientations such as those that guide the present study were severely criticized and largely ignored until the 1980s. Below we argue that such criticisms, appropriate to many of the studies reported in the 1950s and 1960s, are not appropriate to the present approach and analysis. In any case, in the 1980s, the literature on social movements experienced a resurgence of interest in individual-level constructs, particularly those related to individual and social identity (see, e.g., Britt 1994; chapter 12, this volume).

Indeed, if one accepts a broad view of individual incentives that reward participation in social movements and punish nonparticipation as including material, solidarity, and purposive incentives, then the point of view that informs the present analyses has much in common with contemporary rational choice perspectives. If possessing material incentives and being the object of approving attitudes by others, along with purposive incentives, contribute to self-judgments of worth, then the instigations toward participation in social movements expounded in self-referent theory and rational choice theory overlap to a great extent. A major difference, however, is that in self-referent theory the decision to participate in social movements need not be a conscious, intentional one.

The evolution of individual stigmatized identities into a collective identity community along with accompanying dispositions to social action has been studied recently in a variety of deviant contexts including those relating to drug abuse (Anderson 1994), physical disability (Bat-Chava 1994; Braithwaite 1990; Groch 1994), transgenderism (Gagné and Tewksbury 1996), racial status (Porter and Washington 1993), and gay and lesbian status (Anspach 1979; Kaufman 1966; Krouse 1994; Tajfel 1978a, 1978b; Troiden 1993). Thus, the notion that stigmatized identities are implicated in the processes leading to participation in many social movements has resurfaced in many different forms as a viable hypothesis.

Method

We use a longitudinal data set to estimate models specifying the relationships between stigmatized identities and indices of disposition to participate in social movements.

Sample

In the analyses reported below, the subjects consist of 1,943 individuals who were tested at four points over their life course. The inclusive sample from which these subjects were drawn comprises a random half of all seventh-graders in the Houston Independent School District in 1971. The subjects in the present study were tested in the seventh grade and in the ninth grade by self-administered questionnaires and by household interviews when the subjects were in their twenties and again when the subjects were between thirty-five and thirty-nine years of age. The 1,943 subjects were tested at all four points in time and provided information on all the study variables. Among these subjects, 40.1 percent are males, and 59.9 percent are females. Regarding racial and ethnic composition, 27 percent are African American, and 9.1 percent are Mexican American.

The remainder, 63.9 percent, are non-Hispanic whites. More than 80 percent of the subjects reported that their mother graduated from high school, including the 34 percent of the mothers who had a college education. The subjects' age fell within a narrow range, since they were initially studied as seventh-graders (generally, twelve or thirteen years of ages) in 1971.

Variables

The models estimated specify relationships between, on the one hand, self-perceived rejection and failure in conventional membership groups and, on the other, indicators of participation in social movements at a later time. These relationships are estimated controlling for an indicator of earlier involvement in social movements (social protest activities in the seventh-grade) and three other control variables. We describe the dependent variables, central explanatory variable (perceived rejection and failure in conventional membership groups), and control variables in turn.

Dependent Variables

Essential to social movements are collective emotional investments in issues and organized efforts to create or resist change outside institutional channels.

> Social movements are organized collective manifestations of issues for which people have considerable concern. The purpose of the movement is to do something about the concern. Movements deliberately attempt to promote or resist change in the group, society, or world order of which they are a part. They do so through a variety of means not excluding violence, revolution, or withdrawal into utopian communities. (Zurcher and Snow 1981, 447)

No face-valid indicators of *self-definition* of being part of a social movement as such were available. However, a number of indicators implied subjective definition of affiliation with collective responses. These included self-reports of social protest–related activities, activities in political organizations concerned with social issues that were personally salient, and a variety of self-reports of behaviors and attitudes that suggested extreme inclination to affiliate with others for the purpose of effecting social change. These variables reflect both participation in social movements, or the disposition to so participate, and the conversion process that is thought to be one of the more extreme outcomes of participation in the movement.

Because earlier participation in social protests has long-term continuity, albeit in milder form (Fendrich and Lovoy 1988; Marwell, Demerath, and O'Leary 1990; McAdam, 1989; Snow and Oliver 1995; Taylor 1989), it is to be expected that self-perceptions of being the object of rejection by others and as one who has failed to achieve according to conventional and presumably self-referent values as an adolescent will anticipate long-term as well as short-term indices of participation in social movements. We use three indices of disposition to participation in social movements.

Social Protests. Social protest activity is measured by a two-item index consisting of subjects' self-reports of having been involved in a social protest at or outside school and having participated in a strike, riot, or demonstration during the previous year. The subjects provided the data when they were in the ninth-grade. The scores ranged from "0" to "2," with higher scores indicating greater involvement in social protest–related activities.

Participation in Political Organizations. Participation in political organizations is measured by a single item that asks whether or not the subjects were active in social organizations that were concerned with personally salient social issues. These data were gathered during the most recent wave of data collection, when the subjects were in their mid- to late thirties. They were first asked a series of questions regarding whether or not they had very strong feelings about a number of political issues, including women's rights, the environment, homosexuality, race relations, animal rights, gun control, and abortion. Following this, the subjects were asked whether they were active in any organization that was concerned with any of these issues or any other political issues. Subjects who reported being active in such organizations were assigned the value of "1"; those who indicated that they were not involved in any of these organizations, the value of "0."

Extreme Behavioral and Attitudinal Indicators. A number of items available in the young adult or later adult data collections had extremely low frequencies but nevertheless reflected disposition to participate in social movements dedicated to effecting social change. Four of the items were reported during the interview administered when the subjects were in their twenties. These included self-reports of participation in a riot, participation in a lawful demonstration, participation in a radical political/social movement, and affirmation that the subject would like to make friends in some of the "far-out" groups. Two of the items were administered during the most recent wave of data collection, when the subjects were between thirty-five and thirty-nine years of age. These items include a self-report of participation in a strike, riot, or demonstration and a self-designation of being extremely liberal in their political views. If the subjects affirmed one or more of the six items, they were coded as "1"; they were coded "0" if they denied all six items. This composite index was taken to reflect a disposition to engage in relatively extreme activities or dispositions to bring about social change during the subject's adult years.

Central Explanatory Variable

The central explanatory variable in the models accounting for the indices of participation in social movements is the social identity of belonging to a social category of those who are objects of stigmatization. Although we have drawn conceptual distinctions between the actual experience of failure and rejection, with self-perception as one of a category of objects of social disapproval and stigmatization (as part of one's personal identity), and self-rejecting feelings, and although we have hypothesized linear causal relationships among these constructs, it is extremely difficult (if not impossible) to operationalize the distinctions between these constructs. For present purposes, in any case, it is not necessary that we do so. Rather, we offer a series of operational indicators that are said to reflect the causal relationships among these constructs. Each of the indicators may variously be interpreted as an indicator of the actual and perceived experience of failure and rejection, the social identity of belonging to a category of individuals who are objects of social disapproval and stigmatization as a result of these experiences, and/or self-rejecting feelings that are the consequence of social identity. The latent construct reflected in these various indicators is said to express the self-rejecting feelings that are associated with a stigmatized social identity stemming from real and perceived experiences of social failure and rejection. This construct is hypothesized to be related to any of a number of indices of disposition to participate in collective movements.

This latent construct is reflected in five measurement variables based on data collected when the subjects were in the seventh grade. The first three variables reflect perceptions of being the object of social rejection. The first variable is a three-item index measuring self-reported experiences of ever having been suspended or expelled from school; ever having had anything to do with police, sheriff, or juvenile officers for something the subject did or that they thought the subject had done; and having been taken to the school office for punishment during the preceding year. The second variable is a four-item index measuring self-perceived rejection by teachers as this is reflected in affirmation of the following items: my teachers are usually not very interested in what I say or do; my teachers do not like me very much; by my teachers' standards I am a failure; my teachers usually put me down. The third variable is a three-item index measuring perceived rejection by parents. This is reflected in affirmation of the following items: my parents put me down; my parents dislike me; my parents are not interested in what I say or do.

The fourth variable is a four-item index measuring the self-perceived absence of desirable attributes and the presence of undesirable attributes. Self-description of having undesirable attributes or of lacking desirable attributes is reflected in self-definition as being dishonest, telling lies, not being kind, and not having good manners. The fifth variable is a seven-item index measuring negative self-feeling (self-derogation). Self-derogation is reflected in the following statements: I wish I could have more respect for myself; on the whole, I am satisfied with myself (reverse coded); I feel I do not have much to be proud of; all in all, I am inclined to feel that I am a failure; I take a positive attitude toward myself (reverse coded); at times I think I am no good at all; I certainly feel useless at times. These self-evaluative responses presumably reflect the perceptions of being rejected and having failed according to conventional standards. For each of the five variables, the items are coded such that higher scores indicate greater perceived rejection and failure.

Implicit and explicit in our operationalization of social identity is the subjective association of perceived experiences of rejection and failure with the conventional membership groups. That is, the subject feels that the basis of his or her own self-derogation and experiences of rejection and failure derives from membership in conventional social groupings.

Control Variables

In order to preclude interpretations of any observed relationship between perceived rejection and failure at time one and later involvement in social movement–related activities in terms of common antecedent variables, the models specified four control variables. The most significant of these is a measure of social protest using data from the first test administration during the seventh grade. This variable is a two-item index consisting of self-reports of having taken an active part in a social protest either at school or outside school within the last month and having taken part in a strike, riot, or demonstration within the last month. The score ranged from "0" to "2." The measure of social protest reported during the seventh grade was modeled as correlated with perceived rejection and failure reported during the seventh grade, as influenced by the other control variables, and as having an effect on the later measures of participation in social movements. This was the only measure of social movement–related activity that was available for use as a control variable. It was more isomorphic with some of the outcome variables than others. In any case, any observed influence between earlier perceived rejection and failure in conventional membership groups and later participation in social movements could not be accounted for by the common association of these variables with earlier social protest activity.

In addition, minority status, gender, and mother's education were modeled as control variables that had effects on perceived rejection and failure in conventional membership groups reported in the seventh grade, social protest activities reported in the seventh grade, and social movement–related indices reported in the ninth grade, as young adults, or in the fourth decade of life. Minority status was defined as self-report of being either African American or Mexican American. Either self-report was coded as "1"; and "0" was assigned to the mutually exclusive category. Regarding gender, male was coded as "1"; female, "0." Mother's education was defined as a three-category variable with "1" indicating that mother's education was less than high school graduation, "2" indicating that mother's education was greater than high school education but less than college education, and "3" indicating that mother's education was college graduation or above.

Analysis

The analyses examined the influences of perceived rejection/failure (stigmatized identity) on each of the three dependent variables of interest, that is, social protest, activities in political organizations (political activities), and adult extreme behavioral disposition (behavioral disposition), while controlling for earlier participation in social protest and sociodemographic variables (including minority status, gender, and mother's education level).

The analyses were conducted using the LISREL VIII statistical program (Jöreskog and Sörbom 1993a, 1993b). Since many of our variables are skewed in their distributions and are dichotomous, we use an Asymptotically–Distribution Free (ADF) Method that does not require the assumptions of multivariate normality and continuity (Jöreskog and Sörbom 1989). Thus, polychoric correlation matrices based on raw data were computed using the PRELIS program, a companion program for LISREL. These matrices, then, served as input to subsequent LISREL analyses, which relied on Weighted Least Squares estimation for parameter estimates.

Results

Three models were estimated that specify effects of self-perceptions of being the object of rejection and failure in conventional membership groups when in the seventh grade on indicators of social movement participation measured at later times. The indicators of social protests are, respectively, (1) self-reports of participating in social protests, or strikes, riots, or demonstrations, measured when the subjects were in the ninth grade (figure 2);

Figure 2. Standardized effect of T1 adolescent perceived rejection/failure on T2 adolescent participation in social protest (significant paths only)

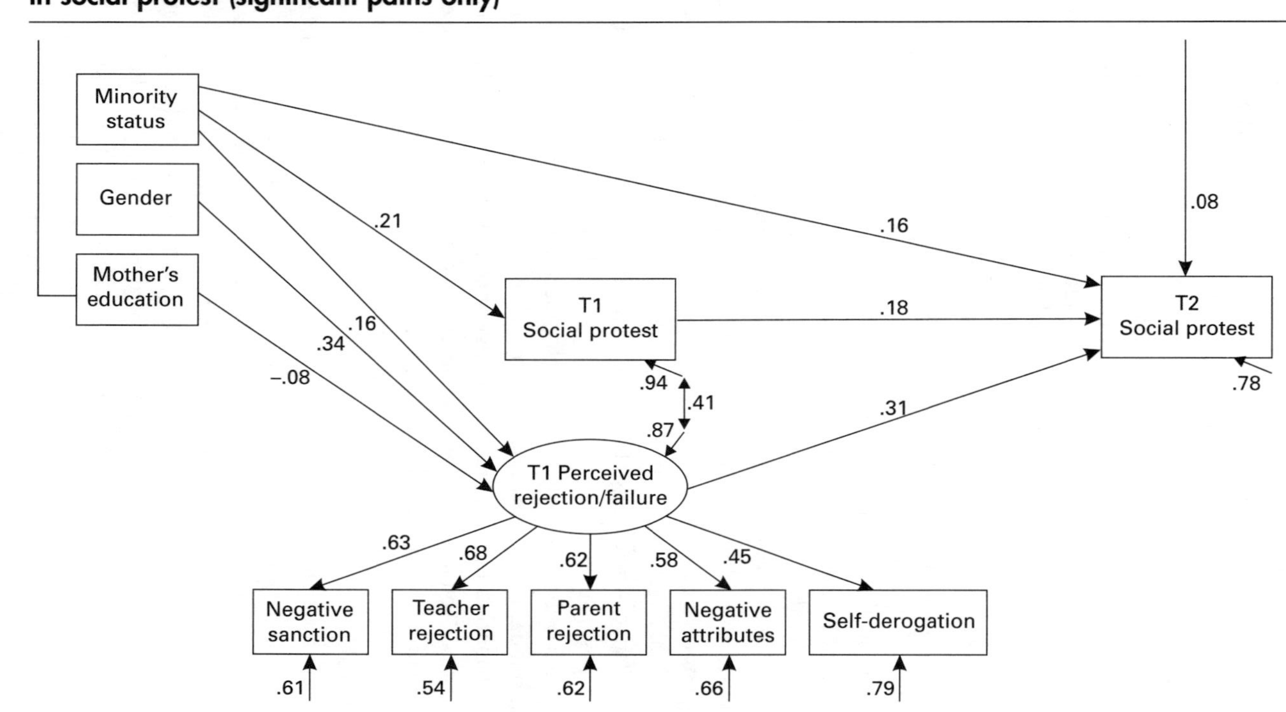

Note: Chi-square = 172.21, d.f. = 25, GFI = .98, AGFI = .97, N = 1,943.

(2) self-reports of being active in political organizations concerned with social issues that are important to the subject, measured when the subjects were between thirty-five and thirty-nine years of age (figure 3); and (3) a composite index of socially extreme attitudinal and behavioral dispositions including wanting to make friends in some of the "far-out" groups and participating in protests, riots, or radical or revolutionary political or social movements (all measured during young adulthood); and, self-descriptions of one's political views as extremely liberal and self-reports of taking part in a strike, riot, or demonstration (measured when the subjects were thirty-five to thirty-nine years of age) (figure 4).

The latent construct of self-perceived experiences of rejection and failure in conventional membership groups (perceived rejection/failure) is reflected in five measurement variables all of which have appreciable and significant loadings on the common factor. The strongest loadings are those that manifestly reflect perceptions of being the object of rejecting attitudes or punitive responses by parents, teachers, and other authorities. However, these variables also, in all likelihood, reflect the possession of attributes or the performance of behaviors that evoke such negative sanctions, as does the measure of negative attributes itself. The measure of self-derogation reflects the negative self-feelings that accompany such perceptions of failure to evoke positive responses and of being distant from salient self-evaluative standards while reflecting, also, the self-perception of failure to approximate such standards. It seems reasonable to interpret this construct in terms of self-attribution of belonging to a category of individuals who have a stigmatized, or spoiled, identity as a consequence of perceived pervasive experiences of rejection and failure according to conventional standards.

In each model, as hypothesized, self-perceived rejection/failure in conventional membership groups had a statistically significant (albeit modest) effect on the indicator of later participation in social movements. The standardized effect was 0.31 for the indicator of social protest measured in the ninth grade and 0.11 or 0.10 where indicators were measured at various points during adulthood. Although the effects were indeed modest (particularly for those indicators measured during adulthood), perhaps the attenuation of effects should not be surprising given the fact that the measures during adulthood were made between ten and twenty-five years after the measure of self-perceived rejection/failure in the seventh grade and that moderating influences were not specified. These findings are consistent with the interpretation that a stigmatized identity sets the individual apart from the mutually exclusive category of nonstigmatized individuals and disposes those with a spoiled identity to participate in social movements that

Figure 3. Standardized effect of adolescent perceived rejection/failure on adult activities in political organizations (significant paths only)

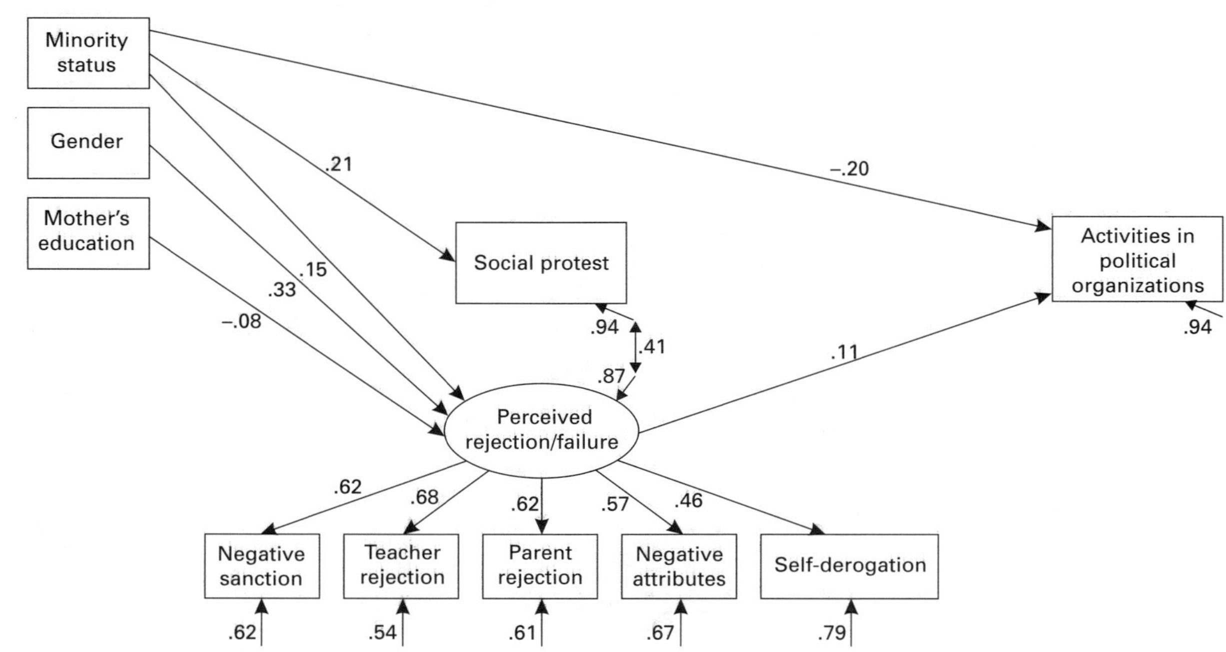

Note: Chi-square = 172.63, d.f. = 25, GFI = .98, AGFI = .97, N = 1,943.

Figure 4. Standardized effect of adolescent perceived rejection/failure on adult extreme behavioral disposition (significant paths only)

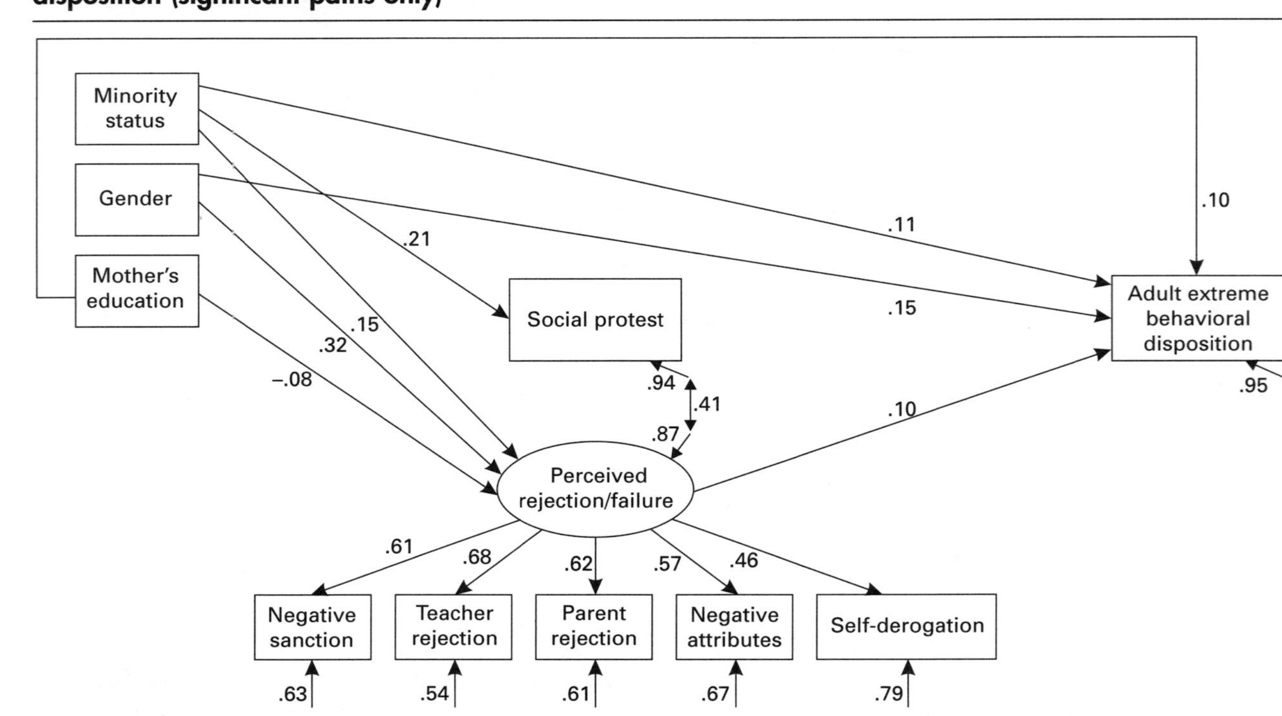

Note: Chi-square = 173.58, d.f. = 25, GFI = .98, AGFI = .96, N = 1,943.

legitimate oneself or serve self-enhancing or self-protective functions with regard to one's self-attitudes.

Discussion

We have argued that possessing a less than satisfactory personal identity incorporating a social identity as part of a stigmatized category creates a need to make the personal identity more estimable and a disposition to behave in ways increasing the likelihood of such an outcome. Participation in a social movement may be consciously or unconsciously intended to enhance personal identity and may do so through a number of mechanisms. The person may, by affiliating with a collective movement, symbolically reject the conventional standards according to which the person is judged to have failed. Affiliation with a movement may symbolically remove the person from occasions for judging oneself as a failure. By becoming a part of a new collective movement characterized by a shared value system, the person may more easily approximate the standards of that movement and so earn social and self-approval. If identification with the movement is now regarded as intrinsically gratifying, the very act of joining the movement increases the perceived value of one's social identity—a collective identity becomes a valued ego extension of one's personal identity and so enhances one's self-worth.

The source of a derogated personal identity may be one's membership in a devalued collective identity, a failure to achieve according to some personally salient value, the experience of social rejection associated with such a failure, or any of a range of other attributes or experiences. Alternatively, a derogated identity may be attributable not to one source but rather to chronic experiences of failure and rejection. In either case, participation in a social movement may represent a personal adaptation to the experience of a spoiled identity. The nature of the movement may or may not reflect the source of personal stigmatization. A person who attributes personal stigmatization to being part of a disvalued minority group may join a movement that has as its goal the enhancement of that group. However, self-enhancing functions of joining that movement may be served as well for individuals whose derogated personal identity is attributable to some other particular experience or attribute, or even for those whose spoiled identity is a series of painful rejections and failures.

We have explored the validity of these speculations using a longitudinal data set. Although the data were not collected with this purpose in mind, we addressed a number of issues relating to the hypothesized relationship between perceived rejection and failure and later behaviors or expressions of attitudes that imply participation in collective movements. The results are compatible with the viewpoint presented.

Individuals who experience pervasive rejection and failure in the context of conventional membership groups, although the source and nature of the specific experiences may differ widely, represent a latent collectivity that is predisposed to protest against the social structure in the context of which self-derogating experiences and consequent spoiled identity emerged. The diverse self-discontented individuals have the potential for affiliating with any of a variety of crosscutting social categories that similarly have reason to resent, distrust, and desire to change the social structure in which the person came to experience highly distressful negative self-feeling (Spencer 1994). However, a confluence of common interests need not project themselves onto one particular movement. Rather, they may at different times and for different purposes ally themselves first with this movement and later with that movement.

We are not hypothesizing that the experience of failure and rejection represents the sole source of motivation for participating in a social movement. Clearly, there are other stimuli for such participation—for example, a sense that injustice is being done to others, a tradition of participating in such movements in one's membership groups in general, and antipathy toward the conventional world—which may operate independently of such self-perceptions.

Certainly, the hypothesis that the need for self-respect exacerbated by stigmatizing experiences and identities leads to social movement is far from universally accepted. It is said that such motives may not provide initial motivation and that in any case participants in social movements would not be so motivated all the time (Olberg 1995). More frequently, critics of such an explanation for participation in social movements do not reject the stigmatized identity and related motivational models out of hand. Rather, they suggest that such explanations are not sufficient to explain participation (Zurcher and Snow 1981).

The criticisms that had been raised against individual-level explanations of participation in social movements in general, and against explanations implicating self-derogation and related constructs in particular, are not apposite to our theoretical orientation. First, pervasive self-devaluing experiences and associated self-rejecting feelings are not regarded as severe pathological traits or as necessarily carrying pejorative connotations. Second, it is not argued that political movements recruit a disproportionate number of individuals characterized by "pathological" personality traits. Rather, it is suggested that individuals with severe self-rejecting feelings associated with self-devaluing circumstances in the context of conventional groups are somewhat more likely to affiliate with social movements. Many other motives are operative that lead individuals to affiliate. Indeed, these alternative motives may be much more prevalent than the need for self-enhancement. Third, we do not argue that psychological traits are *necessarily* translated into political beliefs. Fourth, we do not argue that the relationship between psychological traits and political beliefs, on the one hand, and political action, on the other hand, is simple. Indeed, we argue that these relationships are contingent upon a large number of factors. Elaboration of the theory requires specification of such conditions. Among these conditions are the availability of an organizational context (McAdam 1982). What our model intends to explain is the disposition to affiliate with collective movements having as their objective changing social conditions already in place rather than the origin of the collective movements themselves.

Fifth, studies that demonstrate integration of participants in social movements in their respective communities do not gainsay the validity of our theoretical model. A person may be integrated in a community yet experience self-devaluing circumstances.

Finally, it has been argued that despite the "apparent theoretical sophistication, empirical support for all of these individually based psychological accounts of participation has proved elusive"(McAdam, McCarthy, and Zald 1988, 705). This is due in large measure to the absence of individual-level longitudinal data that could test the hypothesized association between earlier psychological states and later participation in social movements, data that are available for the present analyses.

The findings reported are compatible with our theoretical model, yet a number of causal linkages remain to be established. In particular, we have not been able to establish whether or not the linkage that we observed between the derogated personal identity and the index of participation in a social movement is mediated by a putative social identity. Does the behavioral or attitudinal response to the derogated identity represent an individual response, or does it represent the reflection of a conscious identification with a group of derogated individuals for self-enhancing purposes? Further, if the consciousness of kind exists, does it develop following the individual's act of social protest, or does consciousness of kind develop prior to acts of social protests and correlated attitudes that dispose one to change the nature of the social order where possible? All of the proceeding questions relate to the basic question of how experiences of self-derogating personal identities, and the antecedents of such identities, influence one's identification with a social category and, via that consciousness of kind, lead to attitudinal and behavioral changes dedicated to reforming, avoiding, or attacking the social system.

Although it is clear that a derogated identity is neither a necessary nor a sufficient condition for participation in social movements, it is equally clear that quite often a disvalued social identity is causally implicated in the initial participation in, and commitment to, social movements. Further determination of the prevalence of this dynamic, and of the variables that intervene in or moderate the dynamic, defines our future research agenda with regard to the relationship between earlier experiences of pervasive social rejection, failure in conventional membership groups, and subsequent association with social movement–related activities.

Note

This work was supported by research grants (R01 DA 02497 and R01 DA 10016) and by a Research Scientist Award (K05 DA 00136) from the National Institute on Drug Abuse to the first author.

References

Anderson, Tammy L. 1994. "Drug Abuse and Identity: Linking Micro and Macro Factor." *Sociological Quarterly* 35:159–74.

Anspach, Renee R. 1979. "From Stigma to Identity Politics: Political Activism among the Physically Disabled and Former Mental Patients." *Social Science and Medicine* 13A:765–73.

Bat-Chava, Yael. 1994. "Group Identification and Self-Esteem of Deaf Adults." *Personality and Social Psychology Bulletin* 20:494–502.

Braithwaite, Dawn O. 1990. "From Majority to Minority: An Analysis of Cultural Change From Able-Bodied to Disabled." *International Journal of Intercultural Relations* 14:465–83.

Britt, Lory. 1994. "From Shame to Pride: Social Movements and Individual Affect." Ph.D. diss., Department of Sociology, Indiana University, Bloomington.

Fendrich, James, and Kenneth Lovoy. 1988. "Back to the Future: Adult Political Behavior of Former Student Activists." *American Sociological Review* 53:780–84.

Gamson, William A. 1992. "The Social Psychology of Collective Action." In *Frontiers of Social Movement Theory,* edited by A. Morris and C. Mueller, 53–76. New Haven: Yale University Press.

Gagné, Patricia, and Richard Tewksbury. 1996. "No 'Man's' Land: Transgenderism and The Stigma of the Feminine Man." *Advances in Gender Research* 1:115–55.

Groch, Sharon A. 1994. "Oppositional Consciousness: Its Manifestation and Development: The Case of People with Disabilities." *Sociological Inquiry* 64:369–95.

Hoffer, Eric. 1951. *The True Believer.* New York: Harper and Row.

Hogg, Michael A., and John C. Turner. 1987. "Social Identity and Conformity: A Theory of Referent Information Influence." In *Current Issues in European Social Psychology,* edited by W. Doise and S. Moscovici, 2:139–77. Cambridge: Cambridge University Press.

Hunt, Scott A., and Robert D. Benford. 1994. "Identity Talk in the Peace and Justice Movement." *Journal of Contemporary Ethnography* 22:488–517.

Jöreskog, Karl, and Dag Sörbom. 1989. *LISREL 7: A Guide to the Program and Applications.* 2d ed. Chicago: Jöreskog and Sörbom/SPSS.

———. 1993a. *LISREL 8: Structural Equation Modeling with the SIMPLIS Command Language.* Hillsdale, N.J.: Lawrence Erlbaum.

———. 1993b. *New Features in LISREL 8.* Chicago: Scientific Software.

Kaplan, Howard B. 1975. *Self-Attitudes and Deviant Behavior.* Pacific Palisades, Calif.: Goodyear.

———. 1980. *Deviant Behavior in Defense of Self.* New York: Academic Press.

———. 1984. *Patterns of Juvenile Delinquency.* Beverly Hills, Calif.: Sage Publications.

———. 1986. *Social Psychology of Self-Referent Behavior.* New York: Plenum Press.

———. 1995. "Drugs, Crime, and Other Deviant Adaptations." In *Drugs, Crime, and Other Deviant Adaptations: Longitudinal Studies,* edited by H. B. Kaplan, 3–46. New York: Plenum Press.

———. 1996. "Psychosocial Stress from the Perspective of Self Theory." In *Psychosocial Stress: From the Perspectives of Self, Theory, Life Course, and Methods,* edited by H. B. Kaplan, 175–244. San Diego, Calif.: Academic Press.

Kaufman, Joanne M. 1996. "Stigmatized Individuals and the Process of Identity: The Case of Gays and Lesbians." Presented at the 1996 Annual Conference of the American Sociological Association.

Klandermans, Bert. 1984. "Mobilization and Participation." *American Sociological Review* 49:583–600.

Klapp, Orrin. 1969. *Collective Search for Identity.* New York: Holt, Rinehart and Winston.

Kornhauser, William. 1959. *The Politics of Mass Society.* New York: Free Press.

Krouse, Mary Beth. 1994. "The AIDS Memorial Quilt as Cultural Resistance for Gay Communities." *Critical Sociology* 20:65–80.

Marwell, Gerald, N. J. Demarath III, and Zena O'Leary. 1990. "Trajectories of Activism: 1960s Civil Rights Workers from Their 20s to Their 40s." Paper presented at the Annual Meeting of the American Sociological Association.

McAdam, Doug. 1982. *Political Process and the Development of Black Insurgency: 1930–1970.* Chicago: University of Chicago Press.

———. 1989. "The Biographical Consequences of Activism." *American Sociological Review* 54:744–60.

McAdam, Doug, John D. McCarthy, and Mayer N. Zald. 1988. "Social Movements." In *Handbook of Sociology*, edited by N. J. Smelser, 695–737. Newbury Park, Calif.: Sage Publications.

Morris, Aldon. 1992. "Political Consciousness and Collective Action." In *Frontiers in Social Movement Theory*, edited by A. Morris and C. Mueller, 351–73. New Haven: Yale University Press.

Olberg, Dag. 1995. "The Theory of Heroic Defeats: A Mixed Motivation Approach." *Sociological Theory* 13(2):178–96.

Porter, J. R., and R. E. Washington. 1993. "Minority Identity and Self-Esteem." *Annual Review of Sociology* 19:139–61.

Skinner, Barbara. 1994. "Identity Formation in the Russian Cossack Revival." *Europe-Asia Studies* 46:1017–37.

Snow, David A., and Leon Anderson. 1987. "Identity Work Among the Homeless: The Verbal Construction and Avowal of Personal Identities." *American Journal of Sociology* 92:1336–71.

Snow, David A., and Pamela E. Oliver. 1995. "Social Movements and Collective Behavior: Social Psychological Dimensions and Considerations." In *Sociological Perspectives on Social Psychology*, edited by K. S. Cook, G. A. Fine, and J. S. House, 571–91. Needham Heights, Mass.: Allyn and Bacon.

Spencer, Martin E. 1994. "Multiculturalism, 'Political Correctness,' and the Politics of Identity." *Sociological Forum* 9(4):547–67.

Tajfel, Henri. 1978a. "Interindividual Behaviour and Intergroup Behaviour." In *Differentiation between Social Groups*, edited by H. Tajfel, 27–60. London: Academic Press.

———, ed. 1978b. *Differentiation between Social Groups*. London: Academic Press.

Taylor, Verta. 1989. "Social Movement Continuity: The Women's Movement in Abeyance." *American Sociological Review* 54:761–75.

Taylor, Verta, and Nancy Whittier. 1992. "Collective Identity in Social Movement Communities: Lesbian Feminist Mobilization." In *Frontiers in Social Movements Theory*, edited by A. Morris and C. Mueller, 104–29. New Haven: Yale University Press.

Thomson, Dale. 1995. "Language, Identity, and the Nationalist Impulse: Quebec." *Annals of the American Academy of Political and Social Science* 538:69–82.

Thumma, Scott. 1991. "Negotiating a Religious Identity: The Case of the Gay Evangelical." *Sociological Analysis* 52:333–47.

Troiden, Richard R. 1993. "The Formation of Homosexual Identities." In *Psychological Perspectives on Lesbian and Gay Male Experiences*, edited by L. D. Garnets and D. C. Kimmel, 191–217. New York: Columbia University Press.

Zurcher, Louis A., and David A. Snow. 1981. "Collective Behavior: Social Movements." In *Social Psychology: Sociological Perspectives*, edited by M. Rosenberg and R. H. Turner, 447–82. New York: Basic Books.

11

Volition and Belongingness: Social Movements, Volition, Self-Esteem, and the Need to Belong

Roy F. Baumeister, Karen L. Dale, and Mark Muraven

Social movements require many individual people to hook their individual selves up to a broad movement that may or may not eventually bring pragmatic, tangible benefits. How does this happen? What happens to the self in the process of belonging to a social movement? How does the social movement need to accommodate the idiosyncrasies and demands of individual selfhood? This chapter examines some current work in understanding the self and applies it to these basic questions about social movements.

What Is the Self?

Psychologists have studied the self for decades. Their biggest emphasis has, however, been on cognitive structures and processes: self-concept, self-schema, self-awareness, self-esteem, and the like. The cognitive representations are indeed an important aspect of the self, but they are probably not the only aspect. This chapter focuses on the two other main aspects of self.

The first of these is the interpersonal self. The self originates in social relationships, insofar as a baby begins to act and learn about itself in the context of its family and caregiver relationships. As the child grows to adulthood, it continues to define itself and be defined by its connections to other people. The self is thus fundamentally and inevitably a member of social groups, from dyads to nations. The self is a tool for forming and maintaining relationships with other people. Selves are developed and shaped so as to help connect the person to other people, as well as to society's institutions.

The other neglected aspect of selfhood is the executive function. This is the part of self that makes choices and decisions, takes responsibility, actively initiates action, and exerts self-control. The frequent effort to exert control is one of the most important functions of the self, and selves are developed and shaped by the demands of exerting control.

Taken together, these three aspects of self form a comprehensive basis that can be used to integrate most or perhaps all of what social psychology researchers have found about the self (see Baumeister 1998). First, the self consists of a cognitive structure based on reflexive consciousness, in which awareness turns around on its source and constructs a meaningful representation of one's own person. Second, the self encompasses a member of relationships and a holder of social roles, and thus the self is defined by its social and interpersonal connections. Third, the self actively makes choices, directs action, assumes responsibility, and alters and controls its own responses.

The Interpersonal Self and the Need to Belong

The fundamentally social nature of human beings makes the interpersonal function of selfhood essential. It seems reasonable to assume that people are driven by a basic motivation to form and maintain social bonds. Indeed, most theories of personality have proposed that people have some sort of innate drive to have social connections or relationships. A literature review by Baumeister and Leary (1995) concluded that people are universally characterized by a "need to belong," which requires two things for satisfaction. First, the person must have an ongoing series of pleasant (or neutral) interactions with the same other person or small set of people. Second, these interactions must occur within the context of an ongoing relationship characterized by mutual caring and concern.

Group competition is one corollary of the need to belong that may be quite relevant to social movements. When one's rivals or opponents are organized into a group, it becomes imperative to be part of a group oneself, insofar as individuals would generally be at a steep disadvantage when competing against groups for scarce resources. Consistent with this view, there are signs that competition enhances the tendency to form groups (Hoyle, Pinkley, and Insko 1989).

Self-esteem is also relevant. Leary and his colleagues have proposed that self-esteem serves as a *sociometer,* that is, an internal measure of one's belongingness (Leary et al., 1995; Leary and Baumeister in press). High self-esteem indicates that one has strong appeal to others (i.e., one is competent, likeable, attractive, and moral) and is likely to be sought out by them to participate in groups and relationships. Low self-esteem is associated with a greater perceived likelihood of being excluded or rejected. Sure enough, self-esteem does seem to rise and fall with actual events of social inclusion or rejection (Leary et al. 1995). Across many studies, there is a fairly substantial negative correlation between self-esteem and social anxiety (averaging about –.50; see Leary and Kowalski 1995).

Implications for Social Movements

These basic views of human selfhood and the need to belong offer a basis for several theoretical propositions about social movements.

Joining, Leaving, and Belonging

People will join movements as a way of satisfying the need to belong. Research has confirmed the importance of belongingness to participation in such groups and movements. Cable (1992) analyzed participation in a women's social movement organization and found that initial recruitment occurs through social networks. McAdam (e.g., 1982) has compiled considerable evidence that people move into social movements, and sometimes out of them as well, on the basis of social ties. The two main paths by which social movements form both rely on such interpersonal connections. One is that a preexisting group of people becomes radicalized as a result of social or circumstantial changes, and so the group takes on a new character as being a social movement, with many or most members now serving as activists. The other is progressive recruitment of individuals into the incipient movement, and here, too, the candidates for joining are often identified and recruited on the basis of preexisting social connections or relationships to other people who have already joined the movement.

Support for the two-path theory can be found in research by Cable, Walsh, and Warland (1988). These researchers studied involvement in protest movements following the Three Mile Island accident. In two communities, alliances based on shared grievances were constructed, and in two larger communities, existing networks were utilized.

Sometimes the quest for belongingness and support is clearly the major factor. Barnett and MacDonald (1986) found that people who joined the National Alliance for Optional Parenthood were more interested in affiliating with other people who chose to remain childless, presumably in order to bolster their confidence in their own decision, rather than to pursue the goal of reducing societal pressures to have children.

Social Conditions

Belongingness theory also makes predictions about the kind of circumstances in which a new social movement can most effectively gain adherents. If people do indeed have a need to belong, then society will be stable and successful only if it enables the vast majority of people to satisfy this need—that is, society has to provide people with a stable, confident network of social relationships. Any event that disrupts these social networks, leaving large numbers of people relatively unattached, will provide a fertile recruiting ground for a new social movement.

Such events may facilitate social movements by making available a reservoir of people who are available to join groups or movements. Another type of event may give rise to a social movement in a quite different fashion. As already noted, some movements begin when an entire community is mobilized into political activism. An event that dramatizes a grievance or need of a particular community may result in the formation of a social movement, insofar as the members of the community begin to work together to secure their rights or other goals. In such a case, the preexisting structure of social bonds facilitates the group, and indeed any individual who is reluctant to become involved in the movement may feel subtle or even overt pressure to join in the work. The structure of social bonds thus forms a useful resource for pulling a significant number of people into the movement.

Charismatic Leaders

Many social movements have highly charismatic leaders. A charismatic leader may appeal particularly to people whose motivation to join the movement is to satisfy a deficit in belongingness. After all, if the motivation is simply to help bring about some social change or to identify with some ideological belief, then it matters little whether the movement is led by a flamboyant and charming figure, or a quiet administrator, or even a committee. In contrast, if the motivation is to achieve a sense of personal connection, then the vivid figure of the charismatic leader is centrally important, because the new recruit can feel that he or she is forming a personal attachment to an important, attractive, powerful individual.

The appeal of charismatic leaders has been linked to self-concept issues by Shamir, House, and Arthur (1993). These authors noted that many charismatic leaders perform actions that engage self-related motivations of their followers, such as maintaining self-esteem, and these motivations help keep people involved in the organization.

The advantages held by a single charismatic leader for satisfying members' belongingness needs may explain the eventual failures of some attempts to run social movements with committees. The most famous such committee in history is probably the Committee for Public Safety that presided over the French Revolution. It is perhaps not surprising that this brief phase of committee rule was followed by the rise of one of the most charismatic figures in history, Napoleon. In our own century, the Russian Revolution was likewise initially led by a group, but gradually it was replaced by the charismatic rule of Lenin and then Stalin. Stalin's charisma is perplexing, both because of the horrific internal violence he directed and because of his rather reclusive lifestyle, but it is undeniable.

Individual Differences

Social groups and movements may appeal to people in different ways depending on the structure of the particular self. Personality traits linked to belongingness (such as attachment style) can dictate how the individual views and experiences participation in the movement.

The most interesting category from the perspective of attachment theory is the people who can be classified as avoidant, that is, people who find intimacy uncomfortable and who feel claustrophobic distress when they start to get too close to other people (Hazan and Shaver 1994). Despite this tendency to avoid intimate attachments, these people are presumably still guided by the basic human need to belong. The result is a thorny problem of how to manage social life so as to satisfy the need to belong without getting too close to other people.

Avoidant people have various ways of addressing this problem. One common solution, apparently, is to cultivate a somewhat broad social circle, so one can interact with a number of people on a regular basis without getting too close to any one of them (Tidwell, Reis, and Shaver 1996). Such an approach would fit in quite well with participation in social movements. Participating in a social movement can help the avoidant person feel that he or she is part of a valuable, important group and can provide plenty of social interactions within a suitable framework of ongoing social connectedness. But no one has to get too close.

Differences in self-esteem may also be relevant. According to sociometer theory, people with high self-esteem normally enjoy the comfortable confidence that they will be included by others, whereas people with low self-esteem may fear that they could end up alone. The direct satisfaction of belongingness that a social movement can provide should therefore be more valuable to people with low self-esteem.

Some signs do link social movement participation with self-esteem. Certainly some organized social movements, such as the women's movement and the NAACP, have included raising group self-esteem as a central feature of their agenda. Ferree (1983) examined working-class women's reactions to the women's movement and found that supporters of the movement emphasized self-esteem benefits of the movements.

This is not, of course, to suggest that people with high self-esteem will never join social movements. Still, they will be less likely than others to join merely for the sake of belonging. To a person with high self-esteem, joining a social movement may, in general, be a pragmatic decision based on whether participation in the movement is seen as likely to confer particular, material benefits to the individual. The cost-benefit calculation, in other words, is likely to make a substantial difference as to whether the person finds the group worthwhile. In contrast, people with low self-esteem may be more readily recruited by many groups, regardless of specific pragmatic benefits. To the person with low self-esteem, being wanted and accepted by the group may be reason enough to join.

High self-esteem may be crucially helpful to the leaders and organizers of social movements. After all, founding a movement requires one to get other people to join. A person with low self-esteem may lack the confidence that other people will want to affiliate with him or her. In contrast, someone with high self-esteem is likely to expect that other people will want to accompany him or her in this work. People with high self-esteem may be more likely than others to be confident that the movement can actually accomplish its goals and change the system. They may also be less daunted by defeats and setbacks.

A final relevant set of differences concerns whether the person has recently experienced a loss of social ties. If significant relationships have been lost, the person should be more desirous of forming new ones, and joining a social movement may offer one method of accomplishing this. Divorce and marital separation, for example, entail the loss of a powerful and important social attachment. There is some evidence that postdivorce adjustment depends on getting involved in various social activities that promote the formation of new bonds (Berman and Turk 1981).

Elderly women often lose their social connections because their children grow up and move away and their husbands die before the women. Cain (1988) found that many such women reported increased community involvement to cope with the social losses and with the resulting anxiety and low self-esteem.

Moving to a new locale may similarly disrupt social connections, particularly when most of one's social circle is left behind. One familiar prototype of that situation involves the young person who leaves home to attend a university, leaving family and friends behind. Many authors have noted the seeming adaptive value of having students get involved in various social movements and groups. Weir and Okun (1989) presented questionnaire data showing a link between satisfaction with college and contact with organizations on campus, although clearly that correlation could be explained in multiple ways. Hood, Riahinejad, and White (1986) found that involvement in campus groups was related to growth in confidence among college students over a four-year period. Such findings suggest that social participation builds self-esteem.

Volition and the Self's Executive Function

A vital but easily neglected aspect of selfhood is its executive function, which is also sometimes called the *agent* or *active principle.* The self makes choices and decisions, accepts responsibility for actions, and initiates responses, all of which are central activities of the executive function. The function is also responsible for altering the self's responses, such as inhibiting a response that would normally occur but that might prove under some circumstances to be maladaptive or undesirable.

Recent research in our own laboratory has begun to suggest that the executive function operates like a muscle or energy: it is a limited, renewable resource that is depleted after exertion. So far, it appears that all the vastly different activities of the executive function draw on the same limited resource. If this is correct, then what the self can accomplish through its own active intervention may generally be quite limited. Judicious management of this limited resource is thus essential to the self's effective operation.

Research Findings on Ego Depletion

To test the energy (strength) model of self-control, we conducted a series of studies in which subjects were typically asked to perform two consecutive but seemingly unrelated acts of self-control, in order to see whether performance on the second would be impaired by the depletion of resources resulting from the first. Thus, in one study (Muraven, Tice, and Baumeister 1998), people were asked to regulate their emotional states (either increasing or decreasing their feelings) in response to an upsetting video, and afterward these people showed lower physical stamina on a handgrip endurance task, as compared with people who watched the same video but did not try to alter their emotions. In another study, people who tried to suppress forbidden thoughts later showed less persistence (than control subjects) in the face of failure on an anagram task.

Making choices and accepting responsibility also draw on this same energy resource (and produce similar impairments of self-control afterward;

Baumeister et al. 1998). In addition, depletion of the self's energy (through initial acts of self-control) made people more passive in their subsequent decision making: they were more likely to go along passively with the status quo rather than make an active choice to change things, even when things were not going well for them.

Two implications are relevant. First, the self uses the same energy resource to do many different things: regulate emotions, make decisions, take responsibility, suppress unwanted thoughts, persist in the face of failure, respond actively. Second, this resource is quite limited. A small exertion seems to deplete it.

Importance of Executive Function

Our findings suggest that volition is costly to the human self, in that it depletes a very scarce resource. To preserve this resource, therefore, it would be sensible and adaptive to let most of one's behavior be guided by habit, routine, external forces, and mindless or automatic responses to simple cues and guidelines.

Is it valuable enough to conserve? Even if only 5 percent of behavior involved volition, that 5 percent could have a widely disproportionate effect on the person's success or failure in life. As an analogy, consider steering wheels in cars. Most cars are probably driven straight ahead most of time, possibly even as much as 95 percent. Some might suggest that one could simply ignore the other 5 percent and build cars without steering wheels. Yet obviously such cars would be seriously deficient in their ability to reach most destinations. A car without a steering wheel is not 95 percent as good as a car with one, even if the steering wheel is only used 5 percent of the time.

Research has particularly confirmed the adaptive value of self-regulation (see Baumeister, Heatherton, and Tice 1994 for review). Deficient self-regulation is implicated in a majority of the personal and social problems that face today's American society, including addiction, crime, violence, alcoholism, teen pregnancy, venereal disease, school dropout and failure, and the like. Meanwhile, longitudinal work by Mischel and his colleagues has confirmed that children who show better self-control (in a delay of gratification procedure) at age four were more successful socially and academically more than a decade later, as they moved into adult life (Mischel, Shoda, and Peake 1988; Shoda, Mischel, and Peake 1990).

Implications for Social Movements

Joining

One set of implications concerns the process of joining a social movement. The act of joining can be made either active or passive, and the appeal and success of the group may differ depending on which it is (and on how those procedures fit circumstances).

If an act of volition is required to join a social movement, then social movements will only flourish when a reservoir of people exists who have *surplus volition.* The availability of such volition is thus one of the important resources that need to be mobilized for the sake of social movements, according to the resource mobilization theory of social movements (see McAdam 1982, chap. 2). The remarkable political activism of American women during the nineteenth century is an important example. As has often been discussed (e.g., Cott 1977; Margolis 1984), the industrial revolution took over many of women's traditional tasks, leaving them with far less to do. For example, innumerable female hours had been spent spinning cloth and weaving clothes, but the new industrial textile mills took over those jobs and produced clothes much more cheaply and efficiently than the home weaving could ever have done. Other tasks, such as processing food for storage and making candles, likewise shifted out of the home and into the factory. The broad result was the nineteenth century's "Woman Question," which was a question of what to do with women, because they no longer had to spend nearly every waking minute in productive work that was essential for the family's survival. For present purposes, the important aspect of this development was the unused surplus of volitional energy that nineteenth-century women (particularly of the middle classes) had. Joining social movements was a way for them to allow their underused selves some exercise.

In contrast, when current circumstances are so oppressive that people must use all their volitional resources to survive, social movements are less likely to find many converts. This does run contrary to the simple prediction that social movements will increase when times are bad (because people want to change the system). It does help explain, however, why the working poor may be less prone than either the middle class or the unemployed to join new social movements.

Consistent with this view, some evidence indicates that some protest movements paradoxically seem to gain force just when conditions have improved. In czarist Russia, the increase in terrorism and revolutionary movements coincided with an improvement in social and living conditions. The same is true of France before the revolution (Tocqueville 1955). In recent American history, it is generally accepted that the 1960s were the decade of maximal protest and other socially activist movements. Yet the 1960s were an era of economic boom. When the economy soured in the 1970s, the protest movements seem to have died off. Although these patterns are undoubtedly the result of complex multicausation, they do fit the hypothesis that people will tend to join protest movements when times are sufficiently good that they have surplus volitional resources that are not needed for the basic economic and material demands of life.

Even today, some protest and activist social movements do not necessarily attract the people who stand to gain the most by them. Many inner cities suffer from severe problems of pollution and environmental degradation, yet African Americans are heavily underrepresented in environmental groups.

In short, this work suggests a key hypothesis about the more fertile, promising preconditions for a social movement: the availability of surplus volition. A movement may be best able to flourish when there is a reservoir of people who have the volitional energy to participate. People who are chronically depleted by keeping up with the demands of everyday life will be less likely to become involved in such a movement. Hence, ironically, sometimes the people who are worst off will not be the ones most likely to join a movement to seek change.

Meanwhile, social movements that actively recruit members may require quite different circumstances, because the individual can join passively, without making an active choice. People who are depleted may be most easily recruited into such groups, because they lack whatever volition would be required to say no.

The difference is far from trivial. Research by Fazio, Sherman, and Herr (1982) indicated that people are more strongly affected by active than by passive choices. Cioffi and Garner (1996) showed that people who made an active choice to volunteer ended up being much more helpful, in fact, than were people who passively consented.

Escape from Choice

A classic work by Erich Fromm entitled *Escape from Freedom* (1965) proposed that people are drawn to join certain groups because they want to be rid of the burden of freedom and the responsibilities and pressures that accompany it. Ego depletion theory can explain this appeal without proposing any pathological or maladaptive causes. Choice is draining, and so a group that dictates behavior patterns (e.g., animal rights activists are encouraged to become vegetarians and avoid wearing leather) may appeal to people who want to conserve their limited resources.

Zealous adherence to the group may be facilitated by the freedom from other decisions and choices, insofar as adopting the party line or movement ethos can dictate how to make a broad variety of choices. Commitment to a group may therefore appeal to people whose daily lives are marked by having to cope with pressures and demands (provided, of course, that these demands are not so extreme and all-encompassing that they preclude any other concerns).

Several findings reported by Freeman (1979) support this reasoning. In the early years of the National Organization for Women, for example, the organization had two separate branches: one consisting of women associated with governmental commissions on the status of women, and another formed by women who had been involved in the protest movements of the 1960s. The policymaker group had more power and prestige than the other women, but they were much less zealous than the women who lacked resources such as money and space. Likewise, evidence about voter registration drives in the South during the 1960s found that the people who had less personal money were more successful registering voters, possibly because of greater zeal.

Conclusion

This chapter has focused on two of the self's most important functions. First, the self is a tool designed to help achieve social connection to other people. Second, the self is an executive agent that makes choices and exerts control. We have proposed that both these functions are relevant to social movements. To the extent that participation in social movements can help the self accomplish these functions, it will be able to attract and sustain the participation of many individual members.

It is noteworthy that these appeals may be largely independent of the actual, pragmatic agenda of the group or movement. We do not mean to imply that the goals or purposes of the group are irrelevant to participation. Undoubtedly they are relevant, and they help determine who joins which movement. Still, we propose that looking only at the group's goals or agenda can furnish an impoverished view of why people join and leave social movements. A significant part of the group's or movement's appeal may lie in how it addresses the needs of the individual self in regard to belongingness and volition.

References

Barnett, Larry D., and Richard H. MacDonald. 1986. "Value Structure of Social Movement Members: A New Perspective on the Voluntarily Childless." *Social Behavior and Personality* 14:149–59.

Baumeister, Roy F. 1997. *Evil: Inside Human Violence and Cruelty.* New York: W. H. Freeman.

———. 1998. "The Self." In *Handbook of Social Psychology,* 4th ed., edited by Daniel T. Gilbert, Susan T. Fiske, and Gardner Lindzey, 680–740. New York: McGraw-Hill.

Baumeister, Roy F., Ellen Bratslavsky, Mark Muraven, and Dianne M. Tice. 1998. "Ego Depletion: Is the Active Self a Limited Resource?" *Journal of Personality and Social Psychology* 74:1252–65.

Baumeister, Roy F., Todd F. Heatherton, and Dianne M. Tice. 1994. *Losing Control: How and Why People Fail at Self-Regulation.* San Diego, Calif.: Academic Press.

Baumeister, Roy F., and Mark R. Leary. 1995. "The Need to Belong: Desire for Interpersonal Attachments as a Fundamental Human Motivation." *Psychological Bulletin* 117:497–529.

Berman, William H., and Dennis C. Turk. 1981. "Adaptation to Divorce: Problems and Coping Strategies." *Journal of Marriage and the Family* 43:179–89.

Cable, Sherry. 1992. "Women's Social Movement Involvement: The Role of Structural Availability in Recruitment and Participation Processes." *Sociological Quarterly* 33:35–50.

Cable, Sherry, Edward J. Walsh, and Rex H. Warland. 1988. "Differential Paths to Political Activism: Comparisons of Four Mobilization Processes after the Three Mile Island Accident." *Social Forces* 66:951–69.

Cain, Barbara S. 1988. "Divorce among Elderly Women: A Growing Social Phenomenon." Special Issue: Life Transitions in the Elderly. *Social Casework* 69:563–68.

Cioffi, Delia, and Randy Garner. 1996. "On Doing the Decision: The Effects of Active vs. Passive Choice on Commitment and Self-Perception." *Personality and Social Psychology Bulletin* 22:133–47.

Cott, Nancy E. 1977. *The Bonds of Womanhood.* New Haven: Yale University Press.

Fazio, Russell H., Steven James Sherman, and Paul M. Herr. 1982. "The Feature-Positive Effect in the Self-Perception Process: Does Not Doing Matter as Much as Doing?" *Journal of Personality and Social Psychology* 42:404–11.

Ferree, Myra M. 1983. "The Women's Movement in the Working Class." *Sex Roles* 9:493–505.

Freeman, Jo. 1979. *Women: A Feminist Perspective.* 2d ed. Palo Alto, Calif.: Mayfield Publishing Co.

Fromm, Erich. 1965. *Escape from Freedom.* New York: Avon Books.

Hazan, Cindy, and Phillip R. Shaver. 1994. "Attachment as an Organizational Framework for Research on Close Relationships." *Psychological Inquiry* 5:1–22.

Hood, Albert B., Ahmad R. Riahinejad, and David B. White. 1986. "Changes in Ego Identity during the College Years." *Journal of College Student Personnel* 27:107–13.

Hoyle, Richard H., R. L. Pinkley, and Chet A.Insko. 1989. "Perceptions of Social Behavior: Evidence of Differing Expectations for Interpersonal and Intergroup Interaction." *Personality and Social Psychology Bulletin* 15:365–76.

Leary, Mark R., and Roy F. Baumeister. In press. "The Nature and Function of Self-Esteem: Sociometer Theory." In *Advances in Experimental Social Psychology,* edited by M. Zanna, vol. 32. San Diego, Calif.: Academic Press.

Leary, Mark R., and Robin Kowalski. 1995. *Social Anxiety.* New York: Guilford.

Leary, Mark R., Ellen S. Tambor, Sonja K. Terdal, and Deborah L. Downs. 1995. "Self-Esteem as an Interpersonal Monitor: The Sociometer Hypothesis.: *Journal of Personality and Social Psychology* 68:518–30.

Margolis, Maxine L. 1984. *Mothers and Such: Views of American Women and Why They Changed.* Berkeley: University of California Press.

McAdam, Doug. 1982. *Political Process and the Development of Black Insurgency: 1930–1970.* Chicago: University of Chicago Press.

Mischel, Walter, Yuichi Shoda, and Philip K. Peake. 1988. "The Nature of Adolescent Competencies Predicted by Preschool Delay of Gratification." *Journal of Personality and Social Psychology* 54:687–96.

Muraven, Mark, Dianne M. Tice, and Roy F. Baumeister. 1998. "Self-Control as Limited Resource: Regulatory Depletion Patterns." *Journal of Personality and Social Psychology* 74:774–89.

Shamir, Boas, Robert J. House, and Michael B. Arthur. 1993.
"The Motivational Effects of Charismatic Leadership: A Self-Concept Based Theory." *Organization Science* 4:577–94.

Shoda, Yuichi, Walter Mischel, and Philip K. Peake. 1990. "Predicting Adolescent Cognitive and Self-Regulatory Competencies from Preschool Delay of Gratification: Identifying Diagnostic Conditions." *Developmental Psychology* 26:978–86.

Tidwell, Marie-Cecile O., Harry T. Reis, and Phillip R. Shaver. 1996. "Attachment, Attractiveness, and Social Interaction: A Diary Study." *Journal of Personality and Social Psychology* 71:729–45.

Tocqueville, Alexis de. 1955. *The Old Regime and the French Revolution.* New York: Anchor Books.

Weir, Renee M., and Morris A.Okun. 1989. "Social Support, Positive College Events, and College Satisfaction: Evidence for Boosting Effects." *Journal of Applied Social Psychology* 19:758–71.

12

From Shame to Pride in Identity Politics

Lory Britt and David Heise

Some social movements engage in "identity politics" and "seek to alter the self-conceptions and societal conceptions of their participants" (Anspach 1979, 765). Anspach describes an example in which physically disabled and former mental patients generated a social movement that resulted in an image of self-determination rather than helplessness. A goal of this movement is to pass on these new self-conceptions to others, and implicit in this process is development of a feeling of pride. Historically, a number of social movements, like the civil rights movement and the gay rights movement, have arisen specifically to alter social responses to and definitions of stigmatized attributes, replacing shame with pride.

Thoits (1990) points out that social movements present a unique opportunity to study affect and suggests that a movement offers social support in terms of shared and legitimized feelings (at least within the stigmatized minority). Although Thoits (1990) seems to suggest that shared feeling (e. g., pride) is what motivates participation in a social movement, participation itself may transform individual feeling so that it mirrors the shared affect of other members. For example, Stein observed that, as white ethnics fight back against cultural and political oppression, "fierce pride reverses a pervasive sense of shame, and righteous indignation inverts an unrelievable sense of guilt" (Stein 1975, 283). For the isolated or closeted homosexual, "just seeing a group of openly gay people together at a pride rally, for example, is often an overwhelmingly good feeling" (Hartinger 1992, 50).

Our aim in this chapter is to explicate how a social movement converts shame and loneliness into pride and solidarity. First, we show that shame and pride are associated with distinctive behaviors and that performing those behaviors can induce the emotions. Next we discuss how social movements build and use emotional capital to mobilize participants and propel them into collective actions. Participation in collective actions generates pride and solidarity. We examine the gay rights movement in order to explicate these processes in more detail. Finally, we encapsulate our findings in a model that describes how social movements engage in identity politics. Throughout we assume that people with a stigma are favorably disposed toward a social movement that ameliorates their stigma, so their consensus is mobilized and they have a latent willingness to participate (Klandermans and Oegema 1987). This assumption derives primarily from self-esteem research that indicates that individuals are motivated to engage in behavior that results in a positive experience of self (Kaplan 1975). Individuals who have been stigmatized are likely to be receptive to discourse that portrays them in a favorable light.

Acknowledgement of passion is lacking in contemporary theories of social movements, yet strong affect is blatantly obvious in social movement activities. In seeking to integrate emotion into the study of social movements, we join a limited though growing number of scholars (e.g., Groves 1995; Taylor 1995) who are reacting to a purely "rationalist" approach to social movement participation (particularly that put forth by resource mobilization theory).

Actions of Shame and Pride

Scheff (1990) argues that shame and pride are social emotions arising from viewing one's self from the standpoint of another. According to Scheff, shame occurs when one feels negatively evaluated by self or others, while pride is evident when one feels positively evaluated by self or others. Other researchers similarly have conceptualized shame and pride as reflexive forms of affect, involving negative and positive self-attention (e.g., Nathanson 1987; Taylor 1985).

Scheff (1990) describes hiding behaviors as indicative of shame, including blushing and averting the eyes. Davitz (1969), in his dictionary of emotional meanings, also says that the desire to hide is an aspect of the experience of shame. There is an urge "to withdraw, be alone, away from others, . . . there is an impulse to hide, to run, to get away" (Davitz 1969, 83). Nathanson (1987) suggests that "true of shame is a wish to conceal" (184).

While Scheff and others have identified these behavioral correlates of shame, a similar treatment of pride is lacking. Yet pride, like shame, involves more than an evaluation of self and is reflected in a manner of interacting with others. Prideful behavior occupies public space, or more simply, involves public display. Clear and powerful public discourse, a steady gaze, and even public demonstrations may be taken as indicators of pride or of attempts to build pride in self or others. Other manifestations include erect posture, chest out, brightness of eyes, and telling others about one's achievements (Kovecses 1990). The public nature of pride is noted by Nathanson (1987), who says that "the experience of pride is a certain tendency to broadcast one's success to the object world" and that pride is that "happy emotion that makes us want to be public" (184). Kovecses's (1990) linguistic work on emotion concepts shows that descriptions of pride often follow a theme of increase in body size. For example, "He swelled with pride," "He was bloated with pride," "He was inflated with pride" (90). Davitz (1969), too, in his work on the language of emotion, found that pride involves feeling "taller, stronger, bigger, expansive" (77).

Although shame may lead to hiding and pride may lead to expansive behaviors in public space, causality also operates in the opposite direction, with the actions generating the emotions. Hiding creates shame, and public displays create pride and solidarity. This idea fits well with several theoretical perspectives.

First, there is William James's classic formulation that emotion emerges from the autonomic and behavioral responses elicited in a situation: "We feel sorry because we cry, angry because we strike, afraid because we tremble" (James [1890] 1950, 450; Laird and Bresler 1990). A natural extension of James's position is that we feel shame as a result of hiding and pride as a result of displaying ourselves publicly.

Affect control theory's treatment of emotions (Smith-Lovin 1990) also posits that emotions emerge from ongoing events. A person's identity defines the kind of presence he or she ideally should have. Meanwhile, specific events modify the person's apparent worthiness, power, and spontaneity. Emotions transform people from their ideal presences into the immediate situated presences that emerge in events. An emotion makes a person in a given role feel and look the way events have made that person seem. We used affect control theory's computer simulation program (Heise and Lewis 1988) to obtain predictions of what kinds of actions a man might enact toward a stranger in order to feel shame or pride. Actions that might make the man feel ashamed include hiding from or begging the stranger. Actions that might make the man feel proud include enthralling or outdoing the stranger.

Collins's (1981) analysis of interaction rituals (IR) does not focus on specific emotions but has themes supporting the argument that shame and pride can emerge from behavior in groups. "Taking a dominant position within an IR increases one's emotional energies. Taking a subordinate position reduces one's emotional energies, the more extreme the subordination, the greater the energy reduction" (1002). "If one encounters a series of situations in which one is highly accepted or even dominating, or in which the emotions are very intense, one's emotional energy can build up very rapidly. The rhythms of mass political and religious movements are based upon just such dynamics" (1003).

Another basis for proposing that expressive actions generate their corresponding emotions comes from analyses of emotion work (e.g., Hochschild 1983; Thoits 1990) showing that people in one way or another often manipulate their subjective feelings through their expressive actions when they make emotion displays to fit the norms. If some feature or action of self warrants shame, that shame might be generated by efforts of concealment. Publicly displaying a feature or action that is supposed to produce pride might produce pride even if none was felt initially.

Finally, Festinger's (1957) cognitive dissonance theory could predict that individuals would feel tension when engaging in public behavior while feeling embarrassed or ashamed. If an individual displays a stigmatized attribute in public yet experiences shame, dissonance would likely result (e.g., "I'm ashamed, so what am I doing out here?"). A change in cognition would reduce the dissonance, and given the strong connection between pride and public display, an individual is likely to decide that the proper emotion associated with such behavior is pride. "I must not be ashamed, I must be proud if I'm out here in public."

Affectual Transformations in Identity Politics

Turning shame to pride is no simple matter, and social movements must be involved in several different kinds of processes in order to get the job done. Social movements involved in identity politics deal with people who initially are ashamed, isolated, and perhaps depressed. The first task is to turn shame and depression into other emotions with higher activation in order to incite and motivate. In the empirical emotion structure described by MacKinnon and Keating (1989) and Morgan and Heise (1988), shame and depression are unpleasant, vulnerable emotions with fairly low activation. Moving to higher activation while leaving the same unpleasantness and vulnerability leads to fear. Thus theory accounts for an emphasis in identity politics on instigating fear.

A strategy in gay identity politics is to instill fear through discussions of homophobic reactions toward gays. Dramatizing existing and proposed legislative discrimination against gay men and lesbians instigates fear, and publicizing violence against homosexuals is even more effective in this regard. Consider, for example, how this merely factual statement might terrify homosexuals. "As lesbians and gay men have become empowered, and issues concerning them have gained national attention, anti-gay hostility has become more open and virulent. . . . State and local ordinances aimed at blocking equal rights for gay people are proliferating nationwide. . . . [There is] a homophobic backlash against gay people or those perceived to be gay, including murder—for example, a 127 percent rise in five major cities that keep anti-gay violence records between 1988 and 1993" (American Civil Liberties Union 1994, 1).

The instigation of fear activates people, preparing them to do something. The trouble is that fear leaves people feeling vulnerable, so they may prefer flight over fight. Yet a vital component of identity politics is to motivate participants to join in the struggle. Thus movement agents must transform vulnerability into dominance and in the process change the emotion of fear into the emotion of anger. This involves several tactics.

Ferree and Miller (1985) apply a social psychological model of cognitive processing to the issue of individual participation in movement activities, focusing on "beliefs about the nature of social relationships, one's position in the social structure, and the causes and consequences of social action" (42). The dominant "western ideological myth" that social position is due to individual achievement, they assert, discourages people from "seeing their outcomes as the result of controllable forces external to themselves" (44). Thus, for example, gays' problems are attributed to their individual nature. "The whole society was telling us it was horrible. A homosexual was a flaky, vacuous, bizarre person. If you wanted to insult somebody then (as now), you accused him of being a faggot. The newspapers always referred to homosexuals and perverts as if they were one and the same. The official line from psychiatrists was that homosexuals were inherently sick. . . . People didn't realize the impact such positions and attitudes had on gay men and women. These attitudes affected the way you thought and lived, what you felt, and how you thought of yourself" (Marcus 1992, 190). Even those who suffer objective hardships will not experience them as grievances if they adopt an explanation that attributes the outcome to their own qualities.

The alternative ideological account offered by many social movements provides justification for making an attribution about the system rather than the self, even though "the persecutor desires the victims to remain ignorant of their oppression" (Katz 1976, 335). Movement communications provide people with a basis for seeing their outcomes as the result of controllable forces external to themselves. This recognition delegitimates the system: "We argue that a perception of stable external causality is a prerequisite to sustained action for change" (Ferree and Miller 1985, 44).

As social movements spread the ideological position that particular identities are not inherently deviant or bad but are defined as such by society and therefore may be challenged, stigmatized individuals are likely to replace feelings of fear with feelings of anger. Not only is the system explicitly held accountable for defining specific attributes as "deviant," but movement ideology also unambiguously denies the personal focus of socially constructed images of inherent inferiority, immorality, or illness. By modifying the frame from one of innate deviance to one of oppression, individuals may come to feel angry not only because the system is unjust but because they have been made to feel ashamed.

Since incorporation of movement ideology likely occurs over a span of time rather than immediately upon exposure, an individual might initially feel ashamed of this fear or anger and then again experience anger about feeling ashamed. Although Scheff (1990) notes that the "shame-anger spiral" of emotion can be endlessly recursive, movement activity provides an opportunity to escape from the interminable cycle. The activated feeling of anger propels stigmatized individuals into public space to behave collectively, and feelings of pride emerge.

Literature from the inchoate gay liberation movement reflects the struggle to arrive at an external attribution. Although the fight for homosexuals' civil liberties and equality under law is now a given, even some early gay rights organizations perceived homosexuality as deviant. Daughters of Bilitis, an early lesbian organization, listed one of its missions as "education of the variant . . . to enable her to understand herself and make her adjustment to society . . . this to be accomplished by establishing a library on the sex deviant theme" (Katz 1976, 426). When the notion that homosexuality was not inherently deviant was proposed, it was a controversial issue, even within the gay community. "When [Frank Kameny] articulated the idea that homosexuality was not a sickness, that was a controversial thing to do in the movement. When Kameny said that in the absence of scientific evidence to the contrary, we are not sick—homosexuality is not a sickness—many movement people disputed him, saying 'We have to leave that up to the experts'" (Katz 1976, 427).

Finally, however, a model of oppression replaced the model of inferiority and sickness, and focus moved from internal to external sources. Anger and indignation began to emerge. "We've got to radicalize, man. . . . Be proud of what you are, man! And if it takes riots or even guns to show them what we are, well, that's the only language the pigs understand" (Marotta 1981, 79). Noting the similarity to activities of blacks during the civil rights movement, a participant in the Stonewall Riots recalled, "This time it was like the black woman who wouldn't give up her bus seat in Montgomery. This time, our own time had come. We took to the streets . . . and we're not going back to the closet, the back-of-the-bus" (Teal 1971, 24).

Fear of the enemy also is replaced by anger by urging individuals to stand and fight in defense of liberty and justice. Early resource mobilization theorists suggested that social movement organizations approach potential participants "with some vision of justice or equity with which they hope to raise some righteous anger" (Fireman and Gamson 1979). Even if considerations of justice do not rouse anger (Scher and Heise 1992), such considerations serve to justify anger, allowing angry individuals to see themselves in a moral war. Describing why she joined a gay pride parade going by a coffee shop in which she was sitting, a New York lesbian claimed, "I wasn't going to let the parade go by. . . . The moral outrage was certainly very personal in my own heart" (Marcus 1992, 176).

Much of the propaganda disseminated by lesbian and gay social movement organizations (SMOs) utilizes the metaphor of battle, with opponents of gay liberation portrayed as the enemy. "In states and communities across the nation, the Religious Right is pushing for new anti-gay civil rights initiatives. . . . Rabid opposition of educational efforts to prevent AIDS . . . the vilification of gays and lesbians. . . . These are just some of the items high on the Far Right's agenda. . . . People for the American Way understands the threat posed by a political movement that thrives on the exploitation of hatred, superstitions, and fear" (People for the American Way 1992). "Virulent homophobes in Pat Buchanan's religious war against equality and freedom for gay and lesbian Americans, with a war-chest of over $10,000,000, are well funded . . . and a force to be reckoned with. . . . To win the ultimate victory all of us must fight together" (Human Rights Campaign Fund 1991).

The possibility of potent action as a member of a powerful collectivity in opposition to the enemy is another factor in transforming fearful vulnerability into an angry sense of dominance. Joining a social movement can evoke the sense of power necessary to transform fear to anger.

Communications of the gay liberation movement allude to grassroots massiveness and political action when transforming fear to righteous anger. "Lesbians, gay men, bisexuals . . . are being assaulted city by city and state by state across the country in the Christian Right's homophobic war against us. We must not back down. We need to take charge of our own struggles for civil rights. But we cannot fight from the closet. Instead, we must build a grassroots movement of visible, out lesbians and gay men from every income, race, and region working together for real social change. A movement in which lesbians . . . and gay men . . . attain visibility and power. A movement of equal voices and common goals, mobilizing against the bigotry and hatred of the Christian Right. We will not sit in silence. We are fighting for our lives" (Greenman 1994, 4).

Gay liberation movement organizations claim to have effective responses to specific threats to inculcate an impression of potency. "The backlash against growing national gay and lesbian visibility and progress has already begun. That's why NGLTF is recommitting itself to fight the Right in 1993. We are mobilizing activists around the nation to turn back extremist attacks. . . . We are unleashing an arsenal of tactics" (National Gay and Lesbian Task Force). "Every year the Pride Agenda develops a Legislative and Public Policy Agenda to outline the legislative, electoral and organizing priorities for the lesbian and gay community of New York State. In 1997, in addition to the Non-Discrimination Bill, constituents will address the need to pass an inclusive Hate Crimes Bill and will speak against a recently re-introduced Anti-Gay Marriage Bill. . . . [On March 4, 1997] over two hundred lesbian and gay constituents came from almost all 61 Senate districts to meet with their representatives [to lobby for the Sexual Orientation Non-Discrimination Bill]" (Empire State Pride Agenda 1997).

Public Demonstrations

The activated sense of dominance and displeasure that is involved in anger can be used in mobilizing a variety of actions, from vigilantism, to voting, to public demonstrations of solidarity. Only the last is relevant to the question of how social movements turn anger into pleasurable feelings of pride. Anger, a powerful and active emotion, creates pride by booting participants out of hiding and into a public arena of collective action. As noted in the *Village Voice* (1992, 111), "Protest activity could be used to encourage homosexuals to become proud, open, and political in ways that would force the public to acknowledge the validity of gay life." The presence of anger, however, does not ensure that individuals will band together into the collectivities needed to instill pride.

Rationalistic approaches to collective behavior emphasized that people who join crowds have experienced some prior frustration. "We shall assume, for instance, that perceived structural strain at the social level excites feelings of anxiety, fantasy, hostility, etc." (Smelser 1963, 11; see also Allport 1924).

Yet McPhail (1991) observed that studies of race riots in the 1960s "demonstrated that participants could not be distinguished from nonparticipants on the basis of deprivations or frustrations shared in common" (xxi). Discontent, and in particular the emotion of anger, may be a precursor and facilitator to collective behavior, yet it is not a sufficient condition for action.

McCarthy and Zald (1977) asked how social movement organizations are able to convince individuals to engage in collective action. In contrast to classical theories of collective behavior, in which the central goal was to explain the actions of individuals behaving collectively, McCarthy and Zald's resource mobilization theory directed the research agenda toward a structural approach in which there is a focus on efforts of movement organizations to manipulate available resources to their advantage (Ferree and Miller 1985; Jenkins 1983). Resource mobilization theorists mainly propose that movement organizations mobilize money and labor, though some have included less concrete resources such as organizational skills or expertise (e.g., Freeman 1979).

Micromobilization research focuses on social networks as the "pull" that turns readers into activists (McAdam 1986). Having gotten mad, people still need to get connected before they will take to the streets. "Citizens are quite often recruited or mobilized to join protests by friends and acquaintances. . . . Personal contacts support people who are ready to participate on attitudinal grounds. They are important in transforming attitudinal affinity toward collective action into real participation (Ohlemacher 1996, 197). This idea fits with Kurt Lewin's group dynamics approach to promoting action (Borgatta 1981) and with the community-oriented strategy of missionaries who operate on networks of family and friends as a means of fostering individual religious conversion (Heise 1967). Such connecting typically occurs in micromobilization contexts, such as churches and schools, that have little relevance to the focal issue (McAdam 1986)—contexts that help legitimize the call to action (Ohlemacher 1996). A lesbian realtor said, "I've organized a little network within my own chain, and I've been the one gay realtor in the New York Gay Pride Parade for the last three years. . . . I'm going to try to get a group behind me this year [1990] who march as realtors" (Marcus 1992, 226).

Public activity of people who are displaying pride might recruit other individuals through emotional contagion. The more people who can be observed emitting pride, the more compelling the contagious draw becomes. At Gay Pride parades, for example, watchers flow into the streets at the end of the parade, becoming part of the parade itself. Hatfield,

Cacioppo, and Rapson (1992) define emotional contagion as the tendency to mimic another person's emotional experience or expressions and thus to experience or express the same emotions oneself. Turner and Killian (1957) suggested that contagion of mood or sentiment is facilitated by the process of milling in crowds. "As milling continues, with an increase of verbal activity and physical movement, it becomes a more compelling stimulus. The individual finds it increasingly difficult to disregard the distracting activity about him" (61).

"Contagion" and "milling" are concepts that derive from pre–resource mobilization theories of collective behavior and are again appropriate as contemporary social movement research begins to embrace the emotional as well as the rational aspects of movement participation. The genre has come full circle, from portraying crowd behavior as irrational, to portraying movement participants as calmly rational while they assemble SMOs, to today's recognition and integration of the affective, cognitive, and structural aspects of collective action.

Solidarity

Although a physical stigma such as race is observable in the cohort of others who have the stigma, their emotions and actions in social predicaments involving the stigma are not likely to be salient while one is engrossed in covering oneself. A behavioral stigma such as homosexuality hampers awareness of others in a more insidious fashion. Multiplied throughout the cohort, hiding isolates those with the stigma and creates a condition of pluralistic ignorance in which all believe they are uniquely afflicted with the stigma, not even being cognizant of the others. It is hard to see one's stigma as deriving from social oppression when one lacks appreciation of anyone else being in a similar predicament. "You feel so afraid. I thought there was nobody out there. As far as I was concerned, I was the only one that was different. I just felt that I was the only gay person, the only faggot in the world, the only person that felt the way that I felt, that was attracted to men" (Marcus 1992, 188). Thus shame over a stigma results in sequestration, undermines empathic unity and a sense of alliance with similar others, and prevents bonding through a shared relation to an oppressor. This condition is the very opposite of solidarity.

Heise (1998) identified the following factors in the emergence of empathic solidarity between persons A and B. Both A and B invest identities that put them in the same relationship with a pivotal figure, P; A and B experience the same event with P, resulting in the same emotions and the same impulses to action with regard to P; A and B observe each other's emotions, whereby each obtains a sense of unified consciousness with the other, and they observe each other's behavioral reactions to P, whereby each obtains a sense of alliance with the other; A and B each assures that the other perceives the self's emotions and actions, whereby each believes the other is reciprocating a sense of unified consciousness and a sense of alliance.

Processes involved in identity politics have an impact on each of these factors, and thereby identity politics not only change shame to pride but also transform sequestration into solidarity. First, social movement writings and activities clarify that someone with the stigma is not an idiosyncratic individual but rather a member of a definable plurality. There are others with the characteristic, and all can identify with their commonality when they get together. For example, the first halting steps of the gay rights movement involved making individual gay men and lesbians known to one another. "For people who are invisible, overcoming invisibility is a major step in improvement of self-image, in coming to grips with who you are. Think of all the isolated gay people for whom the sheer existence of groups of their own, that they could turn to, was an enormous improvement over the old situation where they felt totally cut off" (Katz 1976, 430).

Additionally, social movement writings define the identity of an oppositional character whose actions constitute the problems of the oppressed and whose identity is defined at least partly by those who are oppressed. For example, the invention of "homophobe" represents a crucial development in the gay rights movement, as reflected in the following statement: "The AIDS crisis has illuminated the issue of homophobia that we talked about in the seventies. All of those issues that we claimed existed—discrimination in jobs, discrimination in housing, hatred for gay people on a very basic level because we're different—have been made more palpable by the AIDS crisis. I don't think that there's new bigotry or homophobia. I think this is the same homophobia, but AIDS has given people permission to say it out loud. We're seeing that, in fact, we were right" (Marcus 1992, 416).

Movement literature that describes cases of persecution of the oppressed by the oppressor allows a secluded reader to identify with other oppressed individuals and to anticipate a sense of empathic solidarity that might be felt in assemblies. Literature that is effective for this purpose involves clear portrayals of typical actions of the oppressor toward the oppressed, vivid descriptions of emotions—such as fear or anger—felt by the oppressed, and details of common, nonheroic reactions enacted by the oppressed. Thereby the reader realizes that he or she feels and reacts the same as others in the oppressed group when encountering the oppressor.

For example, a gay rights history (Marcus 1992) reports: "As gay life became more visible and gay men, women, and organizations became more vocal, police harassment and repression kept pace. Police raids of gay bars continued, and despite the volatility of the times, this traditional police action most often inspired more fear than resistance among the patrons" (171). Another document reports: "We retreat into a bar. Outside, a police car swoops down on a hapless demonstrator. He is dragged kicking and punching into the car, and it roars off. 'They'll come in here next,' says Bittor. The bar empties, and we run to the far end of the square" (Jackson and Persky 1982, 215). An autobiographical statement by Shirley Willer (Marcus 1992) allows readers to identify with the other pole of response: "Just the assumption that I was gay was justification enough for one policeman to pick me up by the front of my shirt and slap me back and forth. He called me names . . . you god-damned pervert. You queer. You S.O.B. . . . I was so angry at the policeman I could have killed him! I wasn't frightened; I was angry! He had no right to do that to me!" (128).

However, movement literature alone cannot transform sequestration into solidarity. If members of an oppressed group merely attend to movement media productions, they are not a solidary group but rather an audience similar to people in a theater identifying with a stage character. Individuals have to demonstrate their emotions and actions to one another so that each becomes an object of identification for others. Then, and only then, can each individual understand that the experience of unified consciousness and alliance is two-way, from self to others and also from others to self. "Each time I extend a casual greeting to an unknown gay man and receive the same in return, we both affirm that which joins us together and come away from the exchange newly knowing that it's good to be gay. We have added to the bond of gay community. And, in both of us, fear and shame, the wounds inflicted on us while we were too young to protect ourselves, heal a little more. Three or four years ago, I got little positive response to my necessarily tentative gestures of solidarity. Now I find that gay men smile more readily. . . . Whether we've been active in it or not, the gay movement has touched us all" (Jackson and Persky 1982, 73).

Seeing one's own feelings and actions in others generates empathic unity and a sense of alliance. Then the two-way bond of solidarity ties tight as one infers that others are gaining strength by observing one's own feelings and actions as well. Thus the move to public demonstrations, in which those with the stigma display their feelings and actions to one another as much as to outside observers, is a powerful step for achieving solidarity, just as it is for achieving pride. Solidarity becomes generated in collective events wherein each participant builds emotional energies (Collins 1981) both by observing others and by knowing others are observing the self. "The march on Washington [in 1987] was an opportunity I couldn't miss. . . . When I got to Washington, it seemed like everybody there was lesbian or gay or supportive of lesbian and gay people. I'd never seen people just be themselves on public streets in daylight. . . . It's not that people were demonstrating their affection for one another. It was just the way people talked, their body language, the way they were so exuberant. People who didn't know each other talked openly about who they were and where they were from. . . . I'd never been so out. I'd never felt so safe" (Marcus 1992, 468).

Development of solidarity is evident in the Gay Pride parades that have become an annual public activity in many major U.S. and European cities. "Being surrounded by thousands of queers extinguishes that terrible loneliness we experienced when we feared we were the only ones on earth who were that way" (Caster 1992, 49). Solidarity also is evident in other kinds of gatherings: "Things have changed much more than I dreamed possible! The sheer growth of the movement in size and the variety of organizations is something I wouldn't have thought possible when I first joined the movement in 1958. I'm just thrilled that we have gay marching bands, gay choruses, gay outdoor groups, the Gay Games, and gay rodeos in addition to the standard political-action groups and legislative efforts. . . . These groups bring gay people together who start talking about their problems and eventually start talking about how they might solve them. It was how the movement got started in the first place" (Marcus 1992, 225).

Conclusion

The resource mobilization model admits emotion in the form of discontent as a resource to be mobilized: "Discontent may be defined, created, and manipulated by issue entrepreneurs and organizations" (McCarthy and Zald 1977, 1215). This point deserves deeper consideration than it has been given, though, especially in the area of identity politics.

Given the instrumental role of anger in motivating protest, one can interpret anger as an important resource for a social movement. Besides money and labor, people bring "emotional capital" to a social movement. As social movement organizations create or define discontent (McCarthy and Zald 1977), they are raising emotional capital to be spent pursuing movement goals. For example, we have seen that pamphlets and newsletters disseminated by prominent SMOs in gay liberation often have an explicitly affective countenance and strive to arouse the emotions of fear and anger. Movement propaganda is specifically designed for this purpose.

Figure 1. Emotion transformations in identity politics

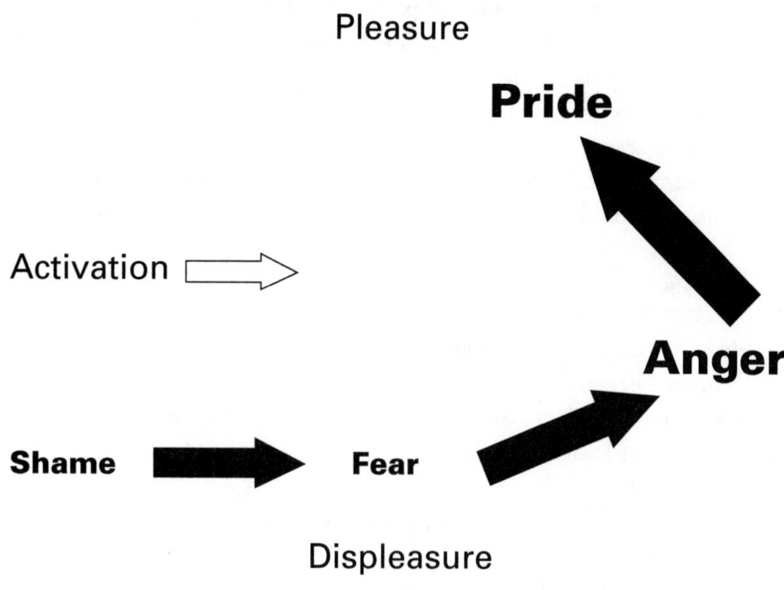

Note: Vulnerable states are shown in small type, dominant states in large type. Arrows represent social processes.

Theories of social movements will benefit by accommodating affect within their frameworks. The concept of emotional capital, although overlooked by resource mobilization theorists, seems implicitly understood by social movement organizations that attempt to incite emotion in potential participants. The role of movement communications not only is to spread information, promote attitudinal change, and urge contributions but also to incite emotion. By understanding that there are important affective precursors (anger and related affective states) to individual participation in movement activity, students of resource mobilization may attend to the "emotion work" that social movement agents and organizations engage in as they create mobilization potentials.

Figure 1 summarizes key parts of our model of emotional transformation in identity politics. Hidden stigma is associated with shame. Ideological campaigns by social movements transform the emotion of shame into fear and anger, thereby creating activated and dominant participants disposed to join collective actions. These individuals get pulled into demonstrations through network ties and crowd contagion. The collective public display of their stigma develops empathic solidarity and pride.

The emotional transformation likely does not end with pride. Pride may be regenerated repeatedly through collective public displays, and that may be necessary to erase earlier feelings of shame, but ultimately individuals come to accept the stigmatized identity as simply another component of the esteemed self. Pride is a prerequisite to incorporating the identity into the positive self and the threshold to the identity's deemotionalization.

References

Allport, Floyd H. 1924. *Social Psychology.* Boston: Houghton-Mifflin.

American Civil Liberties Union. 1994. "Lesbian and Gay Rights." Briefing Paper Number 19:1.

Anspach, Renee R. 1979. "From Stigma to Identity Politics: Political Activism among the Physically Disabled and Former Mental Patients." *Social Science and Medicine* 13A:765–73.

Borgatta, Edgar. 1981. "The Small Groups Movement: Historical Notes." *American Behavioral Scientist* 24:607–18.

Caster, Wendy. 1992. "Of Parades and Progress." In *Outlines.* Chicago: Lambda Publications.

Collins, Randall. 1981. "On the Microfoundations of Macrosociology." *American Journal of Sociology* 86:984–1014.

Davitz, Joel R. 1969. *The Language of Emotion.* New York: Academic Press.

Empire State Pride Agenda. 1997. "Demanding Lesbian and Gay Equality, Hundreds of New Yorkers Lobby the Senate." Press release. March 4.

Ferree, Myra Marx, and Frederick D. Miller. 1985. "Mobilization and Meaning: Toward an Integration of Social Psychological and Resource Perspectives on Social Movements." *Sociological Inquiry* 55:38–61.

Festinger, Leon. 1957. *A Theory of Cognitive Dissonance.* New York: Harper and Row.

Fireman, Bruce, and William A. Gamson. 1979. "Utilitarian Logic in the Resource Mobilization Perspective." In *The Dynamics of Social Movements,* edited by Mayer N. Zald and John D. McCarthy. Cambridge, Mass.: Winthrop Publishers.

Freeman, J. 1979. "Resource Mobilization and Strategy." In *The Dynamics of Social Movements,* edited by Mayer N. Zald and John D. McCarthy. Cambridge, Mass.: Winthrop Publishers.

Greenman, Jessea. 1994. "Out against the Right." Article posted May 26 on World Wide Web site of Lesbian Avengers Civil Rights Organizing Project, 208 W. 13th St., New York, NY 10011.

Groves, Julian-McAllister. 1995. "Learning to Feel: The Neglected Sociology of Social Movements." *Sociological Review* 43:435–61.

Hartinger, Brent. 1992. "Internalized Homophobia: An Inside Look." In *Outlines.* Chicago: Lambda Publications.

Hatfield, Elaine, John T. Cacioppo, and Richard Rapson. 1992. "The Logic of Emotion: Emotional Contagion." In *Review of Personality and Social Psychology,* edited by M. S. Clark. Newbury Park, Calif.: Sage.

Heise, David. 1967. "Prefatory Findings in the Sociology of Missions." *Journal for the Scientific Study of Religion* 6:49–58.

———.1998. "Conditions for Empathic Solidarity." In *The Problem of Solidarity: Theories and Models,* edited by Patrick Doreian and Thomas Fararo, 197–211. Amsterdam: Gordon and Breach.

Heise, David, and Elsa Lewis. 1988. "Programs Interact and Attitude: Software and Documentation." Debuque, Iowa: Wm. C. Brown Publishers, Software.

Hochschild, Arlie Russell. 1983. *The Managed Heart: The Commercialization of Human Feeling.* Berkeley: University of California Press.

Human Rights Campaign Fund. 1991. Pamphlet.

Jackson, E., and S. Persky. 1982. *Flaunting It: A Decade of Gay Journalism from the Body Politic.* Vancouver: New Star Books.

James, William. [1890] 1950. *The Principles of Psychology.* Vol. 2. New York: Dover Publications.

Jenkins, J. Craig. 1983. "Resource Mobilization Theory and the Study of Social Movements." *Annual Review of Sociology* 9:527–53.

Kaplan, Howard B. 1975. *Self-Attitudes and Deviant Behavior.* Pacific Palisades, Calif.: Goodyear.

Katz, Jonathan. 1976. *Gay American History.* New York: Thomas Y. Crowell.

Klandermans, Bert, and Dirk Oegema. 1987. "Potentials, Networks, Motivations, and Barriers: Steps towards Participation in Social Movements." *American Sociological Review* 52:519–31.

Kovecses, Zoltan. 1990. *Emotion Concepts.* New York: Springer-Verlag.

Laird, James D., and Charles Bresler. 1990. "William James and the Mechanisms of Emotional Experience." *Personality and Social Psychology Bulletin* 16:636–51.

MacKinnon, Neal, and Leo Keating. 1989. "The Structure of Emotion: A Review of the Problem and a Cross-Cultural Analysis." *Social Psychology Quarterly* 52:70–83.

Marcus, Eric. 1992. *Making History: The Struggle for Gay and Lesbian Rights—An Oral History.* New York: Harper Perennial.

Marotta, Toby. 1981. *The Politics of Homosexuality.* Boston: Houghton Mifflin.

McAdam, Doug. 1986. "Recruitment to High-Risk Activism: The Case of Freedom Summer." *American Journal of Sociology* 94:502–34.

McCarthy, John D., and Mayer N. Zald. 1977. "Resource Mobilization and Social Movements: A Partial Theory." *American Journal of Sociology* 82:1212–41.

McPhail, Clark. 1991. *The Myth of the Madding Crowd.* New York: Aldine de Gruyter.

Morgan, Rick L., and Heise, David. 1988. "Structure of Emotions." *Social Psychology Quarterly* 51(1): 19–31.

Nathanson, Donald L. 1987. "The Shame/Pride Axis." In *The Role of Shame in Symptom Formation,* edited by Helen Block Lewis. Hillsdale, N.J.: Lawrence Erlbaum.

Ohlemacher, Thomas. 1996. "Bridging People and Protest: Social Relays of Protest Groups against Low-Flying Military Jets in West Germany." *Social Problems* 43:197–218.

People for the American Way. 1992. Pamphlet.

Scheff, Thomas J. 1990. "Socialization of Emotions: Pride and Shame as Causal Agents." In *Research Agendas in the Sociology of Emotions,* edited by Theodore D. Kemper, 281–304. Albany: State University of New York Press.

Scher, Steven J., and David R. Heise. 1992. "Affect and the Perception of Injustice." *Advances in Group Processes* 10:223–52.

Smelser, Neil. 1963. *Theory of Collective Behavior.* New York: Free Press.

Smith-Lovin, Lynn. 1990. "Emotion as the Confirmation and Disconfirmation of Identity: An Affect Control Model." Chapter 9 in *Research Agendas in the Sociology of Emotions,* edited by T. D. Kemper. Albany: State University of New York Press.

Stein, Howard F. 1975. "Ethnicity, Identity, and Ideology." *School Review* 83(2): 273–300.

Taylor, Gabriele. 1985. *Pride, Shame, and Guilt.* Oxford: Clarendon Press.

Taylor, Verta. 1995. "Watching for Vibes: Bringing Emotions in the Study of Feminist Organizations." In *Feminist Organizations: Harvest of the New Women's Movement,* edited by Myra Marx Ferree and Particia Yancey Martin, 223–33. Philadelphia: Temple University Press.

Teal, Donn. 1971. *The Gay Militants.* New York: Stein and Day.

Thoits, Peggy A. 1990. "Emotional Deviance: Research Agendas." Chapter 7 in *Research Agendas in the Sociology of Emotions,* edited by Theodore D. Kemper. Albany: State University of New York Press.

Turner, Ralph H., and Lewis M. Killian. 1957. *Collective Behavior.* Englewood Cliffs, N.J.: Prentice-Hall.

Part III
Studies in Social Movements and Identity

13

Emotions and Identity in Women's Self-Help Movements

Verta Taylor

The concept of collective identity has emerged in the field of social movements as a tool for examining the way social injustices are translated into the everyday lives of collective actors (Gamson 1992b; Melucci 1989; Taylor and Whittier 1992). The rationale behind the use of this concept, according to some analysts, is that the unique forms of power exercised in modern societies give rise to new repertoires of contention focused on the self and everyday experience (Giddens 1991; Habermas 1984; Melucci 1989). Research on the collective identities of social movement participants points to the strong convictions that underlie identity politics (Robnett 1997; Taylor and Raeburn 1995; White 1989; Whittier 1995). Most of this work, however, takes as its focus the cognitive frameworks activists use to draw boundaries around themselves and ignores the emotions that can motivate people to organize around a common identity in the first place (Hunt, Benford, and Snow 1994). Research on the sociology of emotions suggests that the social inequalities and injustices that set the stage for social protest are associated with a host of negative—or what medical anthropologists term "devitalizing"—emotions such as shame, anger, fear, and depression (Kleinman 1986; Mirowsky and Ross 1989; Scheff 1990). At the same time, social movement research demonstrates that developing solidarity with others almost inevitably elicits positive or "vitalizing" emotions such as pride and joy in connection with the group's new positive collective self-definition (Fantasia 1988; McAdam 1988; Morris 1984; Rupp and Taylor 1987).

This chapter examines the way social movements contribute to the reconstruction of social identities by mobilizing around collective identities that translate negative and stigmatized emotions into positively valued self-definitions. The analysis is based on field research on the postpartum depression movement, a self-help movement that emerged out of the women's movement of the 1960s and 1970s and gained wider national support through media attention in the 1980s and 1990s. I use the case of the postpartum support group movement to analyze the process by which activists utilize the movement's collective identity both to accept their negative feelings and as a basis to negotiate and resist dominant conceptions of motherhood.

The analysis combines two different theoretical traditions concerned with the relationship between self and society: sociological theories of emotion that focus on the role of emotions in identity construction, and social movement approaches that accentuate the importance of collective identity in contemporary social activism. After a discussion of the data and methods of the study, I begin by describing the postpartum support group movement and demonstrating how the strategies of community building and collective identity construction associated with self-help exert a powerful influence on the emotions and identities of participants. I then draw from Thoits's (1985) self-labeling theory to examine the ways in which self-help activists' own sense of motherhood becomes engaged with dominant and competing cultural norms of socially appropriate mothering. Whereas self-labeling theory takes into account the importance of women's agency in the recognition and labeling of their non-normative feelings, social movement theory shifts the focus to the collective processes involved in the construction and use of new cultural frameworks as a means of redefining groups and challenging the moral order. I conclude by arguing that the recognition of emotions as an integral part of personal and collective identities is the key to understanding some contemporary forms of collective action.

Theoretical Links between Emotions and Identity

Over the past decade, scholars of social movements interested in the processes that generate and sustain collective action have turned their attention to identifying the micromobilization processes that link the individual and sociocultural levels (McAdam, McCarthy, and Zald 1988; Morris and Mueller 1992). Much of this work attempts to broaden the resource mobilization paradigm's overemphasis on strategic, organizational, and structural factors by elaborating the social psychological and cultural dimensions of social movements (Gamson 1992b; Klandermans 1984; Marwell and Oliver 1993; McAdam 1982; Morris 1984; Snow et al. 1986; Snow and Benford 1992; Tarrow 1994). This new culturally oriented research has been largely cognitive in orientation, advancing concepts such as collective identity, cognitive liberation, and collective action frames. Only a few scholars of social movements have examined the feelings and emotions that inevitably come into play when people band together to challenge and change the social order (Gamson 1992a; Goodwin 1997; Hercus 1999; Jasper 1997; Jasper and Poulsen 1995; Lofland 1985; Morris 1984; Robnett 1997; Taylor 1995b, 1996, 1999; Taylor and Whittier 1995). The lack of attention to the emotions of protest is not surprising, since resource mobilization theory emerged as the dominant perspective, in part, by challenging the "irrationalist" assumptions of classical collective behavior theory (Jenkins 1983; McCarthy and Zald 1977; Tilly 1978).

In response to the troublesome mind-body split that has plagued the social sciences, the sociology of emotions has emerged as an important topic in the field of sociology (Gordon 1981; Hochshild 1979, 1983; Kemper 1978, 1990). A growing body of this work brings together the study of emotions and identities by emphasizing the role emotions play in the construction of self and identity (Howard and Callero 1991; Stryker 1987). Affect control theory (Smith-Lovin 1990, 1995; Smith-Lovin and Heise 1988) treats emotions as messengers that signal to the self the degree to which events confirm or disconfirm identities. The theory predicts that, because the character of one's emotions is determined by his or her identity, people construct events in ways that corroborate fundamental meanings for their own and others' identities so as to create positive emotions. Emotion comes into play in Stryker's (1987) structural theory of identity through norms that specify the type and extent of emotion associated with particular roles and situations. Recognizing the centrality of emotions to social control, Hochschild (1979, 1983) developed the concept of feeling rules to depict the cultural norms specifying the type, extent, and the duration of feeling appropriate in a given role or situation.

Particularly relevant to the study of social movements is the way sociological models of emotions address the matter of non-normative identities. Affect control theory postulates that occupying stigmatized, deviant, or marginal identities gives rise to strong negative emotions, such as shame, guilt, and fear, that can set into motion a search for new ways to characterize the self (Smith-Lovin 1990). One of the predictions of the normative perspective on emotions, developed by Thoits (1985, 1990), is that when people's emotions routinely fail to match cultural expectations, they are likely to doubt their sanity and relabel themselves as mentally ill. The main assumptions of Thoits's self-labeling theory are two: that emotional disorders can best be understood as violations of feeling norms and expression rules, and that it is individuals' own recognition of the discrepancy between their private emotions and the emotional states perceived as normative that triggers self-attributions of mental illness.

Whereas this self-labeling perspective helps us understand the process by which individual women accept, negotiate, and resist the emotion norms of motherhood, social movement theory directs our attention to the collective processes involved in the construction of labels, identities, and other cultural tools as a means of redefining groups. Social movement scholars have used the concept of collective identity to research the question of how groups define and make sense of the question "who we are" (Gamson 1992; Giddens 1991; Melucci 1989, 1995; Taylor 1996; Taylor and Whittier 1992; Whittier 1995). Collective identity is the shared definition of a group that derives from members' common interests, experiences, and solidarity (Taylor 1989). In order for people to pursue collective rather than individual solutions to problems, they must come to some common understanding of their experiences.

Once we acknowledge the body of research by organizational scholars who find purpose, cognition, and emotions intertwined in seemingly the most rational of organizations, we must then grasp the fact that emotions do not belong to individuals any more than does rationality; rather, they are situated in organizational contexts (Albrow 1997). Self-help movements, like most social movement organizations, create distinctive emotion cultures that include expectations about how members should feel about themselves and about dominant groups, as well as how they should manage and express the feelings evoked by their day-to-day encounters with dominant groups. Prior research has demonstrated that the rituals developed by organizations are capable of changing the quality of emotions experienced by individuals (Smith-Lovin and Douglass 1992; Taylor and Whittier 1995). In this analysis I link theories of emotion that focus on the way emotion supports and reaffirms individual identity with collective identity approaches to social movements that explicate the role of social movement culture in identity reconstruction.

Data and Methods

The analysis is based on individual- and organizational-level data on the postpartum support group movement I obtained through field research over the course of ten years, between 1985 and 1995. I generated three sources of individual-level data: semistructured tape-recorded interviews with 29 participants (24 women and 5 men) in the movement, a mailed survey to 220 telephone support contacts around the country, and semistructured tape-recorded interviews with 52 women who described themselves as having experienced postpartum illness.

I constructed the sample of women with postpartum illness from a list of 300 women who responded to notices posted at home birthing centers, day-care centers, mental health centers, physicians' offices, hospital maternity units, social service agencies, restaurants, and a citywide Baby Fair and in local newspapers. Despite attempts to the contrary, the interview sample is biased in favor of older white women with higher levels of income and education. Ninety percent of the women were white, with the remaining 10 percent African American, Mexican American, and American Indian. About a third of the women were high school graduates, a third had some college, and the remaining one-third had B.A. or, in several instances, advanced degrees. A little more than half (54 percent) of the women were employed in a variety of blue-collar, pink-collar, clerical, and administrative and professional positions. Although annual family incomes ranged from $5,000 to a high outlier of more than $100,000, the mean household income was $39,000, somewhat higher than the national family average of $35,000. Most of the women were married at the time of the interview, although 11 percent were not. A little less than half (43 percent) had only one child; 41 percent had two, 12 percent had three, and 4 percent had four or more children. Along certain lines, the sample was diverse; it included women in traditional nuclear families as well as single women, coupled lesbians, and adoptive mothers of American and non-English-speaking children.

Additionally, the analysis draws from three types of organizational data: archival data in the national offices of the two key social movement organizations; participant observation at local, regional, and national conferences and board meetings; and television talk shows and news programs that featured self-help activists. To gain insight into emotion norms surrounding new mothers, these data were supplemented with fifty-six semistructured interviews with medical and mental health providers and an analysis of the self-help and medical and scientific discourse on childbirth, postpartum illness, and motherhood published between 1975 and 1993. (Fuller descriptions of the data and methods are available in Taylor 1996.)

Self-Help Emotion Culture and Collective Identity

The social movement that participants refer to as "the postpartum depression self-help movement" consists of two separate but interacting national social movement organizations, Depression After Delivery (DAD) and Postpartum Support International (PSI). Both groups formed in the mid-1980s out of the experiences of women who suffered serious postpartum psychiatric illness and were unable to find sources of treatment and support that confirmed their self-diagnoses. The postpartum self-help movement gathered steam between 1986 and 1988 through sweeping publicity that began with the founder of DAD's appearance on the "Phil Donahue Show." Widespread media attention helped Depression After Delivery grow into a network of more than 250 support groups tied together in some cases by state- or regional-level associations. The movement operates through a "warm line" that links women with support groups, national and regional conferences, newsletters and publications, and a network of lay and professional leaders and experts whose perspective on postpartum illness is sanctioned by the movement. Consistent with the composition of the organizations that historically have made up the feminist movement in the United States (Buechler 1990), participants in the postpartum support group movement come mainly from the white, educated, upper middle class thought to make up the demographic base of the new social movements (Eder 1993). This constituency calls attention to the movement's structural origins among white middle-class women struggling to balance work and family roles as their participation in paid employment has caught up with that of African American, single, and working-class women (Reskin and Padavic 1994).

In the postpartum self-help movement, women find support and community not only through face-to-face groups but also through telephone networks, self-help reading and talk shows, and pen-pal networks, all of which serve to confirm shared experiences and open windows on new identities. The construction of community that occurs through getting and giving support can be such a vibrant force that it functions as a form of what Breines (1982) has termed "prefigurative politics" by fostering a unique set of feeling rules and expression norms that supports new shared identities (Taylor 1995b). I focus here on the way in which the emotion culture of the postpartum support group movement (1) advances an ethic of care that justifies organizational structures and strategies consistent with female bonding; (2) cultivates different standards for expressing and evaluating emotions to reflect more desirable identities or self-conceptions; and (3) promotes a collective identity that allows participants to make a clear and visible break with the contemporary cultural model of socially appropriate mothering.

To take up the first point, most women's self-help movements make a special claim to a better way of organizing society by constructing a distinctive *culture of caring* in which participants can find emotional support as well as receive practical help and information to understand and overcome their problems (Ferree and Hess 1994; Taylor 1995b). Activists draw heavily from the emphasis on emotional expressiveness, self-transformation, collectivism, and caring advocated by feminist organizations. In 1987 Jane Honikman, a feminist steeped in the political culture of participatory democracy that propelled the movements of the 1960s and 1970s, established Postpartum Support International out of her own feminist consciousness-raising group in Santa Barbara, California. Depression After Delivery board meetings are run by collective decision making that not only allows participants to develop their leadership skills but also gives priority to the kinds of personal and family concerns that ordinarily take a backseat in the modern impersonal workplace (Acker 1990).

The emphasis on caring is also conveyed through open expressions of love and affection among participants. One woman summarized the intensity of women's relationships when she wrote to thank Jane Honikman for starting a pen-pal network for incarcerated mothers serving prison sentences for infanticide:

> For me this has been the best therapy. I feel so close to these women. I mean, we truly know and understand each other's pain and the craziness that accompanies PPP [postpartum psychosis] and other people's misconceptions. It is amazing what an understanding ear can do.[1]

Even the name of Depression After Delivery's newsletter, *Heartstrings,* signifies the emphasis placed on caring and nurturant relationships in self-help.

Some activists in the postpartum support group movement assert the existence of a distinctive set of "female values" that include egalitarianism, collectivism, an ethic of care, emotional expressiveness, and respect for experiential knowledge and base these claims chiefly on women's primary identity as mothers. It is not uncommon for participants to use maternal metaphors to characterize the woman-to-woman support provided by self-help, as in a recent popular self-help book on postpartum depression that begins, "If it were possible to put a big motherly hug into words, that is what we'd do for every postpartum mom who picked up this book" (Dunnewold and Sanford 1994, 5). The postpartum support group movement gives caring a public and moral significance in a society that some scholars have argued devalues women's caring labor (Huber and Spitze 1983).

The second characteristic of feminist emotion cultures is the *redefinition of feeling and expression rules* that apply to women. In "speaking out" about the guilt, anxiety, depression, anger—even the psychosis—connected with motherhood, postpartum depression activists challenge the emotion norms that support the maternal role. Questioning the cultural idea that an emotional response to children akin to love is somehow natural, essential, and inevitable, a recent popular book on postpartum survival explains:

> Society is quite clear about what your emotions are supposed to be once your baby is born. Television, movies, magazines, newspapers all give you the message that happiness, calm satisfaction, joy and pride are the norm when a new baby arrives. Family, friends, and medical professionals tell you to "relax and enjoy your baby," as if relaxation played even the smallest role in the drama of life with a brand new child. (Dunnewald and Sanford 1994, 3)

Like most self-help groups, the postpartum support group movement makes use of survivor narratives, or public testimony, as a means to transform what were once private experiences into public events and to normalize sentiments generally thought of as deviant. Women speak of postpartum illness in stark terms as "shattering" their lives, leading them to feel "trapped in a dark tunnel with no escape," going through "our own living hells," "living a nightmare," and experiencing a "tortured and slow death."

Survivor narratives are a principal means by which the postpartum support group movement has been able to garner widespread media attention. Women who have suffered postpartum illness are encouraged to tell their stories on television and radio talk shows and news magazines, at conferences attended by health and mental health professionals, at the office, in church, and to countless others they encounter in the course of their daily lives. They make their stories public by writing about them in popular books and magazines, newspapers, and even professional and scholarly publications. The collective identity of "survivor" functions, therefore, as a marker that sets off participants who express their deviant emotions publicly.

Finally, the emotion culture of the postpartum self-help movement *promotes a collective identity* that encourages women to connect their problems to the burdens of motherhood and to male-dominated medicine. The sharing of common experiences that takes place in self-help has larger social significance because it promotes the development of a collective identity that connects women's private feelings to the problem of gender subordination. In order to mobilize people to pursue collective solutions to their problems, all social movements ultimately must find a way to bridge the individual and societal levels by finding similarities in the biographies of a group of people and emphasizing them in such a way that the group's definition, or collective identity, becomes a part of individuals' self definitions. The single most important benefit of women's telephone contact with DAD's "warm line," as one woman put it, "was finding out that I was part of something bigger than myself."[2]

It is no coincidence that women in the postpartum support group movement describe the willingness of women and their families to share their experiences as "coming out" (Kleiman and Raskin 1994, 25), for when women admit to having suffered postpartum illness, they make a clear and visible break with conventional views by providing concrete illustrations of motherhood as a role that can be oppressive to women (Taylor 1995a). Furthermore, they place their negative emotions in a larger feminist framework that identifies postpartum illness as an injustice linked to gender inequality. Such a framework justifies opening the curtain on the intimate dramas of women's personal lives as a strategy both to empower women and to demand institutional- and societal-level solutions. Almost from the start, the mainly white middle-class activists in the postpartum support group movement tied their problems to the gender division of labor in American society that designates women primarily responsible for the care and nurture of children. Activists also hold that women are disadvantaged by the male-dominated structure of medicine. By providing authentic representations of their own negative feelings, activists intend to call into question the erasure of postpartum conditions by the medical establishment.

The culture of the postpartum self-help movement grows out of a conscious awareness of the significance of emotional control for upholding gender differences. Activists struggle to resist this imperative through collective practices that encourage the expression of emotions and redefine feeling and expression rules that apply to women to reflect more desirable identities. When postpartum activists express their negative feelings, they experience themselves as different from traditional—and ideal—mothers. Solidarity with other women and the group consciousness that grows out of participation in self-help make it possible, however, for women to use violations of cherished ideals about motherhood for their own purposes. Activists openly discuss the "need, as women, to replace the myth of maternal bliss with a more inclusive view of motherhood that is more realistic and accurate" and places more emphasis on "the challenges and difficulties that are part of the territory" (Dunnewald and Sanford 1994, 142). That activists use the expression of emotions as a deliberate tool for change goes along with the insistence, which is fundamental to women's self-help, that collective self-expression is political. In the next section, I examine the emotions women define as postpartum illness and demonstrate how the collective identity promoted by the postpartum self-help movement fosters emotions more conducive to protest.

Postpartum Illness as Gender Resistance: Reconstructing the Emotion Norms of Motherhood

The term *postpartum depression* is often meant in popular and self-help discourse to convey a complex of distressing emotions. Race, class, ethnicity, religion, sexual orientation, and gender ideology affected the ways women described their emotions (Glenn 1994; Hays 1996; Segura and Pierce 1993). My emphasis here is on the commonalities in the accounts provided by the predominantly white and middle-class women to whom the postpartum depression self-help movement is pitched and on the way their emotions are shaped by their awareness of the strong cultural imperatives—or "feeling rules"—that govern maternal emotion. The feelings that new mothers find to be the most disturbing cluster around the four basic emotions of guilt, anxiety, depression, and anger. These feelings can be thought of as constituting the lived experience of postpartum mental illness. To illuminate the connection between women's emotional distress and the feelings mothers expect following the birth or adoption of a child, my discussion relates these four emotions to the "emotion norms" of motherhood as described by the interviewees and debated in popular, self-help, scientific, and medical writings on postpartum depression. The women interviewed for this study clarified that it was not the reactions of physicians, nurses, and medical providers that led them to assess their feelings as a sign of postpartum depression. Nearly three-fourths of the women interviewed identified their main sources of socialization into motherhood as books, magazines, and pamphlets on pregnancy, childbirth, and parenting; interactions with close women friends; and formal childbirth education courses. The significance of self-help for women's definitions of postpartum depression is clear from one woman's story published in the newsletter of Depression After Delivery ("Postpartum Depression Feels Like a Thief" 1989):

> Until I attended the support group, I wasn't sure if I had postpartum depression. Now I know that I suffered it. Because of the encouragement of others in the group, I sought help with the right doctor, changed therapists to someone who understood and could deal with my guilt over PPD. Thanks to those who listened, cared, and offered support, I was able to accept myself as a loving mother who was suffering illness. (3)

Guilt and Shame and Mother-Infant Bonding

For about half of the women interviewed, the feeling that signals the onset of postpartum depression is guilt, described as "at times overwhelming," brought on by the fact that their feelings for their newborn or adopted child did not match what they expected. The experience of the following woman, who suffered a year-long depression that began almost immediately following the delivery of her first child, is fairly typical:

> I read every book there was, including horrible little old pamphlets. But nobody ever told me there is a chance you might not like her. I got her as this clean bundle at the hospital plopped on my stomach. And when I recognized that I felt absolutely nothing for her, I fell into deep depression.

That so many women expect, as one popular advice book on pregnancy and childbirth puts it, "to bathe in the glow of maternal love" (DeLyser 1989) is undoubtedly linked to the idea of maternal infant bonding, which holds that there are innate emotional and psychological processes that commit a mother to her newborn infant in the first few moments following the baby's birth (Eyer 1993). The following passage from an advice book for new mothers popular in the 1980s contrasts postpartum depression with what Arney (1980) terms the instinctive "falling in love with your child" implied by the concept of bonding:

> Some of the new mother's emotions bother both herself and those closest to her. . . . These symptoms are usually labeled "postpartum depression." On the other hand, when the new mother thrills at feeding and holding her baby, and when her tears are tears of joy, these actions are labeled "maternal." (Korte and Scaer 1984, 185)

In the training materials distributed to its telephone volunteers, Depression After Delivery attempts to counter the myth of instant bonding by encouraging volunteers to reassure women concerned about failing to bond with their babies "not to feel guilty about how they are feeling toward their child" ("Telephone Contact Guidelines"1991, 6). At the same time, by communicating to women that "when the PPD begins to lift and the symptoms begin to lessen, loving feelings will begin to come," DAD nevertheless holds maternal attachment to be synonymous with normal motherhood. The emphasis in the self-help and advice literature is on a gradual "falling in love" that occurs between mother and child. One popular advice book compares motherhood to a "prearranged marriage" and urges women who are not "automatically infused with a joyous desire to love and nurture a new baby" to "ease into it slowly" (Hotchner 1984, 538). The overriding theme, however, is that a mother's detachment from her child should "not be judged harshly but rather seen as an indication that she may be ill and unable to function" (Harberger, Berchtold, and Honikman 1992, 48).

Sociologists of emotions generally think of shame and guilt as among the most fundamental of emotions because they serve as a powerful negative motivation for behavior and imply a degree of personal insufficiency that raises serious questions about the adequacy of the self (Scheff 1990). For many of the women I interviewed, the shame and guilt experienced when the "overwhelming rush of love and instant maternal bonding" they expected did not "come right away" have such a corrosive effect that, as one woman writes, it "steals away their sense of motherhood" (O'Meara 1992, 2; "Postpartum Depression Feels Like a Thief" 1989, 3). By identifying guilt and shame as components of postpartum depression, women are permitted the latitude of expressing what are seen as normal feelings brought on by women's fears of being an "unfit mother" (Hotchner 1984, 11). The advice contained in a popular self-help guide to recovery from postpartum depression written by two women, one a physician and another a social worker, both members of DAD, clarifies the importance of using collective strategies to manage guilt:

> The key to overcoming shame is to risk reaching out to someone and talking about whatever is making you feel so badly. It sounds very simple, yet it is very hard to do. Once you can talk about it, you can begin to free yourself of the shame attached to your feelings. (Kleiman and Raskin 1994, 47–48)

The discourse of the postpartum depression movement, then, encourages women to "off-load much of the guilt" they have accepted by turning away from "the traditional and socially acceptable standards" about being a "good mother and wife" that induce feelings of inadequacy (Dix 1985, 185, 196).

Anxiety and Fear and Mother-Care

All the women interviewed express some degree of anxiety and fear connected to mothering. Initially, women were inclined to link their feelings to the burdens of caring for an infant and, especially for first-time mothers, to inexperience and uneasiness about how to meet the child's needs. To the extent that care and nurturance are central to the definition of motherhood, an inability to care for the child strikes at the very core of maternal identity. A successful dentist in private practice recalls being so worried about whether she was "taking care of the baby properly" that on some days she telephoned her closest friend as often as ten times a day for advice:

> I was so anxious that I would do things like, I couldn't bathe the baby. I couldn't give her a bath because I was afraid I would drown her. I didn't want to change her diaper because something made me afraid I would stick her with the pin. Everything I did with that baby I was afraid to do. I was so paranoid sometimes that I was even afraid to feed her.

Although anxiety almost always began with concern over the child's well-being, for several women these feelings gave way to full-fledged panic attacks and obsessive thoughts of harming or killing their babies. One woman had visions of drowning her baby in the bathtub, another thought about cooking her baby in the oven, another woman envisioned dropping her baby off a freeway overpass, and one woman was haunted by "these goofy thoughts of cutting off the baby's nose."

At the heart of women's concerns about providing good mothering is the gendered model of parenting in American society that designates women primarily responsible for the care and nurturance of children (Berry 1993; Huber and Spitze 1983). The dominant line reflected in the obstetrics and gynecology literature is that, even if women are urged to receive "a certain amount of 'special' help, either from their husbands, or from another woman, often the maternal grandmother or aunt of the new baby," child care ultimately remains the province of mothers (Romito 1989, 1433). Medical treatments of postpartum depression increasingly are written by women who take as the standard the liberal feminist image of the "supermom" who combines marriage and child care with employment (Ball 1987; Beck 1992, 1993; Romito 1989, 1990). The popular advice literature on pregnancy and childbirth tends to parallel the medical overemphasis on the plight of the supermom, thereby ignoring the experiences of other groups of mothers (DeLyser 1989; Eisenberg, Murkhoff, and Hathaway 1988). These sources define motherhood primarily as a voluntary decision and a learned skill acquired through medical consultation, formal childbirth education, the advice of child-rearing experts, and self-help reading. With so many choices available to a woman and so many resources at her disposal, the new mother who experiences anxiety, fear, and ambivalence over her caring labor, although no longer a biological misfit, is nevertheless someone who has failed at "accommodating the female role" (Danforth 1982, 524).

The postpartum self-help movement offers women an alternative to both the traditional and the new views of maternal caring. In its support groups, literature, and media campaign to raise public awareness, the movement gives voice to women whose feelings defy the expectation of unselfish nurturing. Because the feelings women associate with postpartum illness challenge the view that motherly love uniquely equips women to care for children, the movement advocates what Berry (1993) terms "father-care" and "other-care." Husbands of women suffering postpartum depression are encouraged to participate in housework, assume responsibilities for child care, and "adapt to the changes they see in their wives" by providing friendship and understanding (Hickman 1991, 1). Owing to the leadership of a lesbian mother in Pennsylvania, an African American woman in Ohio, and a Mexican American woman in Santa Barbara, at least some groups are struggling to expand the notion of mothering to include the distinct forms of community caring and nonexclusive mothering of racial/ethnic and lesbian mothers.

The emotional requirement that mothers love and care for their infants is so central to the meaning of motherhood that it is not surprising that women find it distressing to feel anxious and fearful about caretaking. In the publications and discourse of the postpartum depression movement, anxiety and fear are taken to be clear signs that a woman is "experiencing PPD" (Harberger, Berchtold, and Honikman 1992). The story told by one woman demonstrates how self-attributions of postpartum depression can be comforting. This woman had two young children, in addition to a three-month-old infant, and recalls the day she knew that she was suffering from postpartum depression. She "lost control" because the baby would not stop crying, smacked "each of the children once," and rocked the baby while repeating, "I hate you, I hate you." By reassuring women that feelings such as these "do not mean that a new mother doesn't love her baby, or is ambivalent about motherhood," the postpartum depression movement permits women to express the anxiety associated with parenting (Lewin 1992). Presenting postpartum illness as a metaphor for less than successful motherhood, especially the failure to demonstrate intense and unswerving love for the child, means, however, that the link between motherhood and caring remains unchallenged. The postpartum support group movement is, nevertheless, a major proponent of a new model of parenting that insists that fathers and mothers share equally in the care of their children and in the anxiety that goes along with a role that is so closely scrutinized.

Depression and Maternal Satisfaction

Women who think of themselves as suffering postpartum depression describe feelings of sadness, hopelessness, worthlessness, and loss in the weeks and months following the birth or adoption of a child when they discover that for them motherhood is not the ultimate road to happiness and fulfillment. A clear majority of the women interviewed mark the beginning of their depression with unexplained episodes of crying that started sometime in the first two weeks after birth and lasted on average about two months. Many describe excessive crying to the point that they "lost control" and were unable to take care of either themselves or their child.

For about one-fourth of the women interviewed, sadness and tearfulness did not subside in the first few months but gave way to major depression that lasted for as long as six months to a year. The major theme that emerges from women's accounts of depression is the loss of self women associate with motherhood. The most common loss reported by women who experienced postpartum depression was leaving a job after the birth or adoption of a child. One woman who quit her job as a secretary for an insurance agency became "depressed about being stuck at home, and being useless, and [the baby] taking all of [her] attention." A school psychologist who took several months of maternity leave before returning to work full-time felt she had made such a mistake that she actually wanted to get rid of her baby: "I resented him, I wanted to get up in the morning and take a shower and eat my breakfast and go to work like I used to. . . . Nothing was the same." An African American woman who took extended maternity leave from her job as a social worker in a family services agency where she worked with black families suddenly found herself feeling "self-centered." Losing her identity as an "other mother" of the black community working on behalf of "race uplift" (Gilkes 1983), she became so depressed that she contemplated getting into her car and driving it "100 miles an hour into a brick wall."

Women describe other kinds of loss of self as well. An eighteen-year-old mother who raised a child as a single parent, while working part-time and attending college, laments the loss of her youth: "I'm a mother now and even though I thought I would be different, I feel old like my Mom." Another single woman, a university professor who wanted a child so badly that she traveled to El Salvador to adopt an eight-year-old girl, describes a "dark cloud" that fell over her life the first year as she began to question her earlier commitment to her career. Her depression made her aware that before having a daughter she had been "only half a person."

The loss described by traditional women who subscribe to a glorified image of motherhood was in a sense more fundamental, as it stemmed from the fact that the societal shift in "the very core of what it means to be a woman" had eroded their status as full-time housewives. One woman who waited until she completed her bachelor's degree to have her first child planned not to begin work or graduate school until her children were in school. Despite her high expectations for motherhood, after the birth of her first child, she experienced a major depression that led to hospitalization. She attributes the depression, at least in part, to disappointment:

> That was the way I was raised, to have my mother there for me all the time. That was the way things were supposed to be. We were going to have kids. And I was going to stay at home and my husband would be a successful college professor. We were going to have everything. . . . I never expected that it would all just come crashing down.

The belief in maternal satisfaction, reinforced by the medical establishment, veils the negative side of motherhood. A growing research literature that reports high rates of depression among mothers of young children is almost entirely omitted from medical discourse (McGrath et al. 1990; Ross, Mirowsky, and Huber 1983). For example, the widely respected and most commonly used text for the education of obstetricians and gynecologists, Williams's *Obstetrics* (1989), contains only one paragraph on women's emotional and psychological response to childbirth. The most recent edition of *The Diagnostic and Statistical Manual of Disorders,* published in 1994, does not list postpartum depression as a separate syndrome or even a subtype. When the emotional distress of mothers is discussed at all in the medical and psychiatric literature, the feelings of irritability, moodiness, weeping, tiredness, fatigue, anxiety, vulnerability, and antagonism toward one's partner reported by between one-half and two-thirds of all women are normalized under the label "baby blues" to distinguish them from the more serious but less frequent psychiatric illnesses (Gabbe, Niebyl, and Simpson 1991). The dominant medical view remains that major depression, manic depression, and psychosis suffered in the postpartum period are not distinct conditions except in timing and are "most likely a variant of primary affective illness and not separate disorders" (Gitlin and Pasnau 1989).

Postpartum psychiatric conditions are beginning to reappear in medical texts, as some medical schools, hospitals, and professional organizations bow to pressure from patients and self-help groups to include discussions of postpartum disorders in medical education, sponsor conferences on the subject, and provide education and treatment. Increasingly, medical accounts of postpartum depression are written by women, and they note "the possible adverse effects of the 'rosy' picture of pregnancy, childbirth, and early parenthood which is painted in many antenatal classes and in most books and magazines for expectant mothers" (Romito 1989, 1443–46).

More often than not, firsthand accounts of postpartum depression and psychosis published in popular sources as well as professional outlets are written by activists associated with the postpartum self-help movement. Reflecting the ongoing struggle between professional and lay definitions that characterize most contemporary self-help campaigns, popular and childbirth education writings pay considerable attention to hormonal and biochemical explanations of postpartum illness, such as those of Katharina Dalton (1980) and James Hamilton (1992), which have had little impact on the mainstream medical establishment.

It is in the discourse of the postpartum support movement that women find the most serious challenge to "the myth of blissful parenthood that is ingrained in our society" (Harberger, Berchtold, and Honikman 1992, 46) and confirmation for the feelings of sadness, unhappiness, hopelessness, and loss that can accompany the changes brought on by motherhood. Whereas medical accounts focus principally on the normalized condition of the "blues," the postpartum self-help movement treats these fairly common feelings as "the little sister" of the "severe illnesses" (Harberger, Berchtold, and Honikman 1992, 45). In face-to-face encounters with physicians and health administrators, at local, regional, and national medical and mental health conferences, through an aggressive letter-writing campaign, and in more than three dozen media appearances on nationally syndicated talk shows, activists publicize the personal tragedies of women and families who have suffered and survived postpartum illness. Participants in the postpartum support group movement have published their own self-help books that warn women of the likelihood of experiencing postpartum disorders and treat these problems in a straightforward manner (see, e.g., Dunnewald and Sanford 1994; Kleiman and Raskin 1994). Through these alternative discourses, self-help activists have opened up a space for public discussion about postpartum psychiatric conditions and provided women with a label for their deviant emotions. The paradox is that, even if the postpartum depression movement holds that maternal satisfaction is not inevitable, its actions reaffirm the cultural myths by promising to restore to women—through support groups, medication, therapy, hospitalization, or whatever it takes—the happiness, joy, and fulfillment of motherhood.

Sociologists generally agree that, although depression is experienced as a personal problem, it can also be understood as a type of social distress that originates in the larger social problems of inequality, alienation, and powerlessness that affect certain groups of people (Mirowsky and Ross 1989). Jack (1991) links women's high rates of depression to the self-silencing women engage in to conform to traditional feminine roles. In telling their stories publicly, self-help activists move the discussion of deviant motherhood into the public domain, bring to light the heavy demands placed on modern mothers, and call attention to the way maternal self-sacrifice undermines women's identities and well-being.

Anger and Maternal Self-Sacrifice

The feeling that women almost universally treat as a sign of postpartum psychiatric illness is anger. Historically, the expression of anger by women has been seen as violating gender norms to such a degree that it has almost always been equated with mental and physical illness (Cancian and Gordon 1988; Ehrenreich and English 1979). Sociologists understand anger to be a distressing emotion provoked by inequity or a sense of unfairness (Kemper 1978). Unlike depression, however, which turns on the self, anger targets those held responsible for the inequity. For the new mother, feeling angry at the very persons she expects to love represents the ultimate failure to feel and act in a motherly and wifely fashion. Women's accounts of postpartum illness reveal strong feelings of hostility and anger directed at their husbands or partners, children, the male-dominated medical establishment that refuses to acknowledge and treat women's suffering as a legitimate concern, and medical and popular representations that glorify motherhood and deny women's subordination.

If there is a single discovery that triggers women's anger, it is the stark realization that motherhood requires that a woman put her feelings at the service of others by enhancing her child's and her husband's or partner's well-being, even at the expense of her own happiness. Well over half of the women interviewed expressed anger, hostility, and resentment toward their husbands or partners for failing to share child care and household responsibilities. The anger articulated by one woman, whose depression persisted for seventeen months after the birth of a third child and was exacerbated by serious marital and financial difficulties, is fairly typical. Even though it was financially necessary for her to work, her husband had traditional ideas about marital roles that were typical of about one-third of the husbands and partners of the women I interviewed who experienced postpartum illness. She began to resent him so bitterly for not sharing household responsibilities that she looked forward to the time when she had the financial independence to seek a divorce:

> I was angry a lot because my husband is not real supportive. He was just there. He was not any help as far as fathers go. He's old fashioned. It's okay if you want to work and everything, but the kids are your responsibility.

More stigmatized, however, are the feelings of anger, resentment, and hostility women direct at their children. One woman, who was so depressed that she was unable to go out of the house for three weeks following the baby's birth, resented her child so much that she dreamed of giving him up for adoption. One-fifth of the women harbored thoughts of harming their babies. The experience of one woman, who like most of the women I interviewed never acted on her feelings, captures such desperation. Prior to her first pregnancy, she had been a successful graduate student working to complete her doctoral dissertation. Her husband had completed his doctoral degree and taken an academic position at a university where the future looked bright for him. The demands of being a mother and wife, in the meantime, required so much of her time and energy that she had fallen behind on her dissertation and decided to let her career temporarily take a backseat to his. One night as she was washing the dishes, while her husband relaxed in the living room, the baby began to cry:

> I recall picking up a butcher's knife to wash it. And for one moment, I considered the possibility that if I went into the baby's room and killed her, my life would return to the way it was before.

Women also direct anger at male obstetrician-gynecologists who downplay their suffering by refusing to treat postpartum depression and postpartum psychosis as illness or who give advice that reinforces gender stereotypes by espousing the view that good mothers sacrifice their own happiness to child rearing. One woman who held a high-level management position waited until her mid-thirties, when her career and marriage were well established, to have a child. After a medically complicated delivery that resulted in an unanticipated cesarean section, she suffered such serious depression that she was forced to take an additional three months of sick leave following six weeks of unpaid pregnancy leave. Her anger was provoked by the fact that her obstetrician-gynecologist "dismissed" her concern over the loss of an independent identity, which she held responsible for her "unrelenting depression." Worse yet, she objected to his advice, which reflected gender stereotypes by setting up expectations about "proper motherly behavior":

> I started crying at the doctor's, saying I was lonely, I needed work, and I needed structure. He said, "this is normal. This will pass. Don't focus so much on yourself. What you have to think of is the baby. In time, you will adjust your priorities and forget that you ever felt the way you do now."

It is not uncommon in medical writings for the burdens of child care and domestic work to be trivialized and women's requests for assistance in these areas to be seen as a sign that they are suffering postpartum illness. Without any explanation of the context and causes of women's anger, the references to mothers' "aggressive thoughts," "homicidal thoughts," feelings of "violence to the infant," "thoughts of harming the baby," and "anger toward the baby" found in medical texts that refer to postpartum psychiatric disorders seem almost baffling (Cherry, Burkowitz, and Kase 1985; Gleicher 1985; Sciarra 1989). Yet women's inappropriate anger is so central to the medical construction that feelings of hostility toward the infant are the most commonly discussed rationale for medical and psychiatric intervention in cases of postpartum illness.

The writings of the postpartum self-help movement acknowledge anger as one of the major "clues" to recognizing postpartum illness (Harberger, Berchtold, and Honikman 1992) and link women's anger to gender inequality. Male physicians are routinely criticized in the movement's publications and confronted in open forums, informal meetings, and medical consultations for dismissing women's complaints by "refusing to treat postpartum depression and psychosis as the illness that it is" ("Depression during Pregnancy" 1988, 4). The movement strikes out at the sexual division of labor in the household that saddles women with the responsibility for child care and maintaining the home, linking postpartum depression to women's subordinate status. One activist, an outspoken feminist with a degree in women's studies, defines her public expression of anger in response to being hospitalized for postpartum psychosis as a deliberate challenge to "patriarchal definitions of mothering" (Celeste 1990). She points to the ways in which self-help activists are struggling to reevaluate motherhood by exposing its "darker side" and are "upsetting the entire gender system."

Anger is a common response to social inequality, and it is the feeling that most clearly indicates the rebellious nature of postpartum depression. Anger positions women's suffering in relation to gender subordination and holds male domination accountable for women's being defined solely in relation to others, as well as for the segregation of roles and loss of an independent identity that can occur when women become mothers. For that reason, anger not only challenges the emotional rules but has the potential to change them. In its public and private discourse, the postpartum support movement encourages women to trade their guilt, shame, and depression for anger and pride over the injustices of motherhood and having "survived" a condition to which "hundreds of mothers have lost their lives" through suicide and infanticide (Berchtold 1991, 3). The overt expression of anger and the refusal to accept the traditional circumscribed roles of mother and wife leave little doubt that postpartum illness can be understood as a form of rebellion and resistance against gendered notions of motherhood.

Conclusion

We cannot fully understand the vitality of modern therapeutic self-help movements without recognizing the wide range of feelings generated by gender subordination and the way they figure into the collective identities, strategies, and organizational forms displayed by these repertoires of collective action. In this chapter, I use research on the contemporary postpartum support group movement to demonstrate that the kind of self-sacrificial love expected of mothers plays an important role in galvanizing women's participation in this movement, as well as in shaping the movement's personalized political strategies, organizational form, and identity-oriented outcomes. The analysis reveals that the emotions women identify as postpartum illness—guilt, anxiety, depression, and anger—represent almost the antithesis of the cultural norms of socially appropriate mothering.

But the emotion work that women do in caring for others not only gives meaning to women's deviant emotions but also organizes women's resistance to gender oppression. The crux of self-help is to be found in the social movement communities that coalesce loosely around the personal relationships stitched out of giving and getting emotional and other very individualized kinds of support. The collective redefinition of self that results from participating in these communities allows women to trade guilt and depression for pride in having survived their ordeals and for anger directed at those who perpetuate the gendered model of motherhood.

Accommodating the centrality of emotions to women's self-help requires us, then, to revisit the claims of scholars who argue that self-help simply reinforces women's subordination (Kaminer 1992). By using postpartum illness as a site for challenging the ideology of intensive mothering, which requires women to dedicate much of themselves to child rearing, activists in the postpartum self-help movement are engaged in defining a new kind of mother who challenges the prevailing gender code. Feminist self-help communities also contribute to the reconstruction of gender through cultivating emotion cultures that dictate open displays of emotion and empathy and legitimate attention to participants' emotions and personal biographies. By moving the discussion of women's deviant identities into the public domain, women who organize around problems as wide ranging as postpartum illness, incest, rape, battering, alcohol and substance abuse, and breast cancer disrupt the divisions between "private" and "public" thought to be basic to the social organization of gender (McMahon 1995; Taylor and Van Willigen 1996).

Although the analysis here focuses on the significance of emotions for the construction of collective identity, it is my view that strong emotions accompany all aspects of social movements. Emotions give ideas the power to motivate people to challenge dominant groups, emotions are the basis of the solidarity that binds participants together in pursuit of a common cause, emotions can be useful tools for mobilizing support and opposition, and protest can evoke intended and unintended emotions in its targets. To suggest that emotions play a part in social movements does not negate the body of scholarship that emphasizes the instrumental and strategic nature of social movements (Gamson 1990; McAdam 1982; McCarthy and Zald 1977; Tarrow 1994). Rather, a full understanding of social movements requires that we attend to both the cognitive and emotional dimensions of social protest.

Notes

This research was supported by grants from the Office of Research and Program Evaluation, Ohio Department of Mental Health, and by funds from the Ohio State University Office of Research and Graduate Studies, the College of Social and Behavioral Sciences, the College of Humanities, the Department of Sociology, and the Department of Women's Studies. I thank Myra Marx Ferree, William Gamson, Elizabeth Kaminski, Doug McAdam, Tim Owens, Jennifer Pearce, Nicole Raeburn, Leila Rupp, Lynn Smith-Lovin, Suzanne Staggenborg, Sheldon Stryker, Marieke Van Willigen, Bob White, Nancy Whittier, and Mayer Zald, who provided comments on earlier versions of this chapter.

1. Reprinted in a letter from Jane Honikman to Friends in the Pen Pal Network, February 25, 1991, Jane Honikman's personal papers.

2. A 1994 mailed survey, conducted by the author, of DAD's 220 telephone support contacts.

References

Acker, Joan. 1990. "Hierarchies, Jobs, Bodies: A Theory of Gendered Organizations." *Gender and Society* 4:139–58.

Albrow, Martin. 1997. *Do Organizations Have Feelings?* New York: Routledge.

Arney, William Ray. 1980. "Maternal-Infant Bonding: The Politics of Falling in Love with Your Child." *Feminist Studies* 6:547–70.

Ball, Jean A. 1987. *Reactions to Motherhood: The Role of Postnatal Care.* Cambridge: Cambridge University Press.

Beck, Cheryl Tatano. 1992. "The Lived Experience of Postpartum Depression: A Phenomenological Study." *Nursing Research* 41:166–70.

———. 1993. "Teetering on the Edge: A Substantive Theory of Postpartum Depression." *Nursing Research* 42:42–48.

Berchtold, Nancy. 1991. "A Note from Nancy . . . Founder-Director." *Heartstrings: The National Newsletter of Depression After Delivery* 2 (Spring): 3.

Berry, Mary Frances. 1993. *The Politics of Parenthood: Child Care, Women's Rights, and the Myth of the Good Mother.* New York: Viking.

Breines, Wini. 1982. *Community and Organization in the New Left, 1962–1968: The Great Refusal.* South Hadley, Mass.: Praeger.

Buechler, Steven M. 1990. *Women's Movements in the United States: Woman Suffrage, Equal Rights, and Beyond.* New Brunswick, N.J.: Rutgers University Press.

Cancian, Francesca M., and Steven L. Gordon. 1988. "Changing Emotion Norms in Marriage: Love and Anger in U.S. Women's Magazines since 1900." *Gender and Society* 2:308–42.

Celeste, Dagmar. 1990. "The Myth of Motherhood: Postpartum Illness from a Feminist Mother's Perspective." Speech at the National Women's Studies Association Conference (June), Akron, Ohio, in the personal papers of Dagmar Celeste, Columbus, Ohio.

Cherry, Sheldon H., Richard L. Burkowitz, and Nathan G. Kase. 1985. *Medical, Surgical, and Gynecologic Complications of Pregnancy.* 3d ed. Baltimore: Williams and Wilkins.

Collins, Patricia Hill. 1990. *Black Feminist Thought: Knowledge, Consciousness, and the Politics of Empowerment.* New York: Routledge.

Dalton, Katharina. 1980. *Depression after Childbirth.* New York: Oxford University Press.

Danforth, David N. 1982. *Obstetrics and Gynecology.* 5th ed. New York: Harper and Row.

DeLyser, Femmy. 1989. *Jane Fonda's New Pregnancy Workout and Total Birth Program.* New York: Simon and Schuster.

"Depression during Pregnancy—One Woman's Story." 1988. *Depression After Delivery Newsletter* (Spring): 4.

Dix, Carol. 1985. *The New Mother Syndrome: Coping with Postpartum Stress and Depression.* New York: Doubleday.

Dunnewald, Ann, and Diane G. Sanford. 1994. *Postpartum Survival Guide.* Oakland, Calif.: New Harbinger Publications.

Eder, Klaus. 1993. *The New Politics of Class: Social Movements and Cultural Dynamics in Advanced Societies.* London: Sage.

Ehrenreich, Barbara, and Deirdre English. 1979. *For Her Own Good.* Garden City, N.Y.: Anchor Press/Doubleday.

Eisenberg, Arlene, Heidi Eisenberg Murkoff, and Sandee Eisenberg Hathaway. 1988. *What to Eat When You're Expecting.* New York: Workman Publishing.

Eyer, Diane E. 1993. *Mother-Infant Bonding: A Scientific Fiction.* New Haven: Yale University Press.

Fantasia, Rick. 1988. *Cultures of Solidarity: Consciousness, Action, and Contemporary American Workers.* Berkeley: University of California Press.

Ferree, Myra Marx, and Beth B. Hess. 1994. *Controversy and Coalition: The New Feminist Movement across Three Decades of Change.* Rev. ed. New York: Twayne.

Gabbe, Steven G., Jennifer R. Niebyl, and Joe Leigh Simpson. 1991. *Obstetrics: Normal and Problem Pregnancies.* New York: Churchill Livingstone.

Gamson, William A. 1990. *The Strategy of Social Protest.* 2d ed. Belmont, Calif.: Wadsworth.

———. 1992a. *Talking Politics.* Cambridge: Cambridge University Press.

———. 1992b. "The Social Psychology of Collective Action." In *Frontiers in Social Movement Theory,* edited by Aldon D. Morris and Carol McClurg Mueller, 53–76. New Haven: Yale University Press.

Giddens, Anthony. 1991. *Modernity and Self-Identity: Self and Society in the Late Modern Age.* Stanford: Stanford University Press.

Gilkes, Cheryl Townsend. 1983. "Going Up for the Oppressed: Career Mobility of Black Women Community Workers." *Journal of Social Issues* 39:115–39.

Gitlin, Michael J., and Robert O. Pasnau. 1989. "Psychiatric Syndromes Linked to Reproductive Function in Women: A Review of Current Knowledge." *American Journal of Psychiatry* 146:1413–22.

Gleicher, Norbert. 1985. *Principles of Medical Therapy in Pregnancy.* New York: Plenum Medical Book Co.

Glenn, Evelyn Nakano. 1994. "Social Constructions of Mothering: A Thematic Overview." In *Mothering: Ideology, Experience, and Agency,* edited by Evelyn Nakano Glenn, Grace Chang, and Linda Rennie Forcey, 1–29. New York: Routledge.

Goodwin, Jeff. 1997. "The Libidinal Constitution of a High-Risk Social Movement: Affectual Ties and Solidarity in the Huk Rebellion, 1946–1954." *American Sociological Review* 62:53–69.

Gordon, Steven. 1981. "The Sociology of Sentiments and Emotion." In *Social Psychology: Sociological Perspectives,* edited by Morris Rosenberg and Ralph H. Turnder, 551–75. New York: Basic Books.

Habermas, Juergen. 1984. *Reason and the Rationalization of Society.* Vol. 1 of *The Theory of Communicative Action.* Boston: Beacon Press.

Hamilton, James. 1992. "Patterns of Postpartum Illness." In *Postpartum Psychiatric Illness: A Picture Puzzle,* edited by James Alexander Hamilton and Patricia Neel Harberger, 5–14. Philadelphia: University of Pennsylvania Press.

Harberger, Patricia Neel, Nancy Gleason Berchtold, and Jane Israel Honikman. 1992. "Cries for Help." In *Postpartum Psychiatric Illness: A Picture Puzzle,* edited by James Alexander Hamilton and Patricia Neel Harberger, 41–60. Philadelphia: University of Pennsylvania Press.

Hercus, Cheryl. 1999. "Identity, Emotion, and Feminist Collective Action." *Gender and Society* 13:34–55.

Hays, Sharon. 1996. *The Cultural Contradictions of Motherhood.* New Haven: Yale University Press.

Hickman, Robert. 1991. "PPD's Impact on Fathers: Starting Support Groups for Men." *Heartstrings: The National Newsletter of Depression After Delivery* 2 (Summer): 1.

Hochschild, Arlie. 1979. "Emotion Work, Feeling Rules, and Social Structure. *American Journal of Sociology* 85:551–75.

———.1983. *The Managed Heart.* Berkeley: University of California Press.

Hochschild, Arlie, with Anne Machung. 1989. *The Second Shift: Working Parents and the Revolution at Home.* New York: Viking.

Hotchner, Tracy. 1984. *Pregnancy and Childbirth: The Complete Guide for a New Life.* New York: Avon Books.

Howard, Judith A., and Peter L. Callero. 1991. *The Self-Society Dynamic: Cognition, Emotion, and Action.* New York: Cambridge University Press.

Huber, Joan, and Glenna Spitze. 1983. *Sex Stratification: Children, Housework, and Jobs.* New York: Academic Press.

Hunt, Scott A., Robert D. Benford, and David A. Snow. 1994. "Identity Fields: Framing Processes and the Social Construction of Movement Identities." In *New Social Movements: From Ideology to Identity,* edited by Enrique Laraña, Hank Johnston, and Joseph R. Gusfield, 185–208. Philadelphia: Temple University Press.

Jack, Dana Crowley. 1991. *Silencing the Self: Women and Depression.* Cambridge: Harvard University Press.

Jasper, James. 1997. *The Art of Moral Protest: Culture, Biography, and Creativity in Social Movements.* Chicago: University of Chicago Press.

Jasper, James M., and Jane D. Poulsen. 1995. "Recruiting Strangers and Friends: Moral Shocks and Social Networks in Animal Rights and Anti-Nuclear Protests." *Social Problems* 42:493–512.

Jenkins, J. Craig. 1983. "Resource Mobilization Theory and the Study of Social Movements." *American Review of Sociology* 9:527–53.

Kaminer, Wendy. 1992. *I'm Dysfunctional, You're Dysfunctional: The Recovery Movement and Other Self-Help Fashions.* Reading, Mass.: Addison-Wesley.

Kemper, Theodore. 1978. *A Social Interactional Theory of Emotions.* New York: Wiley.

———. 1990. *Research Agendas in the Sociology of Emotions.* Albany: State University of New York Press.

Klandermans, Bert. 1984. "Mobilization and Participation: Social Psychological Expansions of Resource Mobilization Theory. *American Sociological Review* 49:583–600.

Kleiman, Karen R., and Valerie D. Raskin. 1994. *This Isn't What I Expected.* New York: Bantam.

Kleinman, Arthur. 1986. *Social Origins of Distress and Disease: Neuresthenia, Depression, and Pain in China.* New Haven: Yale University Press.

Korte, Diana, and Roberta Scaer. 1984. *A Good Birth, A Safe Birth.* New York: Bantam.

Lewin, Barbara R. 1992. "The Moon and the Mythbegotten: Distortions about PPD." *Heartstrings: The National Newsletter of Depression After Delivery* 3 (Winter into Spring): 2.

Lofland, John. 1985. *Protest: Studies of Collective Behavior and Social Movements.* New Brunswick, N.J.: Transaction Books.

Marwell, Gerald, and Pam Oliver. 1993. *The Critical Mass in Collective Action: A Micro-Social Theory.* New York: Cambridge University Press.

McAdam, Doug. 1982. *Political Process and the Development of Black Insurgency, 1930–1970.* Chicago: University of Chicago Press.

———. 1988. *Freedom Summer.* New York: Oxford University Press.

McAdam, Doug, John D. McCarthy, and Mayer N. Zald. 1988. "Social Movements." In *Handbook of Sociology,* edited by Neil Smelser, 695–737. Newbury Park, Calif.: Sage.

McCarthy, John D., and Mayer N. Zald. 1977. "Resource Mobilization and Social Movements: A Partial Theory." *American Journal of Sociology* 82:1212–41.

McGrath, Ellen, Gwendolyn Puryear Keita, Bonnie R. Strickland, and Nancy Felipe Russo. 1990. *Women and Depression: Risk Factors and Treatment Implications.* Washington, D.C.: American Psychological Association.

McMahon, Martha. 1995. *Engendering Motherhood: Identity and Self-Transformation in Women's Lives.* New York: Guilford Press.

Melucci, Alberto. 1989. *Nomads of the Present: Social Movements and Individual Needs in Contemporary Society.* Philadelphia: Temple University Press.

———. 1995. "The Process of Collective Identity." In *Social Movements and Culture,* edited by Hank Johnston and Bert Klandermans, 41–63. Minneapolis: University of Minnesota Press.

Mirowsky, John, and Catherine E. Ross. 1989. *Social Causes of Psychological Distress.* New York: Aldine de Gruyter.

Morris, Aldon D. 1984. *The Origins of the Civil Rights Movement: Black Communities Organizing for Change.* New York: Free Press.

Morris, Aldon D., and Carol McClurg Mueller, eds. 1992. *Frontiers in Social Movement Theory.* New Haven: Yale University Press.

O'Meara, Therese. 1992. "Out of the Darkness . . . into the Light," *Heartstrings: The National Newsletter of Depression After Delivery* 3 (Summer into Fall): 2.

"Postpartum Depression Feels Like a Thief." 1989. *Heartstrings: The National Newsletter of Depression After Delivery* (Fall): 3.

Reskin, Barbara, and Irene Padavic. 1994. *Women and Men at Work.* Thousand Oaks, Calif.: Pine Forge Press.

Robnett, Belinda. 1997. *How Long? How Long? African American Women and the Struggle for Freedom and Justice.* New York: Oxford University Press.

Romito, Patrizia. 1989. "Unhappiness after Childbirth." In *Effective Care in Pregnancy and Childbirth,* edited by Iain Chalmus, Murray Emkin, and Marc Keirse, 1433–46. New York: Oxford University Press.

———. 1990. "Postpartum Depression and the Experience of Motherhood." *Acta Obstetricia et Gynecologica Scandinavica* 69 Suppl. 154:5.

Ross, Catherine E., John Mirowsky, and Joan Huber. 1983. "Dividing Work, Sharing Work, and In-Between: Marriage Patterns and Depression." *American Sociological Review* 48:809–23.

Rupp, Leila J., and Verta Taylor. 1987. *Survival in the Doldrums: The American Women's Rights Movement, 1945 to the 1960s.* New York: Oxford University Press.

Scheff, Thomas J. 1990. *Microsociology: Discourse, Emotion, and Social Structure.* Chicago: University of Chicago.

Sciarra, John J., ed. 1989. *Gynecology and Obstetrics.* Philadelphia: Lippincott.

Segura, Denise A., and Jennifer L. Pierce. 1993. "Chicana/o Family Structure and Gender Personality: Chodorow, Familism, and Psychoanalytic Sociology Revisited." *Signs: Journal of Women in Culture and Society* 19:62–91.

Simonds, Wendy. 1992. *Women and Self-Help Culture: Reading between the Lines.* New Brunswick, N.J.: Rutgers University Press.

Smith-Lovin, Lynn. 1990. "Emotion as the Confirmation and Disconfirmation of Identity." In *Research Agendas in the Sociology of Emotions,* edited by Theodore D. Kemper, 238–70. Albany: State University of New York Press.

———. 1995. "The Sociology of Affect and Emotion." In *Sociological Perspectives on Social Psychology,* edited by Karen S. Cook, Gary Alan Fine, and James S. House, 118–48. Boston: Allyn and Bacon.

Smith-Lovin, Lynn, and William T. Douglass. 1992. "An Affect Control Analysis of Two Religious Subcultures. In *Social Perspectives on Emotions,* edited by David D. Franks and Victor Gecas, 217–47. Greenwich, Conn.: JAI Press.

Smith-Lovin, Lynn, and David R. Heise. 1988. *Analyzing Social Interaction: Advances in Affect Control Theory.* New York: Gordon and Breach Science Publishers.

Snow, David A., and Robert D. Benford. 1992. "Master Frames and Cycles of Protest." In *Frontiers in Social Movement Theory,* edited by Aldon D. Morris and Carol McClurg Mueller, 133–55. New Haven: Yale University Press.

Snow, David A., E. Burke Rochford Jr., Steven K. Worden, and Robert D. Benford. 1986. "Frame Alignment, Micromobilization, and Movement Participation." *American Sociological Review* 51:464–81.

Stryker, Sheldon. 1987. "The Interplay of Affect and Identity: Exploring the Relationships of Social Structure, Social Interaction, Self, and Emotion." Paper presented at the Annual Meetings of the American Sociological Association, Chicago.

Tarrow, Sidney. 1994. *Power in Movement: Social Movements, Collective Action, and Mass Politics in the Modern State.* New York: Cambridge University Press.

Taylor, Verta. 1989. "Sources of Continuity in Social Movements: The Women's Movement in Abeyance." *American Sociological Review* 54:761–75.

———. 1995a. "Self-Labeling and Women's Mental Health: Postpartum Illness and the Reconstruction of Motherhood." *Sociological Focus* 28:23–47.

———. 1995b. "Watching for Vibes: Bringing Emotions in the Study of Feminist Organizations." In *Feminist Organizations: Harvest of the New Women's Movement,* edited by Myra Marx Ferree and Patricia Yancey Martin, 223–33. Philadelphia: Temple University Press.

———. 1996. *Rock-a-by Baby: Feminism, Self-Help and Postpartum Depression.* New York: Routledge.

———. 1999. "Gender and Social Movements: Gender Processes in Women's Self-Help Movements." *Gender and Society* 13: 8–33.

Taylor, Verta, and Nicole C. Raeburn. 1995. "Identity Politics as High-Risk Activism: Career Consequences for Lesbian, Gay, and Bisexual Sociologists." *Social Problems* 42:252–73.

Taylor, Verta, and Marieke Van Willigen. 1996. "Women's Self-Help and the Reconstruction of Gender: The Postpartum Support and Breast Cancer Movements." *Mobilization: An International Journal* 1:123–42.

Taylor, Verta, and Nancy Whittier. 1992. "Collective Identity and Lesbian Feminist Mobilization." In *Frontiers in Social Movement Theory,* edited by Aldon D. Morris and Carol McClurg Mueller, 104–29. New Haven: Yale University Press.

———. 1995. "Analytical Approaches to Social Movement Culture: The Culture of the Women's Movement." In *Social Movements and Culture,* edited by Hank Johnston and Bert Klandermans, 163–87. Minneapolis: University of Minnesota Press.

"Telephone Contact Guidelines." 1991. *Volunteer Update, Depression After Delivery Newsletter* (January): 6.

Thoits, Peggy A. 1985. "Self-Labeling Processes in Mental Illness: The Role of Emotional Deviance." *American Journal of Sociology* 91:221–49.

———. 1990. "Emotional Deviance: Research Agendas." In *Research Agendas in the Sociology of Emotions,* edited by Theodore D. Kemper, 180–203. Albany: State University of New York Press.

Tilly, Charles. 1978. *From Mobilization to Revolution.* Reading, Mass.: Addison-Wesley.

White, Robert W. 1989. "From Peaceful Protest to Guerilla War: Micromobilization of the Provisional Irish Republican Army." *American Journal of Sociology* 94:1277–1302.

Whittier, Nancy E. 1995. *Feminist Generations: The Persistence of the Radical Women's Movement.* Philadelphia: Temple University Press.

14

Developing Working-Class Feminism: A Biographical Approach to Social Movement Participation

Silke Roth

The relationship between the women's movement and the labor movement traditionally has hovered between conflict and cooperation (e.g., Milkman 1990). In addition, the women's movement has often been described as a "white middle-class movement," implying that working-class women and "women of color" do not identify with feminist ideas.[1] Buechler (1990), for instance, argues that women align themselves with respect to the category in which they feel most oppressed. According to this notion, white middle-class women are assumed to stress gender, whereas working-class women supposedly focus on class and African American women are believed to emphasize the oppression due to their race.[2] Collins (1990) mentions the sometimes conflicting demands between Afro-centricity and feminism. However, surveys indicate that working-class women and "women of color" are at least as strong supporters of feminist ideas as white middle-class women, if not more so (e.g., Rinehart 1992). These findings suggest that supporting feminist ideas does not necessarily mean joining organizations of white middle-class feminists. Rather, according to recent studies on organizations of "women of color," the concept of feminist organizing needs to be expanded (e.g., Barnett 1995; Pardo 1995).

There have been several attempts to organize women across class lines and to integrate multiple memberships (Abrahams 1996; Albrecht and Brewer 1990; Bookman and Morgen 1988; Leidner 1993; Naples 1992). Organizations that aim at crossing racial, class, gender, and other lines have an especially difficult task in creating a collective identity that reflects the identities of a diverse membership. As Stryker (chapter 1, this volume) has pointed out, identities are rooted in groups, and thus commitments to social networks and social relationships, rather than in social categories. Members who belong to different social categories might develop a common identity through interaction in an organization. Thus the formation of new organizations can be employed as a strategy to reconcile conflicting identities. Kiecolt (chapter 5, this volume) analyzes how social movements change the self-concept. She identifies narrative, texts, and rituals as three means of identity work. Resnick (1996) analyzed how the tensions between Jewish identity and feminist identity were resolved through the formation of a Jewish feminist spirituality group.

In this chapter I provide a case study of the Coalition of Labor Union Women (CLUW), an organization that seeks to bridge the women's movement and the labor movement and provides a place for developing working-class feminisms. CLUW was formed during the mobilization for the Equal Rights Amendment (ERA), a key issue of the new women's movement. The AFL-CIO did not endorse the ERA before 1973, and women in the labor movement took different stances on the issue. Some saw it as a threat to hard-won protective legislation, whereas others welcomed it as a means for fighting discrimination at the workplace. I argue that CLUW members developed a variety of working-class feminisms as a result of differences in political socialization. I distinguish four membership types in this organization: founding mothers, rebellious daughters, political animals, and fighting victims. The collective identity of CLUW is affected by the participation of these types in the organization.

In the first part of the chapter I address the role of collective identity in social movement theory and describe the methodology I employed. Then I turn to my case study of the Coalition of Labor Union Women and introduce the four types of membership. Finally, I discuss how identities and participation of members are related to the collective identity of the organization. I conclude that activists developed a range of working-class feminisms and that there is a difference between the collective identity of an organization and the identities of its members.

Social Movements and Collective Identity

Collective identity plays a crucial role in the emergence and development of social movements and social movement participation (Laraña, Johnson, and Gusfield 1994; Melucci 1995; Morris and Mueller 1992; Whittier 1995). Processes of identity formation and framing link individuals and groups ideologically (Hunt, Benford, and Snow 1994). Although identity constructions were first analyzed in the context of "new" social movements, they are inherent in all social movements (Calhoun 1993). So far, the social constructivist approaches share with earlier social movement theories an emphasis on recruitment processes (e.g., Gamson 1992; Klandermans 1992).

Collective identity both precedes and results from collective action (Klandermans 1992) and can be analyzed with respect to movement participants and movement organizations. Students of social movements have addressed collective identity in four different ways: first, cognitive liberation (McAdam 1982; Piven and Cloward 1979) and group consciousness (Briet, Klandermans, and Kroon 1987; Klandermans and Oegema 1987; Klein 1987) as preconditions for collective action; second, collective action (Fantasia 1988), social movement communities (Evans and Boyte 1986; Melucci 1989), and social movements (Taylor and Whittier 1992) as sites for the development of collective identities; third, the effects of membership turnover on the collective identity of a social movement or social movement organization (Klandermans 1994; Mueller 1995; Whittier 1995); and, finally, the impact of movement participation and collective identities on activists' lives (Andrews 1991; McAdam 1988; Whalen and Flacks 1988).

Compared with processes of recruitment into activism, sustained participation and disengagement have found less attention among students of social movements (Klandermans 1997). Activists tend to remain committed to social change goals they pursue in social movements, and this commitment has significant effects on their work lives and personal relationships (Andrews 1991; McAdam 1988). Thus not only do collective identity and political consciousness arise out of "cultures of solidarity" at the workplace, in the neighborhood, in the street, and in the family; they also shape everyday interactions over the life course.

Although it has been noted that life histories of activists inform about the development of social movements (Evans 1979; McAdam 1988), a biographical perspective has found less use in the analysis of social movement organizations (but see Moore 1996; Whittier 1995). Moore (1996) argues that scientists' attempts at reconciling their political identity and their professional identity resulted in the invention of a new organizational form—the public interest science organization. Based on a comparison of three such organizations, Moore concludes that the background of the founding members has an impact on the collective identity that defines the legitimate strategic choices of the organization.

For instance, some feminists argue that feminism and bureaucratic structures are mutually exclusive (e.g., Ferguson 1984). According to this view, "nonhierarchical" grassroots organizations represent the only organizational form that is compatible with feminist principles. Others have argued that feminist goals are compatible with a wide range of organizational structures (Ferree and Martin 1995; Martin 1990). These authors suggest disentangling organizational forms and feminist goals and outcomes and overcoming a normative approach to feminist organizations. This does not mean that organizational form does not matter—on the contrary: the choice and the development of the organizational structure have an impact on the recruitment of new members (Staggenborg 1995; Strobel 1995), interaction with the state (Reinelt 1995), and coalitions with other movement organizations (Arnold 1995). Furthermore, the choice and the development of the organizational form are influenced by the political opportunity structure (Clemens 1993; Spalter-Roth and Schreiber 1995).

Thus, organizational form is not separable from, but is an expression of, the collective identity of a social movement or social movement organization. The collective identity defines what strategies and resources are compatible with the goals of the organization. Only when a strategy is perceived congruous with the collective identity of an organization does it become available. Especially in coalitions and in organizations with heterogeneous memberships, certain strategies might not be adopted because they are inconsistent with the identities of some of the participants.

A biographical perspective on social movement participation captures how collective identity of movements and movement organizations are shaped by their participants and vice versa.[3] Such an approach takes into account that some activists move from one movement to another and sustain multiple memberships over time. On the individual level, this results in processes of political socialization; on the organizational and movement level, this leads to social movement interaction and diffusion processes. Frames, strategies, and repertoires of action are transported from one movement to another through overlapping memberships and coalitions.

Data

My analysis is based on a case study of the Coalition of Labor Union Women (CLUW), which was founded in 1974. The goals of the organization are to bring women into union leadership, to organize unorganized women workers, to bring women's issues onto the labor agenda, and to involve women in political action. Regular membership is limited to union members. Nonunion members can hold associate membership, but they are excluded from the decision-making process in the organization. Members can be active at the local level in chapters and at the national level as delegates to the National Executive Board (NEB), which meets about three times each year. The constituency of CLUW comes from "old" and "new" social movements, the labor movement and the women's movement, and also attracts women who previously were not active in either one of these. The organization has a high proportion of "women of color," especially African American women, among the membership and the leadership. According to a survey (N = 524) I conducted in 1994 during an internship with the CLUW Center of Education and Research, about one-third of the respondents were minorities: 21 percent were African Americans, 6 percent were Hispanic Americans, 1 percent were Asian Americans, 2 percent were Native Americans, and 2 percent indicated that they belonged to "other" racial/ethnic groups. CLUW mirrors the higher unionization rate of "women of color" compared with white women: According to the Bureau of Labor Statistics, in 1996, 11 percent of the white women, 17 percent of the Afro-American women, and 12 percent of Hispanic women were unionized.

This chapter is based on the evaluation of life-history and in-depth interviews with members of the Coalition of Labor Union Women.[4] I interrogated current and former members of CLUW who were active at different levels of the organization, belonged to different racial and ethnic groups, were members of a variety of different unions, and represented union participation from voluntary local rank-and-file activism to national leadership. I conducted sixteen life-history interviews in which I employed an interview guide. Most of these life-history interviews were carried out with rank-and-file unionists and business agents of public sector and service sector unions in New England. I asked interviewees to start with their childhood and to tell me how their life developed and how they became involved in the labor movement and in the Coalition of Labor Union Women. These interviews lasted between two and four hours and were conducted with members who were active at the chapter level.

In addition, I interviewed officers and other activists at the national level as well as other activists representing the diversity of the membership of the organization with respect to regions (East Coast, West Coast, Midwest, South), union membership, and race and ethnicity. These interviews were conducted during conventions and breaks from work, mostly lunch breaks. Because of these time constraints, I therefore changed my interview strategy in the course of my research and simply asked interviewees to tell me *how they became involved in the union and in the Coalition of Labor Union Women.* These twenty-nine additional in-depth interviews varied in length from thirty minutes to two hours. Some interviewees referred to their childhood and the union membership of their parents, but others did not, depending on whether or not they found it relevant in the context of the interview. All forty-five interviews were entirely transcribed.

For the evaluatzion, I first summarized the context of the interview and the life history of the interviewee. I paraphrased her description of growing up, going to school, starting to work, and her family life or private relationships if she chose to talk about them, the circumstances under which she became involved in the labor movement and if she had been involved in other social movements, how she had learned about CLUW, what expectations she had about the organization, and how her participation in CLUW and the labor movement developed. In addition, I coded these interviews along six dimensions of political socialization: biographical continuity, agency, identity, interaction, injustice, and resources (Roth 1997).

These six dimensions of political socialization are overlapping rather than mutually exclusive and served as lenses through which I focused on different aspects of the socialization process and captured the development of social movement participation and political consciousness. Under the dimension *biographical continuity* I collected the accounts of the recruitment into and the development of the participation in the union, CLUW, and other social movement activities and voluntary associations. Some interviewees traced their political involvement to their childhood, when they joined parents or grandparents in demonstrations or on picket lines. Other interviewees related their involvement to turning points such as divorce or the death of a spouse or a child. Under the dimension *agency* I compiled accounts of power and powerlessness, efficacy and empowerment with respect to participation in the union and in CLUW. The dimension *identity* focused on accounts of political consciousness such as feminist consciousness or class consciousness as well as race or ethnic consciousness. Here I looked for self-definitions as "feminists" and "union people" as well as interviewees' references to their Christian or Jewish upbringing and their accountability to these traditions. For the dimension *interaction* I searched for accounts of conflict and cooperation within the context of CLUW and the union. Under the dimension *injustice* I looked for descriptions of discrimination experiences. Some interviewees reported that they had been discriminated against, for instance, through lower pay or sexual harassment. Others did not speak about such personal experiences but described how they observed that others were discriminated against. For instance, some white women spoke about racial discrimination from the perspective of an observer, while "women of color" shared experiences of race discrimination. In the dimension *identity* the focus lies on the self-definition of the interviewee, whereas the dimension *injustice* emphasized experiences of interviewees. Finally, the dimension *resources* encompassed accounts of skills, knowledge, and connections that activists brought to social movement activism and those they acquired through activism. I compared the interviews across the six dimensions. In this process the membership typology I present in this chapter emerged.

Developing Working-Class Feminism

The four ideal types—founding mothers, rebellious daughters, political animals, and fighting victims—vary in how they became involved in the labor movement. I found that members' recruitment processes and their positions in their unions are related to their political identities (identifications with the labor movement, feminist consciousness, and race consciousness), their identification of CLUW as part of the women's movement and the labor movement, and their participation in the Coalition of Labor Union Women. The four versions of working-class feminism I have identified relate to members' varying perceptions of and participation in the Coalition of Labor Union Women. Founding mothers and most rebellious daughters participated in the founding convention of CLUW or joined the organization in the early years. The political animals and the fighting victims became members of the Coalition of Labor Union Women later on.

The *founding mothers* were already leaders in the labor movement and familiar with the women's movement before they came together to form the Coalition of Labor Union Women. Most of them were born in the 1920s and 1930s and looked back on long-standing involvement in the labor movement; some of them participated in the organization of the CIO unions in the 1940s. The founding mothers took different paths to the labor movement: from the assembly line or graduate school, from progressive movements, from the Jewish community, the Roman Catholic Church, and some Protestant churches. They joined the union as rank-and-file members, volunteer organizers, or staff members. What unites the founding mothers across these differences was that they were pioneers in the labor movement—they were the first women, whether white, African American, or Hispanic, to hold offices or staff positions in their unions. They are officers or staff at the national or regional level in their unions, or they held these positions prior to retirement. They are active at the national level of CLUW as officers or members of the National Executive Board. Some of the founding mothers are also active in the civil rights and the women's movements and seek to integrate women's and civil rights issues into the labor movement. The founding mothers constitute a considerable portion of the officers and activists at the national and the local level. Aleeta Walker, an African American woman and former director of the women's and civil rights department of an international union who was in her seventies and retired at the time of the interview, described the motivation of the founding mothers in the following words:[5]

> There were networks building up in the political arena, religious women, women of other groups were building networks. And many of us who were in the organized labor movement were a part of these networks but we did not have our *trade union identity* and we thought that was most important. And then we sought to call together women trade unionists wherever they were and we formed the Coalition of Labor Union Women.

Walker described the founders of CLUW as part of the women's movement but emphasized their identity as women trade unionists. Mansbridge (1995) describes the women's movement as a discourse consisting of a set of aspirations and understandings that provide "conscious goals, cognitive backing, and emotional support for each individual's evolving feminist identity" (27). The identification with the labor movement is expressed in the accountability toward the labor movement. The founding mothers emphasize that the organization worked within the framework of the labor movement. They seek the approval of the labor movement and perceive the endorsement and support through the AFL-CIO or individual unions as success. Some refer to CLUW as the "women's AFL-CIO." This is reflected in the structure of the organization. At the conventions, CLUW members come together as representatives of their unions. Union delegates are seated together with members of their union, rather than with other CLUW members from the same state or region.[6] Participants in floor discussions were asked to identify themselves by stating their name and their union affiliation before they made a statement.

In contrast to the founding mothers, the *rebellious daughters* see CLUW more as a *working women's movement.* They are a more homogeneous group than the founding mothers with respect to their recruitment into the labor movement. They were born in the 1940s and 1950s and were active in the social movements of the sixties and seventies before they became active in the labor movement. For a number of rebellious daughters, the farmworkers union represents their first contact with the labor movement; others were members of feminist organizations such as Nine to Five or Union Wage. June Feldman, a white woman in her forties and a staff member of a service sector union, recalled how she felt about the formation of CLUW:

> So, I was excited, I thought, "great, we got a *working women's movement.*" . . . And CLUW had been a forum and a central focus for a lot of women who have feminist concerns but as working class women don't see the feminist movement as their primary movement. . . . I came out of an interesting background. And I have always been a feminist. And when I started working in the labor movement my class consciousness became much more . . . uncovered. . . . Much more. I had a political consciousness. I was part of the socialist movement in this country. But CLUW was a place where I could merge the two, I could be a feminist and I could be a class conscious working woman.

Rather than seeking the approval of the AFL-CIO and the unions, the rebellious daughters are interested in organizing and empowering unorganized working women. Organizing the unorganized is one of the four stated goals of the Coalition of Labor Union Women. However, it is interpreted differently by the founding mothers and the rebellious daughters. For the founding mothers it means supporting organizing drives when they are invited by a union and providing organizing training. The rebellious daughters are disappointed by the lacking effort of the AFL-CIO and many unions to organize women workers more aggressively. Therefore, rather than asking these unions to organize women workers, the rebellious daughters became organizers, business agents, and labor lawyers of unions that organize sectors of the labor market in which women are working. They tend to work for unions that represent, for instance, clerical workers and health care workers. These are the unions with a higher proportion of women among the union leadership that are supportive of pay equity, sexual harassment education, and abortion rights. Furthermore, some of the rebellious daughters work with unorganized working women outside the labor movement, for instance, through providing legal advice or information about sexual harassment.

Founding mothers and rebellious daughters perceive the women's movement as a movement of white middle-class feminists who overlook the interests of working-class women and "women of color." They emphasize not only that CLUW bridges the women's movement and the labor movement and thus creates an organization for working women but also that CLUW is the most racially integrated women's organization. Shelley Turner, a white woman in her thirties and staff member of a state AFL-CIO, who lives in an interracial marriage and has been involved in antiracist work for a long time, recalled that she was very attracted by CLUW's diversity of membership.

> When I walked into the general plenary session of the NEB as an observer and saw a mixed race group, I was floored. To be honest with you, I hadn't seen a mixed race group like that in the labor movement, in the women's movement, anywhere before, and I remember that moment very clearly. [Turner is very moved.] I felt that there was hope. And it was something I had always been looking for.

The integration of different racial and ethnic groups is also a concern of My Chang, a Chinese American woman in her forties and a staff member of a textile workers union. Chang went to college during the sixties and participated in the civil rights movement and the antiwar movement and supported the strike of the farmworkers. After graduating from college, she was involved in the formation of a new Asian American studies program. For about twenty years she worked as a community organizer, a teacher in the immigrant community, and an adjunct professor in ethnic studies. Her interest in women's issues and her support for women's rights began when she went to college. She said, however:

> One problem that I always had with the white feminist movement in the United States was that sometimes their issues became very divorced from say the minority women in the United States who mostly . . . had children, had families. The feminist movement at different stages . . . really rejected marriage, rejected families and so in that sense seemed to reject the experience of a lot of women of color because all of us had kids, had families. . . . We didn't view women's rights as one, as being against all men, or rejecting the whole question of families and children. So we looked at issues like child care, . . . health care and all those issues were very important. And I think at different stages the feminist movement in the U.S. tended to just kind of ignore or that was not an essential thing to them.

According to Chang, CLUW broadened the agenda of the women's movement and the labor movement. Chang became involved in the labor movement when some strikes of restaurant workers and garment workers were carried out in the Chinese community. After starting to work for a union, Chang had to learn to "shift gears" from community activism to labor movement activism. Chang gives CLUW credit for keeping her in the labor movement, because she felt "very alienated" from the labor movement. CLUW offers her the opportunity to continue the fight for women's rights and to address the concerns of working women.

The founding mothers come from the "old" labor movement; the rebellious daughters, from the "new" social movements. Thus, the two types represent to a certain extent different styles of organizing and empowerment in these movements. For the founding mothers it is important to develop a working-class feminism that is consistent with their trade union identity: they aim at seeking the approval of the labor movement and joining it. Part of the political socialization of the rebellious daughters was the participation in the prefigurative politics (Breines 1982) of the New Left. As a result, the rebellious daughters are much more vocal than the founding mothers about the racism and sexism in the labor movement—and racism in the women's movement—and seek more "union democracy." Although most of the rebellious daughters continue to be active in the labor movement, at times they still feel like outsiders in it.

Most of the political animals and the fighting victims joined CLUW later and were not involved in the founding of the organization. Thus the conflicts between the labor movement and the New Left, and the women's movement and the labor movement, are less salient and less relevant to them. Like the founding mothers, the *political animals* were born in the 1920s and 1930s. After graduating from high school, some of the political animals attended business school or a teachers college. Marriage and motherhood were the next important steps in the biographies of the political animals. They became involved in community organizing and local politics, PTAs, Girl Scouts and Boys Scouts, and the like. These involvements were connected to their lives in the neighborhood and to motherhood. Some became involved in labor organizing prior to becoming union members themselves as a result of their involvement in the community.

The political animals perceive their union participation as an extension and natural progression of their political involvement in community politics and the Democratic Party. They belong to the executive boards of their local unions and to the labor council and committees of the state AFL-CIO and are outspoken rank-and-file activists. The political animals are telephone operators, clerical workers in the public sector, and teachers. Thus they have occupations that are female-dominated and organized by public sector unions and other unions that have a high proportion of women members and support women's leadership at the local level as well as the participation of their women members in the Coalition of Labor Union Women. The political animals came into contact with the women's movement through the Coalition of Labor Union Women. From their perspective, the distinction between the labor movement and the women's movement appeared much less pronounced or even blurry. Heather Stone, an Irish American woman in her sixties and a business agent of a public sector union, perceives CLUW as her *springboard for women's issues* and answered my question, how she would situate CLUW with respect to the women's movement and to the labor movement, in the following way:

> It's more a part of the women's movement or the labor movement? I don't think you can separate them. . . . I think it's *women who happen to be in labor who are pushing for issues.* . . . The women's movement or the labor movement? . . . Which will become secondary? Good question. I think it's issues. Do we push for work place issues? Maybe not. What issue do we push for in the work place? Just sexual harassment, otherwise it's all women's issues and reproductive rights and rights for women. So it probably was women's rights.

This example shows that it is not obvious for Stone how to draw boundaries around the women's movement and the labor movement. Although she finally concluded that CLUW pursues "women's issues," it does not appear relevant for her to distinguish between women's issues and workers' issues in the context of CLUW.

The example of the political animals exemplifies that political socialization is an ongoing process and that through participation in political and other organizations members acquire and share knowledge and skills. Although the political animals are self-confident participants in mixed-sex political organizations, they appreciate the all-female support that they experience at the local CLUW chapter and the meetings of the National Executive Board. CLUW is a resource and "another hat" for this type.

In contrast to the previous three types, who had been politicized in social movements and community politics and emphasize that they are active on behalf of others who are less resourceful and articulate, the *fighting victims* became politically active after they had been discriminated against.[7] The fighting victims differ with respect to age, marital status, race, and nationality. The white fighting victims married shortly after graduating from high school and started to work outside the home after a divorce. The African American and Chinese fighting victims worked for pay before they became divorced. All fighting victims started their professional career in low-level clerical and factory jobs. The participation of the political victims in the labor movement and the Coalition of Labor Union Women is grounded in the experience of being treated unfairly. They experienced that union membership and education improved their job opportunities. The union became instrumental in changing their life situation, by providing them with benefits, job security, and in several cases an opportunity for upward mobility within the union. Furthermore, the fighting victims became politicized through their union activity, for instance, in the fight for comparable worth or against sexual harassment. After they improved their own lives, they wanted to contribute to the betterment of other people's lives as shop stewards or volunteer organizers. Then they moved up from rank-and-file activists to officers and staff members. Samantha Torrel—a white woman in her sixties, an administrative assistant in a hospital, and the president of a public sector union local—explained how she became a feminist:

> The civil rights movement had a lot to do with it and getting divorced had a lot to do with my becoming more of a feminist because I had to do a man's job in order to earn a living. Then I went to [work at the hospital] and it was rammed down my throat again that I was in a women's job. When there's somebody who's an illiterate who can make more money than you doing something that you do home for free—carry boxes around and scrape dishes. I mean that was his job. Was my job more valuable to the state while I was a secretary or was his job more valuable? . . . So it just grew. You know, it wasn't my saying: "I'm going to be a feminist." It just kind of grew like topsy, that's all. Things like that happen to you, I guess. I don't know. It wasn't a conscious thing, my saying "I'm going to become a feminist." It was deciding what was right and going in that direction.

Torrel was not active in the civil rights movement, but the events during the Freedom Summer campaign, to which she referred in the interview, opened her eyes to injustice. The civil rights movement thus provides an injustice frame (Gamson 1992) within which she interprets her experience at work.

The fighting victims see the union as a tool for supporting women's interests. Like the political animals, most fighting victims belong to unions that are strong supporters of the Coalition of Labor Union Women. They joined CLUW in order to acquire leadership skills and tended to leave CLUW when they found that the organization no longer offered them training or other support.[8]

The contrast between the rebellious daughters and the founding mothers suggests that the types can be perceived in terms of generational units (Mannheim 1952; Whittier 1995). Mannheim (1952) distinguishes between *generation location,* or being born within the same historical and social region, and *generation as an actuality,* "where a concrete bond is created between members of a generation by being exposed to the social and intellectual symptoms of a process of dynamic destabilization" (303). Furthermore, within the actual generation Mannheim identifies separate *generation units* that respond to their common experience in different specific ways (304). Whittier (1995) introduced the term *microcohorts* in order to account for variations within political generations.

However, although there are certain affinities, none of these concepts fully corresponds with my typology. First, only one of the types, the rebellious daughters, represents generation as an actuality. The rebellious daughters have experienced the emergence of the social movements of the sixties and seventies when they attended college. But these movements also represent an important context for the political socialization for the other types. Second, the founding mothers, political animals, and fighting victims encompass more than one generation. Mannheim's (1952) concept of generational units and Whittier's (1995) concept of microcohorts emphasize the differences within generations, whereas I observed similarities and differences across generations. Third, the four types experienced the labor movement and the women's movement differently not only because these movements changed over time but also because within the movements different branches need to be distinguished. Thus women who joined the labor movement at the same time but became members of different unions experience the labor movement differently. Furthermore, rank-and-file members have a different perspective on the labor movement than staff members and officers. The four types of members with their different working-class feminisms have shaped the collective identity of CLUW in different ways and have conflicted on some points.

Organizational Structure, Participation, and Collective Identity

The Coalition of Labor Union Women experienced a number of conflicts at its founding convention and throughout the following years. These conflicts concerned the question of membership, the support for the farmworkers union, and union democracy (Glick 1983). The founding mothers argue that the membership should be restricted to union members. They emphasize that the organization takes up women's issues and broadens the agenda of the women's movement and the labor movement *within the framework of the labor movement.* Some of the rebellious daughters initially wanted to open CLUW membership to women who are not yet union members. Mildred Sequira, a white woman in her forties and a staff member of a service sector union, is one of the rebellious daughters who remained active in the Coalition of Labor Union Women and is now convinced that it was the right decision to restrict the membership to union members:

> We lost on that question. And in retrospect I am not certain it was a bad decision at all. I mean at that time I felt very strongly that we should be including all working women. But as the years have gone by, I think the fact that CLUW does just represent women in unions has given us more credibility within the labor movement than we would have had if we would have been viewed just as a women's movement or organization. It gave us an *official status within the labor movement.* That's important I think to help push the agenda that we are fighting for. So that issues like child care, working family issues, pay equity had to be taken more seriously by the leadership of our unions. Because *we were part of the unions* and pushing for it.

Sequira represents those rebellious daughters who adopted the perspective of the founding mothers. Sequira thus provides an example of socialization processes that take place through participation in the Coalition of Labor Union Women.

Margitta Guirard, another rebellious daughter, is a white woman in her early fifties, a former union organizer and labor educator who quit her activity in CLUW and the labor movement. She left the organization after attending a national CLUW convention in 1977. She explained her disappointment in the Coalition of Labor Union Women with her description of CLUW's national convention in 1977, which she compared to AFL-CIO conventions.

> But [at AFL-CIO conventions] there was always that little expectation that you could start a floor fight [laughs]. That you could somehow throw a wrench in the works. There was always this feeling that it was not completely sewed up. But that feeling completely was gone in Washington [at the CLUW convention], there was not a desire to throw a wrench in the works. There wasn't, everything was like silk, or every speaker was positive, . . . nobody said anything nasty, there were no fights. Everybody agreed to everything. It was like a convention of the Stepford Wives. It was like surreal, it was so weird. Everything was like this choreographed, you know. Part of it was, I think that people loved CLUW so much at that time that they thought that everything they wanted was happening. . . . Somehow they had resolved the Teamsters issue. They had resolved the Farmworker issue, they had resolved the who's-gonna-run-it-issue. All the resolutions were great, everybody was great, everyone was happy, everything was fine. . . . And there were very few people there. And like after a few hours, I got, I either have to get out of there or I am gonna fall asleep. . . . And I

> knew then, that there was something irrelevant about CLUW. I couldn't explain it. It wasn't like anybody had sold out or anybody had like, it was not like anybody was really fucked up. It was just, *it was just another inside organization.*

Guirard represents the rebellious daughters who are convinced that CLUW should be an outside organization. Outside organizations in this sense do not seek the endorsement of, for example, the labor movement, nor do they feel accountable to the labor movement. Such a strategy has costs and benefits. Outside organizations do not receive financial support, but they are free to criticize the practices of—in this case—the labor movement.

Some rebellious daughters perceive the cooperation with the AFL-CIO and the unions as co-optation. This group of rebellious daughters is no longer active in CLUW, although some are still dues-paying members. Some of them formed or became involved in outside organizations that target unorganized women workers.

The "Teamsters issue" and the "Farmworkers issue" constituted the second major conflict at CLUW's founding convention. Some participants thought that CLUW should support the United Farmworkers in a dispute with the Teamsters. Others argued that such an endorsement would alienate the Teamsters and hamper a broad coalition among union women. Through the decision not to support the farmworkers union, CLUW demonstrated that it would take a neutral position in jurisdictional disputes. This demonstration of neutrality was an important sign not only for the Teamsters but also for the entire labor movement. Glick (1983) argues that the leadership took this position against the will of the rank-and-file members, including rank-and-file Teamster members. The dispute signified the loyalty and accountability of the founding mothers toward the labor movement. Furthermore, the outcome of the dispute was a setback for the rebellious daughters, some of whom first became involved in labor issues through the farmworkers campaign.

In contrast to Klandermans's (1994) findings, in the case of CLUW the collective identity of the organization is shaped more by the *persisters* (the founding mothers) than by the *shifters* (the rebellious daughters). The bureaucratic structure of the organization makes it easier to maintain the original structure and reduce the influence of incoming members (Mueller 1995; Staggenborg 1989). However, there have been organizational changes as well. In 1978, the CLUW Center for Education and Research was created as a tax-exempt, nonprofit organization designed to seek funds for projects such as training programs, research about working women, and the development of materials. Compared with CLUW as a whole, the CLUW Center for Education and Research appears to be less accountable to the labor movement and more involved with organizations of the women's movement.

Furthermore, in the 1980s a Hispanic caucus and a Chinese caucus were formed within the New York City chapter of the Coalition of Labor Union Women. These caucuses allow immigrant women workers to communicate in their native language and to pursue their cultural traditions. At the same time the women become acquainted with the U.S. labor movement and learn about current political issues and women's rights.[9] The caucuses allow them to develop working-class feminisms that include their ethnic identities. This is expressed in the symbol of the Chinese CLUW caucus. Angela Itt, a Chinese American woman in her fifties and a staff member of a textile workers union, described the symbol to me.

> So this is our symbol for the Coalition of Labor Union Women. This symbol was designed from one of our members [a Chinese activist], and, he is artist, he is teacher, he designed this for us.[10] So this is a Chinese symbol. You know we are asking for equal. And this bamboo means "stay strong.". . . If you see that flower, you know it is from China. This means "stay strong" and this means "equal."

The symbol of the Chinese caucus of the Coalition of Labor Union Women consists of the Chinese symbols representing power and equality. In traditional Chinese society women are not equal. The creation of the symbol of the Chinese CLUW caucus, however, stands for continuity with respect to ethnic identity and transformation of this identity in a way that allows for a Chinese feminist identity that did not have a place in Chinese women's homeland. The symbol therefore exemplifies the construction and reconstruction of culture (Tuchman and Levine 1993) and is an example of cultural appropriation (Fantasia and Hirsch 1995; McAdam 1994).

Conclusion

The membership typology encompasses a variety of working-class feminisms that were formed in political socialization processes over the life course. The working-class feminism of the founding mothers emphasizes their trade union identity, whereas the working-class feminism of the rebellious daughters is anchored in a feminist critique of the labor movement and a critique of the racial and class biases of the women's movement. The working-class feminism of the political animals is issue-oriented and values the labor movement and the women's movement as equally important and mutually supportive. The working-class feminism of the fighting victims evolved from discrimination experiences and the fight against discrimination in the context of the labor movement and the Coalition of Labor Union Women. All four types of working-class feminism emphasize equality and justice regardless of race, class, and gender and see these as dimensions that need to be addressed equally.

The formation of the Coalition of Labor Union Women is cause and consequence of these working-class feminisms. The structure, and thus the collective identity, of the organization reflect this variety only to a certain extent. The collective identity of the Coalition of Labor Union Women spans the working-class feminism of the founding mothers, political animals, and fighting victims, but not that of the rebellious daughters. Some rebellious daughters left the organization, but others adopted the view of CLUW as an inside organization. The formation of the Hispanic caucus and the Chinese caucus was possible because the identification with the labor movement was guaranteed. However, the inclusion of nonunion members in some chapters, which reflected the desire of rebellious daughters to include more—nonunionized—working women, was discouraged.

My case study of the Coalition of Labor Union Women demonstrates that personal and social change are interrelated and take place in interaction in socialization processes and the reconstruction of collective identity. The analysis of the life histories of activists captures the construction of collective identity on the individual and the organizational levels. The interactions between these membership groups and the negotiations through which they assess the political opportunity structure constitute the collective identity of the organization.

The formation of the Coalition of Labor Union Women is a result of the emergence of the new women's movement and the diffusion of feminist consciousness. Those who participated in the founding of CLUW sought to reconcile feminist identities, trade union identities, and activist identities. CLUW contributes role models, training possibilities, "free spaces," and visibility for women in the labor movement. Although the number of women in leadership positions is still limited, CLUW contributes to bringing child care, sexual harassment, and pay equity to the labor agenda and thus successfully engages in discursive politics (Katzenstein 1995). In addition, the organization is acknowledged as one of—if not *the*—most inclusive feminist organization in the United States.

Notes

This chapter was originally presented as a paper at the conference "The Relation of Social and Personal Identities and Self-Esteem: New Frontiers, New Implications," organized by Timothy J. Owens, Sheldon Stryker, and Ligaya Lindio-McGovern. I gratefully acknowledge the generosity of my interview partners for sharing time and insights with me. I thank Danielle Currier, Myra Marx Ferree, Timothy Owens, Lynn Resnick, Clint Sanders, Sheldon Stryker, Gaye Tuchman, and Bob White for helpful comments on earlier versions of this chapter. This research was supported through a dissertation stipend of the Hans Böckler Foundation, a Dissertation Fellowship from the Graduate School of the University of Connecticut, and a Summer Fellowship of the Department of Sociology of the University of Connecticut.

1. By putting the phrase *women of color* in quotation marks, I seek to distance myself from the notion that white women do not have race (Frankenberg 1993).

2. This differentiation is far from exhaustive. Not only are Asian women and Hispanic women neglected, and therefore ethnicity, but also religion and sexual orientation.

3. Of course, social movements and movement organizations are embedded in the political opportunity structure, while activists are also influenced by the experiences they make, for instance, at work or in the family.

4. In addition to the life-history and in-depth interviews, I conducted about forty expert interviews with members of the Coalition of Labor Union Women and with members of women's movement organizations and labor movement organizations. Furthermore, I attended meetings at the national and local levels between 1993 and 1995.

5. The name Aleeta Walker and all the following names are pseudonyms.

6. Chapter delegates are seated together with other members of the chapter. However, chapters are rarely represented by more than one delegate and one alternate.

7. This does not mean that the other three types have not been discriminated against or that they did not talk about such experiences, but that they did not frame these experiences as a trigger for their political participation and involvement in the women's movement or other social movements.

8. CLUW offers leadership training at the local level and the national level through educational workshops and conferences. The activities at the local level are mostly designed for rank-and-file members with little experience. There are fewer activities for union officers and staff members.

9. The inclusion of social, recreational, and cultural activities has a tradition in women workers education programs (Kornbluh and Frederickson 1984).

10. Men are admitted to CLUW membership. According to the survey that I conducted in 1994, 13 percent of the respondents were men.

References

Abrahams, Naomi. 1996. "Negotiating Power, Identity, Family, and Community: Women's Community Participation." *Gender and Society* 10:768–96.

Albrecht, Lisa, and Rose M. Brewer, eds. 1990. *Bridges of Power: Women's Multicultural Alliances.* Philadelphia: New Society Publishers.

Andrews, Molly. 1991. *Lifetimes of Commitment: Aging, Politics, and Psychology.* Cambridge: Cambridge University Press.

Arnold, Gretchen. 1995. "Dilemmas of Feminist Coalitions: Collective Identity and Strategic Effectiveness in the Battered Women's Movement." In *Feminist Organizations: Harvest of the New Women's Movement,* edited by Myra Marx Ferree and Patricia Yancey Martin, 276–80. Philadelphia: Temple University Press.

Barnett, Bernice McNair. 1995. "Black Women's Collectivist Movement Organizations: Their Struggle during the Doldrums." In *Feminist Organizations: Harvest of the New Women's Movement,* edited by Myra Marx Ferree and Patricia Yancey Martin, 199–219. Philadelphia: Temple University Press.

Bookman, Ann, and Sandra Morgan, eds. 1988. *Women and the Politics of Empowerment.* Philadelphia: Temple University Press.

Breines, Wini. 1982. *Community and Organization in the New Left.* New Brunswick, N.J.: Rutgers University Press.

Briet, Martien, Bert Klandermans, and Frederike Kroon. 1987. "How Women Become Involved in the Women's Movement of the Netherlands." In *The Women's Movements of the United States and Western Europe: Consciousness, Political Opportunity, and Public Policy,* edited by Mary Fainsod Katzenstein and Carol McClurg Mueller, 44–63. Philadelphia: Temple University Press.

Buechler, Steven. 1990. *Women's Movements in the United States: Woman Suffrage, Equal Rights, and Beyond.* New Brunswick, N.J.: Rutgers University Press.

Calhoun, Craig. 1993. "'New Social Movements' of the Early Nineteenth Century." *Social Science History* 17:385–428.

Clemens, Elisabeth S. 1993. "Organizational Repertoires and Institutional Change: Women's Groups and the Transformation of U.S. Politics, 1820–1920." *American Journal of Sociology* 98:755–98.

Collins, Patricia Hill. 1990. *Black Feminist Thought: Knowledge, Consciousness, and the Politics of Empowerment.* London: Routledge.

Evans, Sara. 1979. *Personal Politics.* New York: Vintage Books.

Evans, Sara M., and Harry C. Boyte. 1986. *Free Spaces: The Sources of Democratic Change in America.* New York: Harper and Row.

Fantasia, Rick. 1988. *Cultures of Solidarity.* Berkeley: University of California Press.

Fantasia, Rick, and Eric L. Hirsch. 1995. "Culture in Rebellion: The Appropriation and Transformation of the Veil in the Algerian Revolution." In *Social Movements and Culture,* edited by Hank Johnston and Bert Klandermans, 144–59. Minneapolis: University of Minnesota Press.

Ferguson, Kathy E. 1984. *The Feminist Case against Bureaucracy.* Philadelphia: Temple University Press.

Ferree, Myra Marx, and Patricia Yancey Martin, eds. 1995. *Feminist Organizations: Harvest of the New Women's Movement.* Philadelphia: Temple University Press.

Frankenberg, Ruth. 1993. *White Women, Race Matters: The Social Construction of Whiteness.* Minneapolis: University of Minnesota Press.

Gamson, William. 1992. "The Social Psychology of Collective Action." In *Frontiers in Social Movement Theory,* edited by Aldon D. Morris and Carol McClurg Mueller, 53–76. New Haven: Yale University Press.

Glick, Phyllis Sharon. 1983. "Bridging Feminism and Trade Unionism: A Study of Working Women's Organizing in the United States." Ph.D. diss., Brandeis University.

Hunt, Scott A., Robert D. Benford, and David A. Snow. 1994. "Identity Fields: Framing Processes and the Social Construction of Movement Identities." In *New Social Movements: From Ideology to Identity,* edited by Enrique Laraña, Hank Johnston, and Joseph R. Gusfield, 185–208. Philadelphia: Temple University Press.

Katzenstein, Mary Fainsod. 1995. "Discursive Politics and Feminist Activism in the Catholic Church." In *Feminist Organizations: Harvest of the New Women's Movement,* edited by Myra Marx Ferree and Patricia Yancey Martin, 35–52. Philadelphia: Temple University Press.

Klandermans, Bert. 1992. "The Social Construction of Protest and Multiorganizational Fields." In *Frontiers of Social Movement Research,* edited by Aldon D. Morris and Carol McClurg Mueller, 77–103. New Haven: Yale University Press.

———. 1994. "Transient Identities?: Membership Patterns in the Dutch Peace Movement." In *New Social Movements: From Ideology to Identity,* edited by Enrique Laraña, Hank Johnston, and Joseph R. Gusfield, 185–208. Philadelphia: Temple University Press.

———. 1997. *The Social Psychology of Protest.* Oxford: Blackwell.

Klandermans, Bert, and Dirk Oegema. 1987. "Potentials, Networks, Motivations, and Barriers: Steps towards Participation in Social Movements." *American Sociological Review* 52:519–31.

Klein, Ethel. 1987. "The Diffusion of Consciousness in the United States and Western Europe." In *The Women's Movements of the United States and Western Europe: Consciousness, Political Opportunity, and Public Policy,* edited by Mary Fainsod

Katzenstein and Carol McClurg Mueller, 23–43. Philadelphia: Temple University Press.

Kornbluh, Joyce L., and Mary Frederickson, eds. 1984. *Sisterhood and Solidarity: Workers' Education for Women, 1914–1984.* Philadelphia: Temple University Press.

Laraña, Enrique, Hank Johnson, and Joseph R. Gusfield, eds. 1994. *New Social Movements: From Ideology to Identity.* Philadelphia: Temple University Press.

Leidner, Robin. 1993. "Constituency, Accountability, and Deliberation: Reshaping Democracy in the National Women's Studies Association." *NSWA Journal* 5:4–27.

Mannheim, Karl. 1952. "The Problem of Generations." In *Essays on the Sociology of Knowledge,* edited by Paul Kecskemeti, 276–321. London: Routledge and Kegan Paul.

Mansbridge, Jane. 1995. "What Is the Feminist Movement?" In *Feminist Organizations: Harvest of the New Women's Movement,* edited by Myra Marx Ferree and Patricia Yancey Martin, 27–34. Philadelphia: Temple University Press.

Martin, Patricia Yancey. 1990. "Rethinking Feminist Organizations." *Gender and Society* 4:182–206.

McAdam, Doug. 1982. *Political Process and the Development of Black Insurgency, 1930–1970.* Chicago: University of Chicago Press.

———. 1988. *Freedom Summer.* New York: Oxford University Press.

———. 1994. "Culture and Social Movements." In *New Social Movements: From Ideology to Identity,* edited by Enrique Laraña, Hank Johnston, and Joseph R. Gusfield, 36–57. Philadelphia: Temple University Press.

Melucci, Alberto. 1989. *Nomads of the Present: Social Movements and Individual Needs in Contemporary Society.* Philadelphia: Temple University Press.

———. 1995. "The Process of Collective Identity." In *Social Movements and Culture,* edited by Hank Johnston and Bert Klandermans, 41–63. Minneapolis: University of Minnesota Press.

Milkman, Ruth. 1990. "Gender and Trade Unions in Historical Perspective." In *Women, Politics, and Change,* edited by Louise A.Tilly and Patricia Gurin, 87–107. New York: Russell Sage Foundation.

Moore, Kelly. 1996. "Organizing Integrity: American Science and the Creation of Public Interest Organizations, 1955–1975." *American Journal of Sociology* 101:1592–1627.

Morris, Aldon D., and Carol McClurg Mueller, eds. 1992. *Frontiers in Social Movement Research.* New Haven: Yale University Press.

Mueller, Carol. 1995. "The Organizational Basis of Conflict in Contemporary Feminism." In *Feminist Organizations: Harvest of the New Women's Movement,* edited by Myra Marx Ferree and Patricia Yancey Martin, 263–75. Philadelphia: Temple University Press.

Naples, Nancy. 1992. "Activist Mothering: Cross Generational Continuity in the Community Work of Women from Low-Income Urban Neighborhoods." *Gender and Society* 6:441–63.

Pardo, Mary. 1995. "Doing It for the Kids: Mexican American Community Activists, Border Feminists?" In *Feminist Organizations: Harvest of the New Women's Movement,* edited by Myra Marx Ferree and Patricia Yancey Martin, 356–71. Philadelphia: Temple University Press.

Piven, Francis Ford, and Richard Cloward. 1979. *Poor Peoples Movements: Why They Succeed, How They Fail.* New York: Vintage Books.

Reinelt, Claire. 1995. "Moving onto the Terrain of the State: The Battered Women's Movement and the Politics of Engagement." In *Feminist Organizations: Harvest of the New Women's Movement,* edited by Myra Marx Ferree and Patricia Yancey Martin, 84–104. Philadelphia: Temple University Press.

Resnick, Lynn. 1996. "Sifting through Tradition: The Creation of Jewish Feminist Identity." Masters thesis, Department of Sociology, University of Connecticut.

Rinehart, Sue Tolleson. 1992. *Gender Consciousness and Politics.* New York: Routledge.

Roth, Silke. 1997. *Political Socialization, Bridging Organization, Social Movement Interaction: The Coalition of Labor Union Women, 1974–1996.* Ph.D. diss., University of Connecticut.

Spalter-Roth, Roberta, and Ronnee Schreiber. 1995. "Outsider Issues and Insider Tactics: Strategic Tensions in the Women's Policy Network during the 1980s." In *Feminist Organizations: Harvest of the New Women's Movement,* edited by Myra Marx Ferree and Patricia Yancey Martin, 105–27. Philadelphia: Temple University Press.

Staggenborg, Suzanne. 1989. "Stability and Innovation in the Women's Movement: A Comparison of Two Movement Organizations." *Social Problems* 36:75–92.

———. 1995. "Can Feminist Organizations be Effective?" In *Feminist Organizations: Harvest of the New Women's Movement,* edited by Myra Marx Ferree and Patricia Yancey Martin, 339–55. Philadelphia: Temple University Press.

Strobel, Margaret. 1995. "Organizational Learning in the Chicago Women's Liberation Union." In *Feminist Organizations: Harvest of the New Women's Movement,* edited by Myra Marx Ferree and Patricia Yancey Martin, 145–64. Philadelphia: Temple University Press.

Stryker, Sheldon. 1980. *Symbolic Interactionism: A Social Structural Version.* London: Benjamin-Cummings.

Taylor, Verta, and Nancy E. Whittier. 1992. "Collective Identity in Social Movement Communities: Lesbian Feminist Mobilization." In *Frontiers of Social Movement Research,* edited by Aldon D. Morris and Carol McClurg Mueller, 104–29. New Haven: Yale University Press.

Tuchman, Gaye, and Harry Gene Levine. 1993. "New York Jews and Chinese Food: The Social Construction of an Ethnic Pattern." *Journal of Contemporary Ethnography* 22:382–407.

Whalen, Jack, and Richard Flacks. 1989. *Beyond the Barricades: The Sixties Generation Grows Up.* Philadelphia: Temple University Press.

Whittier, Nancy. 1995. *Feminist Generations: The Persistence of the Radical Women's Movement.* Philadelphia: Temple University Press.

15

Personal and Collective Identities and Long-Term Social Movement Activism: Republican Sinn Féin

Robert W. White and Michael R. Fraser

In August 1994, the Provisional Irish Republican Army declared a cease-fire, fully supported by its political wing, Provisional Sinn Féin. Six weeks later, Protestant paramilitaries declared their own cease-fire. Peace had broken out; it appeared this was the beginning of the end of political conflict in Northern Ireland. Yet, in January 1996, it was announced in *Saoirse,* Republican Sinn Féin's paper, that a Continuity Army Council (CAC) of the IRA had been created in 1986. In July 1996, soldiers of the Continuity IRA blew up the Killyhevlin Hotel, in Enniskillen, County Fermanagh, demonstrating that the cease-fire did not apply to them.[1]

Who are Republican Sinn Féin and the Continuity IRA? An easy answer to this question is that they are the traditionalists who split from Provisional Sinn Féin and the Provisional IRA in 1986 when these two organizations embraced constitutional politics, as described below. A more complete answer requires an understanding of the personal and collective identities of those involved in these organizations. We posit that there has developed in Ireland a group of Irish Republicans who, consistent with their interpretation of what it is to be a Republican, will support and organize military activity for as long as there is a British presence in Ireland. When the Provisional IRA declared its cease-fire in 1994, this made the need for "true" Republicans that much more pressing. Recent events have not yet satisfied this need.

We examine the personal and collective identities of the founders of Republican Sinn Féin. Members of this organization have internalized a particular interpretation of what it is to identify as an Irish Republican—

the biographical, historical, and political circumstances of these persons' lives have shaped their understanding of Irish Republicanism and framed their movement activism.[2] Their interpretation of who they are—their identities and their belief systems—motivates their participation in the Republican movement. We also show how a collective Irish Republican identity, the shared sense of "we" experienced by members of a social movement (e.g., Cohen 1985; Eyerman and Jamison 1991; Tarrow 1992; Touraine 1981, 1985), developed out of the personal identities of these people.

Data Sources

Our data are primarily from intensive interviews with Irish Republicans, part of a larger project begun in 1984 focusing on why people become involved in the Irish Republican movement.[3] Since 1995, attempts have been made to reinterview 1984/85 respondents. One topic of this research is how and why splits occur in revolutionary organizations.

Three key respondents, founding members of Republican Sinn Féin (RSF), were reinterviewed in 1995. Also interviewed in 1995–97 were twelve other RSF activists. These interviews are complemented by data from several sources, including reinterviews with former and current members of Provisional Sinn Féin (PSF) and/or the Provisional IRA (PIRA) who were first interviewed in 1984; interviews with former Republican activists and non-Republican political activists in Ireland; and a 1994 interview with an officer of RSF. We have also examined Irish Republican literature, including pamphlets and newspapers. Finally, our data are informed by regular, personal interaction with Irish Republicans and former Republicans.

Republican Identities and Abstentionism: The Origins of Republican Sinn Féin

Personal and Collective Identities

The personal identity of a social movement activist refers to the unique, individual nature of the activist's self as a member of a social movement. It is the sense of continuity and identification with, integration in, and differentiation from a social movement that is not structured in terms of the individual's cultural and community expectations but rather the individual's subjective experiences as a movement activist (Hewitt 1989). Personal identities exist situationally, as individuals engage in relationships with other people and recognize and agree with the identity others in the relationship use to describe them. Personal identities act as "internalized positional designations" (Stryker 1980, 60–61) that locate and define individuals within a group, such as a social movement. Identities have "salience" for individuals (Stryker 1968, 1980). For example, in certain situations, an activist identity may be more salient for an individual than his husband identity. Further, the importance of identities may change over time. For long-term movement activists, their movement participant identity remains salient throughout the course of their participation.

Melucci (1995) defines the collective identity of a social movement as "an interactive and shared definition produced by several individuals (or groups at a more complex level) and concerned with the orientations of action and the field of opportunities and constraints in which the action takes place" (44; see also Melucci 1985, 1989). Collective identity is defined similarly by Taylor and Whittier (1992). For them, a movement's collective identity "derives from members' common interests, experiences, and solidarity" (104).

As we view it, the collective identity of a social movement develops from shared aspects of the personal identities of movement activists (Fraser 1996; see also Gamson 1992, 60). For activists, what it means to be an activist has many dimensions and may vary greatly across activists in the same social movement organization (SMO). The key to their involvement for some may be a high commitment to the movement's goal; for others, high solidarity with other activists. At the individual level, some aspects of the meaning of activism for one activist may even conflict with aspects of the meaning of activism for other activists. Collective identity develops when aspects or dimensions of being an activist are congruent across groups of activists.[4] Thus, a goal-oriented activist may also appreciate the solidarity benefits of activism, and presumably an activist primarily motivated by solidarity also supports a movement's goals (see also Brown and Williams 1984).

Social movement organizations are composed of subgroups of activists. We suspect that, among members of subgroups, their individual-level movement identities are relatively homogeneous. Across subgroups of activists, however, the degree to which these movement identities mesh into a collective identity may vary.[5] By its nature, then, a social movement's collective identity is negotiated and subject to change (Klandermans 1992, 1994). Further, individual activists, and subgroups of activists, have a solidarity with and commitment to ("we-ness") fellow activists and a movement in general, but these are varied and subject to change (Gamson 1992, 61).

In locating the origin of a movement's collective identity in the personal identities of the movement's founders, we recognize that a movement's collective identity exists at the sociocultural level (e.g., Gamson 1995, 100). As we view it, collective identity links personal identities, and from this emerges a "we-ness." This "we-ness," however, need not be exclusively solidarity-like. The individuals who come together probably share high levels of solidarity and friendship, but it may also be commitment to a goal that brings them together. Further, although a movement's collective identity may develop out of the personal identities of its founders, over time new recruits may reconstruct their personal identities to fit the collective identity of what has become an ongoing movement (chapter 13, this volume). Thus, a movement's collective identity is influenced by and influ-ences the personal identities of its activists (chapter 14, this volume).

Republican Identities

An Irish Nationalist is a person who wants all of Ireland to be ruled by Irish people. An Irish Republican, at its most basic level, is someone who "seeks to separate Ireland from England by force" (Cronin 1980, 23). Most Irish are Nationalists; few are Republicans.

The identity of an "Irish Republican" is, like all personal identities, rooted in social interaction. At the personal level, there are several dimensions to the Irish Republican identity. For Republicans in general, their most significant interactions are with three groups: (1) fellow Republicans; (2) the British government and other authorities who uphold British rule in Ireland; and (3) former Republicans who reject Republicanism. Two key beliefs of Irish Republicans—the belief that a British withdrawal from Ireland can be gained only through force and that constitutional politics are corrupting—developed from interaction with the British and from interaction with former Republicans who opted for constitutional politics.

Because Republicans advocate revolutionary goals and support political violence, they are in the minority, kept under close surveillance, and often harassed by security forces in Northern Ireland, the Irish Republic, and Britain. These conditions restrict interaction such that Republicans tend to interact with other Republicans, ultimately strengthening the movement's collective identity, because it reinforces participants' identification with the movement and strengthens the solidarity among activists.

The following is from a member of Provisional Sinn Féin. She joined the Republican movement in the early 1970s. From Northern Ireland, she was forced to flee because of the political situation there. She now lives in southern Ireland. In describing her friendships with other Republicans, it is clear that harassment by the security forces—north and south—framed her involvement in the movement:

INTERVIEWER: Today would most of your friends be Republicans?
RESPONDENT 1: All my friends are Republicans.
I: Okay. Is that because of the nature of Republicanism?
RESPONDENT 1: No, it's the nature of censorship and black propaganda. . . . There's a huge effort to isolate and marginalize and demonize Republicans not just in the political sense but also in the very much social and personal sense as well. . . . [The authorities want] to crush it—us, to isolate you totally. And they did that in the North. They did that by killing people of course. Ehm, down here they did it by demonizing you. But also by, like, a whole campaign of anybody that had contact with you would get a visit from the [Special] Branch [of the police], or their workplace [would be visited], or if they were young people their parents would be visited and told, you know, who they're associating with. The IRA—that sort of stuff.
I: So if somebody would move in near you and—
RESPONDENT 1: Oh, like a neighbor or even children that played with your children [would be visited by the Special Branch]. . . . I had that happen to my children, yes. . . .
I: Does that—does that pressure then make the camaraderie among Republicans greater?
RESPONDENT 1: Well, obviously, yeah.

Republicans maintain that Britain is the source of the problems facing the Irish nation. Britain, centuries ago, conquered Ireland. In 1920, against the wishes of the vast majority of the Irish people, Britain partitioned Ireland, creating Northern Ireland and the Irish Free State (declared a republic in 1949). The British also created two parliaments on the island, one in Belfast for Northern Ireland (populated primarily by descendants of seventeenth-century colonizers who tend to be pro-British and Protestant) and one in Dublin for the Free State (where the vast majority of the people are Catholic and view themselves as Irish). Today, Britain maintains the partition just as it maintained its presence in Ireland for centuries—through force.

Irish-British interaction has produced an "oppositional dimension" that is part of the Republican identity (e.g., Taylor and Whittier 1992). Central to this dimension are two beliefs: (1) the British government cannot be trusted, and (2) the only thing the British government responds to is force. This is revealed in the following discussion with a member of Republican Sinn Féin, during the Provisional IRA cease-fire in 1995.

INTERVIEWER: Given the current situation in the North, is there still a role for armed struggle?
RESPONDENT 2: . . . Going on the history of the past you look at it and you say the British never moved out of any place, they never did

> anything until their backs were to the wall with a gun. Maybe present day England are going to have a different way of doing it. I don't know. Of course, I certainly—at the moment in the situation that we're in there is no way that the IRA should decommission their weapons. And leave themselves to the mercy of the British government at the moment.

These comments were echoed by a member of Provisional Sinn Féin, also interviewed in 1995. Asked to comment on the possibility that the IRA might decommission its weapons, he stated:

> INTERVIEWER: If the IRA would change its mind and decommission, in your opinion, do you think the British would then be forthcoming in, in—
>
> RESPONDENT 3: No. I think that the British have a history and a record of being the most devious bastards—and I am not going to change my opinion.

For Republicans, former comrades opting for constitutional politics are sellouts. Abstention from the Dublin parliament dates from 1922.[6] When Britain partitioned Ireland in 1920, Irish rebels, of the Irish Republican Army and the political party Sinn Féin, ignored this and fought on for a united Irish Republic, which had been declared by earlier rebels in 1916. In 1922, however, a rebel parliament in Dublin, Dáil Éireann, ratified a treaty with the British maintaining partition, containing an oath of allegiance to the British monarch, and keeping the "Irish Free State" in the British commonwealth. For those opposed to the treaty, those who voted for the treaty "betrayed the Republic" (Cronin 1980, 132). The former referred to the Dublin government as Leinster House, where it meets, rather than the Dáil. In their eyes, the Second Dáil Éireann, in power at the time of the treaty, remained the true government of Ireland (it had never been formally dissolved).

The split in 1922 was a precursor to additional splits in the Republican movement in 1926, 1946, and 1969/70. Prior to each split, those who advocated political participation claimed they would remain true to their Republican ideals. After each split, in the eyes of those who remained "true," those who left opted for political gain over principle. Each split heightened and made more homogeneous the collective identity of the Republican movement; always, a more "pure " movement remained. On several occasions, converts to constitutional politics virulently denounced, and some who achieved political power actively repressed, their former comrades, confirming the purist's belief that constitutional politics corrupt.

In December 1969, at its convention, the IRA voted to endorse the participation of Irish Republicans in constitutional politics. A minority of the delegates agreed that this violated Republican principles. They met again soon after the convention and formed the "Provisional" IRA, in contrast to the "Official" IRA, which endorsed constitutional politics. In January 1970, the political wing of the Republican movement, Sinn Féin, also split. Those who rejected constitutional politics walked out of the Sinn Féin Ard-Fheis and formed Provisional Sinn Féin. Those who supported the Official IRA were then referred to as Official Sinn Féin. From the foundation of the Provisional IRA and Provisional Sinn Féin through the early 1980s, abstention from constitutional politics was accepted as part of being a Provisional Irish Republican. If elected to either the Dublin parliament, the parliament in Belfast, or the Westminster Parliament, Republicans refused to take their seats. For Republicans, the partitionist parliaments in Dublin and Belfast were imposed on the Irish by the British government; they were illegitimate. Westminster was a legitimate parliament, but only in Britain, not in Ireland. These beliefs formed an uncontested dimension of the Irish Republican collective identity. Beginning in the early 1980s, however, an increasing number of Republicans came to believe that the movement would benefit tactically if it participated in the constitutional politics of the Irish Republic (Bell 1993). Ultimately, disagreement over the implications of involvement in constitutional politics became so important that it split the movement. A key concern of those in Republican Sinn Féin is the belief that Provisional IRA cease-fires, in 1994–96 and 1997 to date, are part of a process, begun in 1986, that will ultimately result in the Provisionals being co-opted by politics and settling for less than "the Republic."

Republican Sinn Féin: The Roots of Their Identities

Republican Sinn Féin was formed in November 1986. At the Provisional Sinn Féin Ard-Fheis (convention) that year, a resolution that the party drop its abstentionist policy toward the Dublin parliament obtained the required two-thirds of the delegates' votes. A number of delegates—one hundred or so—walked out of the convention, reassembled elsewhere, and formed RSF (Bell 1993).

In 1986, opposition to dropping abstentionism was rooted in both Republican principle and practical politics. As a principle, how could ending abstentionism be reconciled with more than sixty years of refusal to participate in Leinster House? Republicans had died for this principle. As a tactic, there was ample evidence that participation in constitutional politics leads to moderation, not a republic.[7] Why would participation in 1986 be different? We examine the development of these beliefs at the personal and collective level of those who created RSF.

Republican Families

The founding board of officers of Republican Sinn Féin had six members. They were Ruairí Ó Brádaigh, Des Long, Cathleen Knowles, Joe O'Neill, Frank Graham, and the late Daithí O'Connell. These people shared many characteristics. For example, each had Republican parents.

Being from Republican families, these people had personal connections through their parents with the events leading to abstentionism. Daithí O'Connell's uncle, Michael Sullivan, was killed by British soldiers in 1921 (*The Last Post* 1985, 133–34). Cathleen Knowles's father, Eamonn Mooney, active in the IRA in Scotland in the 1920s, spent five years in prison for his efforts. She describes her mother as "an unrepentant Republican" (personal interview; "Cathleen Knowles" 1990).

Ruairí Ó Brádaigh describes himself as a "ready made" Republican (personal interview). Born in 1932, he joined Sinn Féin in 1950 and the IRA in 1951. By 1959, he was chief of staff of the IRA. In 1969, he was on the initial Provisional IRA Army Council. From 1970 until 1983 he was president of Provisional Sinn Féin. Currently, he is president of Republican Sinn Féin. In 1919, Ó Brádaigh's father, while attempting to seize arms, was shot, never fully recovering. Until his death in 1942, he was an uncompromising Republican. Ó Brádaigh's mother was in Cumann na mBan, the women's wing of the Republican movement, in the 1918–22 time period. A lifelong Republican, she allowed her home to be used as a safe house in the 1950s.

The following is from a lifelong Republican. Born in 1933, he joined the Republican movement in 1956. In 1986, he joined Republican Sinn Féin.[8] He offers a sense of the people who joined RSF.

> RESPONDENT 4: My mother's, mother, was [pause] a great Republican, she was. But prior to—all our lives, and up to the very end, when she died in the early 1960s, she remained true. And her brother died in 1933, who would be a granduncle of mine. I didn't know him now, he died the year I was born, but he was a man—he never accepted any Free State, good, bad, or indifferent. And uh, my grandmother always told me that he would never have changed. There's a funny thing that I, sort of thing there, that I nearly couldn't be anything else only. I was born to that tradition, and that faith.

There was a cost associated with the path his family chose. His father was offered a job with the new Free State government. He refused it:

RESPONDENT 4: As a matter of fact, when the Free State was set up, my father—[was offered a] court clerkship. It mightn't have been such a great job at that time, but it grew into a good job down to here, but he refused to take it.

For the respondent, the refusal to recognize the Dublin government is a moral decision, and the commitment to Republicanism is like a religious commitment. He describes this.

RESPONDENT 4: Nationality and religion and all this sort of— but that was one thing my grandmother always taught was that religion and Republicanism sort of went hand in hand.
INTERVIEWER: Oh really?
RESPONDENT 4: Aye, you know, went hand in hand there.
I: In what way?
RESPONDENT 4: Well, in the sense that you lived up to certain standards. And Republicanism is something that you have to be very honest—you just can't change for the sake of changing, or you can't change because somebody says to you, "Ahh, we'll go another path." There's a moral thing in it, you know, that kind of thing.

The belief that the Dublin government is illegitimate was passed from one generation to another.

INTERVIEWER: In your opinion is Leinster House a legitimate government of Ireland?
RESPONDENT 4: No, no, no, it was, they are the result of the British Government of Ireland Act [1920]. In no way, morally or any other ways, it's not. And that's one of the reasons why I would oppose it. In no shape or form there. The best of men could be alive today, Cathal Brugha [killed during the Irish civil war] and all those others, if they wanted to accept it then. And that was the sort of thing there, the pressure that was put on them. Liam Mellows [executed December 8, 1922] for instance. They postponed his execution, to see would he accept it. . . . They, they postponed it for a short bit of a time to see would he accept it. This sort of thing there. The pressure was on the—to accept this as legitimate. In no way. No way, no way, I have no doubt at all about that there.
I: Would you have always thought that?
RESPONDENT 4: I always, I always, but I had learned that, as I said, from my grandmother, and then I came along there and reading history and all that, I found out for myself. I have no doubt at all about that there.

For many of those who joined Republican Sinn Féin, their decision to do so was made in 1986, but it was a decision that was informed by a mix of their upbringing and an identification with the movement's ideology. For many, joining RSF was a decision also informed by their personal experience with previous splits in the Republican movement.

Previous Experience with Splits in the Republican Movement

Several of those who formed Republican Sinn Féin have twice walked out of a Sinn Féin Ard-Fheis and created a rival Republican organization. In December 1969, at its convention, the IRA voted to drop its ban on entering Westminster, Stormont, and Leinster House. Those opposing the change met again and formed the Provisional IRA. In their eyes, dropping abstentionism was unconstitutional and, therefore, those who did it were no longer Republicans (Bell 1979; White 1993). In January 1970, an attempt to drop abstentionism at the Sinn Féin Ard-Fheis failed to achieve the required two-thirds majority. Those supporting the change proposed a motion that endorsed the leadership of the "Official IRA." This only required a majority vote. At this, those supporting the Provisionals walked out and formed Provisional Sinn Féin.

The people on the first Provisional IRA Army Council were Seán MacStiofáin (chief of staff), Ruairí Ó Brádaigh, Daithí O'Connell, Paddy Mulcahy, Sean Tracey, Leo Martin, and Joe Cahill. The Caretaker Executive of Provisional Sinn Féin was formed in January 1970. Many of those who founded the Provisional IRA were on the Executive, including Ruairí Ó Brádaigh, Seán MacStiofáin, and Paddy Mulcahy. Sixteen years later, almost all who formed the Provisionals and were still active in Republican politics joined Republican Sinn Féin. Of the twenty-four people on either the 1969 PIRA Army Council or the 1970 PSF Caretaker Executive, twelve were still involved in Republican politics. Ten of the twelve joined Republican Sinn Féin, including three of the party's first officers: Ruairí Ó Brádaigh (PSF, PIRA), Daithí O'Connell (PIRA), and Des Long (PSF) (see White 1993).

The "young" people who formed the Provisionals in 1969–70 were Republican veterans of the 1950s (e.g., Ruairí Ó Brádaigh, Daithí O'Connell, and Seán MacStiofáin). They were complemented by a number of older Republicans who had experienced earlier splits in the movement. These were people such as Joe Clarke, Larry Grogan, and Tony Ruane. By 1970, each had been in the Republican movement for more than half a century.

Larry Grogan's career is particularly interesting. He joined the IRA after the 1916 rebellion, remaining involved in the movement the rest of his life. He was arrested in the 1920s, the 1930s, the 1940s, and the 1950s. In the 1950s, his son Tommy was interned with him in the Curragh Camp.

Grogan was elected to the IRA Army Council in 1938. In that year, then IRA chief of staff Sean Russell sought out the surviving members of the Second Dáil Éireann who had remained faithful to the Republican cause. He asked them to authorize the 1939–45 IRA campaign, which they did. They also codified the illegitimacy of the governments at Stormont and Leinster House by transferring to the IRA Army Council the right to establish a de jure government of the Republic. At this, abstentionism formally became a principle, and Larry Grogan became, in Republican eyes, a member of the government of the "true" Irish Republic (see Bell 1979, 154–55, 178–80).

The influence of people like this on those who formed first the Provisionals and later Republican Sinn Féin was very important. Ruairí Ó Brádaigh gave the oration at Grogan's funeral in 1979. Ó Brádaigh described Grogan's career:

> Larry was interned once more, this time in Mountjoy jail [in Dublin], and was one of the Republican prisoners filing through the central circle of the prison to Mass on the Feast of the Immaculate Conception, December 8th 1922, when they heard the volleys which executed Rory O'Connor, Liam Mellows, Dick Barrett and Joe McKelvey. All four IRA leaders had been taken from their cells during the night and executed without trial on the orders of the Free State government. . . .
>
> [In the 1930s] he was arrested with other Republican leaders, brought before the military tribunal operated by the collaborationist Dublin government and imprisoned again in Mountjoy.
>
> He took part in the jail confrontations that followed and suffered the trauma of the fifty-six day hunger strike for political status of his brother and fellow prisoner Tommy Grogan, during which Tony D'Arcy of Galway and Sean McNeela of Mayo died.
>
> From Mountjoy to Arbour Hill and thence to the Curragh went Larry Grogan, while the Free State firing-squads executed Republicans and even the British hangman was brought over to Dublin in 1944 to end the life of the twenty-six year old IRA Chief-of-Staff of the time, Charlie Kerins from Tralee.
>
> Released in 1945, Larry resumed once more the path of duty. He was denied his employment in the local government service in Drogheda because he would not sign an undertaking to cease Republican activity.
>
> These were the events which had moulded Larry Grogan when those of us of a younger generation came to know him and to serve

> alongside him. Dr. Bowyer Bell, the American historian of the IRA, whose book *"The Secret Army"* is littered with references to Larry refers to him as a *"solid, taciturn man from Drogheda."*
>
> But to us he was a father-figure, an inspiration, a direct link with the past. Padraig Pearse, the centenary of whose birth we have just celebrated, has said that service was the great test of a person's nationalism and Larry surely has qualified many times. ("Larry Grogan" 1979)

The founders of the Provisional IRA and Provisional Sinn Féin were viewed by those who stayed in what became the Official IRA and Official Sinn Féin as "custodians of an irrelevant past" (Bell 1979, 368). The Provisionals did view themselves as "custodians," but saving the movement from ruin by keeping it Republican. This interpretation was confirmed for them. The Official IRA and Official Sinn Féin, they believed, were destined for extinction because of their decision to become involved in constitutional politics. According to the Provisionals, the prediction came true. On the military side, in the early 1970s, the Official IRA carried out a limited military campaign. Then, on May 29, 1972, it declared a unilateral cease-fire (Flackes and Elliott 1994). In "true Republican" terms, they abandoned armed struggle against the British presence. On the political side, in the late 1970s Official Sinn Féin changed its name to Official Sinn Féin/The Workers' Party. In 1982, the party became simply The Workers' Party. Even to external observers the name change "was clearly designed to dissociate itself from charges of paramilitarism" (Flackes and Elliott 1994, 356). That is, they were rejecting their Republican past. The Officials also became severe critics of their former comrades.

Consider the following from a member of Republican Sinn Féin. Not from a Republican family, he joined Sinn Féin in the 1950s. In 1970, he helped form Provisional Sinn Féin. In 1986, he helped form Republican Sinn Féin. He describes why participation in constitutional politics will corrupt the Republican movement.[9]

> INTERVIEWER: Is Leinster House the legitimate government?
> RESPONDENT 2: . . . If you go with the old Republican Parliament and we go back to the time of Tom Maguire [the Second Dáil Éireann, in 1922] . . . they'll say that Leinster House is not [legitimate]—that they never got a mandate to do what they did.
> I: Uh-hmm. So what's your opinion on it?
> RESPONDENT 2: Well, it may not be legitimate—but it is the de facto [government]. . . . It may not be the de jure but I think at this stage there's no one going to change it. It is the de facto now at the moment and . . . what can you do about it like? It's just there, a

> clause in an argument now I suppose. It's gone so deep into history.
>
> I: If that's your opinion, why did you go with Republican Sinn Féin?
>
> RESPONDENT 2: Well, I, I went with Republican Sinn Féin because they—I could see that the other lads were, you see, and I knew from my own background too that when you get a taste of politics after a while a lot of people want to go for the political scenario. And the political scenario, once you accept it you're bound by it. So then, where does the Republican movement go for it to keep a legitimate Republican movement? The heart and soul has gone out of it.
>
> I: What do you mean by a legitimate Republican movement?
>
> RESPONDENT 2: One that would keep, you see, the primary purpose for the Irish Republican movement on the card. And that is the British go and we have a united Ireland. Now, you see, if you take all the people that joined the Workers' Party and all these, they're all gone out of it. They've gone the full circle of the wheel and they have just forgotten about [a united Ireland]. As a matter of fact, some of them are maybe the worst adversaries that the Republican movement has.

Ideologically, two dimensions of the general Republican identity were key to the creation of Republican Sinn Féin. First, many founders rejected the validity of participation in the Dublin parliament. Fundamentally, such participation was immoral. Second, even for those willing to accept the Dublin government as a fait accompli, participation in that government is bad politics. It leads to corruption, a focus on politics, and the loss of the "heart and soul" of the Republican movement. Agreement across individual Republicans on these two dimensions of the general Republican identity forms the core of the collective identity of Republican Sinn Féin.

Embedding Identities in Social Interaction

The founders of Republican Sinn Féin share several characteristics. Many are from Republican families, and many were involved with the split of the movement in 1969–70. In addition, many were recruited into the Republican movement in the 1950s (e.g., all but Cathleen Knowles of the first board of officers), and many were born and raised in the Republic/Free State (nineteen of twenty-one persons on the founding board of officers and organizing committee).

They also share interaction with one another, routinely confirming their personal and collective commitment to the movement. For example, Respondent 4 was asked a question concerning interaction with other Republicans prior to the Ard-Fheis in 1986:

INTERVIEWER: Going into the Ard-Fheis, would you have pretty much been aware that there's a very good chance there's gonna be a split?
RESPONDENT 4: Well, there was great rumors and talk sort of thing, yeah, there was rumors and talks. All that sort of thing there. . . .
I: Would you have—would you have, talked to people about it?
RESPONDENT 4: Oh yeah, oh yeah, I talked to—within my own county sort of thing there. . . . I talked to people around, and you know, I talked to people, I talked to other Republicans, too—sort of thing. Looking for ordinary people who, that might be just—well, for their advice, even though I had my own mind made up. . . . You just can't be doing things just because, you know? You have to have grounds, and moral grounds for doing a thing before you.
I: Of the people you went—you were talking to about it, would most of them have thought like you, and—
RESPONDENT 4: Well, they would, they would. Some of them would. . . . [Some] might be saying there's some other way, that sort of thing. Eh, but, yeah, they wouldn't be so sure, you know? . . .
I: Would you have talked to Ruairí Ó Brádaigh before the split?
RESPONDENT 4: Oh, I would, I would. Because he was always like, in communication with us, by virtue of the fact that we were in the next county and he is a Longford man . . . and we'd be at meetings, and he'd be at them and I'd be at them and it could come up for discussion. You know?

For those who created Republican Sinn Féin, joining the party was a natural extension of their interaction with other like-minded people, their upbringing, and their shared experiences. Respondent 4 describes his reaction and the reaction of his friends to the events at the Ard-Fheis.

INTERVIEWER: Did uh, many of your friends leave also for Republican Sinn Féin?
[Pause]
I: Friends who are Republicans?
RESPONDENT 4: Ah yes, a lot, yes, aye, aye, the majority of whom I was involved with . . . even the prior ones [splits] there when the Officials and all that, I hadn't nearly hadn't to think of which was right and which was [wrong]. I wouldn't count that a problem at all to know what side I should be on.

Similar comments were offered by Respondent 2.

INTERVIEWER: You would have been in a local cumann [local Sinn Féin organization], right?

RESPONDENT 2: Yeah.
I: Of your local cumann did any of those people go with Provisional Sinn Féin?
RESPONDENT 2: Eh, no.
I: No?
RESPONDENT 2: No, no, none of them.

These accounts are consistent with data collected from a third supporter of Republican Sinn Féin. He is from Belfast and was born in the 1930s. From a Republican family, he joined the IRA in the early 1950s. He helped form the Provisional IRA in 1969 and joined Republican Sinn Féin in 1986. He has known Ruairí Ó Brádaigh for more than forty years. When asked if he was surprised that Ó Brádaigh had walked out of the Ard-Fheis when abstentionism was dropped, he replied that he would have been more surprised if Ó Brádaigh had not walked out.

These accounts may be contrasted with accounts from members of Provisional Sinn Féin who stayed with the Provisionals in 1986. These respondents were interviewed in 1984; two were reinterviewed in 1996, the third in 1997. They were asked questions about the split in 1986.

Respondent 5 was born in 1948. From North Belfast, he joined the movement in 1970. Respondent 6 was born in 1953. From West Belfast, he joined the IRA in the mid-1970s. Respondent 7 was born in 1957. From County Monaghan, he joined Sinn Féin in 1979. None of the three is from a Republican family. Each is significantly younger than many of the people who joined Republican Sinn Féin. Each of them supported the dropping of abstentionism. They were asked to comment on the choice their friends made in 1986. Although they knew people who left for RSF, or who opposed the dropping of abstentionism, their accounts show that the "vast majority" of their Republican contemporaries remained with Provisional Sinn Féin.

INTERVIEWER: Any of your friends leave for Republican Sinn Féin?
RESPONDENT 5: Yeah, [prominent Republican], from [outside of Belfast].
I: Oh yeah [Name deleted].
RESPONDENT 5: Aye. [Name deleted is] a friend of mine. . . .
I: Yeah. Would most of the people in Belfast, though, have stayed with the leadership?
RESPONDENT 5: Vast majority. Vast majority . . . very [few] people from Belfast went with RSF.
I: Are you in a local cumann?
RESPONDENT 5: Yeah.

I: Would anybody in the cumann have left?
RESPONDENT 5: No.
I: No?
RESPONDENT 5: No, nobody from North Belfast went with RSF at all.
I: Would you have had any friends—close friends, Republican friends—walk out, go with Republican Sinn Féin?
RESPONDENT 6: No close friends walked out. I certainly had one good friend who didn't walk out. She didn't, eh, allow herself to be used by the media. But who would not work for Sinn Féin afterwards and hasn't since.
I: Really. Okay, one out of—I mean—
RESPONDENT 6: Well, one out of, I don't know, scores.
I: When the split came [in 1986] would you have had any close friends who left for Republican Sinn Féin, or—
RESPONDENT 7: No, but I've known several of them. And I would respect several of them I would have liked while I worked with them [in the movement]. . . . But I tell you what, I didn't respect their decision [pause] at all.

Among Republicans, who left for Republican Sinn Féin and who did not was, with some exceptions, not a surprise. Many who left came from similar backgrounds and had shared experiences with previous splits in the Republican movement. They also tended to interact with other Republicans who had similar opinions with respect to participating in Leinster House. Those who left knew that comrades like themselves were likely to go with RSF. Those who stayed with the Provisionals knew that comrades like themselves were likely to stay with the Provisionals. Within each group—those who created Republican Sinn Féin versus those who stayed in Provisional Sinn Féin—their interpretation of what it is to be a "Republican" had similar origins and, over the course of their movement careers, had been reinforced because they shared both personal and, through their involvement in Republican politics, organizational network ties (see also chapter 2, this volume; McAdam and Paulsen 1993, 659, 663). RSF's founders had internalized movement goals, shared collective beliefs and experiences, and defined and situated themselves personally as Republicans through their interactions with others. Walking out of the 1986 Sinn Féin Ard-Fheis was behavior highly consistent with their Republican identities.

Interpreting Behavior

We argue that the internalization of a Republican identity and collective identification with Republican ideology led a small group of Irish

Republicans to form Republican Sinn Féin. They did this because they believed that by dropping abstentionism from Leinster House Provisional Sinn Féin had begun the process of transforming the Republican movement into a political group that would become ensnared in the compromises of constitutional politics. This interpretation is supported by comparing the social movement conditions that this group faced when they formed Republican Sinn Féin in 1986 with the conditions faced they when they formed Provisional Sinn Féin in 1969–70.[10]

RSF's founders have twice started a new social movement. In forming the Provisionals, they took a risk and left behind virtually all the movement's resources, including property (e.g., party headquarters). Provisional Sinn Féin had to secure a loan to start its paper, *An Phoblacht* ("Birth of the Provos" 1990). In 1969–70, however, conditions were ripe for mobilization of a new Republican movement. Northern Ireland had erupted in violence, and there was a large amount of discontent in the Northern Nationalist community (e.g., Bell 1979).

In 1986, conditions were different. The founders of the new movement again gave up property and a newspaper, but, in the short term, there was little chance of eclipsing the Provisionals—their previous creation. It was years before Republican Sinn Féin was able to secure a permanent party headquarters. RSF's founders had fewer resources for two reasons. First, the Provisional IRA, nonexistent prior to December 1969, was still active in 1986. Many Republicans, even if reluctantly, will stick with Provisional Sinn Féin as long as the IRA is active. Second, changes in the Republican movement from 1969–70 contributed to a decreased likelihood of success for those who formed Republican Sinn Féin. In 1969–70, the IRA and Sinn Féin were a conspiratorial clan dominated by IRA veterans of the 1950s. By 1986, the movement was a large-scale social movement dominated by young, post-1969 recruits who were mostly from Northern Ireland (White 1993). In 1969–70, the movement split roughly down the middle. If little else, the Provisionals had themselves and a countermovement of the same size. In 1986, a minority of the delegates walked out of the Ard-Fheis and formed Republican Sinn Féin. They not only gave up resources but also faced competition from a much larger movement that laid claim to the same goals.

RSF's founders recognized the difficulties of creating a new Republican party. Yet, they were still willing to do so because they were behaving consistently with their personal identities and their interpretation of the collective "Republican" identity, no matter the personal costs and the costs to the social movement they feared was being led to ruin.

Conclusion and Implications

In Ireland, there are two groups of people referring to themselves as "Republicans." They support two different political parties, Republican Sinn Féin and Provisional Sinn Féin, and two different guerrilla armies, the Continuity IRA and the Provisional IRA.[11]

In general, the identities of these people are very similar. All of them seek a united Ireland, free of British interference. All (at least until recently) believe that without military activity, or at least the threat of military activity, the British will not disengage from Ireland. Their identities differ on the question of whether or not Republicans should participate in the Dublin parliament. For those in Republican Sinn Féin, to be a true Republican is to reject such political participation. This rejection is based on two beliefs. First, the Dublin parliament is illegitimate. Participating in that government ignores decades of principled refusal and the price paid for that refusal. Second, participation in constitutional politics will lead to moderation and corruption and the demise of the Republican movement.

For many members of Republican Sinn Féin, the belief that the Dublin parliament is illegitimate stems from their upbringing; they internalized the beliefs of their parents, who were also Republicans. Others, not born into Republican families, developed this belief over the course of their Republican careers. Through experience with Republicans who opted for constitutional politics and, ultimately, turned on their former comrades, these people came to believe that participation in constitutional politics is corrupting, if not also immoral. Across a group of like-minded people who interact with one another, these two dimensions of a personal Republican identity combine with two beliefs—the belief that Ireland should be free of British interference and the belief that physical force is required to remove this interference—and form the core of the collective identity of those in Republican Sinn Féin.

Several implications may be gleaned from our findings. First, the collective identity of the Irish Republican movement is complex and involves both solidarity among activists and shared ideological beliefs. The collective identity of Republican Sinn Féiners is not just an outgrowth of social solidarity or "we-ness" among a small clique or faction of the Provisional Irish Republican movement. Certainly the level of solidarity among those who formed Republican Sinn Féin is high. There was enough in-group interaction, trust, and preorganization that prior to the walkout of the Ard-Fheis they rented a location in which they could regroup. Yet, we learned in several key interviews, those leading the walkout had more followers than they expected. Close ties to those who organized the split do not account for all who split. Disagreement with the proposed changes in policy—ideology—most likely accounts for many of these additional walkouts.

We do not wish to underemphasize the "we-ness" aspect of the collective identity of Republican Sinn Féiners. We do want to emphasize that the evidence suggests two important dimensions to this collective identity: (1) "we-ness" and solidarity and (2) ideology in the form of opposition to constitutional politics. This finding may in part reflect the nature of the general Irish Republican movement. Republicans are involved in a traditional, goal-oriented, political movement. This may be contrasted with many "new" social movements, which may be less goal-oriented and more organized as "self-help" or consciousness-raising movements (e.g., chapter 13, this volume).

Second, the beliefs that coalesce across activists and form the collective identity of a social movement need not be totally agreed on among movement activists. With respect to the Irish Republican movement, from the early 1980s until the split in 1986 there was broad agreement on movement goals (the British out of Ireland) and the general necessity of physical force methods. Yet there was also disagreement over the impact of Republican participation in constitutional politics. An increasingly larger portion of the movement came to believe that such participation would benefit the movement. An increasingly smaller portion of the movement rejected this belief, but these people were willing to maintain their activism as long as the belief was not adopted as policy. If those voting for an end to abstentionism had lost in 1986 (which is what happened in 1985), there would not have been a split. For those opposed to dropping abstentionism, their commitment to the movement's goals would have overridden their opposition to (unsuccessful) change. Further, in 1986, there were persons who voted against the change but did not participate in the walkout. For these people, solidarity with those proposing the change greatly influenced their behavior (see also Johnston, Laraña, and Gusfield 1992, 16–17; and White 1993).

Finally, social movement researchers have noted that there are cycles of social protest (e.g., Tarrow 1989). We agree with this and note that in this century Republicans have mobilized and carried out significant amounts of political violence in the following time periods: 1916, 1919–23, 1939–45, 1956–62, and from 1969 to the present. We add to this, however, the important note that Irish Republican political activism spans these cycles. The activism of some individual Republicans almost spans the entire century: their Republican identity links periods of high movement activity and carries across these periods. For some Irish Republican activists, there is a "permanence of protest"; part of being an Irish Republican is to persist. These are people like Tony Ruane. Ruane joined the IRA in the 1918–21 era. He remained active in either the IRA or Sinn Féin, or both, until his death in 1991. His activism spanned four military campaigns by the Irish Republican Army and five significant splits in Sinn Féin. We suspect that in other movement settings there is a similar permanence of protest. Many social movements contain members who continue their struggle, no matter the odds or the consequences. Some of these movements and activists ultimately succeed, such as the African National Congress (ANC) and Nelson Mandela. Others, at least thus far, fail, for example, the Communist Party in the United States (Gornick 1977). Either way, noncompromisers, diehards, traditionalists, and the like play a key role in the generation and continuation of social protest.[12]

Notes

This research was supported by grants from the Harry Frank Guggenheim Foundation; the Department of West European Studies, Indiana University, Bloomington; the IUPUI Office of Faculty Development; and the National Science Foundation (grant SES-8318161). We thank Tim Owens, Shel Stryker, and Eric Wright and the SISM Conference participants for their comments, and we thank Lori Langdoc and Libby Laux for their research assistance.

1. The media link Republican Sinn Féin with the Continuity IRA, a link regularly denied by party members, who acknowledge that the two organizations share the same goals and ideology.

2. Here, "Republican" and "Republicans" refer to persons involved with or veterans of four organizations: the Provisional IRA, Provisional Sinn Féin, Republican Sinn Féin, and the Continuity IRA.

3. Procedures for collecting data between 1984 and 1992 are described in White (1993, 179–88). Information on data collection from 1995 to 1999 is available from the authors.

4. The collective identity of a social movement reflects the interests of individuals who create that movement. A movement's collective identity may also reflect aspects or dimensions of identities of people who are not members of the movement, including people who reject the movement. In Ireland many people are Nationalists—they seek an end to British involvement in Irish politics. Part of their Nationalist identity is consistent with the collective identity of the Irish Republican movement. Thus, when the IRA pulls off a "spectacular" or suffers excessive repression, some non-Republican Irish people will express support or sympathy for Republicans. Because they also reject the physical force aspect of the Republican collective identity, it is unlikely they will be recruited. Our conceptualization also accounts for "hangers-on," who identify with aspects of

the Republican identity but may not be welcome in the movement (e.g., because they are unreliable or unstable).

5. Individual-level (personal) movement identities of activists are relatively homogeneous within subgroups of a movement but relatively heterogeneous across subgroups of a movement. There may be considerable variation, even within subgroups, in the strength of nonmovement identities (e.g., family identities, work identities). The solidarity and commitment of subgroups of activists probably increase with activism, as does the homogeneity of the nonmovement identities of subgroups of activists (see chapters 1 and 2, this volume).

6. For a history of abstentionism by Irish Republicans, see Bell (1979) or Ó Brádaigh (1997).

7. Irish Republicans draw on several examples in support of these views. They may be found in Bell (1979) or White (1993).

8. Respondent 4 joined Provisional Sinn Féin soon after it was formed in 1970.

9. Tom Maguire, an IRA veteran of the 1920s, was a member of the Second Dáil Éireann. Following the treaty, he stayed with the Republican side and refused to acknowledge Leinster House. Through the 1920s and 1930s, he and other members of the Second (All-Ireland) Dáil Éireann continued to meet as the "true" government of Ireland. Maguire was among those who assigned to the Army Council of the IRA the authority to represent the Irish people as their legitimate government. In 1969, as the sole surviving member of the Second Dáil who refused to support Leinster House, he asserted that the IRA Convention "had neither the right nor the authority" to recognize the parliaments in Belfast, Dublin, and London. In 1986, he again refused to "recognize the legitimacy of any Army Council styling itself the Council of the Irish Republican Army which lends support to any person or organisation styling itself Sinn Fein and prepared to enter the partition parliament of Leinster House" (Ó Brádaigh 1997, 44–48). Maguire was the "patron" of Republican Sinn Féin, until his death in 1993 at the age of 101.

10. Some argue that Republican Sinn Féin was not caused by dropping abstentionism but rather by the egos of Ruairí Ó Brádaigh and Daithí O'Connell, who (reportedly) were unable to (1) accept criticism of their leadership of the movement and (2) let new leadership assert itself. This interpretation is problematic for a number of reasons. When formed, Republican Sinn Féin attracted more recruits than would be expected if its primary appeal had been to assuage Ó Brádaigh's and O'Connell's egos. In addition, there were occasions prior to 1986 when Ó Brádaigh and O'Connell could have created an alternative movement but did not (see White 1993, 165 n. 8).

11. Recent PIRA cease-fires, another split in the Republican movement in late 1997, and participation of the Provisionals in elections in Northern Ireland have increased the complexity of internal differences among Republicans.

12. These are often movement participants who organize "abeyance" structures, allowing for movement continuity even in times of organizational or activist doldrums (see Taylor 1989).

References

Bell, J. Bowyer. 1979. *The Secret Army: The IRA, 1916–* . Dublin: Academy Press.

———. 1993. *The Irish Troubles: A Generation of Violence, 1967–1992.* New York: St. Martin's.

"Birth of the Provos: Not an Inch" [interview with Ruairí Ó Brádaigh]. 1990. *Irish News,* January 29, 6.

Brown, Rupert, and Jennifer Williams. 1984. "Group Identification: The Same Thing to All People?" *Human Relations* 37 (7): 547–64.

"Cathleen Knowles." 1990. Biographical statement.

Cohen, Jean. 1985. "Strategy or Identity: New Theoretical Paradigms and Contemporary Social Movements." *Social Research* 52:663–716.

Cronin, Seán. 1980. *Irish Nationalism: A History of Its Roots and Ideology.* Dublin: Academy Press.

Eyerman, Ron, and Andrew Jamison. 1991. *Social Movements: A Cognitive Approach.* University Park: Pennsylvania State University Press.

Flackes, W. D., and Sydney Elliott. 1994. *Northern Ireland: A Political Directory, 1968–1993.* Belfast: Blackstaff Press.

Fraser, Michael. 1996. "Identity and Representation as Challenges to Social Movement Theory: A Case Study of Queer Nation." In *Mainstream(s) and Margins,* edited by Michael Morgan and Susan Legget, 32–44. Westport, Conn.: Greenwood Press.

Gamson, William A. 1992. "The Social Psychology of Collective Action." In *Frontiers in New Social Movement Theory,* edited by Aldon D. Morris and Carol McClurg Mueller, 53–76. New Haven: Yale University Press.

———. 1995. "Constructing Social Protest." In *Social Movements and Culture,* edited by Hank Johnston and Bert Klandermans, 85–106. Minneapolis: University of Minnesota Press.

Gornick, Vivian. 1977. *The Romance of American Communism.* New York: Basic Books.

Hewitt, John P. 1989. *Dilemmas of the American Self.* Philadelphia: Temple University Press.

Jenkins, J. Craig, and Charles Perrow. 1977. "Insurgency of the Powerless: Farm Workers Movements." *American Sociological Review* 42:249–68.

Johnston, Hank, Enrique Laraña, and Joseph R. Gusfield. 1992. "Identities, Grievances, and New Social Movements." In *New Social Movements: From Ideology to Identity,* edited by Enrique Laraña, Hank Johnston, and Joseph R. Gusfield, 3–35. Philadelphia: Temple University Press.

Klandermans, Bert. 1992. "The Social Construction of Protest and Multi-organizational Fields." In *Frontiers in Social Movement Theory,* edited by Aldon D. Morris and Carol McClurg Mueller, 77–103. New Haven: Yale University Press.

———. 1994. “Transient Identities?: Membership Patterns in the Dutch Peace Movement.” In *New Social Movements: From Ideology to Identity,* edited by Enrique Laraña, Hank Johnston, and Joseph R. Gusfield, 168–84. Philadelphia: Temple University Press.

“Larry Grogan.” *An Phoblacht/Republican News,* December 1, 1979, 11.

The Last Post: Details and Stories of Irish Republican Dead, 1916–1985. 1985. 3d ed. Dublin: National Graves Association.

McAdam, Douglas, and Ronnelle Paulsen. 1993. “Specifying the Relationship between Social Ties and Activism.” *American Journal of Sociology* 99:640–67.

Melucci, Alberto. 1985. “The Symbolic Challenge of Contemporary Movements.” *Social Research* 52:789–816.

———. 1989. *Nomads of the Present: Social Movements and Individual Needs in Contemporary Society.* Philadelphia: Temple University Press.

———. 1995. “The Process of Collective Identity.” In *Social Movements and Culture,* edited by Hank Johnston and Bert Klandermans, 41–63. Minneapolis: University of Minnesota Press.

Ó Brádaigh, Ruairí. 1997. *Dílseacht: The Story of Comdt. General Tom Maguire and the Second (All-Ireland) Dáil.* Dublin: Irish Freedom Press.

Stryker, Sheldon. 1968. “Identity Salience and Role Performance.” *Journal of Marriage and the Family* 30:558–64.

———. 1980. *Symbolic Interactionism: A Social Structural Version.* Menlo Park, Calif.: Benjamin-Cummings.

Tarrow, Sidney. 1989. *Democracy and Disorder: Protest and Politics in Italy, 1965–1975.* Oxford: Clarendon Press.

———. 1992. “Mentalities, Political Cultures, and Collective Action Frames: Constructing Meaning through Action.” In *Frontiers in Social Movement Theory,* edited by Aldon D. Morris and Carol McClurg Mueller, 174–202. Philadelphia: Temple University Press.

Taylor, Verta. 1989. “Social Movement Continuity: The Women’s Movement in Abeyance.” *American Sociological Review* 54:761–75.

Taylor, Verta, and Nancy E. Whittier. 1992. “Collective Identity in Social Movement Communities: Lesbian Feminist Mobilization.” In *Frontiers in Social Movement Theory,* edited by Aldon D. Morris and Carol McClurg Mueller, 104–29. Philadelphia: Temple University Press.

Touraine, Alain. 1981. *The Voice and the Eye.* New York: Cambridge University Press.

———. 1985. “An Introduction to the Study of Social Movements.” *Social Research* 52:750–87.

White, Robert W. 1993. *Provisional Irish Republicans.* Westport, Conn.: Greenwood Press.

Contributors

PAMELA J. ARONSON is currently a postdoctoral fellow in the training program in Identity, Self, Role, and Mental Health in the Department of Sociology at Indiana University. Her research examines connections between women's identities and the larger social context, adolescent development, and the transition to adulthood. Her most recent project focuses on young women's life course pathways, identities, and contemporary attitudes toward feminism.

ROY F. BAUMEISTER holds the E. B. Smith Professorship in the Liberal Arts at Case Western Reserve University. He has written approximately two hundred research publications.

MARILYNN B. BREWER is Professor and Eminent Scholar in social psychology, Department of Psychology, The Ohio State University. Her work has long focused on intergroup attitude and relationships. Currently editor of *Personality and Social Psychology Review,* and a past associate editor of *Social Cognition,* she is a past president of the Western Psychological Association, the Society for the Psychological Study of Social Issues, the Society for Personality and Social Psychology, and, most recently, the American Psychological Society. She is a recipient of the Donald T. Campbell Award for Distinguished Research in Social Psychology from the SPSP and of the Kurt Lewin Award from SPSSI. Her recent research brings social identity to the study of intergroup relations.

LORY BRITT is quality systems manager for a corrugated box company in the Colorado Front Range. Her current sociological interests include the role of affect in the growing opposition to increasing development of the prairie ecosystem in the Front Range.

KAREN L. DALE completed her M.S. at the University of Canterbury, New Zealand, before studying at Case Western Reserve University. She is currently conducting research in psychology at the University of Plymouth, United Kingdom.

KAY DEAUX is Distinguished Professor of Psychology and Women's Studies at the Graduate School and University Center of the City University of New York. She has contributed extensively to the literature on gender stereotypes and gender-related behavior. Most recently, her work has focused on social identification, including ethnic identity, the nature of collectivism, and the functions that social identities serve for those who hold them. She has served as president of the American Psychological Society and the Society for Personality and Social Psychology.

MARGA DE WEERD is a member of the research staff at the Institute for Social Work and Organizational Psychology at Vrije Universiteit, Amsterdam.

MICHAEL R. FRASER is a program manager at the National Association of County and City Health Officials. His current research interests include health movement organizing and mixing sociological and public health perspectives. He has published several articles on HIV/AIDS and social movements that developed in response to the epidemic.

VIKTOR GECAS is Professor of Sociology and Rural Sociology at Washington State University. His scholarly interests have focused on the social psychology of self and identity, especially on the motivational significance of self-processes.

DAVID HEISE is Rudy Professor, Department of Sociology, Indiana University, and the past editor of *Sociological Methodology* and *Sociological Methods and Research.* His methodological research ranges from issues in quantitative modeling to computer applications in qualitative research. His social psychological research focuses on the affective and logical foundations of social interaction—in particular, affect control theory and event structure analysis. He has received the Cooley-Mead Award for lifetime contributions from the social psychology section of the American Sociological Association.

HOWARD B. KAPLAN is Distinguished Professor of Sociology and Mary Thomas Marshall Professor of Liberal Arts at Texas A&M University. He directs an NIH-funded multigenerational longitudinal study of drug abuse and other deviant adaptations to stress. Among his publications are *Patterns of Juvenile Delinquency; Social Psychology of Self-Referent Behavior; Deviant Behavior in Defense of Self; Drugs, Crime, and Other Deviant Adaptations;* and *Psychosocial Stress: Perspectives on Structure, Theory, Life Course, and Methods.*

K. JILL KIECOLT is Associate Professor of Sociology at Virginia Polytechnic Institute and State University. Her research interests include social structural influences on changes of the self-concept over the life course. Her other publications focus on the effects of mate availability and economic opportunity on marital status and family formation.

BERT KLANDERMANS is Professor in Applied Social Psychology at Free University, Amsterdam. His work focuses on the social psychological consequences of social, economic, and political change. He has published extensively on the social psychological principles of participation in social movements and labor unions and is one of the leading experts in the world in this area. He is the editor of Social Movements, Protest, and Contention, a book series published by the University of Minnesota Press, and the author of *The Social Psychology of Protest.*

XIAORU LIU is Assistant Professor of Sociology at San Diego State University. Her recent publications are in the areas of gender, deviance, psychosocial stress, and intergenerational processes. Her interests include crime and deviance, longitudinal analysis, life course and psychosocial stress, and methodology.

DOUG MCADAM is Professor of Sociology at Stanford University and the author of numerous books and articles on social movements and the dynamics of collective action. His books include *Political Process and the Development of Black Insurgency, 1930–1970; Freedom Summer;* and, with John McCarthy and Mayer Zald (editors), *Social Movements in Comparative Perspective.*

MARK MURAVEN is a postdoctoral research fellow at the Research Institute on Addictions in Buffalo, New York. He is interested in how people set and reach goals, particularly self-control goals.

TIMOTHY J. OWENS is Associate Professor of Sociology at Purdue University and is on the faculty of the National Institute of Mental Health training program in Self, Identity, Role, and Mental Health at Indiana University. His research interests are self and identity, life course analysis, the sociology of mental health, and the sociology of children and adolescence. The author of numerous books and articles, he is currently the series editor for Advances in Life Course Research and coeditor of the forthcoming volume *Extending Self-Esteem Theory and Research: Sociological and Psychological Currents.*

ELIZABETH C. PINEL is Assistant Professor of Psychology at Pennsylvania State University. Her research emphasizes the social construction of the self-concept as it pertains to targets of stereotypes and intergroup processes, and her work explores the most effective strategies for individuals and groups to discourage out-group members from stereotyping them. She argues that people's need to feel known plays an important role in determining which strategies they use to combat stereotyping, as well as how out-group members will react to those strategies.

ANNE REID is Assistant Professor of Psychology at Baruch College, where she teaches statistics and psychometrics. She was previously a research associate at Yale University, where her work focused on connecting social identity with health-related behaviors and outcomes. Her research interests include collectivism, social identity, and structural components of the self.

SILKE ROTH received her Ph.D. in sociology at the University of Connecticut. Together with Myra Marx Ferree, she has published articles on new social movements from an American perspective and on the cooperation between the German labor and women's movements. Recently, she conducted research at the Bauhaus University Weimar analyzing the opportunity structure that big events such as *Weimar 1999 Culture City of Europe* offer. She is currently working on a book about the Coalition of Labor Union Women.

MICHAEL D. SILVER is a Ph.D. candidate in social psychology at The Ohio State University. His research interests include the use of experimental and survey methods to explore intergroup perception, intergroup relations, group identification, and group loyalty. He is particularly interested in the psychological perception of relationships among multiple group identifications and the consequences of those multiple identifications.

DAVID A. SNOW is Professor of Sociology at the University of Arizona. He has published widely on various aspects of social movements, framing processes in the context of movements, conversion processes, self and identity, ethnographic field methods, and homelessness. He is author of *Shakabuku: A Study of the Nichiren Shoshu Buddhist Movement in America, 1960–1975;* coauthor (with Doug McAdam) of *Social Movements: Readings on Their Emergence, Mobilization, and Dynamics;* and coauthor (with Leon Anderson) of *Down on Their Luck: A Study of Homeless Street People,* winner of a number of distinguished book awards.

SHELDON STRYKER, Distinguished Professor of Sociology at Indiana University, has long-standing interests in a symbolic interactionist perspective in social psychology emphasizing structural constraints on self and the consequences of self, and in the development and test of identity theory, deriving from that perspective. He is a past editor of *Sociometry* (now *Social Psychology Quarterly*) and the *American Sociological Review* and the recipient of the American Sociological Association's Cooley-Mead award for lifetime achievement in social psychology. His current research, with Richard Serpe and Matthew Hunt, investigates the impact of social structural location on commitments to social relationships.

WILLIAM B. SWANN JR. is Professor of Psychology at the University of Texas at Austin. He has been a fellow at Princeton University and at the Center for Advanced Study in the Behavioral Sciences and is the recipient of multiple Research Scientist Development Awards from the National Institutes of Mental Health. His research has focused on the interplay between beliefs about others and the self in interpersonal relationships. He has written numerous articles on these topics, as well as a book, *Self-traps: The Elusive Quest for Higher Self-Esteem.*

VERTA TAYLOR is Professor of Sociology and a member of the graduate faculty of women's studies at The Ohio State University. She is the author of *Rock-a-by Baby: Feminism, Self-Help, and Postpartum Depression;* coauthor (with Leila J. Rupp) of *Survival in the Doldrums: The American Women's*

Rights Movement, 1945 to the 1960s; and coeditor (with Laurel Richardson and Nancy Whittier) of *Feminist Frontiers.* She has also published numerous articles on social movement theory, women's movements, and the gay and lesbian movement. She is currently completing an edited volume with Nancy Whittier, *Gender and Social Movements,* and collaborating with Leila Rupp and Josh Gamson on a historical and ethnographic study of cross-dressing as a collective action repertoire.

ROBERT W. WHITE is Associate Professor of Sociology and Associate Dean for Faculty Affairs at the School of Liberal Arts, Indiana University (Indiana University–Purdue University at Indianapolis). He is the author of *Provisional Irish Republicans: An Oral and Interpretive History.* His work has appeared in *American Sociological Review, American Journal of Sociology,* and other scholarly journals.

Index